TOWARDS AN ELEGANT SYNTAX

Recent developments in the study of natural language syntax have suggested that theoretical elegance is an aim that should be more central in this area of investigation.

This collection of essays, written between 1980 and 2001, places the search for theoretical elegance at centre stage. The author shows that although the conceptual difference between "elegance" and the minimalist search for "perfection" may appear to be subtle, its consequences are in fact wide ranging and radical. These considerations lead to a markedly different and novel theory of syntax where most of the major features of minimalism, such as derivation, economy, merge, move, phrases and projection, are not just reanalyzed or shifted to other components but in a majority of cases are dispensed with completely or reduced to much simpler notions.

The four-part structure of this book essentially corresponds to the stages in the development of elegant syntax. Articles in the first part of the book examine the search for theoretical elegance within the principles and parameters approach. Essays in the second part show how elegance becomes an organizing principle in the study of syntax. The second and third parts of this volume chronicle some of the various directions that were taken in the search for syntactic elegance. The fourth part is devoted to mirror theory, the theory of syntactic representation in elegant syntax.

Towards an Elegant Syntax makes available some better known and some less easily accessible publications together with a new introduction for the first time.

Michael Brody is Professor of Linguistics at University College London and Scientific Advisor at the Linguistics Institute of the Hungarian Academy of Sciences.

ROUTLEDGE LEADING LINGUISTS
Series editor Carlos P. Otero

1 ESSAYS ON SYNTAX AND SEMANTICS
James Higginbotham

2 PARTITIONS AND ATOMS OF CLAUSE STRUCTURE SUBJECTS, AGREEMENT, CASE AND CLITICS
Dominique Sportiche

3 THE SYNTAX OF SPECIFIERS AND HEADS
Collected essays of Hilda J. Koopman
Hilda J. Koopman

4 CONFIGURATIONS OF SENTENTIAL COMPLEMENTATION
Perspectives from Romance Languages
Johan Rooryck

5 ESSAYS IN SYNTACTIC THEORY
Samuel David Epstein

6 ON SYNTAX AND SEMANTICS
Richard K. Larson

7 COMPARATIVE SYNTAX AND LANGUAGE ACQUISITION
Luigi Rizzi

8 MINIMALIST INVESTIGATIONS IN LINGUISTIC THEORY
Howard Lasnik

9 DERIVATIONS
Exploring the dynamics of syntax
Juan Uriagereka

10 TOWARDS AN ELEGANT SYNTAX
Michael Brody

TOWARDS AN ELEGANT SYNTAX

Michael Brody

LONDON AND NEW YORK

First published 2003
by Routledge
2 Park Square, Milton Park, Abingdon, Oxon, OX14 4RN

Simultaneously published in the USA and Canada
by Routledge
711 Third Avenue, New York, NY 10017

Transferred to Digital Printing 2005

First issued in paperback 2012

© 2003 Michael Brody for selection and editorial matter

Typeset in Garamond 3 by
Newgen Imaging Systems (P) Ltd, Chennai, India

All rights reserved. No part of this book may be reprinted or reproduced or utilised in any form or by any electronic, mechanical, or other means, now known or hereafter invented, including photocopying and recording, or in any information storage or retrieval system, without permission in writing from the publishers.

British Library Cataloguing in Publication Data
A catalogue record for this book is available
from the British Library

Library of Congress Cataloging in Publication Data
A catalog record for this book has been requested

ISBN13: 978-0-415-29959-6 (hbk)
ISBN13: 978-0-415-65459-3 (pbk)

CONTENTS

Acknowledgements   vii

Introduction   1

Principles and parameters   5

1 On circular readings   7

2 On contextual definitions and the role of chains   17

3 On the complementary distribution of empty categories   40

Beyond principles and parameters   75

4 On Chomsky's *Knowledge of Language*   77

5 A note on the organization of the grammar   87

6 θ-theory and arguments   93

Towards an elegant syntax   115

7 Projection and phrase structure   117

8 Perfect chains   150

9 The Minimalist Program and a perfect syntax   176

CONTENTS

10 On the status of representations and derivations   185

Aspects of mirror theory   **203**

11 Mirror theory   205

12 "Roll-up" structures and morphological words   232

13 Word order, restructuring and mirror theory   251

   Notes   266
   Index   301

ACKNOWLEDGMENTS

I am grateful to Carlos Otero for asking me to put this volume together. Previously published papers are reprinted here with the kind permission of

Elsevier

On Circular Readings: (1982) in Neil Smith (ed.) Mutual Knowledge, pp. 133–148.

Blackwell Publishing

On the status of derivations and representations. (2002) in Derivational Explanation Sam Epstein and Daniel Seely (eds).

On Chomsky's "Knowledge of Language" (1987) Mind and Language, 2(2): 165–177.

The Minimalist Program and a Perfect Syntax. (1998) Mind and Language, 13(2): 205–214.

John Benjamins

Word Order, Restructuring and Mirror Theory. (2000) in Peter Svenonius (ed.) *The Derivation of VO and OV.* pp. 27–43.

Roll-up Structures and Morphological Words. To appear. É. Kiss, K. and H. van Riemsdijk (eds) Verb clusters in West Germanic and Hungarian – a Sprachbund?

Kluwer Academic Publishers

Perfect Chains. (1997) in Liliane Haegeman (ed.) *Elements of Grammar*, 139–167.

MIT Press

On Contextual Definitions and the Role of Chains. (1984) *Linguistic Inquiry*, 15(3).

On the Complementary Distribution of Empty Categories. (1985) *Linguistic Inquiry*, 16(4).

ACKNOWLEDGMENTS

Theta Theory and Arguments. (1993) *Linguistic Inquiry*, 24(1): 1–23.
Projection and Phrase Structure. (1998) *Linguistic Inquiry*, 29(3): 367–398.
Mirror Theory: Syntactic Representation in Perfect Syntax. (2000) *Linguistic Inquiry*, 31(1): 29–56.

INTRODUCTION

This volume attempts to track aspects of the prehistory and development of the research hypothesis first explicitly suggested around 1996, according to which the narrow syntactic component of language is a system whose properties are ultimately determined by gene-independent natural law. There are certain typical properties that, everything else being equal, make theories less elegant and so less highly valued than their respective competitors that do not suffer from such shortcomings. These include, for example, redundancies among theoretical principles, the non-unified treatment of apparently unifiable phenomena or the need for auxiliary hypotheses. Under the assumption that properties of natural language syntax are determined gene-independently, that is, independently from evolutionary *bricolage*, such methodological considerations carry over fully to the study of this component of the human mind.

Recent and not so recent developments in the study of natural language syntax suggest that theoretical elegance is an aim that may well be worth taking to be more central than usual in this domain. The concept of elegance apparently differs quite significantly from the notion of perfection as used in the mainstream minimalist literature. Before looking at this, let me quickly try to put aside a point that to my mind confuses the issue, at least in the form it is usually presented.

It is sometimes suggested that the notion of perfection used in the minimalist approach does not refer to the theory (of language) but to the object (language) the theory is a theory of. This sense of perfection is difficult to understand. In particular it is not clear how at some point in time t we can say anything about what some object is or what properties it has, over and above what our best theory of that object tells us – on the basis of all available evidence at t.

Let us ignore potential alternative interpretations of this suggestion, which as far as I know have never been explicated. In one sense in which it has been used, perfection is just a synonym for elegance – at best a terminological issue. This terminology now appears to obscure rather than clarify in that it is (and has been) easily associated with other senses in addition to that of theoretical elegance.

In a related but different second sense, perfection (and near-perfection) are effectively "engineering" terms. They presuppose a task and an evaluation measure – where both task and measure may be complex. Degrees of perfection tell us how well (in the simplest case, how elegantly) the task has been accomplished by a particular system. This approach clearly involves more conceptual apparatus than whatever is involved in the search for theoretical elegance. Elegance is embedded here in a logically prior frame involving the predetermined task and the task-relative evaluation system. In other words the question of what counts as elegance is complicated under this approach, at least by the added issue of having to determine the task for which elegance will be measured. Given that there are in principle many potential tasks from which to choose, this assumption at the very least makes the search for the best theory more complex. At the same time, the approach has a less ambitious aim than the one that simply requires a theory to be elegant: the best theory now need not be elegant, only the optimal one for some adopted purpose.

Although facts might conceivably force us eventually to a stance in the spirit of task relevant (near-)perfection, the approach is clearly an undesirable one when a less complex alternative is available that additionally assumes that the best case obtains. Furthermore I think it is generally fair to say that assuming the task-relevant perfection approach typically has a somewhat demoralizing effect: it has made it respectable to come up with inelegant analyses, that is, less than optimal explanations, and defend them as containing somewhow inevitable imperfections. In my view, this has invariably led into blind alleys. As a prominent example of this phenomenon, take the case of move, which has invariably been regarded as an imperfection in the minimalist view[1] until very recently.[2] In the framework of elegant syntax taking a syntactic relation to be "imperfect" has been ruled out on principled grounds essentially from the outset: "... Move cannot be ... [an imperfection]. It is therefore necessary to find a different conceptualization for this relation."[3] The approach which allows move/chain not to be an inelegant addition in fact has much in common with the more recent minimalist proposal.

Thus it seems to me that the effectively used sense of (near-)perfection is exploited in actual practice only to deflect even the apparently satisfiable requirements of theoretical elegance. Both for this reason and for the theoretical undesirability of the engineering sense of perfection noted above, I shall continue to adopt the theory that more simply aims for elegance. To avoid confusion I shall not use perfection as a synonym of elegance. In my earlier publications I have, however, followed the minimalist terminology for some time, and used perfection in this sense, with the implicit suggestion that the term perfection is best understood in the sense of elegance. This led to some misunderstandings and after some hesitation I have switched terminology somewhere around the end of the 1990s, and started to refer to the approach as elegant syntax. I have not changed the original wording in this volume, so in various earlier papers perfection and perfect syntax should be read as elegance and elegant syntax, respectively.

The distinction between task-oriented perfection and theoretical elegance may appear to be subtle, but a strict adherence to the latter resulted in the last eight years or so in noticeable simplifications. The resulting theory of syntax (one of potentially infinitely many that are compatible with the central role accorded to elegance) eliminates or simplifies many or most characteristic properties of the minimalist approach.

It is not the case of course that all outstanding theoretical problems have found their solutions. However, it seems clear that elegant syntax leads to a rather different picture from the more standard view. Concepts like derivations, economy, merge, move, phrase, projection, c-command, jointly provide a reasonable characterization of the apparatus of the minimalist framework. Syntax internally now all these appear to be either fully redundant or reducible to much simpler notions (see the parts on "Towards an elegant syntax" and "Aspects of mirror theory").

Although elegant syntax and the minimalist approach apparently differ significantly, there are also aspects in which they are parallel enterprises that are near enough not only to adopt ideas from each other but sometimes even to transplant specific solutions and mechanics with minor modifications. There are in particular a number of cases where considerations of elegance led to results that were later apparently independently arrived at in the minimalist framework in which considerations of elegance are less prominent but of course not missing altogether.

I have already cited one case relating to the question of whether the move/chain relation is an imperfection. Another example is the idea that LF is the basic syntactic level. This has also originated from considerations of architectural elegance already in the early 1980s.[4] In the late 1980s when the claim was slightly more elaborated,[5] Chomsky (1987) took this claim to deny the existence of other syntactic levels, essentially as later proposed by Chomsky himself in 1992 and 1995. At this earlier time however, he argued quite strongly against it on (admittedly weak) empirical grounds. It was in fact in the early 1990s (Brody 1992, 1993),[6] where the argument for eliminating D-structure was more carefully presented. Almost identical arguments for this point were independently given by Chomsky 1995.[7] In this work the centrality of LF (as opposed to D- or S-structure) was also prominently and strongly adopted.

Or take another instance, where expletive-associate chains[8] share crucial properties with later minimalist feature movement and probe-goal Agree structures.[9] Or the arguments that even if one adopts a derivational view, syntax should involve a single cycle[10] – although in part for additional reasons, the mainstream minimalist view is now in agreement with this point.[11] There are various other cases of this kind that an attentive reader of the volume will no doubt notice, from the early treatment of empty categories within the Principles and Parameters theory[12] to the approach to checking theory and in particular to the role of deletion and invisibility.[13]

The relative systematicity of such cases, where focusing on theoretical elegance makes it possible to reach certain types of results that the minimalist approach can adopt or rediscovers, sometimes much later, is suggestive. On the view that such results are not completely insignificant, the situation may be taken to hint at the correctness of the view that considers elegance a primary objective, perhaps even a tautologous requirement of (syntactic) theory construction.

Articles in the first part of this book search for theoretical elegance only within the Principles and Parameters approach. From the late 1980s, (here from the second part onwards) elegance becomes an organizing principle that in certain crucial respects dictates the choice of the framework. As indicated above, these considerations eventually lead to a quite different theory of syntax where most of the major features of minimalism are not just reanalyzed, or shifted to other components, but where many, perhaps their majority, are either dispensed with completely or reduced to what is perhaps their genuinely conceptually inevitable core – in any case to a rather more impoverished conceptual apparatus. The second and third parts of the volume chronicle some of the various directions and stages in the search for elegance in the theory. The final part is devoted to mirror theory, the theory of syntactic representation in elegant syntax.

References

Brody, M. 1985. On the Complementary Distribution of Empty Categories. Linguistic Inquiry 16:4. pp. 505–546.

Brody, M. 1987. On Chomsky's "Knowledge of Language." Mind and Language 2:2 Blackwell. pp. 165–177.

Brody, M. 1992. Three Theories of the Organization of the Grammar. UCL Working Papers in Linguistics Vol. 4, UCL.

Brody, M. 1993. Theta Theory and Arguments. Linguistic Inquiry 24: 1. pp. 1–23.

Brody, M. 1995a. *Lexico-Logical Form: A Radically Minimalist Theory*. Cambridge, Mass.: MIT Press.

Brody, M. 1995b. Perfect Chains. Working Papers In the Theory of Grammar 2:2. Research Institute for Linguistics, Hungarian Academy of Sciences.

Brody, M. 1997. Perfect Chains. In Liliane Haegeman (ed.) *Elements of Grammar*, Kluwer. pp. 139–167.

Brody, M. 1998a. The Minimalist Program and a Perfect Syntax. In *Mind and Language* 13: 205–214.

Brody, M. 1998b. Projection and Phrase Structure. Linguistic Inquiry 29: 3. pp. 367–398.

Chomsky, N. 1987. (Reply to Comments by Alexander George and Michael Brody) Mind and Language 2:2 Blackwell. pp. 178–197.

Chomsky, N. 1992. A Minimalist Program for Linguistic Theory. MITWPL No. 1.

Chomsky, N. 1995. *The Minimalist Program*. Cambridge, Mass.: MIT Press.

Chomsky, N. 1999. Derivation by Phase. Ms. MIT.

Chomsky, N. 2000. Minimalist Inquiries: The Framework. In Martin *et al.* eds. *Step-by-step – Essays on Minimalist Syntax in Honor of Howard Lasnik*, Cambridge, MA: MIT Press.

Chomsky, N. 2001. Beyond Explanatory Adequacy Ms. MIT.

PRINCIPLES AND PARAMETERS

1

ON CIRCULAR READINGS

1. Introduction

It is well known that there are a number of constraints determining what are the possible positions of a linguistic antecedent of a given anaphoric expression. (1a,b) for example are ill-formed on the reading indicated; they cannot legitimately express the meaning of (2a,b). (Co-indexing marks anaphoric relationship between constituents.)

(1) a. *He_x said Tom_x was ill
    b. *Tom_x saw him_x
(2) a. Tom_x said he_x was ill
    b. Tom_x saw $himself_x$

Consider now (3), which contains a structure where the antecedent includes the anaphoric expression:

(3) *I met [$_x$$her_x$ childhood friend's wife]

The meaning that we should expect (3) to have is something like (4).

(4) I met the one_x who_x is her_x childhood friend's wife

Just as in the case of (1a,b) a structural constraint can be stated that rules (3) ungrammatical.[1] In this chapter, I shall consider the further question of whether the effect of this constraint follows from some independent considerations. An account of such structures has recently been proposed in a paper by James Higginbotham and Robert May (1979), (henceforth HM), to which I shall refer as the pragmatic solution. This crucially involves a pragmatic principle that is often assumed in some form in the different approaches to the problem of the interaction of content and context, represented at this conference. I should like to argue below that this solution, although at first sight plausible, is not tenable. I shall present an alternative explanation, one that involves what are probably not pragmatic principles but rules of grammar.

According to the pragmatic solution, a structure like (3) with the referential dependency as indicated (henceforth Circular Reading (CR)) "is in a certain sense absurd, for the reference of some of the terms that it contains is given only circularly" (HM, pp. 20/21). This absurdity is due to the general condition of use "that speakers are expected to provide sufficient cues for the determination of deictic reference" (HM, p. 21). So in the case of a CR, the reference of a pronoun is dependent on some NP, NP*, hence varying the context cannot, by hypothesis, provide contextual cues for the determination of the pronoun's reference. On the other hand, it is assumed, that NP* is unable to supply this reference, since the reference of NP* is itself dependent on that of the pronoun. "Intuitively, the reference of a pronoun cannot be 'given' in terms of itself" (HM, p. 109).

This solution then rests on the truth of two claims: (a) that there is a pragmatic condition that the reference of a pronoun must be identifiable and (b) that CR structures fail to satisfy this condition. The first of these claims has an air of naturalness about it, which I think is misleading. Suppose that the reference of a pronoun P is not determinable in some context. Why could not P be interpreted as a free variable? Since there seems to be no a priori reason why there could not be expressions with free variables in them in natural language, the pragmatic principle is in need of independent motivation. The second crucial premise of the pragmatic solution is that the reference of the pronoun in a CR structure is not determinable. I shall argue that this premise is false, and therefore whatever the status of the pragmatic condition, it cannot provide an explanation of the unacceptability of structures like (3). But before doing this, I should like to present some more relevant data and introduce some terminology with the help of which the problems the new data gives rise to can be stated.

Consider (5) and (6):

(5) a. *[$_x$her$_x$ childhood friend's wife]
   b. *[$_x$the fact that you believed it$_x$]
   c. *Tom [$_x$wanted to appear to $\emptyset_x$]
(6) a. *[$_y$her$_x$ employer] respects [$_x$his$_y$ secretary]
   b. *Everybody who says [$_y$Fred proved it$_x$] agrees [$_x$that Mike denies it$_y$]
   c. *The boy who [$_y$mentioned that Bill will $\emptyset_x$] saw the girl that [$_x$announced that someone had $\emptyset_y$]

(5b,c) show that the full explanation of the unacceptability of CRs will have to take into acount not only co-reference relationships but anaphoric connectedness in general. (The sense in which I shall use the term "anaphora" here is meant to exclude rules of sentence grammar.)[2] As (6) shows, the description of CR structures as ones in which the antecedent contains the anaphor, is not exhaustive: the same type of unacceptability results also if the antecedent of an anaphor A contains anaphor B whose antecedent contains A.

Let us call the relation in which the interpretation of an anaphor stands to that of its antecedent "anaphoric dependency"; and the relation in which the interpretation of some segment stands to that of its constituents "compositional dependency." Let us furthermore define the relation "a-c dependency" as holding between two interpretations A and B iff A is anaphorically dependent on B, or A is compositionally dependent on B. The ungrammaticality of (5) and (6) could now be described by stipulating that (a) a-c dependency is transitive and that (b) the a-c dependency of an anaphor's interpretation on that of its antecedent is asymmetric, that is if A a-c depends on B, and A is an anaphor's interpretation, then B does not a-c depend on A. The CRs now lead to contradiction. In (5a), for instance, the interpretation of the anaphor *her* is a-c dependent on that of the NP *her childhood friend's wife*. The asymmetry of this dependence (stipulation (b)) entails that the interpretation of *her childhood friend's wife* does not a-c depend on that of *her*. But it does in consequence of the compositionality principle. Given the transitivity of a-c dependence, we can similarly derive contradictions from the CRs of (6).

A-c dependence incorporates only anaphoric and compositional dependencies. The fact that these two are under a transitive "super-relation" cannot be a consequence of a general property of dependencies between interpretations. The interpretation of a variable, for instance, depends in some sense on that of its quantifier: its reference varies within the limits set by its binder. Nevertheless, this dependency must not be included under a-c dependency, if it was, (7) would be incorrectly excluded.

(7) a. Tom [$_x$kissed every girl Peter did $\emptyset_x$]
    b. [$_y$Every girl Peter did $\emptyset_x$] Tom [kissed y]
       $\qquad\qquad\qquad\qquad\qquad\qquad$ VP$^*_x$

On some level of analysis (7a) will have to have a representation like (7b), evidence for Quantifier Raising and for the identity condition on VP-anaphora converge to support this.[3] Assume that the stipulations about a-c dependency made above refer to this level. Here the zero VP asymmetrically a-c depends on VP* by stipulation (b). VP* in its turn a-c depends on the variable (related to the extracted quantifier phrase), as does the quantifier phrase on the zero VP. Thus given the transitivity of a-c dependence, if the variable a-c depended on the quantifier, we should end up with a contradiction and the structure would be incorrectly excluded. VP* a-c depends on VP (by transitivity of a-c dependence) and VP* does not a-c depend on VP (by asymmetry of the a-c dependence of an anaphor's interpretation on that of its antecedent). Thus "behaving transitively" with respect to anaphoric or compositional dependence is not a general property of interpretive dependencies.

At least three questions arise at this point. First, why do anaphoric and compositional dependencies interact, and why in this particular way by forming a transitive chain? Note that described in these terms, the fact that the structures in (6) are just as ungrammatical as the apparently related ones in (5) is not a logical necessity, hence surprising in a linguistically interesting sense. Second, from what independently motivated consideration could it be made to follow that it is just these two and no other relations that form such a chain that can create contradictions with the entailments of the principle of asymmetry? Again it is worth noting that the grammaticality of (7a) seems to be an unexpected and genuinely puzzling fact when this structure is compared with (5) and (6). Third, the same question could be asked about the principle of asymmetry. Could some independently motivated consideration explain the asymmetry of the a-c dependence of the interpretation of an anaphor on that of its antecedent? We shall see in the next section that this is not a property of dependencies between interpretations in general either.

The two stipulations concerning a-c dependency are *ad hoc*. Nevertheless, they are quite natural and it is not obvious if they should not be taken as axioms. But I shall attempt to search for explanations.

2. The inadequacy of the pragmatic solution

Returning now to the pragmatic solution, we note that in this only examples like (5a) and (6a) are considered, that is, ones containing pronouns and dependencies between referents. Given this limitation of the data, the problem of explaining why anaphoric and compositional dependencies interact does not arise. In (5a) and (6a), only referential dependencies (both anaphoric and compositional) occur. It is indeed difficult to imagine how this relation could fail to be transitive. However, the problem of explaining the asymmetry of anaphoric dependence does show up. Why is it that sentences in which the reference of some pronoun A depends on that of some segment B, where B's reference depends on that of A, are unacceptable? I shall return to the problem of explaining the interaction of anaphoric and compositional dependencies in later sections. First I should like to reconsider the explanation given by the pragmatic solution of the unacceptability of CRs with referential linkages. From our present point of view, this is an attempt to explain the asymmetry of referential dependence, i.e. to give a partial answer to problem (3) of section 1. I shall then go on to examine the potential of this solution to serve as a basis for an explanation for the asymmetry of the a-c dependence of anaphors other than pronouns.

Recall that according to the pragmatic solution, the reference of a pronoun in a CR structure is not determinable, this being due to it "being given in terms of itself."

"In this respect, pronouns are no different from other singular or plural terms. If one wanted to know who the name *Cicero* refers to, it is of no use to be told that it refers to the person people refer to when they use that name, for what we wanted to know was *who* that was." (HM, pp. 19/20). HM appear to assume then that some principle like (8), call it the Circularity Principle, is logically necessary:

(8) If the reference of some segment A is given circularly, that is, if it is dependent on that of another segment B, and the reference of B is dependent on A, then the determination of the reference of A cannot be effected.

If this was indeed a necessary principle, then the asymmetry of referential dependence would be explained. Whenever the pronoun both depends on and is depended on by some segment, this leads to leaving the pronoun without a determinate referent and hence to the exclusion of the structure by the pragmatic constraint. However, the Circularity Principle is not logically necessary, and even if it was, the solution would not be generalizable to the whole range of data.

The "Cicero" example appears to be misleading. The absurdity there is not due to circularity, but simply to the uninformativeness of the answer. Thus someone who would like to know who the name "Cicero" refers to can be informatively, though "circularly," answered by stating that it refers to the person who just uttered the name "Cicero." The explanation can be proper and truthful in appropriate circumstances. The example is irrelevantly complicated since "Cicero" is being mentioned in it instead of used as pronouns in CRs are. To take another, perhaps more perspicuous analogy, consider (9):

(9) $c = 1/c$

Suppose that "c" may take values in the domain of integers. The specification that the actual value of "c" equals the value of "1/c" may be circular, but is perfectly adequate, picking out 1 and -1.

It is neither necessary nor sufficient for a proposition to be a syntactic definition in order for it to pick out determinate referents that satisfy it. Of course it can be assumed that the relation between antecedent and anaphor is that of definiens and definiendum, or that the interpretation of an antecedent must be computable independently of (without access to) the interpretation of the anaphor. If some such step was made, asymmetry of the dependence of the interpretation of an anaphor on that of its antecedent would follow. But these assumptions, although perhaps natural, are neither necessary nor independently motivated, so they represent no improvement on the equally natural axiom of asymmetry of a-c dependence of the anaphor's interpretation, which I set out to explain.

Circularity in and of itself does not make the computation of the anaphor's and the antecedent's interpretation a difficult or even unparalleled task either. Computing the interpretation of an anaphor participating in a CR could be similar to disambiguation. Thus in (10), one of the possible meanings of *ball* is filtered out by selectional restrictions.

(10) the ball's trajectory

In (10), the interpretation of *ball* depends on that of the whole NP, whose interpretation in turn depends on that of *ball*. CRs could be dealt with in an exactly parallel fashion. Take (5a) for instance. Here the reference of *her* depends on that of *her childhood friend's wife*, whose reference in turn depends on that of *her*. In both cases, the contained NP (*ball/her*) has a number of possible interpretations/referents from which that or those will be picked out that meet(s) further conditions imposed by the container NP. It will have to be checked, for each possible interpretation/referent of the contained segment, whether it meets these: the selectional restrictions of the whole NP's interpretation in the former case, the identity requirement with the whole NP's reference in the latter. We can then conclude that the Circularity Principle is not logically necessary, and neither is the asymmetry of the dependence of a pronoun's reference on that of its antecedent.

But even if the Circularity Principle was necessary or independently motivated, no satisfactory solution could be based on it for the full range of data in (5) and (6). Asymmetry of a-c dependence is a property of the interpretation of all anaphors, it is not characteristic only of pronouns' referents. To explain this in the spirit of HM's solution, a stronger version of the Circularity Principle would have to be necessary, which refers not only to referential dependencies but to dependencies between interpretations in general:

(11) If the interpretation of some segment A is given circularly, that is if it is dependent on that of another segment B, and the interpretation of B is dependent on A, then the determination of the interpretation of A cannot be effected.

But this revised principle is not just not necessary or motivated, it is false. As the cases of disambiguation and of the antecedent-contained VP-anaphor (7) show, it is possible to have circular dependencies between interpretations in grammatical structures.

Summarizing so far, I have argued that the pragmatic solution is unsatisfactory for several reasons. This account of the unacceptability of CRs with referential linkages makes use of two assumptions: the pragmatic principle that the reference of a deictic expression must be determinable, and the Circularity Principle according to which CRs fail to satisfy this condition. Neither of these assumptions seems to be necessary or independently motivated.

But even if the account was accepted as an answer to the problem of why referential dependency is asymmetric, it would not be generalizable to explain the asymmetry of anaphoric dependency in general. Hence at best, the pragmatic solution could only have been a partial answer to one of the three central problems of CRs. It does not contribute at all to the solution of the problems of why anaphoric and compositional dependencies, and only these, interact by forming a transitive chain.

3. Referential chains and asymmetry

I shall persist in trying to find an answer to the asymmetry problem, whose solution, as will be seen, provides the answers automatically to the other two problems posed in section 1. I will approach this by gradually modifying the framework presented in Higginbotham and May's paper.

According to HM, structures with CRs have "referential chains" that may be infinitely long. Referential chains are hypothetical objects, part of a full semantic representation. Briefly, if the reference of a pronoun A depends on that of the NP B, then "A $\rightarrow$ B" may form part of the chain representing that B is the antecedent of A. Furthermore, if a segment C *contains* another, D, where C and D are in the referential chain by virtue of being on the right-hand side and on the left-hand side respectively of an arrow, this will be shown by linking C and D in the following notation: "C $\supset$ D."

So for example the referential chain of (6a) "[$_y$her$_x$ employer] respects [$_x$his$_y$ secretary]" on the reading marked may contain "her$_x$ → [$_x$his$_y$ secretary]" and "his$_y$ → [$_y$her$_x$ employer]." Since both "[$_x$his$_y$ secretary]" and *his$_y$* are in the chain they are linked by "⊃":

(12) her$_x$ → [$_x$his$_y$ secretary] ⊃ his$_y$ → [$_y$her$_x$ employer]

"[$_y$Her$_x$ employer]" includes *her$_x$* so (12) can continue as (13):

(13) her$_x$ → [$_x$his$_y$ secretary] ⊃ his$_y$ → [$_y$her$_x$ employer] ⊃ her$_x$

But now the reference of the last *her* in (13) again depends on that of the NP "[his secretary]," so the construction of the chain need not stop here.

Let us make the following natural assumption:

(14) All pronouns and pronoun containers in the referential chain must initiate an element of the form "A → B" or "A ⊃ B" respectively.[4]

Now the chain of (6a) appears to have to be infinite. Referential chains and (14) can be generalized as anaphoric chains in the obvious way. Since the chain is part of the semantic representation, structures with CRs can be excluded by the assumption that grammars must not assign an infinite representation to a finitely long sentence. Semantic representations must be accessible. This it would seem should be considered as a necessary property of grammars. Asymmetry of the a-c dependence of an anaphor's interpretation on that of its antecedent seems to fall out now.

This solution, however, does not work as it stands. Note first that even if it did explain asymmetry, it would not be satisfactory. It offers no hope of an explanation to the first two problems of section 1: why do anaphoric and compositional dependencies interact transitively, and why is it just these two dependencies between interpretations that do so? Anaphoric chains only stipulate and do not explain this. It would be, for instance, incorrect to include the dependence of the interpretation of a variable on that of its quantifier in the anaphoric chain (cf. (7)), but no motivation independent of the present problem can be given against this. But asymmetry is not explained either. The idea that referential chains for CRs will be infinite is crucially used (and generalized to anaphoric chains). But in HM's framework, this is incorrect even if (14) is accepted. This is because according to HM, the annotations of the chain only relate entities: "The items themselves in the referential chain are definite occurrences of NPs in the logical form" (HM, p. 19).

To see the problem, with this in mind, reconsider the referential chain of (6a). At the stage where the first four steps have been constructed, it may look like (13). But under the present assumptions about the status of the items in the referential chain, there will be no fifth step, since the last item in (13) is the same as the first: a definite occurrence of an NP in the logical form. The last *her* in (13) must of course initiate an element of the form "A → B" under (14), but it already has. This is the one that the first *her* in (13), with which the last one is identical, has initiated. It seems then that if the explanation of the unacceptability of CRs based on the infiniteness of the relevant anaphoric chains is to be maintained, then it must be ensured that the first

13

and the last *her* in (13) are not identical. To do this, the assumption that the annotations of the anaphoric chain only *relate* entities must be given up; they have to create new ones.

4. Anaphoric expansion

Is there any independent evidence for such a modification? To show that there is, I have to describe some data first noted and analysed by Jacobson (1977). She pointed out the difference in acceptability between (15a) and (15b) and the fact that it can be accounted for under the assumption that the first pronoun in (15a,b) (*her*), is represented at some level as a full NP identical to the pronoun's antecedent, as in (16a,b).

(15) a. [$_y$The man who$_y$ y loved her$_x$] kissed [$_x$his$_y$ wife]
 b. *[$_y$The man who$_y$ she loved y] kissed [$_x$his$_y$ wife]
(16) a. [$_y$The man who$_y$ y loved [$_x$his$_y$ wife]] kissed [$_x$his$_y$ wife]
 b. [$_y$The man who$_y$ [$_x$his$_y$ wife] loved y] kissed [$_x$his$_y$ wife]
(17) a. *[$_y$the man who$_y$ y loved [$_x$his$_y$ wife]]
 b. [$_y$the man who$_y$ [$_x$his$_y$ wife] loved y]

Some constraint will have to differentiate between (17a) and (17b) marking only the latter as deviant. Assume that it will be sensitive to the relative order of the variable (related to the *wh*-phrase) and the co-indexed pronoun. But whatever the precise formulation of this condition, it can automatically account for the difference between (15a) and (15b) provided that it has access to the level at which (15a,b) are represented as (16a,b) respectively.

HM build this into their framework in the following way. They stipulate what I shall call the Target Condition:

(18) The target of an annotation entry (i.e. the right hand side of an arrow "A → B") must not "contain a free variable, as such targets have reference only relative to an assignment of values to variables. In general a target NP$_i$ which gives the reference of a pronoun$_j$ must be *closed*, where NP$_i$ is closed iff every anaphor contained in NP$_i$ has a c-commanding antecedent in NP$_i$ (understanding containment as a reflexive relation)." (HM, pp. 18/19)

(Keep in mind that "anaphor" in this quotation refers to dependent elements participating in sentence grammar binding processes. This is in contradistinction to the way the word is used elsewhere in this chapter to mean the dependent members of "discourse grammar" associations.) Furthermore, it is stipulated that there is to be an exception from the Target Condition: annotations that violate it are permitted "where their semantic interpretation is determined by the result of substituting the target for the pronoun" (HM, p. 25), in other words, where the substitution will result eventually in a well-formed semantic representation.

In the derivation of (15a), the annotation that associates *her* with *his wife* has a target that violates the Target Condition; *his* is not bound from within the NP *his wife*.[5] Therefore this annotation is only legitimate if *his* can end up bound when *his wife* is substituted for *her*. After substitution, as in (16a), *his* can be properly bound.

(15b) is not similarly derivable since the pronoun *his*, in the substituted NP *his wife*, cannot have the same index as the variable that is linked to the *wh*-phrase and is to its right in consequence of the constraint that excludes (17b).

This analysis relying on substitution presupposes just like Jacobson's the existence of a level where certain pronouns are represented *in situ* by their antecedents, and not in abstraction from the rest of the structure. This is necessary in order to check whether conditions of proper binding are met by the substituted segment. Here we have evidence, then, for reinterpreting, at least in some cases, the annotation "A → B," relating logical form entities as a rewriting rule expanding A as B. It is natural to think of this rule as part of the mapping to a full representation of meaning.[6] Note that the analysis creates unmotivated distinctions between the interpretations of parallel structures. For instance, different structures are assigned to (15a) and (19). Since in (19), *her* has a closed target (*Mary*) there is no substitution:

(19) The man who loved her$_x$ kissed Mary$_x$

Suppose that the generalization is made that *all* anaphoric pronouns (i.e. those not bound by some antecedent in a sentence grammar process) have to be expanded when they have linguistic antecedents. (15a) and (19) will now have parallel mappings. The expansion of the first pronoun in (15a,b) will fall out from general principles: all anaphors expand. Note that the second pronoun in (15a,b) need not expand since the relation between it and its c-commanding antecedent is not anaphora in our sense, but that of sentence grammar binding.[7] The Target Condition becomes superfluous here as does its *ad hoc* exception covering the case of substitution. Since the "all expansion" account does not have recourse to anything not assumed in HM's theory, it is also more parsimonious in being able to dispense with anaphoric chains.

5. Some consequences

Equipped with evidence that all anaphoric pronouns must be substituted by a copy of their antecedents at some level of representation, I can return to the three problems that were posed at the outset. This theory can explain the asymmetry of the dependence of the pronoun's reference on the reference of its antecedent. It is now genuinely a consequence of the inadmissibility of inaccessible semantic representations. Given that an antecedent has to be copied in for all anaphoric pronouns, no fully expanded semantic representation will ever be reached for a CR. In (5a) for example, the anaphor *her* expands as *her childhood friend's wife*; in which *her* expands again as *her childhood friend's wife*, and so on.

The arguments originally advanced for the syntactic treatment of a great number of anaphoric processes (Grinder and Postal 1971, Hankamer 1973, Ross 1969, etc.) do not stand up when turned against more sophisticated interpretive theories. But they are as yet unrefuted if constructed as showing the necessity of countenancing the existence of some level where anaphors are expanded, represented by a copy of their antecedents. These arguments taken together with Jacobson's, discussed briefly in section 4, would seem to argue strongly for generalizing the expansion treatment to all anaphoric processes of discourse grammar (in the sense of Williams 1977).[8] If so, then the generalization of the explanation given for the ungrammaticality of (5a) to examples like (5b,c) is independently motivated. This solves the third problem of section 1, the asymmetry of the anaphor's interpretation on that of its antecedent.

Why does the ungrammaticality of CRs extend from the self-embedding patterns of (5) to the crossing ones of (6), the first of the three problems posed at the outset? The present theory provides an answer to this too. Anaphoric dependency interacts transitively with compositional dependency because expansion rules translate, as it were, the former into the latter. So to take (6a) for example, the interpretation of *her employer* compositionally depends on that of *her*, the interpretation of *her* anaphorically on that of *his secretary*. But at the level where the expansion rule has applied to *her*, it is represented as *his secretary* (copy). So *her employer* will simply compositionally depend on *his secretary* (copy). The makeshift notion of a-c dependency becomes superfluous.

This solution automatically provides an answer to the second problem of section 1, for which, just like for the first, anaphoric chains held no promise of an explanation. Only anaphoric dependency interacts with compositional dependency because expansion is motivated only for anaphors. There is no syntactic motivation for the substitution of a variable by a copy of its quantifier or of course for the expansion of a lexical item in the shape of a segment whose selectional restrictions disambiguate it. Expansion in these cases would also produce semantically nonsensical results.

In summary, I have argued that the condition that deictic expressions must have determinable referents has no role to play in the explanation of the unacceptability of CRs. An alternative explanation was put forward that was based on independently motivated rules and which was able to account for some interesting properties of CR constructions.

Acknowledgment

I am grateful to James Higginbotham, Robert May, Geoff Pullum, Neil Smith and Deirdre Wilson for helpful conversations on this material.

References

Brody, M. (1979) "Infinitives, Relative Clauses and Deletion," ms. UCL.
Grinder, J. and P.M. Postal (1971) "Missing Antecedents," *Linguistic Inquiry* 2, 269–312.
Higginbotham, J. and R. May (1979) "Crossing, Markedness, Pragmatics," in GLOW proceedings.
Hankamer, J. (1973) "Unacceptable Ambiguity," *Liguistic Inquiry* 4, 17–68.
Jacobson, P. (1977) *The Syntax of Crossing Coreference Sentences*. Doctoral dissertation University of California, Berkeley.
Postal, P.M. (1972) "An Invisible Performance Argument," *Foundations of Language* 9, 242–245.
Ross, J.R. (1969) "Guess Who," Proceedings of CLS, 5, 252–286.
Sag, I. (1977) "Deletion and Logical Form," Indiana University Linguistics Club.
Vergnaud, J.-R. (1974) "French Relative Clauses," Doctoral dissertation. MIT.
Williams, E. (1977) "Discourse and Logical Form," *Liguistic Inquiry* 8, 101–139.

2

ON CONTEXTUAL DEFINITIONS AND THE ROLE OF CHAINS

1. Introduction

1.1. Contextual definitions

A basic assumption of the Government-Binding theory of Chomsky (1981) (henceforth LGB) is that NPs are (exhaustively) partitioned by the properties $+/-$ pronominal, $+/-$ anaphor. This makes it possible for various subtheories of grammar that are sensitive to these distinctions to operate. Empty categories are not overtly marked with respect to these properties, but they must still be assigned to the appropriate subclass.

(1) a. *Tom_x is illegal e_x to go there
    b. *Tom_x hit e_x
(2) a. It's illegal e_x to go there
    b. Tom_x tried e_x to go there
(3) a. Tom_x seems e_x to go there
    b. It_x seems e_x to be obvious that Mary left
(4) Who_x did Tom hit e_x

For example, the Empty Category Principle (ECP), which rules out ungoverned non-pronominal empty categories, will exclude (1a) only if the empty category in this structure is taken to be a nonpronominal (trace). The condition that an empty pronominal anaphor (PRO) must be ungoverned, a consequence of the binding theory of LGB, rules out (1b) only if the empty category here is a pronominal anaphor. We may assume that for principles of interpretation to function correctly, the empty categories in (2)–(4) must also be assigned to the appropriate subclasses. In the system of LGB the empty category is a pronominal anaphor in (2), a non-pronominal anaphor (NP-trace) in (3), and a non-pronominal nonanaphor (*wh*-trace/variable) in (4).

In LGB Chomsky also postulates principles that characterize empty categories as $+/-$ pronominal, $+/-$ anaphor on the basis of their context. These so-called *contextual definitions* are reproduced in (5) (LGB 330).[1]

17

(5) a. α is a pronominal iff $\alpha = [_{NP} \, F,(P)]$, where P is a phonological matrix and $F \subset \phi$ and either (i) or (ii)
  (i) α is free
  (ii) α is locally A-bound by β with an independent θ-role.
 b. α is a variable iff α is locally $\bar{A}$-bound.
 c. If α is an empty category and not a variable, then α is an anaphor.

The conditions in (5) ensure that the empty categories in (1)–(4) are properly characterized. Consider first (5a). ϕ is the set of features that pronouns and empty categories are allowed to have (e.g. gender, number). Thus, (5a) from right to left entails that the empty category in (1b) and (2) is a pronominal. Since it is empty, all of its features are drawn from ϕ. It is free in (2a), satisfying (5ai), and A-bound by an element with an independent θ-role in (1b) and (2b), satisfying (5aii). From left to right (5a) predicts that the empty categories in (1a), (3), and (4) are nonpronominals, since they are either bound by an NP with a dependent θ-role (that is, one that has been assigned in the position of the empty category and then transmitted by it to its antecedent), as in (1a) and (3a), or by a category without a θ-role, as in (3b) and (4). Given (5b), the empty category in (4) – and it alone of the empty categories in (1)–(4) – is a variable, since it alone is $\bar{A}$-bound. (5c) requires all nonvariable empty categories to be anaphors; therefore, all empty categories in (1)–(3) are anaphors.

But the conditions in (5) are really superfluous here, since the above classification of the empty categories in (1)–(4) follows from independently motivated principles. Thus, the fact that the empty category is a nonpronominal in (1a) follows from the assumption that pronominal categories break the chain.[2] (If they did not, then control structures like (2b) would violate the θ-Criterion; the chain containing the antecedent of the pronominal and the pronominal itself would have two θ-positions.)[3] If the empty category in (1a) were taken to be a pronominal, then the chain containing its antecedent, the argument *Tom*, would have no θ-rule, violating the θ-Criterion. (If it is a nonpronominal, the structure is still excluded by the ECP.)

The empty category in (1b) cannot be a nonpronominal, since in that case it would form a chain with its antecedent, which would have two θ-positions, again violating the θ-Criterion. (The assumption that nonpronominal empty categories form a chain with their antecedent, at least when this is in A-position, is also independently motivated by NP-movement structures like (3a). Without this assumption (3a) would be analyzed as containing two chains, [Tom] and [e] – yet another θ-Criterion violation.)[4] This empty category cannot be a pronominal nonanaphor (pro), since it is not in an "identified" position (in the sense of Chomsky (1982)).[5] Moreover, as noted earlier, it cannot be a pronominal anaphor, since it is not ungoverned. Thus, the statements in (5) are not necessary to ensure that (1a) and (1b) are excluded; nor are they necessary to ensure that the empty categories in (2)–(4) have the appropriate NP-type status.

The empty category in (2) is not nonpronominal, since it is in an ungoverned position and hence would violate the ECP. Again, it is not a pronominal nonanaphor, since it is not identified. Hence, it is a pronominal anaphor.

The empty categories in (3) and (4) are nonpronominal, since they are neither ungoverned nor identified. Furthermore, those in (3) must be anaphors: since they are A-bound, if they were nonanaphors then they would violate principle (C) of the binding theory.[6]

(6) *Binding Theory*
    A. An anaphor is A-bound in its governing category.
    B. A pronominal is A-free in its governing category.
    C. A pronominal nonanaphor is A-free.

Finally, the empty category in (4) must be a nonanaphor (this incidentally does not follow from (5)), since it is governed but not A-bound. Taken as an anaphor, it would violate principle (A) of the binding theory.

These examples show that the conditions in (5) are largely redundant. Clearly, it would be methodologically best if they were fully redundant and could be eliminated from the grammar. I shall argue that the minimal hypothesis is in fact correct here – that the "contextual definitions" do not exist, and all their effects follow from other independently motivated principles. Indeed, I shall show that not only their effects but also the definitions themselves, at least in those respects in which they are correct, follow from independently necessary subsystems of grammar.

1.2. Complementary distribution and feature composition of empty categories

In LGB and in Chomsky (1982) the assumption that empty categories are characterized with the help of contextual conditions is contrasted with the position that empty categories differ inherently, in feature composition. Chomsky gives a directly empirical and a more conceptual argument against the latter claim.

The direct empirical argument is as follows. Agreement processes that suggest that PRO has features (person, number, etc.) behave in exactly the same way in constructions with traces. Thus, assuming that (7) (for example) involves an agreement requirement between the subject of the embedded clause and the postverbal NP makes it necessary to accept that PRO has number features. But the same assumption also leads to the conclusion that traces have number features, given the evidence in (8) and (9).

(7) a. Tom tried PRO to become a doctor
     b. They tried PRO to become doctors
(8) a. Tom appears t to be a doctor
     b. They appear t to be doctors
(9) a. Who does Tom believe t to be a doctor
     b. Which men does Tom believe t to be doctors

The argument shows that traces share some features with PRO, if the assumption is granted that agreement in these cases really involves the empty category. But it appears to have no bearing on the problem of whether trace and PRO differ in feature composition. Even though they may share some features, they may differ in others, just like lexical pronouns and anaphors. Still, even if the argument were valid that all empty categories have the same features, it would be irrelevant to the real issue: the question of the existence of NP-type definitions like (5).

The contrast between characterizing empty categories in terms of their feature content and classifying them by contextual conditions seems misleading to me. The issue here is not between contextual conditions and differences in feature composition. It is between the existence of the statements in (5) (or indeed of any condition that is motivated solely by the fact that it contributes to establishing a typology of empty categories) on the one hand and the lack of such stipulative conditions (that is, random characterization of empty categories constrained by independently motivated principles) on the other. Whether empty categories differ in feature composition is of tangential interest only. Both the negative and the positive answer to this question are compatible with both the existence and the nonexistence of contextual conditions in general and the statements in (5) in particular.

The main ("conceptual") argument for the existence of contextual definitions in LGB and in Chomsky (1982) is based on the complementary distribution between trace and PRO and their combined ability to appear in (almost) any NP position. Chomsky argues in LGB that these striking facts are explained if there is only one basic type of empty category. "PRO" and "trace" are then simply names of the various functions or occurrences in different contexts of what is always the same empty category. If contextual definitions exist and associate the names "PRO" and "trace" with the appropriate contexts, this makes it possible to maintain the assumption that there is only one basic empty NP, and thus to explain the appearance of complementary distribution and the fact that this empty category may appear in any NP position.

This argument involves two claims: first, that the assumption that there is only one basic type of empty category explains the phenomena of complementary distribution, and second, that this assumption entails the existence of contextual definitions.

Let us start with the latter point. In order to assume that there is only one basic type of empty category, it is not necessary to countenance contextual definitions (i.e. additional principles for identifying empty category types). Given independently necessary conditions on these types, random characterization of empty categories as $+/-$ pronominal, $+/-$ anaphor might do just as well. (This is essentially the same point that was just made: the issue is not between definitions and differences in feature composition but between definitions and the lack thereof – that is, random characterization.) Random characterization of empty categories does not entail the claim that there are feature differences between them; hence, definitions are not necessary in order to maintain that there is only one basic empty category with varying properties.

Furthermore, assuming that there is only one basic type of empty category does not explain the complementary distribution; it only pushes the problem to a different level.[7] Instead of asking why the two kinds of empty categories – trace and PRO – are in complementary distribution, we must now ask why the two functions/occurrences of the same empty category are in complementary distribution.

In fact, the theory of LGB offers a nonexplanatory answer to this question. The complementary distribution of trace and PRO is due to the curious conspiracy between the ECP and the binding theory: the former restricts traces to governed positions, the latter restricts PRO to ungoverned positions. From this it appears that an approach that tries to explain the complementary distribution by deepening our understanding of the *concept* of PRO and trace is doomed to failure. For a genuine explanation we should look instead at the principles that induce the complementary distribution, trying to reformulate them in such a way that this phenomenon ceases to appear to be an accidental conspiracy. (See Brody (forthcoming) for such an attempt.)

I should also mention here the argument – implicit in Chomsky (1982) but often made explicitly – that the existence of derivations in which empty categories change their (+/− pronominal, +/− anaphor) status shows the necessity of contextual definitions. It seems unclear whether such derivations in fact exist – certainly the evidence adduced in favor of this hypothesis is unconvincing.[8] But it is important to note that the basic problem with this argument is not empirical but conceptual. Whether empty categories change status is irrelevant to the present problem. Suppose that such changes do take place. Then empty categories must be recharacterized at some or every level of the derivation. This says nothing about the method of characterization, which therefore need not involve definitions and can be random. (Of course it also says nothing about whether empty categories differ in feature composition.)

2. On variables

2.1. *The definition of variables*

Let us start our discussion of the redundancy of conditions (5a–c) with the definition of variables in (5b), repeated here:

(10) α is a variable iff α is locally $\bar{\text{A}}$-bound.

We might understand (10) as a principle of NP typology, as a principle of interpretation, or as both. If it is a principle of NP typology, then the notion of variable here is like that of PRO or trace – it is simply an abbreviation referring to certain NPs with a given feature composition, namely, to nonpronominal nonanaphor empty categories.[9] Thus, one way of understanding (10) is as an abbreviation of (11).

(11) α is a nonpronominal nonanaphor empty category iff α is locally $\bar{\text{A}}$-bound.

Another way of understanding (10) is to consider it as a principle of interpretation, as in (12),

(12) α is interpreted as a variable iff α is locally $\bar{A}$-bound.

which says that locally $\bar{A}$-bound categories, whatever NP-type they happen to belong to, are interpreted as variables. (10) may also mean the conjunction of (11) and (12).

Since our aim is to show that NP-type definitions do not exist, we must demonstrate that (10) should be understood only as a principle of interpretation, and not as (11). I shall argue that (11) is partly redundant and partly incorrect.

Consider (11) from left to right, as in (13).

(13)   If α is a nonpronominal nonanaphor empty category, then α is locally $\bar{A}$-bound.

(13) may be taken to contribute to the account of the ungrammaticality of structures with crossover violations, for example (14a), and of examples like (14b).

(14)   a. *[Who$_x$ did] he$_x$ like e$_x$ (cf. Who$_x$ t$_x$ liked himself$_x$)
       b. *He$_x$ liked e$_y$

(14a,b) are excluded if the empty category in them is taken to be a pronominal, since it is neither ungoverned nor identified. If the empty category is a nonpronominal anaphor, then (14a) is excluded by the θ-Criterion (since the chain [he,e] contains two θ-positions), and (14b) by principle (A) of the binding theory (since it contains an anaphor that is not A-bound in its governing category). If the empty category in (14) is a nonpronominal nonanaphor, then (13) excludes the structure, since the empty category is not locally $\bar{A}$-bound in it.

However, it is not necessary to appeal to (13) here. (14a) with a nonpronominal nonanaphor empty category is excluded by the θ-Criterion. Since all nonpronominal empty categories form a chain with their local A-binder, (14a) still contains the chain [he,e] to which two θ-roles are assigned. (14a) is now also excluded by principle (C) of the binding theory, since it contains an A-bound nonpronominal nonanaphor.

As for (14b), it has often been suggested in the literature that natural language grammar includes a – presumably interpretive – condition that excludes free variables. If we assume that nonpronominal nonanaphor empty categories are necessarily interpreted as variables, then this interpretive condition will entail (15).

(15)   *The V-Element Condition (VEC)*

   If α is a nonpronominal nonanaphor empty category, then α is bound.

Since being a nonpronominal nonanaphor empty category is not (as I shall soon argue) a necessary condition of being a variable, I use a different term for these categories – namely, *V-elements* – and call (15) the *V-Element Condition* (VEC).

The VEC immediately excludes (14b) if the unbound empty category in it is nonpronominal. In fact, (13) in general is a consequence of the VEC and principle (C) of the binding theory. Consider a nonpronominal nonanaphor empty category. By the VEC it must be bound, by principle (C) it must be A-free. Hence, such a category must be locally Ā-bound. Since this exhausts the full content of (13), (13) can be dispensed with.

Now consider (11) from right to left, that is, (16):

(16) If α is locally Ā-bound, then α is a nonpronominal nonanaphor empty category.

That locally Ā-bound categories must be empty excludes structures like (17a).

(17) a. *Who$_x$ did Tom see Mary$_x$
b. *Who$_x$ is it illegal e$_x$ to see Tom

This, however, is a natural result of the fact that categories with features not drawn from ϕ are overspecified to function as variables. Given (12), all locally Ā-bound categories are interpreted as variables, and a conflict results. The part of (16) stating that locally Ā-bound categories can only have ϕ-features is therefore redundant; the same result follows from principles of interpretation.

Condition (16) also states that locally Ā-bound elements must be nonpronominal nonanaphors. This restriction correctly appears to exclude the ungrammatical (17b). In (17b) the empty category cannot be nonpronominal (by the ECP), since it is ungoverned. (16) excludes (17b) if the empty category is taken to be a pronominal.

As (18) shows, however, there exist both Ā-bound pronominals and Ā-bound anaphors.[10]

(18) Who$_x$ did PRO$_x$ losing his$_x$ way annoy e$_x$

The first of the two empty categories here must clearly be a pronominal, since otherwise it would be excluded by the ECP; moreover, it must be an anaphor, since it is not identified as a pronominal nonanaphor would have to be. The claim that locally Ā-bound categories are all nonpronominal nonanaphors then appears to be false.

From this we may conclude that the definition of variables in (5b)/(10) should not be interpreted as an NP-type definition, i.e. (11).[11] Apart from making the false claim that locally Ā-bound categories are nonpronominal nonanaphors, (11) is in fact redundant.

It remains to account for the ungrammaticality of (17b). As (19) shows, PRO is nonreferential when it has a nonreferential antecedent.

(19) It$_x$ often rains without PRO$_x$ snowing

(The empty category in (19) must be a pronominal anaphor, since it is in an ungoverned, nonidentified position.) In (17b) PRO also has a nonreferential antecedent: the *wh*-phrase. It follows that PRO itself is nonreferential; therefore, it is not an argument and cannot function as a variable. (17b) then violates the θ-Criterion, since there is no argument for the subject θ-role of the verb *see* to be assigned to. In addition, (17b) is ungrammatical because, although the principle of interpretation in (12) requires all locally Ā-bound categories to be interpreted as variables, PRO in (17b) cannot be so interpreted since it is a nonreferential element. In contrast, (18) is not excluded, since here PRO does have a referential antecedent: the other empty category in the structure, which itself functions as a variable. The PRO in (18) therefore can be an argument and a variable.[12]

2.2. *On which categories are interpreted as variables*

We now understand (5b)/(10) as a principle of interpretation, an abbreviation of (12).

Let us look more closely at the notion of variable. We may think of a variable as a category whose reference varies within the limits set by its quantifier. We may or may not assume further that the reference of a variable varies *independently* within these limits. This matters when there is more than one element bound to the same quantifier, as for example in (20):

(20) Who$_x$ t$_x$ likes his$_x$ friends

In such cases all these elements – in (20) the trace and the pronoun – must corefer for each choice of referent. Suppose also that there is a priority ordering between the two Ā-bound elements in (20): the trace varies independently, and the pronoun takes up whatever value the empty category happened to take. This further assumption appears to be incorporated in (12), the principle stating that only locally Ā-bound categories are interpreted as variables. The pronoun in (20) then is interpreted as a pronoun that happens to have a variable antecedent; therefore, coreference between it and its antecedent happens to involve a set of coreference relations. If, however, we do not assume that variables must vary independently, then we will propose that all (and only) Ā-bound elements (whether or not *locally* Ā-bound) are interpreted as variables. Under this alternative, then, the pronoun in (20) would be interpreted as a variable.

Structures in which two locally Ā-bound elements are linked to the same quantifier, e.g. (18), provide clear evidence that this is the correct analysis for (20).[13] If locally Ā-bound elements vary independently, then we predict that in all structures where more than one element is locally bound to the same quantifier, these elements will vary independently; they need not take the same values for each choice of referent. As the interpretation of (18) shows, this is not true. But if we do not assume that variables must vary independently, then there seems to remain no difference in the semantic behavior of locally and nonlocally Ā-bound elements, and therefore no reason to restrict the concept of variable to locally Ā-bound categories. Let us then reformulate (12) as (21).[14]

(21) α is interpreted as a variable iff α is Ā-bound.

3. Why certain empty categories are anaphors

Let us now turn to principle (5c), which requires nonvariable empty categories to be anaphors. The main motivation for this condition in LGB appears to be the assumption that empty pronominals are always anaphors. Given this consequence of (5c), the binding theory ensures that empty pronominals never appear in governed positions (they would have to be both bound and free; see (6) and LGB).

In light of the arguments in Chomsky (1982) for the existence of a pronominal nonanaphor empty category (pro), we must modify (5c) as (22), which requires only *nonpronominal* nonvariable empty categories to be anaphors.

(22) If α is an empty category and α is neither a variable nor a pronominal, then α is an anaphor.

The work of the part of (5c) that we have eliminated (the requirement that empty pronominals must be anaphors) is taken over by the identification principle. Empty pronominals are now restricted to ungoverned positions when they are anaphors (PRO) and to identified positions when they are nonanaphors (pro).

The remaining part of (5c) – that is, condition (22) – ensures that the empty category in (23) is an anaphor.

(23) a. *Tom_x seems that it was seen e_x (by Mary)
b. *Tom_x seems that it is certain e_x to like Mary

The empty category in (23) is not Ā-bound, so it is not a variable. It is neither ungoverned nor identified, so it cannot be a pronominal. It follows from (22) that this category must then be an anaphor. This makes it possible for principle (A) of the binding theory to exclude (23): the anaphor is not bound here in its governing category.

Though there might well be independent reasons for the ungrammaticality of (23), we have seen that it can be attributed to the binding theory. Even then, however, (22) is dispensable. As we have seen, the empty category cannot be a pronominal. Therefore, it is either a nonpronominal anaphor, in which case it is excluded by principle (A) of the binding theory, or a nonpronominal nonanaphor. But then principle (C) will require it to be A-free and thus exclude the coindexing in (23).

In fact, (22) follows in general from the VEC, principle (C) of the binding theory, and the principle for the interpretation of variables. Consider a nonpronominal nonanaphor nonvariable empty category. By principle (C) it must be A-free, since it is a nonpronominal nonanaphor. Since it is not a variable, it is Ā-free. Thus, it must be free. But by the VEC it must be bound: it is a nonpronominal nonanaphor empty category. Hence, this category is both free and bound; it cannot exist. A nonpronominal nonvariable empty category must be an anaphor.

4. The definition of pronominals

4.1. Right to left

4.1.1. Restatement and elimination

The definition of pronominals (5a) from right to left (24) is equivalent to the conjunction of (25a) and (25b).

(24) If ($\alpha = [F,(P)]$ and α is locally A-bound by β with an independent θ-role or α is free), then α is a pronominal.

(25) a. If $\alpha = [F,(P)]$ and α is free, then α is a pronominal.
b. If $\alpha = [F,(P)]$ and α is locally A-bound by β with an independent θ-role, then α is a pronominal.

(25a) states that free categories that have ϕ-features only are pronominal; (25b) says that categories that are locally A-bound by an element with an independent θ-role and have ϕ-features only are also pronominal. The pronoun and the empty category in (26a,c) are pronominals by (25a), the ones in (26b,d) are pronominals by (25b).

(26) a. He$_x$ left
b. Tom$_x$ said he$_x$ left
c. It's illegal PRO$_x$ to go there
d. Tom$_x$ tried PRO$_x$ to go there

I have been assuming throughout that lexical pronouns and lexical anaphors are inherently characterized as pronominals and anaphors, respectively. Given this natural assumption, the prediction of (24) that *he* is a pronominal in (26a,b) is superfluous. Let us then consider the effect of (24) for empty categories, starting with (25a) and (26c).

The fact that the empty category is pronominal in (26c) also follows from the ECP (since it is ungoverned). In fact, it is easy to see that (25a) is redundant in general for empty categories. By the VEC, a free empty category cannot be a nonpronominal nonanaphor. By the ECP (which would require it to be governed) and principle (A) of the binding theory (which entails that governed anaphors are bound), it cannot be a nonpronominal anaphor, either. Hence, a free empty category must be a pronominal.

Next consider (25b). Apart from predicting that the empty category in (26d) is a pronominal, the claim that categories that have ϕ-features only and are locally A-bound by β with an independent θ-role are pronominals appears to contribute to the account of the ungrammaticality of the examples in (27).

(27) a. *Tom$_x$ hit e$_x$
b. *Tom$_x$ believes e$_x$ to seem that Mary left

In (27) the empty category is bound by an argument in a θ-position, thus by an element with an independent θ-role. By (25b), it is then a pronominal. Since it is in a position that is neither ungoverned nor identified, (27) is excluded.

I shall argue that (25b) is partly tautologous and partly incorrect, hence that it should not be part of the grammar. (25b) involves the rather problematic assumption that lexical anaphors have features not drawn from φ. As (28) exemplifies, lexical anaphors can also be locally bound by a category in an A-position that has an independent θ-role. (In fact, they probably must be bound by such a category.)

(28)   Tom$_x$ likes himself$_x$

If lexical anaphors drew all their features from φ, (25b) would incorrectly predict that *himself* in (28) and lexical anaphors in general are pronominals.

But if lexical anaphors must have features not in φ, this entails that empty and lexical anaphors systematically differ in ways other than the presence or absence of a phonetic matrix. (Within the LGB theory, empty anaphors cannot have features not drawn from φ, since this would preclude the existence of empty pronominal anaphors.) This systematic difference in the feature composition of empty and lexical anaphors seems highly undesirable, since we have a fully explanatory account of the properties of empty categories only to the extent that they are the same as those of their lexical counterparts – apart from differences that follow from the lack of a phonetic matrix. Let us therefore extend from pronominals to anaphors the assumption that all the differences between lexical and empty instantiations are a consequence of the optionality of a phonetic matrix: lexical anaphors also draw all their features from φ. As a result, (25b) must be revised to take account of the fact that lexical anaphors can also be locally A-bound by an element with an independent θ-role.

(29)   If α = [F,(P)] and α is locally A-bound by β with an independent θ-role, then α is a pronominal or α is an anaphor.

(29) states that categories with φ-features only that are locally A-bound by an element with an independent θ-role are either pronominals or anaphors. (29) follows trivially from principle (C) of the binding theory. Principle (C) requires nonpronominal nonanaphors to be A-free; (29) states (with the conditional turned around) that nonpronominal nonanaphors are either (locally) A-free or not = [F,(P)] or not bound by β with an independent θ-role. Thus, whatever appears to be correct from (25b) (that is, (29)) follows from the binding theory. Of course, neither (29) nor principle (C) of the binding theory tells us any more that the empty category in (26d) and (27) is a pronominal.

Apart from the above argument concerning lexical anaphors, (25b) cannot be part of a definition of pronominals since it is circular. As (30a,b) show, having an independent θ-role is not the same property as being in a θ-position.[15]

(30)   a. After PRO$_x$ reading, John$_x$ was shot t$_x$
       b. John$_x$ seems to his$_x$ friends t$_x$ to like Mary

Here the pronominal is bound by an element in a θ-position that inherits from its trace a θ-role that is independent from the pronominal. In order for (25b) to tell us which categories are pronominal, we must therefore know which elements have an independent θ-role. But in order to know that, we must know which categories are pronominal, since if a category is not in a θ-position, then whether or not it has an independent θ-role will depend on what sorts of empty categories it binds. In (30a), for instance, if we had to rely solely on the definition of pronominals, we could never find out which empty category is a pronominal and which is not. In order to know whether either of the two empty categories is a pronominal, we first need to know if the other one is.

There are good reasons, then, to reject (25b). How can it be ensured now that the empty category in (26d) is taken to be a pronominal and that (27a,b) are excluded? As we have seen in section 1, the empty category in a structure like (26d) (= (2b)) must be a pronominal because of the ECP, which excludes ungoverned nonpronominal empty categories. Moreover, structures like (27a) (= (1b)) are excluded whatever NP-type the empty category belongs to. It cannot be a pronominal, since it is neither ungoverned nor identified, and it cannot be a nonpronominal, since then it would form a chain with its antecedent that would have two θ-positions and thus violate the θ-Criterion. (If the empty category is a nonpronominal nonanaphor, then the structure would also be excluded by principle (C) of the binding theory.)

Consider (27b). The empty category here is again a nonpronominal, since it is governed and nonidentified. But the θ-Criterion does not exclude the chain [Tom,e] in (27b), since only one θ-role is assigned to it – the empty category is in a $\bar{\theta}$-position. As discussed in LGB, the movement derivation of structures like (27b) is excluded by the θ-Criterion operating at D-structure under the Projection Principle. Under the movement derivation, the D-structure of (27b) is essentially like (31).

(31) np believes Tom to seem that Mary left

In (31) the argument *Tom* is in a $\bar{\theta}$-position, violating the θ-Criterion. Furthermore, there is no argument in the matrix subject position to bear the relevant θ-role. There cannot be an argument in this position in the D-structure of (27b), since it would have to disappear by S-structure, deleted by the moved NP *Tom*. The disappearance of an argument during the derivation can plausibly be considered to be a violation of the Recoverability Condition.

This account, however, does not extend as it is to the derivation of (27b) where all NPs have been base-generated in their surface position. Restricting our attention to NP-movement structures, we may consider the assumption that D-structure is a *pure* representation of GF-θ (that is, of thematically relevant grammatical functions) to mean that at D-structure only θ-positions may contain arguments. This excludes the base-generation of structures like (32),

(32) Tom_x was believed t_x to have left

since here the argument *Tom* is in a $\bar{\theta}$-position at S-structure. The assumption, however, requires the base-generation of (27b); here, since the matrix subject is a GF-θ and the embedded subject a GF-$\bar{\theta}$, the argument *Tom* must occupy the former position at D-structure as well. The θ-Criterion is then satisfied at both D-structure and S-structure.

Suppose that we think of D-structure not as a pure representation of GF-θ but as the pure representation of GF$_n$ – that is, of the most embedded GFs of chains. Instead of saying that at D-structure arguments may have only GF-θs, we assume that at this level arguments may only have GFs that correspond to GF$_n$s at S-structure.

This view of D-structure forces the movement derivation not only in (32) but also in (27b), if the empty category in the structure is taken to be a nonpronominal. As discussed earlier, the empty category in (27b) must be a nonpronominal, since it is neither ungoverned nor identified; thus, it will form the chain [Tom,e] with the matrix subject. The GF$_n$ in this chain is the embedded subject. Since this is the only GF in the chain that may contain an argument at D-structure, the D-structure of (27b) must be (31). (31) is excluded as before by the θ-Criterion and the Recoverability Condition.[16]

To sum up, we have seen that the definition of pronominals from right to left is partly redundant ((25a) is a consequence of the VEC, the ECP, and principle (C) of the binding theory) and partly incorrect: (25b). We have also seen that the cases (25b) was meant to account for can be handled by independent principles.

4.1.2. D-structure as a pure representation of GF$_n$

The assumption that at D-structure only GF$_n$s may contain arguments (let us call it the GF$_n$-hypothesis) entails that at this level all chains contain a unique member. From this it follows that here only GF-θs may contain arguments. Since all chains have only one member at this level, there is no θ-role transmission; thus, an argument in a $\bar{\theta}$-position could not receive a θ-role at D-structure, violating the θ-Criterion.

Another reason why only GF-θs may contain arguments at D-structure is the following. Consider an argument NP that has a chain at S-structure in which the GF$_n$ is a GF-$\bar{\theta}$. If there is no GF$_i$ in the chain that is a GF-θ, the structure is excluded, since the chain that contains the argument is not assigned a θ-role in any position. If there is a GF$_i$ ($i \neq n$) that is a GF-θ, then (by the θ-Criterion and the Projection Principle) it must contain an argument at D-structure. This may be ruled out for two reasons. First, an argument in a GF$_i$ ($i \neq n$) at D-structure violates the GF$_n$-hypothesis. Second, if there is movement to GF$_i$, then this argument will have to be deleted by S-structure in violation of the Recoverability Condition (cf. the discussion of (31)). Hence, the fact that at D-structure only GF-θs may contain arguments – the main content of the assumption that D-structure is a pure representation of GF-θ – follows from the GF$_n$-hypothesis.

The GF$_n$-hypothesis, together with the Recoverability Condition and the Projection Principle, also entails the uniqueness requirement of the θ-Criterion. We can separate two components of the θ-Criterion: the basic condition requiring that each argument containing a chain have some θ-position and each θ-marked chain contain some argument, and the uniqueness condition, according to which a chain cannot have more than one θ-position or contain more than one argument. The principle that a chain cannot have more than one θ-position follows immediately from the GF_n-hypothesis since, as discussed earlier, the only GF of a chain that may be a θ-position without violating the GF_n-hypothesis (and in movement structures the Recoverability Condition as well) is GF_n.

Consider now a chain with two arguments. Suppose that both arguments are present at D-structure. Again, only one of them may be in GF_n; hence, the GF_n-hypothesis is violated (and in movement structures the Recoverability Condition as well). The only remaining case in which uniqueness could not be observed then is one in which an argument is created during the derivation. For example: Why can *Tom was seen e* not mean *Tom was seen somebody*, i.e. *Tom and someone were seen*? We should of course want to answer this without a stipulation like "NP-traces are nonarguments." Recall that the direction in which Move α operates is immaterial; that is, a theory in which Move α derives S-structures from D-structures (moves GF_n to GF_1) is a notational variant of one in which this rule derives D-structures from S-structures (moves GF_1 to GF_n). But then the Recoverability Condition would be inadequate, if it would prevent the deletion of an argument only in one direction, that is, when Move α is viewed as replacing GF_1 by GF_n but not vice versa. The Recoverability Condition should be a bidirectional principle, ensuring a one-to-one mapping between arguments at D-structure and at S-structure, thus preventing both the deletion and the "creation" of arguments during the derivation. (Note that this approach allows an argument-role to be transferred, as for example in *Wh* Movement from the *wh*-phrase to the variable.) The uniqueness conditions now follow completely.

The movement derivation of *Wh* Movement structures follows from the assumption that D-structure is a pure representation of GF-θ but not from the formulation that at D-structure only GF-θs may contain arguments. Given the definition of chains in LGB, the assumption that D-structure is a pure representation of GF_n does not entail this either.

Suppose that we strengthen the assumption that D-structure is a pure representation of GF_n to mean that at D-structure only GF_n may contain "contentive" elements, where these include Operators and arguments. This will also exclude the nonmovement derivation of *Wh* Movement structures if the restriction of the notion of chains to A-chains is dropped. Instead of the hypothesis that all categories in Ā-position break the chain, we may assume that only Operators do.[17,18]

The GF_n-hypothesis entails that the concept of chains and not that of Move α is basic, in the sense that the definition of the latter makes reference to the former.[19] We now think of Move α as operating in the domain of chains, relating GF-Ās and GF-θs only derivatively, as a consequence of its basic function of relating GF_1s and GF_ns.

This account of the relationship between Move α and chains raises the following question, to which we return in the next section: if chains are not an encoding at S-structure of the operations of Move α during the derivation, then what are they? What is their function in the grammar?

4.2. Left to right

4.2.1. Restatement and elimination

Let us now consider the definition of pronominals from left to right:

(33) If α is a pronominal, then α = [F,(P)] and (if α is bound, then it is locally A-bound by β with an independent θ-role).

In part, (33) says that a pronominal has only φ-features. This is preserved in the assumption made earlier that both pronominals and anaphors have only φ-features. Moreover, (33) states that pronominals are either free or locally A-bound by β with an independent θ-role, or equivalently that bound pronominals are locally A-bound by β with an independent θ-role.

Now the θ-role of β (if it has one) will be necessarily independent from α if α is a pronominal because of the assumption discussed in section 1 that pronominals do not transmit θ-roles. We can therefore omit the proviso in (33) that the θ-role of β must be independent.

Second, as argued earlier, locally Ā-bound pronominals exist in cases like (18). It seems, then, that (33) must be restricted to cases where the pronominal is locally A-bound. Given these observations, (33) reduces to (34).

(34) If α is a pronominal locally A-bound by β, then β has a θ-role.

This last remnant of the definition of pronominals appears to contribute to excluding structures like (35).

(35) *It$_x$ is clear that Mary left yesterday without e$_x$ being obvious that she was forced to.
(Compare with *It is clear that Mary left yesterday without it being obvious that she was forced to.*)

(34) predicts that the expletive-bound empty category in (35) cannot be taken as a pronominal. As a nonpronominal it is excluded by the ECP since it is ungoverned. Are there any independent reasons why the empty category in (35) cannot be a pronominal?

In LGB Chomsky proposes that θ-roles are assigned not to categories but to chains. We may then assume that β, the element that functions as the antecedent of a pronominal, is also not a category but a chain.[20] Therefore, in (30a,b) the entity that functions as the antecedent of the pronominal and has a θ-role is not the NP *John* but the chain [John,e] containing this NP and its trace. We accordingly revise (34) as (36):

(36) If α is a pronominal locally A-bound by a chain C, then C has a θ-role.

Returning to (35), if the empty category is taken to be a pronominal, then its antecedent is not the expletive NP *it*; instead, according to the proposal just made, it is the whole chain that contains both this NP and the postverbal S′ [it,S′]. But this explains, without any reference to the definition of pronominals or to its modification in (36), why the empty category in (35) cannot be a pronominal. We can assume that the chain [it,S′] refers by virtue of containing an argument, the postverbal S′. A pronominal must be coreferential with its antecedent when the latter refers. Therefore, if the empty category is pronominal in (35), then it must refer, and it must be an argument. This will be excluded by the θ-Criterion at D-structure, however, since there would be two arguments in the *without*-clause but only one θ-role. (By the bidirectional Recoverability Condition, the empty category cannot be a nonargument at D-structure.)[21] If the empty category is nonpronominal, it is of course still excluded by the ECP.

In contrast to the stipulation in (34), this account claims that (35) contains an element that can function as the antecedent of the pronominal. Evidence for this is provided by (37).

(37) It was clear without PRO being obvious that Mary left yesterday.

(37) differs from (35) only in that it does not contain a postverbal S′ cosuperscripted with PRO. In (37) the empty category has the same antecedent as the one in (35). However, in (37) the θ-Criterion is not violated, since the *without*-clause here contains only one argument (the pronominal empty category) for the one available θ-role.

(37) shows that it was correct to revise (34), the condition that requires the binder of a locally A-bound pronominal to have a θ-role. This condition would have excluded the grammatical (37) alongside the ungrammatical (35), since in both cases the local binder of PRO is an expletive.[22] The revised condition in (36) allows both (35) and (37). Since (35) is excluded by the θ-Criterion, once it is assumed that the antecedents or pronominals are not categories but chains, neither (35) nor (37) shows the necessity of countenancing (36).

There are reasons to think, however, that (36) is descriptively correct. Together with certain other assumptions, (36) entails that PRO can never be expletive, if we generalize it from chains that are binders to all chains that are antecedents of pronominals, as in (38) (that is, if we extend it from structures like Tom_x *likes his$_x$ friend* to cover *His$_x$ friend likes Tom$_x$* as well).

(38) If chain C is the antecedent of a pronominal, then C must have a θ-role.

Because of its essentially variable-like interpretation, we can assume that an antecedentless PRO must be an argument. Given (38), all pronominals that have antecedents must also be arguments. Since a chain that is the antecedent of a pronominal must have a θ-role, it must contain an argument. If so, then either this argument will refer or it will be a quasi-argument like the weather-*it* in (19), for example. If it refers, then the pronominal of which it is the antecedent must be coreferential with it. Hence, the pronominal must also refer and must also be an argument. If the antecedent is a quasi-argument, then so is the pronominal (cf. (19)). Hence, again, the pronominal must be an argument.

PRO then cannot be an expletive, whether or not it has an antecedent. Note that (38) entails more generally that expletive pronominals must be free, since by the above argument expletives must not have an antecedent.

If the stipulation in (38) is useful, then we should consider whether it is a consequence of some more general principle. Let us approach this by recalling that the discussion of (27b) ended with the conclusion that the notion of chain and not that of Move α is the more fundamental of the two, since Move α operates in the domain of chains, and chains are not the encoding of the operations of Move α. What exactly, then, is a chain?

Chomsky's proposal that θ-roles can be assigned to chains leads to the hypothesis that chains are on a par with arguments: they are to S-structure (and LF, if this is distinct) what arguments are to D-structure. From a slightly different viewpoint, we may say that instead of, or parallel with, projecting the θ-Criterion from S-structure to D-structure, the Projection Principle projects this condition from the level of chains (C-structure) to the level of arguments (A-structure). The θ-Criterion should then be stated as (39a,b), and its effect at the level of arguments will be (39c,d):

(39) a. Each chain is assigned some θ-role.
      b. Each θ-role is assigned to some chain.
      c. Each argument is assigned some θ-role.
      d. Each θ-role is assigned to some argument.

(39c,d) contain the original core idea of the θ-Criterion. The further consequence of the proposed view of this condition and the Projection Principle is that the relation holds not only between arguments and θ-roles, as stated in (39c,d), but also between chains and θ-roles, as required by (39a,b).

By (39a), all chains must have a θ-role. But then (38) – the requirement that those chains that serve as antecedents for pronominals have a θ-role – follows in general. This means that we have dispensed with the definition of pronominals completely.[23] From right to left it was partly incorrect and circular (i.e. (25b) and partly a consequence of the VEC, principle (A) of the binding theory, and the ECP (25a)). From left to right it was partly incorrect (in excluding Ā-bound pronominals) and partly a consequence of the revised formulation of the θ-Criterion, according to which all chains have θ-roles.

4.2.2. S-structure as chain-structure and uniformity of θ-role assignment

In LGB Chomsky suggests that grammars of a well-designed theory of UG that incorporates the Projection Principle should not make it possible for derivations to violate a condition like (40):

(40)   If α θ-marks β (β a category or a position) at some level, then α θ-marks β at all levels.

"Grammars conforming to this theory [a theory of UG that includes the Projection Principle] should simply not provide devices" that on the one hand permit the requirement that syntactic representations are projections from the lexicon (i.e. the Projection Principle, essentially) to be satisfied but on the other hand permit condition (40), that positions and categories are θ-marked in the same way at all syntactic levels, to be violated (LGB 38–39).

If we are correct in assuming that the Projection Principle projects the θ-Criterion from arguments to chains, then it is regularly a different entity that receives a given θ-role at A- and at C-structure. We can preserve the essential content of Chomsky's suggestion if we assume that grammars should not provide devices that would permit a violation of (41).

(41) If α θ-marks an argument β in position P_i at A-structure and a chain γ in P_j at C-structure, then $P_i = P_j$ and β is contained in γ.

The requirement in (40) that a θ-role must be assigned to the same category throughout the derivation is met by NP-movement structures under the assumption that chains transmit the θ-role assigned to them to the argument that they contain. This account does not work for *Wh* Movement constructions, however. Consider the analysis according to which chains transmit θ-roles to arguments. In a standard *Wh* Movement structure like (4), the θ-role that is assigned to the chain at S-structure that contains a unique member, the variable, is taken up at D-structure by the *wh*-phrase. This chain cannot transmit the θ-role to the *wh*-phrase, since the *wh*-phrase is not contained in it. Extending chains to Ā-chains does not help, since even if the θ-role could be transmitted to the *wh*-phrase at S-structure, it should not be, as this element is not an argument at this level.

There is no problem in the present framework, however. Once chains are extended to include Operators, the *wh*-phrase satisfies (41); in general, a moved *wh*-phrase W is always in the chain at C-structure that receives the θ-role assigned to W at A-structure.

Assuming that the lexicon specifies the GFs to be θ-marked, the condition of (41) that an element α θ-marks the same (corresponding) positions at all levels can be taken to follow from the Projection Principle. Consider the requirement that the argument β that α θ-marks at A-structure must be in the chain γ that is given (the same) θ-role by α at C-structure. To violate this condition, a grammar would have to contain some device to make β external to γ. When β is in its A-structure position at C-structure, it is in γ. Therefore, this device must be either movement or deletion. Deletion is ruled out by the Recoverability Condition; β must be an argument at A-structure, since by hypothesis it receives a θ-role. Movement is also ruled out in a Universal Grammar in the grammars of which all movement is chain-internal – be this because chains are defined as the encoding of the derivation at S-structure, or (as proposed here) because movement is defined as an operation on the members of some chain.

5. Crossover

As another illustration of how the grammar functions without NP-type definitions, let us consider strong crossover structures.

(42) a. *[I wonder who$_x$] he$_x$ saw e$_x$
 b. *[I wonder who$_x$] he$_x$ said e$_x$ Mary liked e$_x$
 c. *[Who$_x$] e$_x$ saw e$_x$
 d. *[Who$_x$] e$_x$ said e$_x$ Mary liked e$_x$

The problem stated in the usual way is this: Why is it impossible to associate the *wh*-phrase and the pronoun *he* in (42a,b)? In other words, why is the reading of (42a,b) missing that is indicated by the indexing and on which (42a,b) would be synonymous with (43a,b), respectively?

(43) a. I wonder who saw himself
 b. I wonder who said Mary liked him (where *him* is related to *who*; that is, *I wonder for which x, x said Mary liked x*)

Although strong crossover is often discussed in the context of *Wh* Movement, the presence of a *wh*-phrase in Comp is irrelevant to the basic issues here. We might consider the general problem to be the following: When are A-bound empty categories permissible? Thus, (42a,b) are simply special cases and the problem is better exemplified if the square-bracketed material in (42) is ignored. The question why the so-called Comp-to-Comp violations exemplified in (42c,d) are excluded also falls under this more general formulation. Comp-to-Comp violations differ from crossover only in that here the binder in A-position is an empty category.

Let us partition the relevant examples into two sets: in (44)–(46) no empty category in Comp is involved, whereas the structures in (47) contain such an empty category.

(44) a. *He$_x$ saw e$_x$
 b. *He$_x$ said Mary saw e$_x$
(45) a. *He$_x$ said e$_x$ seemed S'
 b. *He$_x$ believed e$_x$ to seem S'
(46) a. *He$_x$ seemed e$_x$ saw Mary
 b. *He$_x$ seemed Mary saw e$_x$
(47) a. *He$_x$ said e$_x$ Mary saw e$_x$'
 b. *He$_x$ said e$_x$ e$_x$' seemed S'
 c. *He$_x$ seemed e$_x$ e$_x$' saw Mary, *He$_x$ seemed e$_x$ Mary saw e$_x$'

Consider first (44)–(46). Here the empty category cannot be a pronominal, since it is neither ungoverned nor identified. If it were, structure (44b) would be grammatical (compare (2b), for example). ((44a) would still be excluded by principle (B) of the binding theory.) (45) with a pronominal empty category, PRO or pro, would be excluded even if this were ungoverned or identified. As discussed in section 4, a pronominal with a referential antecedent must refer, and hence is an argument. Therefore, the θ-Criterion is violated at A-structure, there being two arguments for the one θ-role assigned by the embedded verb (the pronominal and the postverbal S'). (By the bidirectional Recoverability Condition, the pronominal must be an argument at A-structure as well.) If the antecedent were not an argument but an expletive, then (45) would be excluded by the θ-Criterion for another reason: there would be no argument to receive the θ-role of the matrix subject. The same problem would also arise in (44) if the matrix subject were an expletive.

(46a,b) would also be excluded by the θ-Criterion at C-structure, even if the empty pronominal in them were in an ungoverned or identified position. Since pronominals break the chain, the matrix subject and the empty category would be in two separate chains, but no θ-role is available for one of them. If the matrix subject is not an expletive but an argument, as in (46), then there is a further violation of the θ-Criterion at S-structure: this argument receives no θ-role.

Consider now nonpronominal empty categories. In (44a,b) and (45a,b) the chain [he,e] contains a θ-position that is not identical to GF_n. If this position contains no argument at A-structure, the construction is excluded by the θ-Criterion; if it does, the construction is excluded by the GF_n-hypothesis. If there is movement to this position from GF_n, then the Recoverability Condition will also be violated; moreover, (45) will violate the θ-Criterion in GF_n, where the argument *he* would receive no θ-role. If the matrix subject is an expletive element, then base-generation of (44) and (45) is ruled out by the θ-Criterion, since there will be no argument for the matrix subject θ-role to be assigned to. Under the movement derivation the expletive in (44), though not in (45), would violate the θ-Criterion in GF_n. Both in (44) and in (45) either the θ-Criterion or both the GF_n-hypothesis and the Recoverability Condition would again not be observed (depending on whether the matrix subject position contains an argument at A-structure).

If it is a nonpronominal anaphor, the empty category in (46) is excluded by principle (A) of the binding theory, because it is not A-bound in its governing category. If it is a nonpronominal nonanaphor, it is ruled out by principle (C), because it is not A-free. Redundantly, if the empty category is a nonpronominal nonanaphor, principle (C) also excludes (44) and (45). If the empty category is a nonpronominal anaphor, then principle (A) also rules out (44b) and (45a), again redundantly. Thus, if the empty category is a nonpronominal, then (44b) and (45a) are ruled out by the θ-Criterion or the GF_n-hypothesis and the binding theory. (44a) and (45b) violate only the θ-Criterion or the GF_n-hypothesis (compare for example *He was seen e*), and (46) violates only the binding theory (compare with *He seemed e to see Mary*).

Let us now turn to the cases with an empty category in Comp. Empty categories in this position may be Comp-to-Comp traces, as in (48a), or Operators, as in (48b).

(48) a. Who_x did you say e_x Mary liked e'_x
 b. I found a $book_x$ e_x PRO to read e'_x

In LGB Chomsky credits R. Freidin with the observation that principle (C) as stated in (6) would exclude structures like (48b) with e' a nonpronominal nonanaphor, since the c-commanding coindexed NP *the book* is in A-position. I adopt the LGB proposal that principle (C) should be interpreted as requiring nonpronominal nonanaphors to be A-free only within the scope (c-command domain) of their Operator. This proviso is vacuous for categories that have no Operator; that is, these must still be A-free throughout.

Let us make the simplest assumption, namely, that empty categories in Comp are optionally taken to be Operators. Suppose that *e* in (48a) is incorrectly taken to be an Operator. (48a) is then excluded because Operators are not allowed in the Comp node related to the matrix verb of (48a), presumably by selectional restrictions. The structure is also ruled out by the principle against vacuous quantification (Chomsky 1982), since it will contain two quantifier-type elements but only one category that can serve as a variable. (48a) with *e* an Operator is like (49), in which the Operator is overt.

(49)   *Who did you say who Mary liked e

Hence, the empty category in Comp in (48a) is not an Operator.

Suppose now that *e* in (48b) is misclassified as a non-Operator. Consider the empty category in object position, *e'*. *e'* cannot be a pronominal, if (as suggested in note 12) Ā-bound pronominals exist only in cases like (18) where the pronominal has an antecedent in A-position linked to the same Ā-binder. (In (48b) *e'* is also in a governed, nonidentified position.) Suppose that *e'* is a nonpronominal. It cannot be an anaphor, since it is not A-bound in its governing category as required by principle (A) of the binding theory. It cannot be a nonpronominal nonanaphor either, since its A-binder is in the scope of its Operator (it does not have one, by assumption, so this holds vacuously), violating principle (C). Thus, if the empty category in Comp is taken to be a non-Operator in (48b), then *e'* cannot be either a pronominal or a nonpronominal. Hence, *e* must be an Operator in (48b).

Returning to (47a–c), these are excluded if the empty category in Comp is an Operator, since selectional restrictions exclude Operators in the Comp node associated with the matrix verbs in (47), just as in (48a).[24] Suppose that this empty category is not an Operator. Again consider *e'*, the empty category in A-position. *e'* cannot be either a pronominal or a nonpronominal, for the same reasons that excluded both of these possibilities in (48b). Therefore, *e* in (47) is neither an Operator nor a non-Operator; the structure cannot exist.

Principle (C) of the binding theory played a central role in eliminating contextual definitions; it was involved in the derivation of each of the three NP-type conditions. I am aware of one more argument for these conditions that I have not discussed so far. This takes the opposite direction: it attempts to eliminate principle (C) with the help of the contextual definition of pronominals. The argument, which Chomsky (1982) attributes to D. Sportiche, is as follows. If the definition of pronominals is assumed, then the empty category in structures like (44) is a pronominal (it is A-bound by a category with an independent θ-role) and is excluded by virtue of being neither ungoverned nor identified. Chomsky suggests that this makes it possible to eliminate principle (C), at least for empty categories.

In LGB, following May (1979), Chomsky assumes principle (C) to exclude structures like (42b). The empty category in A-position in the embedded clause is locally Ā-bound by the empty category in Comp, so it is a variable. It is also A-bound by the matrix subject that is in the c-command domain of the Operator related to the variable, i.e. the *wh*-phrase. But variables are R-expressions in the LGB framework, constrained by principle (C), so the structure is excluded. Chomsky (1982) points out that if the Comp-to-Comp trace in (42b) is not considered to be a binder, then the account of (44) that uses the definition of pronominals carries over to (42b), making principle (C) superfluous here.

But this cannot be an argument for contextual definitions, since (44) is also excluded by principles independent of principle (C), even if the definition of pronominals is not assumed. If in (44) the empty category is not taken to be a pronominal, then (44) contains the chain [he,e], which has two θ-positions. As we have seen, this is excluded either by the θ-Criterion or by the GF_n-hypothesis (and by the Recoverability Condition if there is movement). This account can be made to carry over to examples like (42b) (which are essentially like (47a)) in the same way as the one that uses the definition of pronominals. If Comp-to-Comp traces do not count as binders for the definition of pronominals, then presumably they do not break chains. As suggested in section 4.1.2, we may assume that only Operators do. We have seen that structures like (47a) and (42b) are excluded if the empty category in Comp is taken to be an Operator. If it is not an Operator, then the structure is excluded not only by the binding theory but also by the principles that prevent the chain [he,(e),e'] from legitimately containing two θ-positions. Hence, whether or not the definition of pronominals is assumed, principle (C) is redundant in the account of the ungrammaticality of (47a) and (42b).[25] Even if it turned out to be desirable and feasible to eliminate principle (C) for empty categories, this would not provide evidence for contextual definitions.

But note that the definition of pronominals does not help to exclude (46) and (47c). Since the empty category in these examples is not A-bound by an element with an independent θ-role, the LGB definition does not predict it to be a pronominal. Correspondingly, the θ-Criterion does not exclude these structures either. Some condition with the effect of principle (C) is still necessary, then, to ensure that these constructions cannot be generated with a nonpronominal nonanaphor empty category.

6. Conclusion

I have argued that the contextual definitions proposed in LGB to achieve the appropriate classification of empty categories have the status of auxiliary stipulations. I have shown that they are partly incorrect and partly consequences of independently necessary principles of grammar, which (given certain modifications) account for all the phenomena that motivated the definitions. One of the proposed modifications is to regard the Projection Principle as projecting the θ-Criterion from the level of chains (C-structure) to the level of arguments (A-structure). C-structure differs from S-structure in that at this level chains play the role that arguments have at

A-structure with respect to θ-roles. A-structure is unlike D-structure in that it is a pure representation of GF_n and only derivatively of GF-θ. This framework explains the fact that both chains and arguments are involved in the θ-Criterion. The uniqueness requirement of this condition and the fact that A-structure is a pure representation of GF-θ follow from it. It explains further some phenomena involving the relationship of pronominals and independent θ-bound categories that the LGB definition of pronominals stipulates. Thus, the assumption that A-structure is a pure representation of GF_n of chains contributes to the explanation of the fact that independent θ-bound empty categories are pronominals. The hypothesis that at C-structure chains are the bearers of θ-roles helps to account for the fact that the antecedent of a pronominal always has a θ-role.

Acknowledgments

I am grateful to Noam Chomsky, Luigi Rizzi, Neil Smith, Jean-Roger Vergnaud, and two LI reviewers for helpful comments. Parts of this material were presented at MIT, University College London, and the 1983 GLOW conference in York.

References

Betts, A. (1983) "A Note on the Intransitive Impersonal Passive Construction in German," ms., University College London.

Brody, M. (1982) "Anaphoric Dependencies and Conditions on Domains," paper presented at the 1982 GLOW conference, Paris.

Brody, M. (forthcoming) "On the Complementary Distribution of Empty Categories," *Linguistic Inquiry* (1985) 505–546.

Chomsky, N. (1981) *Lectures on Government and Binding*, Foris, Dordrecht.

Chomsky, N. (1982) *Some Concepts and Consequences of the Theory of Government and Binding*, MIT Press, Cambridge, Massachusetts.

Higginbotham, J. (1980) "Pronouns and Bound Variables," *Linguistic Inquiry* 11, 679–708.

Koopman, H. and Sportiche, D. (1981) "Variables and the Bijection Principle," paper presented at the 1981 GLOW conference. Göttingen.

May, R. (1979) "Must COMP-to-COMP Movement Be Stipulated?," *Linguistic Inquiry* 10, 719–725.

Rizzi, L. (1983) "On Chain Formation," paper presented at the 1983 GLOW Conference, York.

Safir, K. (1983) "Multiple Variable Binding," ms., University of Pennsylvania.

Sportiche, D. (1983) *Structural Invariance and Symmetry in Syntax*, Doctoral dissertation, MIT, Cambridge, Massachusetts.

3

ON THE COMPLEMENTARY DISTRIBUTION OF EMPTY CATEGORIES

1. Introduction

1.1. *The phenomenon*

Consider phonetically unrealized NPs that are coreferential with their antecedents when they have one (as in (3b)) and are interpreted (roughly) as "for someone" when they do not (as in (3a)). These NPs are in complementary distribution with launching sites of movement rules, as (1) through (7) illustrate.

(1) *Who is it illegal e to go there
(2) *Tom is illegal e to go there
(3) a. It's illegal e to go there (= "It's illegal for someone to go there")
     b. Tom thinks it's illegal e to shave himself (= "Tom thinks it's illegal for him (Tom) to shave himself")
(4) a. Who does Tom believe e likes Mary
     b. Who does Tom believe Mary likes e
(5) Tom seems/is believed e to like Mary
(6) a. *Tom believes e to like Mary (≠ "Tom believes someone/himself to like Mary")
     b. *Tom believes Mary to like e (≠ "Tom believes Mary to like someone/him (Tom)")
(7) Tom thinks it seems/is believed e to like Mary (≠ Tom thinks it seems/is believed someone/he to like Mary; i.e. "Tom thinks someone/he seems/is believed to like Mary")

Consider the position the phonetically unrealized NP takes in (3), where the "for someone" and the "coreferential" interpretations are available. As (1) and (2) show, movement is not possible from this position. Conversely, launching sites of movement, exemplified in (4) and (5), are not legitimate positions for phonetically null NPs with these special interpretations, as (6) and (7) show.

Assuming that nonovert subjects (as in (3)) and launching sites of movement (as in (4) and (5)) are syntactically represented by empty categories (ECs) and assuming the notion of government developed in Chomsky (1981), the above distribution can be described in the following terms: ECs in launching sites of movement are governed; ECs with the special "for someone/coreferential" interpretation must be ungoverned.

In Government-Binding (GB) theory the EC that is coreferential with its antecedent or has the "for someone" interpretation is a pronominal anaphor (PRO), whereas the ECs left by movement rules in their launching sites are traces, in general nonpronominal NPs. In standard versions of this theory the complementary distribution between trace and PRO is a consequence of the Empty Category Principle (ECP) and the binding theory. The ECP requires nonpronominal ECs to be properly governed – a stronger condition than the Trace Condition (8a), but from which (8a) follows. The binding theory entails the PRO Condition (8b); see Chomsky (1981) for discussion.

(8) a. *Trace Condition*
    Trace (nonpronominal EC) is governed.
  b. *PRO Condition*
    PRO (pronominal anaphor EC) is ungoverned.

Thus, under standard GB theory this regularity follows from the accidental interaction of two unrelated modules of grammar. This conspiracy between the two subtheories is quite curious, and it seems to cast doubt on the correctness of the principles involved. This is different from the situation where some surface irregularity is explained as the result of the accidental interplay of two subsystems. Here we have a regularity, and a regularity is explained only if the theory tells us why it is necessary. So a crucial regularity of the system like the one exemplified in (1)–(7) should presumably follow from some deep principle of Universal Grammar. I shall attempt to develop such a principle. Note that this argument holds against all theories where (the effects of) the PRO Condition and (the effects of) the Trace Condition are derived independently from each other, for example, the theories of Brody (1981), Aoun (1982), Bouchard (1982), Vergnaud (1982), Zubizarreta (1982), Sportiche (1983), and Manzini (1983). (Theories that are concerned with and derive the conditional "If a trace is governed, then it is properly governed" – for example, the treatment of the ECP in Aoun (1982) or Pesetsky (1982) – are of course immune from this criticism.)

1.2. *Contextual definitions*

Chomsky (1981; 1982) emphasizes that the complementary distribution of trace and PRO requires an explanation and claims that his proposed contextual definitions of ECs provide a solution. The striking fact of complementary distribution is explained, Chomsky argues, if there is only one basic type of EC, "PRO" and "trace" then being just names for the occurrences in different contexts of what is always the same EC, whose various functions/occurrences are picked out by the contextual definitions. As I argue in Brody (1984a), the argument is incorrect, essentially because the assumption that there is only one basic type of EC does not solve the problem of complementary distribution but only changes it into the question of why the two functions of the same EC are in complementary distribution. And this is still due to the conspiracy between the binding theory and the ECP – a nonexplanatory answer. "For a genuine explanation we should look instead at the principles that induce the complementary distribution, trying to reformulate them in such a way that this phenomenon ceases to appear to be an accidental conspiracy" (Brody (1984a, 360)).

In Brody (1984a) I argue further that contextual definitions are in fact auxiliary stipulations, and that these stipulations can be dispensed with. ECs can be characterized as +/− pronominal, +/− anaphor in a random fashion, the incorrect assignments all being excluded by other independently motivated conditions. For ease of reference I shall call the version of GB theory incorporating these assumptions, which I shall adopt, the *Random Characterization* (RC) system.

2. Chains and the complementary distribution

2.1. *Stipulations in the definition of chains*

Let us start with the simplified definition of chains in (9) and Chomsky's (1981) statement of the θ-Criterion, essentially as in (10).

(9) $[x_1, \ldots, x_n]$ is a chain iff
   a. x_1 is an NP
   b. x_i locally A-binds x_{i+1}
   c. for $i > 1$, x_i is an EC

(10) *θ-Criterion*
   a. Each argument is in a chain that has a unique θ-position.
   b. Each θ-position is in a chain that contains a unique argument.

According to (9), a set of categories $[x_1, \ldots, x_n]$ is a chain only if they are all coindexed, x_1 is an NP, all others are ECs, and each member c-commands the next.

Consider (11) and (12).

(11) Tom$_x$ tried e$_x$ to go there often
(12) Tom$_x$ seems e$_x$ to go there often

By definition (9) there are three chains in both (11) and (12): [Tom], [e], and [Tom,e]. Let us assume that an EC is optionally taken to be an argument. In (11) the chain [Tom,e] would not satisfy the θ-Criterion since it contains two θ-positions. However, the chains [Tom], [e] do comply with this condition when the EC is an argument. In (12) the chains [Tom], [e] would not satisfy the θ-Criterion since the former contains an argument but receives no θ-role. The chain [Tom,e], where the EC is a nonargument, does satisfy the θ-Criterion: it is assigned a unique θ-role and contains a unique argument. Thus, as far as the grammatical examples in (11) and (12) are concerned, there is no need to complicate the definition of chains and/or the theory of ECs. Some such move appears to become necessary, however, when we consider the ungrammatical cases in (2) and (6a), the standard examples of Trace Condition and PRO Condition violations.

(2) *Tom_x is illegal e_x to go there
(6) a. *Tom_x believes e_x to like Mary

The assumptions in (9) and (10) do not suffice to exclude these structures. (2) could be analyzed like (12): since according to definition (9) it contains the chain [Tom,e], it satisfies the θ-Criterion. (6a) could be analyzed like (11): since according to definition (9) it contains the chains [Tom], [e], it satisfies the θ-Criterion requirements that each chain be associated with at most one θ-position and argument.

In Chomsky (1981), where it is assumed that ECs cross-classify as +/− pronominal, +/− anaphor categories, the contextual definitions ensure that the EC in (2) is a non-pronominal (anaphor), while the EC in (6a) is a pronominal anaphor. This enables the PRO and Trace Conditions to exclude these structures.

Since we have rejected the contextual definitions of ECs, other assumptions are necessary to make the PRO and Trace Conditions operative. In standard GB theory, as in the RC system, it is not true that movement rules always leave behind nonpronominal ECs; nor is it true that the presence of nonpronominal ECs is conditional on movement having taken place. Given the distinction between + and − pronominal ECs, the EC in the Italian example of subject inversion in (13) is naturally considered a free pronominal element despite its having been left behind by the rule that moved the subject into postverbal position. Conversely, the parasitic gap EC in (14) is a nonpronominal EC, although it has been base-generated in its S-Structure position. (See Chomsky (1981; 1982) for discussion.)

(13) e parla Giovanni
      speaks Giovanni
      "Giovanni speaks"
(14) Which book did he criticize e without reading e

In the RC system, if the EC in (2) is taken to be nonpronominal, then it is excluded by the Trace Condition, and ultimately by the ECP, since it is ungoverned. But what if it is taken to be pronominal? Contextual definitions do not prevent this, since the RC system dispenses with them. The θ-Criterion and the Projection Principle force a movement derivation on (2). The NPs cannot be in their base-generated position in (2) since then the construction would violate the θ-Criterion at D-Structure. But as (13) shows, this by itself does not entail that the EC in (2) cannot be a pronominal. It might be that if the EC is taken to be a pronominal nonanaphor (pro), the Identification Principle of Chomsky (1982) excludes it; but what if it is a pronominal anaphor?[1] The PRO Condition is satisfied, since the EC is ungoverned. The Trace Condition is irrelevant, since the EC is pronominal. The θ-Criterion is also satisfied: given the definition of chain in (9), (2) contains the chain [Tom,e], which fulfills the requirements in (10).

Various other assumptions could be adopted to exclude (2) in the RC system. Let us accept temporarily the stipulation proposed in Chomsky (1981) (where, in the analysis incorporating contextual definitions and a statement of the θ-Criterion as in (10), it in fact appears to be redundant): pronominal categories break the chain.[2] Given the assumption that nonhead members of chains are ECs, the stipulation can be restricted to ECs.

(15) A pronominal EC is always the head (x_1) of the chain.

(15) ensures that (2) is also excluded when the EC in it is taken to be pronominal. If it is, (2) will contain two chains, [Tom] and [e], at least the former violating the θ-Criterion.

(6a) presents a similar situation. If the EC is a pronominal, it may be an anaphor or a nonanaphor. If the latter, it is excluded by the Identification Principle, since it is not identified. If the former, it is excluded by the PRO Condition, since it is governed. But suppose that it is analyzed as a nonpronominal category. The PRO Condition and the Identification Principle are irrelevant, since they only constrain pronominals. On the other hand, the Trace Condition (and the ECP) is satisfied, since the EC in (6a) is (properly) governed. The chains [Tom] and [e], which conform to definition (9), also satisfy the θ-Criterion. To ensure the exclusion of (6a), we might choose from the range of possible stipulations to strengthen (15) to a biconditional. That is, equivalently, in addition to (15) we could also adopt (16).

(16) A nonpronominal EC is never the head (x_1) of the chain.

(16) again follows Chomsky (1981). In the context of a requirement that nonpronominal ECs must be bound (see the definition of pronominals in Chomsky (1981) and the interaction of the V-Element Condition, the ECP, and binding principle (A) in the system proposed in Brody (1984a)), (16) entails the effects of Chomsky's maximality requirement on chains, in the domain of chains not involving cosuperscripting. (Again, given statement (10) of the θ-Criterion and the contextual definition of pronominals, the maximality requirement seems to be redundant, at least in the context of the present problem.)[3]

(16) ensures that (6a) is excluded even if the EC in it is taken to be nonpronominal, which circumvents the effect of the PRO Condition. If the EC is nonpronominal, then by (16), (6a) will contain only one chain, [Tom,e], violating the θ-Criterion.

As stated, (16) entails the extension of chains to Ā-chains. Assuming that of categories in Ā-positions all and only Operators break the chain, an Operator may be defined as an NP in Ā-position that is not locally Ā-bound. An assumption more in keeping with the RC system would be that ECs are optionally taken to be Operators when they occur in Ā-position. Those lexical NPs that can function as Operators are then inherently characterized as such. (See Brody (1984a) for discussion.) The extension of chains to Ā-chains assumed here is not crucial to the central argument, as appendix 2 will show.

2.2. Further problems

The θ-Criterion is crucially involved in excluding both (2) and (6a). If the EC in (6a) is taken to be a nonpronominal, then the θ-Criterion rules out the resulting doubly θ-marked chain [Tom,e]. This predicts that an example that differs from (6a) in that only one of the two positions of the corresponding chain is θ-marked should be grammatical.

(5)   Tom seems/is believed e to like Mary
(17) *Tom believes e to be obvious that Mary left

The prediction is fulfilled when the $\bar{\theta}$-position is that of the head of the chain (5) but not when it is a nonhead (17). Brody (1984a) suggests that D-Structure is a representation, not of GF-θ (as in Chomsky (1981; 1982), for example), but of GF_n – that is, at this level an argument must be in the most deeply embedded position of its chain[4] – and points out that under this assumption (17) violates the θ-Criterion at D-Structure. See Sportiche (1983) for another approach to the problem created by examples like (17).

Now consider (2). If the EC is taken to be pronominal, then again the resulting chain structure [Tom], [e] violates the θ-Criterion since the former chain will receive no θ-role. The θ-Criterion in (10) then will not exclude structures that differ from (2) to the extent that this chain does not contain an argument and thus does not need a θ-role.

(3)   a. It's illegal e to go there
(18) a. *There is illegal e to be a man in the garden
      b. *It was clear that Mary left without e being obvious that she wanted to
         (Compare: It was clear that Mary left without it being obvious that she wanted to)
(1)   *Who is it illegal e to go there

The EC in (18) and (1) is PRO, other possibilities being excluded by the Trace Condition and the Identification Principle. Suppose first that PRO is not coindexed with anything. Then it is an argument interpreted "quantificationally" as "for someone." Its argument status creates a θ-Criterion violation in (18), though not in (3a). The prohibition against vacuous quantification (Chomsky (1982)) excludes (1). Suppose now that PRO is coindexed with the matrix subject (*it, there*) in (3a) and (18) and with the *wh*-phrase in (1). (18a) would be excluded by the system of Case and θ-theory of Chomsky (1981) (the chain [e,the man] being headed in these terms by a cosuperscripted pronominal that has no Case and is therefore not eligible for θ-role assignment); however, this account will not translate into the theory being developed here. In any event, some further assumption is needed to deal with (3a), (18b), and (1). (19) appears to be a natural hypothesis.

(19) The antecedent of PRO (if it has one) must be an element with a θ-role.

(19) excludes the coindexed versions of every example in the above set. (3a), (18a), and (1) contain only nonthematic categories as possible antecedents. In (18b) the postverbal S' may also be taken as antecedent, but then the PRO must be coreferential with it, hence an argument. This would create a θ-Criterion violation in the second clause. In Brody (1984a) I argue that given the assumption that the antecedent of a PRO is a chain, (19) is a consequence of a revised formulation of the θ-Criterion requiring that all chains have a θ-role.

Let us assume that some explanations can be given for the ungrammaticality of (1), (17), and (18a–b) under these remaining problematic analyses, perhaps along the lines just suggested. Concentrating on the central cases of PRO and Trace Condition violations, (6a) and (2), we see that these are excluded by the assumptions in (9) (the definition of chains), (15), (16) (stipulations on (9)), and (8) (PRO and Trace Conditions), together with (10) (the θ-Criterion). This account cannot be very highly valued, however, since practically every crucial component of it is stipulative in nature. The following questions arise immediately.

(20) Why must pronominal ECs break the chain? (That is, why does (15) hold?)
(21) Why must nonpronominal ECs not break the chain? (That is, why does (16) hold?)

Since we began by rejecting the hypothesis that the Trace and PRO Conditions follow from the ECP and the binding theory, our original two problems must be added to these.

(22) Why must pronominal anaphor ECs be ungoverned? (That is, why does the PRO Condition hold?)
(23) Why must nonpronominal ECs be governed? (That is, why does the Trace Condition hold?)

2.3. PRO as a nonpronominal

The accounts of examples like (2) and (6a) based on the PRO and Trace Conditions make crucial use of the assumption that PRO as opposed to trace is a pronominal category. This is true both of the theory that invokes contextual definitions and of the RC system as so far described. All of the four stipulations of the RC account – (8a), (8b), (15), and (16) – refer to this distinction. It is problematic, however, since PRO does not appear to have the characteristic properties of other pronominals.

Thus, lexical pronouns either are expletive, like *it* in (24a), or have independent or dependent specific reference, like *he* in (24b) and (24c), respectively.

(24) a. It seems that S
b. He left
c. Tom$_x$ said he$_x$ left

PRO, on the other hand, cannot function as an expletive and cannot normally have independent reference. Thus, (18b) is ungrammatical and (3a) cannot be interpreted as "It's illegal for him/her/it (specific entity) to go there."

(18) b. *It was clear that Mary left without e being obvious that she wanted to
(3) a. It's illegal e to go there

PRO can have specific reference when it has an antecedent; thus, parallel to (24c) is (25).

(25) Tom expected e to go there
(26) Tom expected himself to go there

However, as (26) shows, this is not an exclusive property of pronominals; a non-pronominal anaphor can also have specific reference when it has an antecedent. Thus, PRO appears to behave like lexical anaphors but unlike lexical pronouns.

The definition of pronominals in Chomsky (1981) implicitly claims that PRO is like a lexical pronoun in that both NP-types are either free or bound by an element with an independent θ-role. But again, lexical anaphors can also be bound by categories with an independent θ-role (as in (26)), and they can also be free (as in (27)).[5]

(27) a. Those pictures of himself disturbed Tom
b. Those pictures of each other disturbed the men

Would it be possible to maintain this point in a different form – namely, that PRO, unlike lexical anaphors, does not need an antecedent?[6] Thus, the antecedentless lexical anaphor in (28b) is excluded, but PRO in (28a) is not excluded even though it has no antecedent. (The NP *Mary* cannot function as a syntactic (coindexed) antecedent of a PRO that binds *oneself*: *Mary tried e to wash oneself.*)

(28) a. e washing oneself in public disturbed Mary
b. *Pictures of himself disturbed Mary
(29) Pictures of myself/yourself/oneself can be made here in five minutes

But, as (29) illustrates, first and second person lexical anaphors and *oneself*, the lexical anaphor that an antecedentless PRO can bind, can also occur without antecedents in certain types of structures. Furthermore, the positions where PRO and these anaphors need/do not need an antecedent appear to correlate exactly. For example, compare (28a)/(29) on the one hand, and (30)/(31), on the other.

(30) *John asked/promised Bill e to wash oneself
(31) a. *John asked Bill about a picture of myself/yourself/oneself
b. *John promised Bill a picture of myself/yourself/oneself

It seems, then, that PRO shares with lexical anaphors the property of needing an antecedent only in certain positions. See section 4 for a version of the binding theory that can capture this parallel.[7]

To summarize: We have found no characteristic that PRO has in common with lexical pronouns but not with lexical anaphors. The assumption that the EC in control structures and the EC in movement structures are differentiated by the $+/-$ pronominal distinction appears to be an artifact of the standard GB account of the ungrammaticality of examples like (2) and (6a). (Of course, this is true both of the account involving contextual definitions and of the RC system as presented so far.) The only independent motivation for the assumption that the EC in control structures is a pronominal (anaphor) is the fact that this makes it possible to derive the PRO Condition from the binding theory. But we have rejected this derivation for the strong conceptual reason discussed in section 1. Therefore, we conclude that the $+/-$ pronominal distinction between anaphoric ECs should be dispensed with if possible. (Manzini (1983) and Sportiche (1983) reach the same conclusion partly on the basis of similar arguments.)

2.4. *Toward a solution*

2.4.1. *NP-trace and PRO*

Let us try to build an alternative account of the complementary distribution of ECs that does not make use of the $+/-$ pronominal distinction and answers the questions in (20) through (23). First, consider once more the RC account of the ungrammaticality of (6a).

(6) a. *Tom believes e to like Mary

The EC in (6a) is nonpronominal, since it is governed but not identified. By (16), a nonpronominal EC cannot head a chain; hence, (6a) does not contain the set of chains {Tom}, {e} and therefore violates the θ-Criterion.

This derivation can be simplified further by collapsing its two steps as shown in (32). I shall call the resulting combined statement the *One Fell Swoop (OFS) PRO Condition*.

(32) *One Fell Swoop PRO Condition*
A governed EC is not the head of a chain unless it is pro. (= A head EC is ungoverned or pro.)

Given (15), (32) entails the PRO Condition (8b). By (15), a pronominal EC is the head of its chain; by (32), a head EC must be ungoverned or pro. Hence, PRO, an EC non-pro (i.e. + anaphor) pronominal, must be ungoverned.

But in fact the OFS PRO Condition makes it unnecessary to invoke (8b), (15), or (16), since the relevant effects of (8b) and (16) follow from (32) alone. The governed non-pro (since nonidentified) EC in (6a) cannot be the head of the chain by (32); hence, (6a) will not contain the two chains [Tom], [e] – the familiar θ-Criterion violation.

Now reconsider the treatment of (2) in the RC system.

(2)   *Tom is illegal e to go there

By the Trace Condition (8a), the ungoverned EC is a pronominal; therefore, by (15), it breaks the chain. Thus, (2) cannot contain the chain [Tom,e] and it violates the θ-Criterion. Again, the two steps in this argument can be collapsed, creating a condition that combines the effects of (8a) and (15): the *One Fell Swoop (OFS) Trace Condition*.

(33)   *One Fell Swoop Trace Condition*
An ungoverned EC is the head of a chain. (= A nonhead member of a chain is governed.)

(33), together with (16), entails the Trace Condition. By (16), a nonpronominal EC is always a nonhead member of a chain, and, by (33), a nonhead EC must be governed. Hence, a nonpronominal EC must be governed.

Given the OFS Trace Condition, however, it is not necessary to refer to either (8a) or (15) or (16) in order to exclude (2). The syntactic effects of (8a) and (15) follow from (33) alone. Since the EC in (2) is ungoverned, it is the head of its chain by (33); hence, (2) does not contain the chain [Tom,e] and again violates the θ-Criterion.

2.4.2. pro

The OFS Trace and PRO Conditions make no reference to the +/− pronominal distinction. As they take the place of the four main conditions (8a), (8b), (15), and (16), whose correct operation depends on the classification of ECs as +/− pronominal, they in effect eliminate the need to distinguish anaphoric ECs in this way.

In arguing for a pronominal nonanaphor EC – namely, pro – Chomsky (1982) points out that given the existence of nonpronominal anaphor, nonpronominal nonanaphor, and pronominal anaphor ECs the lack of a pronominal nonanaphor EC would be a surprising, unexplained gap in the paradigm: no principled reasons appear to exist to rule out this combination of features. But this argument – to my knowledge the only serious argument for the existence of pro – collapses if PRO is not a pronominal category. This assumption has provided the only strong independent reason to think that the paradigm in which the nonexistence of a pronominal nonanaphor EC would have created a gap existed at all. In other words, the assumption that PRO is a pronominal EC has been the only strong reason to assume that ECs may be pronominal. Let us assume, then, that all ECs are nonpronominal – pronominal ECs do not exist.[8]

This assumption is compatible with both Chomsky's (1981) and Rizzi's (1982a) analyses of "subject pronoun drop" and other phenomena associated with pro. I shall henceforth adopt Rizzi's analysis. Thus, I shall adopt a version of GB theory in which ECs associated with Clitics and certain types of Agr(eement) elements are nonpronominal anaphors bound by the Clitic, and are nonhead members of chains headed by the Clitic. Given the extension of chains to Ā-chains in general, in A-position ECs that are heads of chains occur only in control structures.

Consequently, we can dispense with the unless-clause in the OFS PRO Condition (32) and state it simply as in (32'), parallel to (33).

(32')   *OFS PRO Condition* (revised)
A governed EC is not the head of a chain. (= A head EC is ungoverned.)

Collapsing (32') and (33) gives the biconditional (34).

(34)   *One Fell Swoop EC Condition*
An EC is the head of a chain iff it is ungoverned.

2.4.3. Wh-trace

In standard versions of GB theory that assume that the +/− pronominal distinction cross-classifies ECs, PRO has various properties: it must have an antecedent with a θ-role, and it is associated with the "for somebody/coreferential" interpretation. These principles of course do not make it necessary to assume that the EC in control structures is of a different NP-type than other anaphor ECs. An EC appears in a control structure iff it is ungoverned and iff it is the head of a chain. Therefore, we may attribute these properties not to ECs that are pronominal but to ECs that are ungoverned or are heads of chains. I shall adopt the latter assumption. Conversely, whatever properties nonpronominal ECs are assumed to possess in standard GB theory now become properties of nonhead members of chains. (Recall that by the definition of chains, these are always ECs.) Since I have rejected the hypothesis that ECs may be pronominal, the terms *PRO* and *trace* should not refer to pronominal (anaphor) and nonpronominal ECs, respectively. Therefore, I shall also change the terminology and use *PRO* to refer to EC heads of chains and *trace* to refer to nonhead (EC) members.

Finally, let us consider how the proposed account of Trace Condition violations extends to locally Ā-bound ECs.

(1)   *Who is it illegal e to go there

The EC in (1) is the head of a chain by the OFS EC Condition, since it is ungoverned. Thus, it has the interpretive properties that PRO has in the standard GB theory.

In particular, its antecedent (if any) must have a θ-role. It therefore cannot be coindexed with the *wh*-phrase in (1), and the structure is excluded since it involves vacuous quantification.

2.4.4. *Complementary distribution of empty heads and nonheads of chains*

The Trace and PRO Conditions (8a) and (8b) did not exclude (1), (2), and (6a) under all analyses. The Trace Condition applied only when the EC in (1) and (2) was taken to be a nonpronominal; the PRO Condition ruled out (6a) only when the EC was a pronominal (anaphor). Other considerations ((15), (16), (19), and the θ-Criterion) excluded these structures when the EC was analyzed as belonging to some other NP-type. Similarly, the OFS EC Condition rules out these structures only under certain analyses. Thus, the OFS Trace Condition excludes (1) and (2) only if they are taken to contain the chain that includes the EC and its binder: [Tom,e] in (2) and [who,e] in (1). Under the alternative analysis where (2) contains the chains [Tom], [e] and (1) contains [who], [e], the θ-Criterion rules out (2) and principle (19) rules out (1). (6a) is excluded by the OFS PRO Condition only if it is taken to contain the two chains [Tom], [e]; when it is taken to contain the single chain [Tom,e], its ungrammaticality is due again to the θ-Criterion.

This seems exactly right. Using the revised terminology, we may describe the situation as follows. The analyses of (1), (2), and (6a) that are not excluded by the OFS Conditions have nothing to do with the complementary distribution of trace and PRO. Thus, the EC that heads its own chain in (1) and (2) is not a trace in an ungoverned position legitimate only for PRO, but a PRO that happens to have an improper antecedent. The EC that is a nonhead member of its chain in (6a) is not a PRO in a governed position legitimate only for traces, but a trace that is part of an "improper movement" structure – that is, it belongs to a chain in which for $i \neq n$, x_i is a θ-position.

To put the point differently, instead of the complementary distribution of pronominal (anaphor) and nonpronominal ECs, the OFS EC Condition ensures the complementary distribution of EC head and nonhead members of chains. If we assume the strong relation between chains and movement that all and only movement is chain-internal (Brody (1984a)), then the complementary distribution between launching sites of movement and ECs in control structures follows immediately.[9]

The OFS EC Condition entails the effects of (8a), (8b), (15), and (16) and does so without distinguishing pronominal and nonpronominal ECs. It thus answers questions (20) through (23). However, the original question of why the two types of ECs (the ones in control structures and the ones locally bound by an element in a $\bar{\theta}$-position) are in complementary distribution still stands, albeit in a modified form. The OFS EC Condition changes the question "Why do pronominal (anaphor) and nonpronominal ECs occur in complementary distribution?" into "Why should EC heads and nonhead members of chains occur in complementary distribution?"

Why should the OFS EC Condition hold? Optimally, we should hope to find a particular type of answer to this. We should try to find principles that not only entail this condition but also provide some insight into why it must be a biconditional – that is, why it restricts EC heads of chains to positions complementary to those of (EC) nonheads.

3. Case-checking theory

3.1. *The OFS EC Condition and Case theory*

The OFS EC Condition (34) is reminiscent of the Case requirement proposed in Chomsky (1981), a version of which is stated in (35).

(35) A head of a chain either has Case or is PRO (i.e. a pronominal anaphor EC).

In the framework adopted here (35) must be restated in a way that does not assume the existence of the pronominal anaphor EC.[10]

(36) A head of a chain either has Case or is an ungoverned EC.

Like (34), (35), and (36) distinguish heads and nonhead members of chains and involve reference to ungoverned EC (PRO) heads. This might suggest that (34) is related to Case theory.

The formulation of (35) and (36) assumes that Case is a property of categories and not of chains. Thus, (36) can be strengthened to a biconditional, making it more similar to (34).

(37) An NP has Case or is an ungoverned EC iff it is the head of a chain.

Thus, (37) adds the requirement to (36) that nonhead members of chains are Caseless and either lexical or governed. Since (by the definition of chains) nonheads are ECs, this means that (by (37)) they must be governed (and Caseless).

Given the extension of chains to Ā-chains, (37) entails that locally Ā-bound traces do not have Case either. Suppose that the fact that these cannot appear in Caseless (governed) positions is due to some requirement other than that they need Case. We may assume then that ECs never have Case.[11] Given this hypothesis, ECs will all fall under the second part of the disjunction of the left side of (37): by this principle, an EC head of a chain must now be ungoverned. Since, as we have seen, (37) also entails that nonheads are governed, the OFS EC Condition follows from this principle.

So far, however, this does not solve the problem of why EC heads and nonhead members of chains are in complementary distribution. The question of why the principle that constrains the positions of these elements is a biconditional is transferred intact from (34) to (37). (37) also creates a further serious problem. (37) is a disjunctive principle, and one might well ask why the same condition should hold for Case-marked NPs on the one hand and ungoverned ECs on the other (and conversely for

Caseless NPs and governed ECs). I shall attempt to answer these problems in the context of a theory of Case-checking.

3.2. Case-checking theory and the case filter

Suppose that NPs are not assigned Case by their governors but have Case inherently, as has occasionally been suggested. For example, in (38) the verb *has* accusative Case but does not *assign* this Case.

(38) a. Mary saw him
      b. *Mary saw he

Since NPs have Case inherently, both *he* and *him* can be inserted freely in the position following the verb. Some condition of Case-checking must then exist to ensure that an NP is inserted whose Case is appropriate in the context. We may say that an NP must be Case-checked and that it is Case-checked iff it is governed by some element with matching Case.[12] In (38a) *him* has accusative Case and so does its governor, the verb *saw*; in (38b) *he* has nominative Case, which does not match that of the governing verb. Hence, the Case-checking condition excludes (38b) but not (38a).

The preliminary statement of the Case-checking condition involves two conceptually distinct requirements. One is that of locality: the Case on an NP must be related to the Case on its governor. Let us call this the *Case-linking requirement*. The other part of the Case-checking condition is the *Case-matching requirement*: the governor of the NP must have the same Case as the NP. Separating these two components, we can state the Case-checking condition as the conjunction of (39) and (40).[13]

(39) *Case-linking Condition* (CLC)
      *NP unless Case-linked.
      NP_x is Case-linked (to y) iff $=_{df} NP_x$ has Case iff NP_x is governed (and governed by y).
(40) *Case-matching Condition* (CMC)
      If NP_x is Case-linked to y, then y has a Case that matches that of NP_x.

(39) defines the Case-linking Condition so that it is satisfied in all and only those instances where an NP has Case iff it has a governor; further, it states that when the condition is satisfied, it is the governor to which the Case of the NP is linked. (40) requires simply that the Case of an NP Case-linked to some governor must be matched by the Case of that governor. Again considering (38a–b), assuming that both *him* and *he* have Case, both of these NPs are Case-linked since they are governed. Each is furthermore Case-linked to its governor, the verb *saw* with which (by the CMC) its Case must match. The CMC is then met by (38a) but not by (38b). Consider now a Caseless lexical NP in an ungoverned position.

(41) *He (Caseless) to go there would be illegal

If the pronoun *he* in (41) is not taken to have nominative Case but is Caseless, then it has neither a Case nor a governor and hence falls under the CLC. Furthermore, since this NP has no governor, there is no element *y* to which it is Case-linked, although it is Case-linked – vacuously. Since it is not Case-linked to any specific category *y*, it also meets the CMC, again vacuously. (The CMC requires Case-match of a category *x* with a category *y* only when *x* is Case-linked to *y*. But in this case there is no *y* to which *x* is Case-linked, since *x* is ungoverned.)

To eliminate this problem, let us assume that lexical NPs always have Case. That is, let us make the natural assumption that a lexical NP cannot have a phonological interpretation if it has no Case. It follows that a lexical NP cannot be vacuously Case-linked or Case-matched. By the CLC, if an NP has Case, it must have a governor; and, by the CMC, the Case of the NP must match the Case of this governor. If in (41) the NP *he* is Case-marked, then (41) will straightforwardly fail the CLC since it contains a Case-marked NP without a governor.

Consider now a lexical NP in a governed Caseless position, as in (42).

(42) a. *It seems Tom to go
b. *It was seen Tom

Given the assumption just made about lexical NPs, the NP *Tom* in (42) both has Case and is governed. It is therefore Case-linked. Is it also Case-matched? Whatever Case this NP happens to have, it could not match that of its governor, which has no Case at all. In general, those governors that would not assign Case in a Case-assigning framework do not have Case in the Case-checking framework.

The effects of the Case Filter of the Case-assignment framework follow from Case-checking theory. NPs with a phonetic matrix cannot appear either in ungoverned positions, by the CLC, or in governed Caseless positions, by the CMC.

3.3. *Case-checking theory and ECs*

What does the Case-checking theory say about ECs? To begin with, let us abstract away from movement phenomena altogether and also from ECs associated with Clitics. The only EC that remains is the ungoverned EC of control structures. The assumption suggested in section 3.1 that ECs have no Case could ensure that this EC is ungoverned. If ECs have no Case, then by the CLC they must be ungoverned, since in a governed position a Caseless category would not be Case-linked. In an ungoverned position the Caseless EC would meet the CLC. Although an ungoverned category is Case-linked, it is not Case-linked to anything, since it has no governor. Ungoverned categories always satisfy the CMC vacuously; the CMC does not require anything of them. Thus, if all and only lexical NPs have Case, then the CLC entails that lexical NPs are governed and ECs are ungoverned. The CMC ensures Case-matching for governed, lexical NPs and holds vacuously for ungoverned ECs.

Of course, if ECs never have Case, then launching sites of movement and ECs associated with Clitics create a problem. These are in governed positions; therefore, if they are Caseless, then they are not Case-linked. Apparently these ECs counter-exemplify the CLC. Given the extension of chains to Ā-chains, launching sites of movement are always nonhead members of chains; this is also true of ECs associated with Clitics under Rizzi's (1982) analysis. ECs in control positions and lexical NPs, on the other hand, are always heads. Therefore, the CLC could be restricted to heads of chains.

If ECs have no Case, then nonhead members of chains not only need not but in fact must not be Case-linked, since a Caseless category is Case-linked only if it is ungoverned. But nonhead members of chains must be governed. Therefore, the CLC should be restated so that it requires only of heads of chains that they be Case-linked but constrains nonhead members by prohibiting them from being Case-linked.

(43) *Case-linking Condition* (revised)
    NP_x is Case-linked iff NP_x is the head of a chain.

Checking the predictions of the revised CLC, consider first lexical NPs. These always have Case. A lexical NP in a governed position is Case-linked to its governor, with two consequences. First, the NP and its governor must be Case-matched, by the CMC. Second, since the NP is Case-linked, it must be the head of its chain, by (43). A lexical NP in an ungoverned position is not Case-linked (recall the discussion of (41)), since it has Case but no governor. It is therefore a nonhead member of its chain. This is ruled out by the definition of chains: nonhead members of chains are all ECs.[14]

Turning now to ECs, which have no Case, consider first an EC in an ungoverned position. It is Case-linked, since it has neither Case nor a governor. Since it has no governor, there is no element to which it is Case-linked; thus, it satisfies the CMC. Since this EC is Case-linked, it is the head of its chain by (43), the revised CLC. Finally, a governed EC is not Case-linked, since it has a governor but no Case. The revised CLC predicts that it must be a nonhead element of its chain.

3.4. Solutions provided by Case-checking theory

The revised CLC entails (a) that the head of a chain is either a governed and Case-marked (lexical) category or an ungoverned and Caseless (empty) category; and (b) that a nonhead element is either a governed and Caseless (empty) NP or an ungoverned and Case-marked (lexical) one. As noted, the last possibility is excluded by independent considerations. The revised CLC entails the positive effects of the earlier Case theory condition (37). In particular, the OFS EC Condition, the requirement that an EC is ungoverned iff it is the head of a chain, also follows from (43).

The revised CLC solves the problem raised by (35), (36), and (37) of what ungoverned ECs and Case-marked NPs have in common that qualifies them to be heads of chains. In the present theory both ungoverned ECs and governed Case-marked NPs are Case-linked. This eliminates the necessity for disjunctive formulation of the basic Case theory condition.

Let us now turn again to the central problem of the complementary distribution of ECs in control and movement-launching positions. We restated this as the complementary distribution of head and nonhead members of chains, ensured by the OFS EC Condition. The problem of why the complementary distribution holds became the question of why the OFS EC Condition is a biconditional that restricts EC heads of chains to positions complementary to those of (EC) nonheads. The same question can be asked about the revised CLC, from which the OFS EC Condition follows.

Chomsky (1981) suggests that the Case requirement of which we discussed the version in (35) is due to a visibility requirement on θ-role assignment. A chain not meeting (35) is not visible at LF and cannot receive a θ-role; thus, it ends up violating the θ-Criterion. Following this idea, we could attribute the CLC to the visibility requirement. Assume then that a chain is made visible for θ-role assignment only if its head is Case-linked. Why is it that only the head of the chain may be Case-linked? I propose that this is due to a prohibition against visibility conflict: a chain may be made visible only in one position.

We began with the idea that the complementary distribution of PRO and trace is not that of +pronominal and −pronominal ECs, but that of head and nonhead EC members of chains. The OFS EC Condition that ensures this follows from the revised CLC in (43), itself a consequence of the θ-Criterion given the proposed version of the visibility condition on θ-role assignment. According to the present theory, ultimately it is this uniqueness requirement on the visibility condition for θ-role assignment that is responsible for the complementary distribution of ECs.

3.5. Case-checking theory and Ā-chains

Extending chains to Ā-chains means that instead of assuming that locally Ā-bound categories break the chain, we assume that Operators do. Unless we restrict the CLC to hold only for elements in A-position, we must arrange for Operator heads of chains to be Case-linked. As noted in section 3.1, we need an account of the fact that locally Ā-bound traces do not occur in (governed) Caseless positions that does not presuppose that these traces need Case, since we assume that no ECs have Case. The natural alternative is that these traces must occur in Case positions because of the Case requirement on the Operator associated with them. This suggests that the CLC should not be restricted to A-positions.

Independent of our assumptions about Case-checking, it must somehow be ensured that the Operator in Comp (at least in the unmarked case) has the same Case as the one authorized by the governor associated with some EC in A-position that it locally binds.[15] In the Case-assignment framework this is achieved by a Case-transmission convention: the Case assigned in the position of the EC is also borne by the Operator. In the Case-checking theory, in which NPs have Case inherently, the equivalent of this convention is the assumption that the Case of an Operator must be checked in the position of an EC in A-position that it locally binds. Given this independently necessary convention, it is natural to consider an Operator to be Case-linked just in case it would be Case-linked if it were in the position of this EC.[16]

Since traces (ECs that are nonhead members of chains) are governed, as a consequence of the CLC, it follows that an Operator is Case-linked iff it is Case-marked. A locally Ā-bound trace will now never occur in a governed Caseless position, since its Operator would be Case-linked to its governor and by the CMC they would have to be Case-matched. But this is impossible here for the same reason that it is impossible in structures like (42) — since the governor has no Case, whatever Case the element Case-linked to it has, it will not match.

Since we assume that only lexical NPs may have Case, the conclusion that Operators always have Case leads us back to the *wh*-deletion rule of Chomsky and Lasnik (1977). Alternatively, we may allow ECs in Ā-positions to have Case.[17]

4. ECs as anaphors

4.1. Binding theory and locally A-bound categories

4.1.1. PRO and lexical anaphor

Consider the definition of governing category proposed in Chomsky (1981, 211), along with the binding theory.[18]

(44) x is a governing category for y if and only if x is the minimal category containing x, a governor of x, and a SUBJECT accessible to x.

(45) Binding Theory
   A. An anaphor is A-bound in its governing category.
   B. A pronominal is A-free in its governing category.
   C. Other NPs are A-free.

Now consider examples (46a–b).

(46) a. John tried e to win
      b. John knows how e to win

The binding theory based on (44) makes no predictions about the choice of antecedents for PRO, since PRO is ungoverned and thus has no governing category. The assumption (adopted here) that PRO is a pure anaphor enables binding principle (A) to ensure that PRO is bound in (46a) if reference to a governor is dropped from (44). Principle (A) would then require an anaphor x to be bound in the minimal category containing x and a SUBJECT accessible to x. However, this would give incorrect results for (46b). PRO in (46b) may (but need not) have *John* as antecedent. In other words, it may have the arbitrary interpretation (it may be free).

Adapting Manzini's (1983) proposal, we shall assume that for an ungoverned category x "governor" in (44) refers to the governor of the *c-domain* of x (where y is the c-domain of x iff y is the minimal maximal category dominating x). We shall assume further that S is the maximal projection of Infl iff a Comp is present. (Thus, the c-domain of PRO is S′ in (46a) and S in (46b).) To make this explicit, let us refer to the notion "governor of x if x is governed, otherwise governor of the c-domain of x" by the term *g-governor*. For a governed category x, then, g-governor of x = governor of x, and the governing category of x remains the same when defined in terms of g-government. In the case of an ungoverned category there are two possibilities. In (46a) *try* g-governs PRO (it governs PRO's c-domain, i.e. S′), whereas in (46b) PRO has no g-governor (neither PRO nor its c-domain (S) is governed). Now in (46a) the governing category of PRO is the matrix S; this is the minimal category that contains a g-governor (*try*) and an accessible SUBJECT. In (46b) PRO has no governing category, since it has no g-governor. Hence, binding principle (A) allows it to be free.

Manzini (1983) points out that, contrary to what is predicted by the various versions of the binding theory in Chomsky (1981), an anaphor inside a nominal in subject position need not be bound, but may corefer freely with a non-c-commanding antecedent, as illustrated in (47).

(47) a. The boys$_x$ thought that $\begin{Bmatrix} \text{[each other's}_x \text{ pictures]} \\ \text{[pictures of each other}_x \text{]} \end{Bmatrix}$ were on sale

b. $\begin{Bmatrix} \text{[Each other's}_x \text{ pictures]} \\ \text{[Pictures of each other}_x \text{]} \end{Bmatrix}$ would please the boys$_x$

Let us adopt the essential component of Manzini's theory: that is, let us assume that the governing category of y is not the minimal category that contains a SUBJECT accessible to y (and a g-governor of y); rather, it is the first category with a SUBJECT (and a g-governor), but only if this SUBJECT is accessible to y. If it is not, then y has no governing category.[19]

(48) y is the governing category of x iff y is the minimal category that contains x, a g-governor of x, and a SUBJECT z; if z is accessible to x.

The anaphors in (47) now have no governing category, since the minimal category that contains (a g-governor and) a SUBJECT is S, where SUBJECT = Agr, and the Agr is not accessible for categories inside the subject. Manzini develops a theory of control, shown here in (49), that uses the same idea to account for the parallel behavior of PRO. (Note that she uses *subject* to refer to a SUBJECT.)

(49) a. An anaphor is bound in its domain-governing category.
b. z is a domain-governing category for x iff
z is the minimal category with a subject containing the c-domain of x and a governor for the c-domain of x, and z contains a subject accessible to x.

But given the assumption that PRO is a nonpronominal anaphor, (49) is redundant; all the major facts that Manzini's control theory entails also follow from principle (A) of the binding theory. Consider the central contrast between a PRO in a sentential subject of a sentence S and a PRO in a sentential object of S. In the latter construction PRO needs a binder inside S, as shown by the impossibility of (50a)

(= (30)) and (50b); in the former it can have a non-c-commanding antecedent, as in (51a), or no antecedent at all, as in (51b) (= (28a)).

(50) a. *[$_S$ John asked/promised Bill [$_{S'}$ e to wash oneself]]
 b. *Mary said that [$_S$ John asked/promised Bill [$_{S'}$ e to wash herself]]
(51) a. [$_S$ e to behave himself in public would help Bill's development]
 b. [$_S$ e washing oneself in public disturbed Mary]

The domain-governing category for PRO in (50) is S: S is the minimal category that contains the c-domain of PRO (i.e. S'), a governor of the c-domain, and a SUBJECT that is accessible. PRO must be bound in S by the control theory in (49). But S is also the first category that contains a g-governor (since PRO is ungoverned, its g-governor is the governor of its c-domain) and a SUBJECT accessible to PRO; hence, PRO must also be bound in S by principle (A) of the binding theory, given formulation (48) of governing category. (49) puts no constraints on PRO in (51), since the SUBJECT of the first category that contains the c-domain of PRO (the subject of S), a governor of the c-domain (Agr of S), and a SUBJECT (again Agr of S) is not an accessible SUBJECT. But principle (A) gives the same result: the first category with a g-governor and a SUBJECT is S, whose SUBJECT is Agr. But this SUBJECT is not accessible, so PRO has no binding category and principle (A) is met vacuously. Other phenomena that motivate Manzini's control theory (the extraposition and purpose-clause cases) similarly fall under principle (A) given formulation (48) of the binding theory domain.

Consider lexical anaphors that do not need antecedents: *myself, yourself, oneself*. When such a lexical anaphor is inside a subject NP, which itself contains no SUBJECT, as in (52a) (= (29)), or inside a category meeting this description and coindexed with a subject, as in (52b), then it has no governing category. This is because the nearest c-commanding SUBJECT (that is, Agr in S) is not accessible. Such an anaphor then meets principle (A) vacuously, just as PRO does in (51).

(52) a. Pictures of myself/yourself/oneself can be made here in five minutes
 b. There were pictures of myself/yourself/oneself on sale
(53) a. *John asked Bill about a picture of myself/yourself/oneself
 b. *John promised Bill a picture of myself/yourself/oneself

The lexical anaphors in (53) (= (31)), however, must be bound in S, just like the PRO in (50), since the SUBJECT of S in (53) is accessible to the anaphor. Thus, binding principle (A) predicts the parallel behavior of PRO and these lexical anaphors, given the assumption that PRO is a pure anaphor.[20]

4.1.2. NP-trace and pronoun

As is well known, lexical pronouns and lexical anaphors related to a given antecedent are not in complementary distribution inside NPs:

(54) The men liked each other's books
(55) The men liked the books about each other
(56) The men$_x$ liked their$_x$ books
(57) The men$_x$ liked the books about them$_x$

Given the definition of governing category in (48), binding principle (A) correctly predicts that the anaphor in (54), (55) must be bound in its governing category, S. But under this definition binding principle (B), which requires a pronominal to be free in its binding theory domain, incorrectly rules out (56), (57): the pronoun does not have to be free in S.

Manzini accounts for (56) by assuming that an element can function as its own (nonaccessible) SUBJECT in the definition of domain for the binding theory. If this proposal is adopted, then the anaphor and the pronoun in (54), (56) have no binding category since the relevant SUBJECT (the pronoun/anaphor itself) is not accessible. This allows the pronoun to be bound by the matrix subject in (56). But in order to ensure that the anaphor in (54) cannot remain free, it is now necessary to invoke the separate condition of control in (49). Furthermore, as Manzini notes, such a treatment of (54), (56) does not extend to (57), where the pronoun is in object position. Since in (57) the first category with a SUBJECT is S and the SUBJECT of S is accessible, the pronoun is incorrectly predicted to be necessarily free in S by binding principle (B).

Anaphors that head chains (PRO and lexical anaphors) are Case-linked. Let us call them *CL-anaphors*. Suppose that whereas a CL-anaphor x must be bound in the minimal category that contains x, a g-governor of x, and a SUBJECT ($\neq x$) (if this is accessible), a pronoun x must be free in the minimal category that contains x and its g-governor and *may* contain a SUBJECT. The anaphors in (54), (55) must be bound in the matrix S, as before. The pronouns in both (56) and (57) now need be free only in NP, the minimal category that contains them and may contain a SUBJECT. (Note that the question of whether this SUBJECT is identical to the pronoun does not arise, since this is a potential rather than an actual SUBJECT.)[21]

NP-traces are chain-internal, non-CL-anaphors. Their binding category is therefore the same as that of pronouns; hence the ungrammaticality of (58).

(58) *John$_x$ seems that it^y is certain [e$_x$ to like Mary]^y

To summarize: In this section I have proposed the following definition of binding theory domain:

(59) The governing category for x is the minimal category with a SUBJECT z, $z \neq x$, which contains x and a g-governor of x; if z is accessible to x. z need not be an actual SUBJECT unless x is a CL-anaphor.

The definition of governing category in (59) captures both the parallel between NP-trace and pronoun and the generalization over lexical anaphor and PRO. The binding theory domain of the former group is defined in terms of a governor and a virtual SUBJECT; they meet the nonidentity and accessibility conditions vacuously. CL-anaphors, on the other hand, have a binding category defined in terms of an actual SUBJECT and a g-governor. The actual SUBJECT is constrained by the nonidentity and accessibility conditions. An English CL-anaphor x always redundantly satisfies the requirement that its binding theory domain must contain its g-governor, in the sense that a minimal maximal category containing a g-governor of *x* never properly includes the minimal maximal category containing a SUBJECT of *x* (nonidentical to *x*). A CL-anaphor may also meet the g-governor requirement vacuously, when it has no governing category, as in (46b), for example.

4.2. Binding theory and locally Ā-bound ECs

The definition of variable taken as a syntactic principle has the import of (60) in standard GB theory (where *V-element* is an abbreviation for *nonpronominal nonanaphor EC*; see Brody (1984a)).

(60)   *x* is a V-element iff *x* is locally Ā-bound.
(61)   *V-Element Condition* (VEC)
       A V-element must be bound.

I argue in Brody (1984a) that (60) should be dispensed with in favor of the V-Element Condition (VEC) in (61). The definition of variable should be understood not as a syntactic condition but as a principle of interpretation (and as such it should not specify that the binding between the variable and its Operator is local).

This result suggests that perhaps the syntactic concept of V-element can be dispensed with completely. If the VEC could be eliminated, then we could claim that this concept has no relevance for the grammar – that there are no grammatical principles that refer to it. A stronger position from which this would follow is that V-elements do not exist, and locally Ā-bound ECs are also all anaphors. We then dispense with the VEC, since there exist no nonanaphor ECs to which it refers. Do its effects follow? Are all those ECs bound that have to be? Principle (A) of the binding theory ensures that ECs that have a governing category must be bound. Consider ECs without a governing category, which are not constrained by the binding theory. These are either ungoverned, like the ECs in (51a–b), or governed, as for example an EC would be in the position of the lexical anaphor in (52a–b). In (51) the EC indeed may be free, but in (52) it would have to be bound. But the fact that governed ECs must be bound follows from Case-checking theory. A free EC is necessarily the head of a chain, and therefore Case-checking theory requires it to be ungoverned.

I have argued that the distinction between +pronominal and −pronominal ECs is an artifact of the standard GB theory description of the complementary distribution of PRO and trace; ECs are all nonpronominal categories. Discussing the VEC leads to reexamining the other distinction between ECs made in this theory: that ECs locally Ā-bound by an Operator – as opposed to PRO, NP-trace, and Clitic-related ECs (as we have assumed with Rizzi (1982a)) – are not anaphors. In fact, the arguments for this distinction also become rather weak in the context of the theory presented here.[22]

Locally Ā-bound ECs appear not to be subject to the Opacity Conditions (Rizzi (1982b), Chomsky (1981)). In the GB framework this means that if these ECs are not V-elements but anaphors, then constructions employing them would not always obey binding principle (A) even if it were stated as in (62). (62) contains no requirement that the binder of an anaphor must be in A-position. Note that some such extension of the condition is necessary anyway if ECs related to Clitics are (nonpronominal) anaphors.

(62) An anaphor is bound in its governing category.

However, this does not seem to be sufficient reason to reject the hypothesis that all ECs are anaphors. One alternative is to restrict (62) so that it is relevant only for A-bound anaphors. That is, we could understand principle (A) as requiring only an A-bound anaphor to be bound in its governing category. Case-checking theory ensures that governed ECs are bound. Another alternative is to retain (62) and assume that Comp and other S-adjoined positions are deemed to be in every governing category of a given structure. (See appendix 1.)

The second main argument for considering locally $\bar{\text{A}}$-bound ECs to be V-elements is that this makes it possible to rule out so-called strong crossover violations (e.g. (63a)) by the same condition (binding principle (C)) that excludes overt locally A-bound nonpronominal nonanaphors (e.g. (63b)).

(63) a. *Who$_x$ did he$_x$ say that Mary liked e$_x$
      b. *He$_x$ said that Mary liked Tom$_x$

The argument presupposes that ECs are not optionally taken to be + and − anaphor categories. In fact, within the RC system the assumption that ECs may be nonanaphors could not contribute to the account of the crossover facts since ECs would be analyzed randomly as + or − anaphors (and as +/− pronominal if this distinction is also countenanced). Thus, even if (63a) is excluded by the same principle that rules out (63b) when the EC in (63a) is taken to be a (nonpronominal) nonanaphor, it is still necessary to ensure that (63a) is ruled out when the EC is taken to be an anaphor. Brody (1984a) shows that strong crossover structures are excluded by independently necessary principles of grammar no matter what NP-type (+/− pronominal, +/− anaphor) the EC belongs to; hence, they are also excluded when the EC is an anaphor.

Assuming the theory of Case-checking, the relevant parts of this demonstration can be summarized as follows.

(64) a. *He$_x$ likes e$_x$
      b. *He$_x$ believes e$_x$ to be obvious that S
      c. *He$_x$ seems Mary saw e$_x$
(65) a. *He$_x$ said e$_x$ Mary likes e$_x$
      b. *He$_x$ believes e$_x$ e$_x$ to be obvious that S
      c. *He$_x$ seems e$_x$ Mary saw e$_x$

I take the central problem of "crossover" to be the question of when A-bound ECs are permitted. Structures with *wh*-phrase binders, such as (63a), introduce a further violation: they contain a locally Ā-bound nonanaphor. Consider (64) and (65). The EC in these examples is not Case-linked. Therefore, (64) contains the chain [he,e] and (65) the chain [he,e,e] – given the hypothesis that in Ā-position only Operators break the chain. (The EC in Comp in (65) cannot be an Operator, because of selectional restrictions.) (64a) and (65a) violate the θ-Criterion at S-Structure, since in these cases the chain contains two θ-positions. (64a), (64b), (65a), and (65b) all violate the θ-Criterion at D-Structure, given the assumption that D-Structure is a pure representation of GF_n. Assuming that the Recoverability Condition has not been violated, there is no argument at this level to which the matrix subject θ-role can be assigned.

(64c) violates the binding theory: the EC anaphor is not bound in its governing category. Given the assumption that Comp positions are in every governing category, it is necessary to understand binding principle (A) as requiring an anaphor to be locally bound in its governing category. Thus, although in (63a) the *wh*-phrase binds the trace from inside its governing category, there is no local binding relationship between them. It is the pronoun *he* and not the *wh*-phrase that locally binds the EC. In order to ensure the exclusion of (65c), we are led to assume that non-Operator ECs in Comp do not count as binders for the binding conditions.

It seems, then, that there are no strong reasons not to return to the assumption of the pre-Government-Binding EST: all ECs are anaphors.[23] On the basis of an argument by D. Sportiche, which makes use of contextual definitions, Chomsky (1982) suggests that principle (C) of the binding theory does not constrain ECs and can perhaps be eliminated entirely. Brody (1984a) argues that given the hypothesis that ECs may be (nonpronominal) nonanaphors, some condition with the effect of principle (C) is still necessary for ECs (whether or not the contextual definitions of Chomsky (1981) are assumed) to rule out structures like (64c) (and also (65c), given certain other assumptions of Brody (1984a)) when the EC in them is analyzed as a nonanaphor. If all ECs are anaphors, then the argument becomes inapplicable: principle (C) ceases to be relevant for ECs, and it becomes plausible to restrict the binding theory to principles (A) and (B).[24]

5. Conclusion

The arguments in this article have shown that the complementary distribution of PRO and trace is not that of pronominal anaphors and nonpronominal ECs but that of EC heads and nonheads of chains. This is a consequence of Case-checking theory, in particular of the uniqueness requirement on the visibility condition for θ-role assignment. Case-checking theory entails the effects of the PRO and Trace Conditions and also the consequences of the crucial stipulations of the RC system that all and only pronominal ECs break the chain. This permits the conclusion that PRO is a pure anaphor and the development of a binding theory that captures the generalization over PRO and lexical anaphors. Since the putative pronominal status of PRO is the only strong argument for the existence of pronominal ECs, it is assumed that ECs are all nonpronominal. Finally, the binding theory has been extended to Ā-positions, allowing the extension of binding principle (C) to ECs, the VEC, and the remaining +/− anaphor distinction for ECs to be dispensed with.

Appendix 1

One way of accounting for the fact that locally Ā-bound traces do not show clear Opacity effects is to retain the version of binding principle (A) that extends to Ā-binding but to assume that S-adjoined Ā-positions are in every governing category of a given structure. If binding principle (B) is also extended so that it does not refer only to binders in A-positions, then the assumption that S-adjoined positions are in every governing category will rule out the central cases of weak crossover violations.[25]

(66)   a.   *Who$_x$ does his$_x$ friend like e$_x$
        b.   Who$_x$ e$_x$ likes his$_x$ friend
(67)   a.   *His$_x$ friend likes everyone$_x$
        b.   Everyone$_x$ his$_x$ mother likes e$_x$

(67b) is the LF representation of (67a). The pronoun in (66a), (67b) is locally bound by an Operator in Ā-position, violating principle (B). (66b) is not excluded if we take *free* in principle (B) to mean *not locally bound*. Thus, although in (66b) the pronoun is bound by a category in S-adjoined position (that is, in its governing category), it is not locally bound by it. The local binder of the pronominal is the trace, which however is outside its governing category, the NP.

(68)   a.   *Tom$_x$ hit him$_x$
        b.   ?*Who$_x$ did his$_x$ father hit e$_x$
        c.   (?)the man$_x$ who$_x$ his$_x$ father hit e$_x$
        d.   the man$_x$ who$_y$ his$_x$ father hit e$_y$

The acceptability contrast between (68a) (where binding principle (B) is violated by a binder in A-position) and (68b) (the weak crossover structure, where the binder is in Ā-position) can be attributed to a rule parasitic on the predication rule that Chomsky (1982) assumes is responsible for the acceptability of relative clause cases like (68c). The rule derives (68c) from (68d). Chomsky assumes that the constraint ruling out weak crossover does not hold at the output level of this rule. Because of examples like (69b), which could be derived from (69a) by the predication rule, this hypothesis is not available in the theory proposed here; binding principle (B) would not be able to exclude this derivation. (Examples like (69) and the consequence that binding principle (B) must be able to apply after the predication rule were pointed out by E. Williams.)

(69)   a.   John$_x$, he$_x$ likes him$_y$
        b.   *John$_x$, he$_x$ likes him$_x$

Let us assume with Sportiche (1983) that part of the effect of the predication rule is to revoke the Operator status of the category in Ā-position. Since non-Operators in Ā-position do not bind, as far as the binding theory is concerned, the resulting structure is not ruled out by principle (B). The analysis that takes the acceptability of (68b) to be parasitic on (68c) seems to be supported by the intuition that weak crossover violations are acceptable to the extent that the speaker has some discourse referent in mind that serves as the antecedent of the pronoun and is forced by the context to be identical to the referent of the variable.[26]

Sportiche (1983) develops a theory in which locally Ā-bound categories are all pronominal. He argues that locally Ā-bound pronouns occur in some languages. He provides only two cases where the local Ā-binding relation cannot be taken to be the result of the predication rule: interrogatives in Egyptian Arabic and Vata. In the first case he is forced to conclude that the Ā-binder is not an Operator (at least in the sense relevant for weak crossover); therefore, in our terms there will be no locally Ā-bound pronoun: binding by non-Operators in Ā-position is not visible for the binding theory. As for the Vata example (70), the evidence presented in Sportiche (1983) and Koopman and Sportiche (1983) may be taken to indicate that the elements Ā-bound in (70) are not pronominals.

(70) Alo$_x$ O$_x$ gugu na O$_x$ ka mlI la
      who he thought that he FUT leave WH
      "Who thought that he was leaving"

(71) Alo$_x$ O$_x$ nO gugu na O$_x$ mlI la
      who his mother think that he left WH
      "Who did his mother think left"

All Ā-bound categories in (70) and (71) are low tone except the leftmost one in (71), which is mid high tone. If only the mid high tone element is a pronominal, this suffices within the present theory to exclude the weak crossover violation in (71).

Given the assumption that PRO is a nonpronominal anaphor, the crucial counterexample to the claim that pronominals cannot be Ā-bound, the "PRO-gate" structure (72) of Higginbotham (1980), ceases to be a problem. Under the present account of weak crossover it is also immediately clear why this structure is not a violation on a par with (66a), (67a) – it contains no locally Ā-bound pronominals.[27]

(72) Who$_x$ did e$_x$ washing himself$_x$ disturb e$_x$

The fact that the proposed account does not exclude parasitic gap structures like (73) should probably also be considered a point in its favor.[28]

(73) What kind of music$_x$ does Raymond discuss e$_x$ without ever hearing e$_x$

The contrast noted by Higginbotham (1980) between examples like (74) and (75) follows from the Bijection Principle of Koopman and Sportiche (1983), as they note, if this is a constraint on LF representations. In the same way, if the binding theory constrains LF, then binding principle (B) will exclude (74) but not (75).

(74) *[$_x$ Which biography of which artist$_y$] do you think he$_y$ (his$_y$ father) wants to read e$_x$
(Compare: [$_x$ Which biography of which artist$_y$] e$_x$ was read by him$_y$ (his$_y$ father))
(75) [$_x$ Which biography of Picasso$_y$] do you think he$_y$ (his$_y$ father) wants to read e$_x$

At LF, (74) but not (75) will have the form (76) in which the pronoun is Ā-bound.

(76) Which artist$_y$ [$_x$ which biography of e$_y$] do you think he$_y$ (his$_y$ father) wants to read e$_x$

Note that the *wh*-phrase *which artist* must be raised into Ā-position in (74); otherwise, the pronoun is not in its scope and therefore cannot be bound by it. Like the Bijection Principle, binding principle (B) allows for the fact that in (77) *some* can bind *him* if *some* has wider scope than *every*, if movement of narrow-scope quantifiers is not obligatory or if they are not necessarily adjoined to S when they move. The LF structures (78a–b) would contain no locally Ā-bound pronominals.[29]

(77) Someone$_x$ played every piece you wanted him$_x$ to
(78) a. Someone$_x$ (e$_x$ played every piece you wanted him$_x$ to)
b. Someone$_x$ (e$_x$ (every piece you wanted him$_x$ to)$_y$ (played e$_y$))

Appendix 2

Suppose that contrary to the assumptions made above, we adopt the definition of chains given in (9), according to which a locally Ā-bound category breaks the chain. A locally Ā-bound category is then always the head of a chain – it must be Case-linked in order to receive a θ-role. A governed category is Case-linked only if it has Case; hence, we are led to assume that governed locally Ā-bound ECs have Case.

Now suppose that whereas lexical NPs must have Case, ECs can also have Case optionally. This assumption makes it necessary to reintroduce some of the concepts and principles we were able to dispense with earlier (in the theory that used Ā-chains), in order to ensure the complementary distribution of ECs. Consider (6a) and (2) again.

(6) a. *Tom believes e to like Mary
(2) *Tom is illegal e to go there
(1) *Who is it illegal e to go there

If the EC has no Case, then on the relevant chain analyses ([Tom], [e] in (6a) and [Tom,e] in (2)) these structures are excluded as before by the Case-checking theory, ultimately by the uniqueness requirement on θ-role assignment. (Recall that under the alternative chain analyses ([Tom,e] in (6a) and [Tom], [e] in (2)) (6a) is an improper movement structure that contains a trace, and (2) is an ungrammatical control construction that contains a PRO; that is, they contain an illegitimate binder for the EC and not an EC in an improper position.) Suppose the EC has Case. Then (6a) is analyzed as containing two chains, [Tom] and [e], since the EC is Case-linked and therefore the head of a chain. Case-checking theory does not exclude (6a) under this analysis. The corresponding problem arises in the case of (2). The EC is not Case-linked; therefore, it is a nonhead member of a chain. The chain [Tom,e] in (2) is not ruled out by the theory as developed above.

Locally Ā-bound ECs raise the converse problem. If the EC in (1) has Case, it is not Case-linked; therefore, the A-chain containing it cannot receive a θ-role, violating the θ-Criterion. But some further condition is needed to ensure that (1) is ruled out when the EC is Caseless and therefore Case-linked in its ungoverned position, thus making θ-role assignment to its A-chain legitimate.

Consider (79), proposed by Manzini (1983). (79) is based on the assumption that the +/− anaphor distinction extends to ECs.

(79) a. If an EC has Case, it is a nonanaphor.
b. If an EC has no Case, it is an anaphor.

The EC with Case in (6a) and (2) will then be a nonanaphor. Nonanaphors (+ or − pronominal) must then be prevented from occurring in these structures. Nonpronominal nonanaphors must not be free or locally A-bound: for these, binding principle (C) together with the VEC is the obvious answer. If the +/− pronominal distinction is also assumed, then we shall have to say that pronominal nonanaphor ECs cannot occur in (6a) and (2) by the Identification Principle. The Caseless EC in (1) is an anaphor by (79b). The fact that it cannot be locally Ā-bound is not due to the binding theory: ungoverned anaphors may be Ā-bound in structures like (72). We can attribute the ungrammaticality of (1) on this analysis to (19): the anaphoric head of a chain must have a θ-marked antecedent.

Alternatively, suppose that we adopt (80), proposed by Sportiche (1983), who assumes that locally Ā-bound categories are pronominals.[30]

(80) a. An EC has no Case iff it is an anaphor.
b. An EC has Case iff it is a pronominal.

Again we may appeal to (19) to ensure that the Caseless anaphor in (1) is ruled out. The ECs with Case in (6a) and (2) are pronominals by (80b). And again we need some condition to ensure that a pronominal that is not identified by its governor (as ECs associated with Clitics would be) must be locally Ā-bound.

There are three objections to restricting the notion of chain used in Case-checking theory to A-chains. First, although it is not unnatural to assume that Case is a necessary condition for a category to function nonanaphorically, it is not clear why ECs with Case should be nonanaphors, as in (79), or pronominals, as in (80). Certainly lexical NPs with Case can be anaphors and nonpronominals.

Second, (79) and (80) make it necessary to resurrect a number of other not very well motivated assumptions that we were able to dispense with above. (79) implies that at least the $+/-$ anaphor distinction is relevant for ECs, and (80) that both this distinction and the $+/-$ pronominal classification extend to them. In order to make (79), (80) rule out (6a), (2), and (1) on the relevant analyses, further assumptions must be readmitted that are unmotivated in light of the Case-checking theory and the binding theory developed above.

Third, in the theory adopted in the text, it is possible to derive from Case-checking theory the generalization that of all ECs, heads and nonhead members of chains are in complementary distribution. However, in a theory that assumes A-chains, optional Case for ECs, and some condition like (79) or (80), only a weaker and more involved generalization follows from Case-checking theory.[31]

(81) In the set of Caseless (not locally Ā-bound) ECs, heads of chains and nonhead members of chains are in complementary distribution. ECs that have Case (and are heads of chains) are in complementary distribution with Caseless (not locally Ā-bound) heads.

Recall that in the framework assumed in the text, where ECs have no Case, the chain analysis relevant for the complementary distribution of PRO and trace (i.e. of EC heads and nonhead members of chains) is the one according to which (6a) contains the chains [Tom], [e], and (2) the chain [Tom,e]. On this analysis, where (6a) and (2) violate the complementary distribution, they are excluded by the Case-checking theory. Now if ECs may optionally have Case, then as we have seen it is necessary to invoke some independent constraint like (79) or (80) that excludes the same chain analysis where the EC has Case, since this is not ruled out by Case-checking theory. Therefore, the complementary distribution entailed by the Case-checking theory in effect becomes a narrower phenomenon. It seems fair to consider this as an indirect argument against the approach in terms of A-chains and optional Case on ECs.

Although our main conclusions about the complementary distribution of ECs in movement and control structures would still hold within this more standard approach, the fact that this framework would have to assume some at present unmotivated principles, together with the observation that it restricts the empirical coverage of the Case-checking theory explanation of the complementary distribution, make it perhaps less plausible than the alternative developed in the text.

Appendix 3

Chains and θ-theory

In order to derive the CLC in full from the θ-Criterion using the visibility requirement (see section 3.4), it is necessary to assume (82).

(82) All chains need a θ-role.

(82) is adopted in Brody (1984a) and also in Chomsky (1985).[32] Both works give independent evidence for (82), although they derive it from different assumptions. In order to maintain (82), the notion of chain must be extended to include not only objects defined in (9) (in Chomsky's terms, chains derived by movement) but also expletive argument pairs in structures like (83a–b) and combinations of such pairs with (9)-type chains (as for example in (84)).

(83) a. There$_x$ is a man$_x$ in the garden
     b. It$_x$ seems S$'_x$
(84) There$_x$ seems e$_x$ to have been a man$_x$ killed e$_x$

Let us then modify (c) in the definition of chains in (9) to allow a nonhead element to be either an EC or an argument.[33] As a result, (83a), (83b), and (84) have the chains [there,a man], [it,S'], and [there,e,a man,e], respectively.

Consider the statement of the D-Structure θ-Criterion in (85), which seems minimal, and the assumptions in (82), (86), and (87).[34]

(85) a. Each argument receives some θ-role.
     b. Each θ-role is assigned to some argument.
(86) All chains contain some argument.
(87) a. (If a chain has a θ-role,) all of its θ-roles are assigned in a unique position.
     b. A chain does not contain more than one argument.
     c. (If a chain has a θ-role,) it is assigned in x_n.

(86) follows from (82) and (85): the θ-role that the chain C has must be assigned to some argument of C at D-Structure.[35] All that remains now from the S-Structure (and/or LF) θ-Criterion of Chomsky (1981) (stated in (10)) is (87a) and (87b). Chomsky (1985) stipulates (87a) as the θ-Criterion.[36] But perhaps the θ-Criterion is more properly considered to be the assumption in (85). Let us ask, then, why (87a) and (87b) should hold.

In Brody (1984a) D-Structure is regarded as a pure representation of x_n – that is, as a level where only the most deeply embedded position of a chain may contain a "contentive" category, where contentives include LF Operators and arguments. As discussed there, the GF$_n$ hypothesis entails (87a) and (87b) (and also (87c), a condition that is not part of the S-Structure θ-Criterion (10)). (87a) (and (87c)) follow because (by the θ-Criterion) at D-Structure all θ-positions *must* contain arguments, but only x_n *may*; hence, all θ-positions must be x_n. Since a chain may contain only one "most deeply embedded position," it may have only one θ-position.[37] Similarly, since at D-Structure a chain may contain only one θ-position, it may contain only one argument at this level, since one position cannot contain more than one category. Assuming that arguments cannot be inserted during the derivation, (87b) must hold.[38]

The GF$_n$ hypothesis is somewhat inelegant as stated; we might wonder why two such parallel conditions as "only GF$_n$ may contain arguments" and "only θ-positions may contain arguments" (the latter an immediate effect of condition (b) of the θ-Criterion; cf. footnote 34) should exist side by side. Let us therefore restate the GF_n hypothesis as (88).

(88) *The Revised GF_n Hypothesis*
Of the set of positions in chains, D-Structure contains all and only x_n's.

We may consider (88) as the definition of D-Structure. Let us assume also that D-Structure is a pure representation of GF-θ, in the strong sense of (89).[39]

(89) All A-positions at D-Structure are θ-positions.

Perhaps (89) is a consequence of the assumption that D-Structure is a derived level of representation: it has only such properties as it is forced to have by some global condition like the Projection Principle. Now each x_n is both a D-Structure position (by (88)) and an A-position, so it must also be a θ-position; hence (82). By the Projection Principle all θ-positions are present at D-Structure, as they are at all syntactic levels. Since all D-Structure positions are x_n, no positions other than x_n may be θ-positions; hence (87a) and (87c).[40]

We continue to assume that Move α operates chain-internally,[41] its operation consisting in replacing x_i by x_{i+1}. Move α is iterative and optional. Since all and only x_n are θ-positions, all and only x_n contain arguments at D-Structure by the θ-Criterion (85). (87b) also follows as before.

Chains and Case theory

In section 3.4, I suggested that the CLC is due to a uniqueness requirement in the visibility condition for θ-role assignment: all and only heads of chains are Case-linked, because a chain must and may only be made visible in the position of its head. The intuitive content of the proposal is that whatever rules apply to LF representations will take a (new) chain to have started in (all and only) Case-linked positions.

Of course, the account allows further questions to be raised. In particular, (a) why should a new chain start in all visible positions (why should the uniqueness requirement hold) and (b) why should a new chain start only in visible positions (why must the visible position be the head of the chain)?

Chomsky (1985) assumes a similar condition.[42] He proposes (in the standard Case-assignment framework) that a chain must contain exactly one Case-marked position, that of the head. He attributes the uniqueness requirement to visibility: a position in a chain is visible iff the chain has a unique Case-marked position. The requirement that this position must be the head of the chain is taken separately. Chomsky implies that the uniqueness requirements on chains of having Case and having θ-position (cf. (87a)) both hold because these properties are properties of chains. ("If θ-role and Case are indeed to be regarded as properties of CHAINs, then we require that each be uniquely assigned to a CHAIN, ... " (p. 188).) But this cannot suffice, since clearly it could be a property of chains that they have 2, 3, any specific, or any arbitrary number of Cases/Case-linked positions and θ-positions. We were able to derive the uniqueness condition for θ-positions (87a); now let us try to do the same for the CLC.

As we have just seen, it is not necessary to assume that θ-roles or θ-positions can be properties of S-Structure and/or LF chains. All the effects of the θ-Criterion stated for such chains could be derived from the minimal D-Structure condition in (85) that involves only the objects that must in any case be θ-role carriers – that is, arguments. Essentially the same might be true for visibility. Clearly, arguments must be visible in some sense for θ-role assignment. Let us then try to eliminate visibility at LF as a property of chains, maintaining it only as a property of arguments (which it must be in some sense in any relevant theory). Accordingly, let us assume the biconditional in (90).[43]

(90)   At LF all and only arguments are visible.

An argument can receive a θ-role at D-Structure iff it is visible at LF. (We assume that a θ-role that is assigned to a position P at some level must be assigned to P at all levels by the Projection Principle, but a θ-role needs to be assigned to a category only once. Alternatively, θ-roles may be taken to be assigned directly to positions only and the θ-Criterion could then be restated in terms of θ-positions and the arguments they contain. See note 34.)

In the text we extended chains to Ā-chains, creating Operator-variable structures in which the EC variable is a non-Case-linked nonhead member of the chain. If this extension of chains is maintained, we apparently need to restrict (90) to D-Structure arguments, or more precisely to D-Structure contentives. This seems reasonable given the assumption we have just made: visibility at LF is a condition for θ-role assignment at D-Structure.[44]

Continuing to suppose that a syntactic object is visible iff it is Case-linked, (90) would entail the CLC if (91) held.

(91) x is a (D-Structure) contentive iff x is the head of some chain at LF.

(91) appears to be false only in expletive-argument structures like (83) and (84). Chomsky (1985) proposes that, as a consequence of the Principle of Full Interpretation, at LF expletives cannot be present;[45] they must be replaced (by Move α) by the argument they are coindexed with at S-Structure. Suppose that this is correct. Then the LF representations of (83) and (84) will be like (92) and (93), respectively, with the chains indicated, so (91) may hold in general.

(92)   a. A man$_x$ is e$_x$ in the garden   [a man,e]
       b. S'$_x$ seems e$_x$ [S',e]
(93)   A man$_x$ seems e$_x$ to have been e$_x$ killed e$_x$ [a man,e,e,e]

Ultimately, then, a chain may be made visible only in a unique position because it must contain a unique argument, essentially a consequence of the GF$_n$ hypothesis.

Acknowledgments

This chapter corresponds to the second half of Brody (1984b). (The first half appeared as Brody (1984a).) I have made no changes to the text apart from adding appendix 3, some clarifying remarks, and a slight revision of the definition of governing category. I am grateful to two anonymous LI reviewers for detailed and helpful comments and for reminding me of some data not accounted for by the formulation of the binding theory domain in Brody (1984b). Sections 1–3 were presented at MIT, at the University of Massachusetts at Amherst, and at University College London in the fall of 1983.

References

Aoun, J. (1982) *The Formal Nature of Anaphoric Relations*, Doctoral dissertation, MIT, Cambridge, Massachusetts.

Aoun, J. and D. Sportiche (1983) "On the Formal Theory of Government," *The Linguistic Review* 2, 211–236.

Borer, H. (1982) *Parametric Variation in Clitic Constructions*, Doctoral dissertation, MIT, Cambridge, Massachusetts.

Bouchard, D. (1982) *On the Content of Empty Categories*, Doctoral dissertation, MIT, Cambridge, Massachusetts.

Brody, M. (1981) "Binding Theory and the Generalized ECP," ms., University College London. Presented in part at NELS XII at MIT, and at GLOW 1982 in Paris.

Brody, M. (1984a) "On Contextual Definitions and the Role of Chains," *Linguistic Inquiry* 15, 355–380.

Brody, M. (1984b) *Conditions and NP-types*, Doctoral dissertation, University College London.

Chomsky, N. (1981) *Lectures on Government and Binding*, Foris, Dordrecht.

Chomsky, N. (1982) *Some Concepts and Consequences of the Theory of Government and Binding*, MIT Press, Cambridge, Massachusetts.

Chomsky, N. (1985) *Knowledge of Language: Its Nature, Origins and Use*, ms., MIT, Cambridge, Massachusetts.

Chomsky, N. and H. Lasnik (1977) "Filters and Control," *Linguistic Inquiry* 8, 425–504.

Cinque, G. (1984) "Ā-Bound pro vs. Variable," ms., Università di Venezia.

Haïk, I. (1983) "On Weak Crossover," in I. Haïk and D. Massam, eds, *Papers in Grammatical Theory*, MIT Working Papers 6, Department of Linguistics and Philosophy, MIT, Cambridge, Massachusetts.

Haïk, I. (1984) "Indirect Binding," *Linguistic Inquiry* 15, 185–223.

Higginbotham, J. (1980) "Pronouns and Bound Variables," *Linguistic Inquiry* 11, 679–708.

Higginbotham, J. (1983) "Some Remarks on Binding Theory and Logical Form," ms., MIT, Cambridge, Massachusetts.

Huang, C.-T. J. (1983) "A Note on the Binding Theory," *Linguistic Inquiry* 14, 554–561.

Jaeggli, O. (1980) "Remarks on *To* Contraction," *Linguistic Inquiry* 11, 239–245.

Jaeggli, O. (1981) *On Some Phonologically-Null Elements in Syntax*, Doctoral dissertation, MIT, Cambridge, Massachusetts.

Kayne, R. (1980) "Extensions of Binding and Case-Marking," *Linguistic Inquiry* 11, 75–96.

Koopman, H. and D. Sportiche (1983) "Variables and the Bijection Principle," *The Linguistic Review* 2, 139–160.

Koster, J. (1982) "Do Syntactic Representations Contain Variables?" ms., University of Tilburg.

Levin, J. (1983) "Case-Linking, Predication and the Distribution of Empty Operators," ms., MIT, Cambridge, Massachusetts. Presented at NELS XIV at the University of Massachusetts, Amherst.

Manzini, M. R. (1983) "On Control and Control Theory," *Linguistic Inquiry* 14, 421–446.

Manzini, M. R. (1985) "On Binding Theory and Control," paper presented at the Cumberland Lodge Conference, "Mental Representation and Properties of Logical Form," Windsor Great Park, England.

Pesetsky, D. (1982) *Paths and Categories*, Doctoral dissertation, MIT, Cambridge, Massachusetts.

Rizzi, L. (1982a) "Negation, *Wh* Movement and the Null Subject Parameter," in *Issues in Italian Syntax*, Foris, Dordrecht.

Rizzi, L. (1982b) "Violations of the *Wh* Island Constraint and the Subjacency Condition," in *Issues in Italian Syntax*, Foris, Dordrecht.

Safir, K. (1982) *Syntactic Chains and the Definiteness Effect*, Doctoral dissertation, MIT, Cambridge, Massachusetts.

Safir, K. (1984) "Multiple Variable Binding," *Linguistic Inquiry* 15, 603–638.

Sportiche, D. (1983) *Structural Invariance and Symmetry in Syntax*, Doctoral dissertation, MIT, Cambridge, Massachusetts.

Stowell, T. (1981) *Origins of Phrase Structure*, Doctoral dissertation, MIT, Cambridge, Massachusetts.

Vergnaud, J.-R. (1982) *Dépendances et niveaux de représentation en syntaxe*, Thèse de Doctoral d'Etat, Sorbonne, Université Paris VII.

Zubizarreta, M. L. (1982) *On the Relationship of the Lexicon to Syntax*, Doctoral dissertation, MIT, Cambridge, Massachusetts.

BEYOND PRINCIPLES AND PARAMETERS

4

ON CHOMSKY'S *KNOWLEDGE OF LANGUAGE*[1]

I

The Preface of *Knowledge of Language* (KL) draws together in a spirited way the two rather disparate areas of Chomsky's work. He presents his contribution to linguistics as an attempt to solve in this domain what he calls Plato's problem: "... to explain how we know so much, given that the evidence available to us is so sparse." In contrast, his political writings can be taken to be a discussion of "Orwell's problem": "why we know and understand so little, even though the evidence available to us is so rich."

Four of KL's five chapters concern linguistics. Three of these are about conceptual–philosophical issues, and one presents a picture of the current state of Government Binding theory. The fifth chapter contains a brief discussion of "Orwell's problem."

In chapter 1, Chomsky notes that generative grammar represents a shift of focus "from behavior ... to states of mind/brain that enter into behavior." This leads to three basic questions: What constitutes knowledge of language? How is this knowledge acquired? And how is it used? Chomsky emphasizes that the question of whether there is a distinct language faculty is an empirical one and goes on to present the poverty of stimulus argument. He argues briefly that knowledge of language is not a practical ability to speak and understand.

Chapter two sets off with a discussion of the usual abstractions involved in the technical concept of language. Chomsky then defines Externalized Language (E-language) and Internalized Language (I-language). E-language is a construct that "is understood independently of the mind/brain," "a collection of actions or utterances or linguistic forms (words, sentences) paired with meanings." I-language is "some element of the mind of the person who knows the language," "an entity abstracted from the language faculty." He then interprets the shift of focus in generative grammar noted in chapter 1 as one from the study of E-language to the study of I-language. The shift is justified by the fact that languages in the sense of E-language "are not real world objects but are artificial somewhat arbitrary and perhaps not very interesting constructs. In contrast the steady state of knowledge attained [i.e. I-language MB] and the initial state S_0 [a Universal Grammar MB] are real elements of particular mind/brains, aspects of the physical world." Earlier use of "grammar" with systematic ambiguity to refer to I-language and also to the linguist's theory of I-language were "unfortunate terminological choices which reinforced inappropriate analogies to the formal sciences." Thus the terminology might suggest taking E-language to be given and the grammar to be that of E-language, a construal under which there is no sense in which one of the extensionally equivalent grammars could be taken as the correct one. But the "E-language is not given, what is given to the child is some finite array of data..." "E-languages... are derivative, more remote from data and from mechanisms than I-languages and the grammars that are theories of I-languages; the choice of E-language therefore raises a host of new and additional problems beyond those connected with grammar and I-language."

Chapter 4 starts with an interesting discussion of Kripke (1982). Next the question of the legitimacy of the (technical) usage of rule following is taken up. A main common thread from commentaries by Quine, Dummett, Searle and others is identified as the objection that "even if there is evidence that S_o [i.e. the initial state of the language faculty, Universal Grammar] includes the principle P and Jones's attained state S_L includes the rule R, and even if these conclusions are specifically and crucially invoked in the best account of Jones's behavior, still none of this would provide any reason to believe that R is a rule that Jones is following or that P has 'causal efficacy'." Chomsky argues that no linguistics-specific problems arise from taking a realist view of the statements of the best theory, and further that nothing more is involved in the assumption that R (of S_L) "guides" behavior or that P (of S_o) has "causal efficacy" "beyond the claim that they are invoked by the best theory." The chapter ends with a discussion of whether the ordinary language term "knowledge" can serve as the right concept for the theory of knowledge. Having emphasized that much of our propositional knowledge is innately determined, Chomsky suggests again that "some of the questions of the theory of knowledge should be recast. Certain systems of knowledge that are central to human thought and action do not have the properties that have often been assumed to be paradigmatic."

Chapter 3 is about Chomsky's current syntactic theory. In many respects this part of the book is a survey, and thus does not lend itself to meaningful summarization. I shall instead take a particular module or subsystem of the grammar, thematic theory and make some comments on Chomsky's treatment. Thematic theory is a central subtheory in the Government-Binding framework, which crucially contributes to the determination of the overall organization of grammar. But its main concepts are likely to have relevance beyond the syntactic levels to which the principles in which they are involved refer. As Chomsky notes, his presentation of this topic is exploratory and, as he also indicates, in parts quite technical. Given the general importance of the subject it might be worthwhile to attempt to discuss it in a way that avoids as much as possible the technical details. "Technicality" is however a relative notion, – a principle may be a "basic idea" from one perspective and a matter of "execution" from another. Also there is a tension between the aim of avoiding generalities and the undertaking to skirt technicalities. I do not expect to be able to resolve this in a fully satisfactory way.

II

I assume some familiarity with the organization of levels of representation in the theory, depicted in Figure 1. Various instantiations of the rule move-α take part in the mapping between D-structure and S-structure and S-structure and Logical Form (LF).

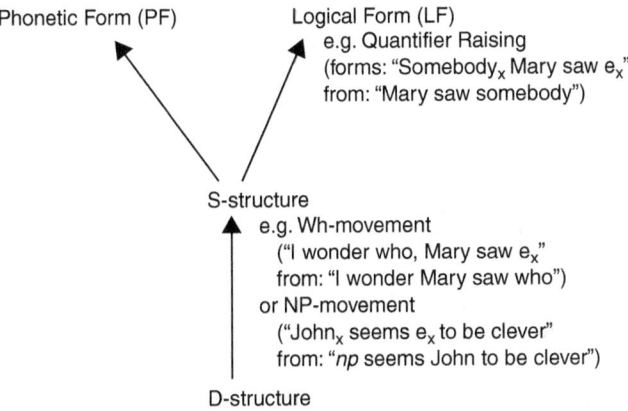

Figure 1

e is the trace of the moved category, interpreted at LF in Wh- and Quantifier movement structures as a variable associated with the appropriate quantifier (-like) phrase. (The status of the element np, the "null category," which appears in pre-NP-movement structures above is not immediately relevant for our present concerns; you might wish to think about it as an orthographic device indicating the position in which the moved category will eventually land.)

A

"We call the semantic properties assigned by heads thematic roles (θ-roles). We refer to the conditions on proper assignment of θ-roles as the 'θ-criterion'." The "intuitive idea" of this condition is "that each argument is uniquely assigned a semantic role and each available semantic role is uniquely assigned to an argument." "Noun phrases that require θ-roles (e.g. *John, the man*) are arguments; nonarguments include such expletive elements as *there* in" (KL 69):

(1) There is a man in the room.

Thus the θ-criterion will for example exclude a structure like (2) below where there are two arguments applying for the one available θ-role. ((11) below is an example of the converse case where there is only one argument for two θ-roles.)

(2) *John seems that Mary left (compare with "it seems that Mary left").

The description of arguments in KL quoted above should of course be taken as an informal statement only, otherwise the θ-criterion would be partly tautologous: categories that require θ-roles require θ-roles. Chomsky (1981) proposed that arguments are "NPs with some referential function, including names, variables, anaphors and pronouns." This characterization has a well-known problematic aspect that relates to the treatment of quantification assumed in Government-Binding theory. In a Wh- movement structure like (3a) below there is only a quantifier (-like element) – a nonreferential category – present at D-structure to receive the θ-role assigned at LF to the corresponding variable. In a structure containing a syntactically unmoved quantifier phrase like (3b) the problem arises both at D- and at S-structure.

(3a) D-S: Mary kissed who
S-S: Who did Mary kiss e
LF: Who did Mary kiss e
(3b) D-S: Mary kissed somebody
S-S: Mary kissed somebody
LF: Somebody Mary kissed e

One possibility would be to require the θ-criterion to hold only at LF, where the θ-roles that appear to be assigned to quantifier-like categories get taken up by variables, elements that arguably have (variable) reference.[2] But consider the case of NP-movement, illustrated in (4).

(4a) D-S: np seems John to like Mary
S-S: John seems e to like Mary
(4b) D-S: np seems np to be certain John to like Mary
S-S: John seems e to be certain e to like Mary
(4c) D-S: np was seen John
S-S: John was seen e

Here it seems clear that the optimal level for the statement of the θ-criterion is D-structure, where the argument *John* is in the position in which its θ-role is assigned. In fact Chomsky assumes that:

(5) "D-structure is a 'pure' representation of theta structure, where all and only the θ-positions are filled by arguments."

But then what should we say about the examples in (3) where a nonreferential category occupies a D-structure θ-position? The picture could be made consistent for instance by assuming that there is a natural class, call it the class of "contentives," that includes not only arguments but also quantifiers and more generally categories that function as operators at LF. The assumption behind this is that contentives are categories that are part of the "referential apparatus," they and only they participate grammar-internally in fixing (variable and nonvariable) reference. (5) could then be rephrased so that it requires a one-to-one correspondence between θ-positions and contentives (instead of arguments). (Cf. Brody 1984 and 1995 for discussion and evidence.)

Note that (5) is in effect a statement of the θ-criterion at D-structure, together with a possible rationalization of why at this level it takes the form it does. Compare (5) with the "intuitive idea" of the θ-criterion quoted at the outset. We shall make use of this observation below.

The examples in (4) contain the empty category *e*, the trace of the moved category. The presence of traces in syntactic representations is well-motivated not only in cases like (4) where they are interpreted as variables, but also in NP-movement structures where such an interpretation seems unwarranted. Trace theory (in the sense of the assumption that syntactic representations contain empty, phonetically unrealized, categories) is often claimed to follow from the projection principle "which states that lexical structure must be represented categorically at every syntactic level." Thus "a consequence of the projection principle is to put it informally, that if some element is 'understood' in a particular position, then it is *there* in syntactic representation, either as an overt category that is phonetically realized or as an empty category assigned no phonetic form ... " Clearly this consequence hinges on the word "categorically" in the statement of the projection principle. But there is no motivation for the assumption that lexical structure must be *categorically* represented apart from the evidence that motivates trace theory. So the usual claim that trace theory falls out of the projection principle seems too strong. Chomsky's discussion should be interpreted as saying that the (otherwise well-motivated) assumption that syntactic representation contain empty categories can plausibly be amalgamated with the statement of the projection principle.

B

Given traces, the concept of chain can be defined: "a chain is the S-structure reflection of a 'history of movement', consisting of the positions through which an element has moved." Thus in (4a, c) we have the chain [John, e]; in (4b) we have [John, e, e]. In (4a, b) there is also the chain [Mary] – "the vacuous case of the single membered chain of an element that remains in its D-structure A-position."[3] In a later section of KL the notion of chain is extended to include not only the movement–history case but also expletive–argument pairs as in (6a) and combinations of the two types as in (6b).[4]

(6a)   There is a man in the room [there, a man]
(6b)   There seems e to have been a man in the room [there, e, a man]

"The expletive argument pair (*there, a man*) is similar to a chain in that the initial member of the pair is in a Case-marked position and the final member is in a θ-position."

In KL (163) very interesting arguments are presented that show that the following assumption has a number of desirable consequences in the grammar:[5]

(7) All maximal chains have a θ-position.

(7) is derived the following way: Chains that contain an argument will contain a θ-position, the D-structure position of the argument. (Recall that (5) ensures that at D-structure all arguments fill θ-positions.) For expletive elements in non θ-positions Chomsky (KL 166) suggests the following: expletives cannot be inserted during the derivation, but they can be linked to an argument (they can form a chain with it) at D-structure. In fact the condition in (8) ensures that they *must* form such a chain.

(8) A D-structure A-position is occuped by α, α nonnull[6] if and only if α is linked to an argument.

Now all chains must contain an argument hence a θ-position, – the D-structure position of the argument. Chomsky considers (8) "a slight relaxation of the definition of D-structure as a pure representation of thematic structure. We now allow a non-θ-position in D-structure to be filled by an expletive linked to an argument." Notice that this way of putting the matter assumes that the hypothesis that D-structure is a pure representation of θ-structure means that at D-structure all and only θ-positions are *filled*. This assumption would need to be supplemented by the θ-criterion to ensure that at D-structure categories that fill θ-positions are arguments. But until now the D-structure θ-criterion was incorporated in the assumption that this level is a pure representation of θ-structure (cf. (5) above). So it now seems necessary to construe this hypothesis as the conjunction of the two interpretations: at D-structure all and only θ-positions are filled and only by arguments. Or equivalently: at D-structure all and only θ-positions are filled by arguments and non-θ-positions are not filled. It is this conjunction of conditions that is relaxed by (8). I am not sure if complicating (5) in this manner genuinely helps to explain why (8) and ultimately (7) holds. I shall return to this problem below.

C

Once chains are defined "the θ-criterion can...be formulated as a property of chains." Before looking at the actual formulation let us first deal with a general question concerning this step. The assumption in (5) that "D-structure is a pure representation of θ-structure where all and only the θ-positions are filled by arguments" is, as we have seen, a statement of the θ-criterion. Let us assume that constraining chains by the θ-criterion is an empirically well motivated move (cf. (11) below). We then have a system where the θ-criterion has to be stated more than once, both at D-structure and at the level(s) where chains are formed. One might wonder if the *prima facie* nonoptimality of this arrangement is real?

One common answer to this worry is to say (following ideas in Chomsky 1981) that the multiple statement of the θ-criterion is due to the projection principle, which projects it to all syntactic levels. I think it should be emphasized here, however, that a projection principle that would do this is rather different from the one whose characterization I quoted above. To require that syntactic structures be projected from the lexicon does not suffice to ensure that particular types of relations hold between some of these positions and some of the elements that can fill these positions. Let us however assume, not at all implausibly, that the projection principle can be appropriately generalized to achieve the desired result. Now since we want the θ-criterion to hold of arguments at D-structure and of chains at other levels, the minimal hypothesis must be that the θ-criterion is projected unchanged to all syntactic levels, the only difference between levels being that elsewhere than at D-structure chains take the place of arguments. Thus the D-structure condition that all and only arguments receive a θ-role (or fill θ-positions) projected to other levels will say that all and only chains receive a θ-role (or fill/contain θ-positions). One desirable consequence of this view[7] is that it entails (7) trivially, thus making the condition in (8) superfluous.

D

The first version of the θ-criterion for chains presented in KL (83) is stated essentially as in Chomsky 1981.

(9) "Each argument α appears in a chain containing a unique visible θ-position P, and each θ-position P is visible in a chain containing a unique argument α."

Let us ignore the visibility requirement which relates to Case theory not considerd here,[8] and consider (9) in the form of (9')

(9') Each argument α appears in a chain containing a unique θ-position P, and each θ-position P is in a chain containing a unique argument.

The condition is now largely redundant, a fact implicit in the later development of the subject in KL. Thus if we think of chains as the recapitulation of the history of movement, including the vacuous case of an unmoved category, then each argument will necessarily be in a chain. Furthermore since D-structure is a pure representation of θ-structure, each chain containing some argument will contain a θ-position (the D-structure position of the argument) and each chain with some θ-position will contain some argument (the one that occupied this position at D-structure).[9] So the principle in (9') really adds only the following two requirements:

(10a) A chain has not more than one θ-position.
(10b) A chain has not more than one argument.

There are various plausible ways of ensuring the effects of (10b) (a problem not considered in KL).[10] Let us concentrate on (10a). This principle ensures that no movement can take place between two θ-positions, as for example in (11):[11]

(11) *John hit e (compare with (4)).

In section 3.4.3 Chomsky formulates the θ-criterion as (10a) (conjoined with the visibility requirement, cf. KL (168)).

Here again we face the same question that arose earlier in connection with stating a θ-criterion at S-structure/LF: why should there be a second θ-criterion in addition to the one incorporated in the assumption that D-structure is a pure representation of thematic structure? Notice that at D-structure the one-to-one nature of the relation falls out since only one argument can be in any given (θ-)position, and it cannot be in more than one (θ-)position. Hence it would be implausible to deal with (10a), as we did in section C above with the principle in (7), by using a generalized projection principle that was taken to project the relevant requirements from arguments to chains. This is because, as we have just seen, it would be redundant to require that an argument is in not more than one θ-position at D-structure. So we cannot take the uniqueness requirement on the number of θ-positions in chains to be a projection of a related requirement on arguments at D-structure.

The discussion of the principle in (10a) above in KL contains the remark that "if θ-role and Case are indeed properties of CHAINS then we require that each be uniquely assigned to a CHAIN...." I am not quite sure how this comment is to be understood, but clearly it cannot be an explanation of (10a), since it would then be circular. We might try to explain (10a) by making use of the recoverability condition. Thus notice that given the θ-criterion at D-structure, the θ-position into which the NP *John* moved in (11) must have contained some argument at D-structure. Since in (11) there is no place where this argument could have moved, the movement of the object NP must have resulted in its deletion. The reasonable assumption that the recoverability condition prevents deletion of arguments will account then for the ungrammaticality of (11). Other principles of the grammar will exclude cases where the D-structure argument has been moved from the θ-position which is the target of another movement, i.e. cases of movement into a trace.[12]

This account in terms of the recoverability condition extends to expletive–argument chains. Thus we can say essentially the same thing about (12) below where an expletive argument chain occupies two θ-positions that we did about (11): in the position of the expletive *there* there must have been an argument at D-structure, which has been illegitimately deleted during the derivation. (Buf cf. the second paragraph of Note 11.)

(12)   There hit John [there, John]

E

Consider now the principle in (13):

(13)   "the θ-position in C [i.e. a chain] must be the position occupied by α_n, in its final term."

(13) is derived in the following way. In chains that recapitulate movement history, α_n, the root of the chain C must be the D-structure position of the category α that

heads C. If α is an argument, then the root position must be a θ-position, since at D-structure all arguments are in θ-positions by (5). This θ-position is unique then in C by (10a). The assumption in (14) is made in KL to deal with expletive–argument chains.

(14) "in an expletive–argument pair the expletive binds the argument, not conversely..."

(14) ensures that a chain always terminates in a subchain that recapitulates movement history (perhaps vacuously, if the argument is in its D-structure position), hence, that (13) holds in general. Again, as in the case of (8), one might wonder why (14), a rather specific condition conspires with general principles to produce the result ((7) and (13) respectively) in the desired general form.

Let us reconsider the three central thematic conditions on chains that are discussed in KL and above:

(15a) All maximal chains have a θ-position ((7) above).
(15b) A chain has not more than one θ-position ((10a) above).
(15c) The θ-position in a chain must be the position occupied by x_n, its final term ((13) above).

All of (15) can be derived as we have seen, with the help of various auxiliary assumptions from other principles in the theory. Thus to get (15a) in KL condition (8) is proposed which backs up the general D-structure θ-criterion in (5). In section C we attempted to improve this analysis by a certain generalized formulation of the projection principle which made the arguably *ad hoc* condition in (8) redundant. In section D we made the suggestion that (15b), the residue of the θ-criterion of Chomsky (1981) (i.e. (9) above), might be attributable to a condition on recoverability. Finally (15c) follows again from (5), given the additional assumption in (14).

We can consider then (15) as the basic thematic chain condition, which requires that the unique θ-position in a chain is its root. But one could argue then that none of the versions of the analysis given in KL or above is really satisfactory, since they make the derivation of this basic simple and general condition contingent on the conspiracy of a number of conditions some of which are not very well understood and motivated. To meet this objection we might try to look at the situation in a somewhat different way.

In KL the definition of chains is based on the concept of movement (in most cases they recapitulate movement history). Suppose that we adopt a theory in which the concept of chains is primary (we have "construct chains" instead of "move-α"), and movement only occurs chain-internally. We now have the option of thinking of D-structure as a representation of the root positions of chains. Let us take this option. Assume in other words that (of the set of positions in chains) at D-structure all and only the root position is present. This means that the concept of D-structure is derived, in the sense that it is abstracted from S-structure, or more precisely from the

S-structure concept of chains. We take the θ-criterion to hold at D-structure as before: at this level all and only θ-positions may contain arguments.

Under such a theory (15c) and (15b) immediately follow from the projection principle. Since available θ-positions must be present at every syntactic level, they must be present at D-structure. D-structure however contains only the root position of chains. Hence only the root position in a chain may be a θ-position (15c), and given the uniqueness of roots in chains this θ-position must be unique in the chain (15b). Now suppose that in consequence of D-structure being a derived level of representation it may contain only such positions that general principles force it to have. Thus the projection principle requires D-structure to contain all available θ-positions but nothing requires it to have non-θ-positions, therefore it must not contain such positions. Now all root positions must be θ-positions (=(15a)).[13]

F

While the evidence presented above for the view that the concept of move-α and not that of chains is derived is certainly not overwhelming, it seems to simplify the picture of grammar in the domain considered. One question that arises immediately is that of LF-movements. Standard S-structures do not contain the chains created by movement rules operating between this level and LF. What happens with these rules if all movement is chain internal? Assuming that LF movement rules in fact exist, the least interesting answer would be to restrict the hypothesis to (strictly) syntactic rules, that is to rules applying between D- and S-structure. Another possibility would be to maintain that S-structure does contain the relevant chains, perhaps in the form of an appropriate indexing.[14] Another version of the hypothesis, however, would maintain the concept of chains unchanged and still assume that all movement is chain-internal. This would be possible if chains were defined not at S-structure but at LF. The idea that this would suggest, is that LF is the basic level of representation. Taken together with the assumption (based on a deficiency of stimulus argument), that there is very little, or perhaps no variation at the LF level between languages, we get very close to giving substantive content to the notion of a "universal base." As the work of generative semanticists in the early 70s and the frequent misquotations of Chomsky's work testify, this is an idea that captures the imagination.

References

Brody, M. 1984: On Contextual Definitions and the Role of Chains. *Linguistic Inquiry*.
Brody, M. 1985: On the Complementary Distribution of Empty Categories. *Liguistic Inquiry*.
Brody, M. 1995: *Lexico Logical Form*. Cambridge, Mass.: MIT Press.
Chomsky, N. 1981: *Lectures on Government and Binding*. Dordrecht: Foris.
Kripke, S. 1982: *Wittgenstein on Rules and Private Language*. Oxford: Basil Blackwell.
May, R. 1985: *Logical Form*. Cambridge, Mass.: MIT Press.
Sportiche, D. 1983: *Structural Invariance and Symmetry in Syntax*. Doctoral Dissertation, MIT.
Williams, E. 1986: A Reassignment of Functions of LF. *Linguistic Inquiry*.

5

A NOTE ON THE ORGANIZATION OF THE GRAMMAR[1]

In Chomsky (1989) the following picture of the grammar is proposed: There are three fundamental levels of representation: Logical Form (LF), D-structure and Phonetic Form (PF). They are interface levels with the central conceptual systems, the lexicon and with motor-perceptual systems respectively. Principles of Universal Grammar (UG) determine properties of these levels of representation, which furthermore have to satisfy "external" constraints that are consequential on their interface status. The three interface levels are taken not to be related to each other directly — the relationship among them is mediated (solely) by S-structure. Properties of S-structure are determined by the fundamental levels and by the requirement that all three be related to it by the postulated system of principles. "The level of S-structure for L [= a given language, MB] is the system that satisfies these conditions, something like the solution to a certain set of equations" (p. 3).

This elegant picture implies that there is a three way symmetry: S-structure in the centre with three (sub-)derivations to relate it to the three fundamental levels. To express this we shall capitalize on a perhaps somewhat tenuous visual analogy and call the system outlined the Ferris Wheel theory. The structure of the grammar is then taken to be along the lines of (1), where S-structure is an axis around which the interface levels appear at the endpoint of three radiuses:

(1) The Ferris Wheel theory

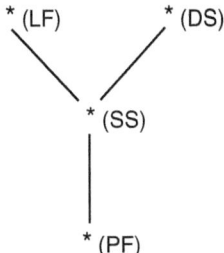

A problem for the three way symmetry implied by the Ferris Wheel theory is posed by the fact that there is little evidence that the principles that relate S-structure to PF have the diagnostic properties of move-α the rule that relates D- and S-structure and also S-structure and LF. We have little reason to think that subjacency, ECP and theta theory would constrain a central principle mapping between S-structure and PF stated in minimal terms, say as affect-α. This fact leads to a modification of the Ferris Wheel view: Since the mapping between S-structure and D-structure and S-structure and LF appears to be of the same type in contradistinction to the mapping between S-structure and PF, we are led to what is probably the more generally accepted version of the standard view: there is a derivation that relates D-structure and LF and S-structure is a level of representation somewhere along this mapping. Let us use the term "syntax" in one of its now standard senses to refer to the principles that characterize the levels of D- and S-structure and LF and their interrelationships. Since we assume that in syntax the derivations on both sides of S-structure are similar in essential respects, syntax-internally S-structure appears to be some arbitrary point on the mapping. We can define this point as the one where the rules that relate PF to syntax branch off.

Let us call this second picture of the grammar that takes account of the different nature of phonological and syntactic principles the Window theory. As the name suggests, under this system S-structure is taken to be a window on the syntactic derivation between D-structure and LF. Phonological rules will relate the representation in this window to PF representations, ultimately to sensory and motor systems. Proponents of the Window theory generally assume that phonological rules relay the information they find at S-structure to PF, i.e. that the phonological component is directional, and it is "interpretive." But we should perhaps not prejudge the issue of whether (in our competence theory) we should think of the mapping between S-structure and PF as (uni-)directional. Thus the Window theory as understood here only claims that at S-structure information is being exchanged and is meant to leave open the question of the directionality of the S-structure–PF mapping.

If we add some indication to our illustration of the Ferris Wheel theory in (1) to show that the mapping between D- and S-structure and S-structure and LF is of the same general type, whereas the mapping between S-structure and PF has different characteristics we have a sketch of the Window theory. I do this in (2) by putting S-structure on a straight line connecting LF and D-structure, thus indicating also that under the Window theory it is natural to take the D-structure/LF derivation to be unitary with S-structure characterized as the point on this derivation where phonology connects to syntax.

(2) The Window theory

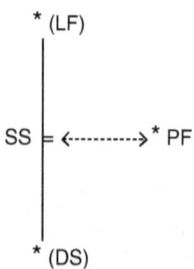

There is a certain feature of the organization of the syntactic subtheory that both the Ferris Wheel and the Window theory share that is quite curious and even on the rather general level of this discussion one might wonder about. Recall that LF and D-structure are taken to be interface levels with the central conceptual systems and the lexicon respectively. The relationship of these levels is mediated by the syntactic derivation. Since it is necessary for the lexicon and our central cognitive processes to interact, everything else being equal, it would clearly be preferable in principle to have just one interface level between them. The lexical constraints on our conceptual systems could then be defined on this unique interface. This would be in contrast to the standard alternative where we have two interfaces with two potentially completely different sets of properties interrelated by a third system devised for precisely that purpose, with precisely the right properties to link up to these two potentially completely different representations.

The argument of the previous paragraph concerning the undesirability of having LF and D-structure as two distinct levels could be repeated with any pair of interface levels, say LF and PF for example. But of course even though abstractly it might be desirable to have a common sensory/motor and conceptual interface, we know that it is most unlikely that such a direct interface exists. The principles of PF organization and the elements they operate on appear to be of a very different nature and completely disjoint from the principles and primitives of LF. Given this fact we are led to assume that there must be two distinct levels related through some mapping. However, no similar situation is encountered in the case of the pair D-structure and LF. The concepts and principles necessary to characterize D-structure, like for example X'- and theta theory constraints and their conceptual apparatus is a subset of the principles necessary to characterize LF. Thus there is no general empirical difficulty in taking DS and LF to be nondistinct.

It is this fact that makes the standard view in both its Ferris Wheel and Window theory incarnation curious. Since it is both desirable and possible to collapse LF and D-structure, why keep them distinct?

It should be emphasized that the argument for adopting a single interface system unless facts force us to do otherwise is not a simpleminded argument from Occam's razor that ignores the overall simplicity of the whole theory of grammar organized in a modular fashion. It is also not simply an argument that has to do with the overall theoretical simplicity and elegance of the theory of grammar, although such a point can validly be made. But there is a further consideration that would seem to strongly favour a single interface syntax, namely that such a system appears to provide a more efficient means of interaction between the lexicon and our conceptual systems. In the standard frameworks there will inevitably be D-structure representations that correspond to no well-formed LF configurations. If we do not take the LF–D-structure mapping to be directional then also conversely, we shall find LF representations that cannot be related to legitimate D-structures. Such overgeneration of structures is unavoidable in a transformational syntax, and clearly makes for a non-optimally efficient system. If on the other hand the lexicon had access to the conceptual interface, the constraints that it standardly imposes on D-structure could constrain LF directly and thus the overgeneration of syntactic interface structures could be avoided.

Suppose that the standard view involving a derivation between two syntactic interfaces is true at some point in the evolution of humans. The two fundamental levels are in principle different in kind but in point of fact one is constrained by a subset of the primitives and axioms that constrain the other. Since a mutation that would make it possible for the lexicon to interact with the conceptual systems directly through a single interface would make the system more efficient, it could result in an evolutionary advantage. Thus we would expect evolution to favour the mutant version and assuming that no hidden advantages exist for the pre-mutation system, we would expect it to gradually disappear. Incidentally, we know on the usual level of abstraction characteristic of current linguistic theorizing what this mutation would have had to be: trace theory.

We are proposing then a theory where there is only a single syntactic interface level, a level that both the lexicon and the conceptual systems have access to. We shall call this level of representation LF, keeping in mind that a different status is now attributed to this level. D-structure can now be thought of a level properly included in LF, or abstracted from LF in a particular way. LF still needs to be related to the interface of sensory and motor systems, PF. Let us call the theory incorporating these assumptions the Lexico-Logical Form (LLF) theory.

Consider now the status of S-structure. The standard framework assumes that this level is somewhere between D-structure and LF and relays information to PF. It is rather unclear however on both the Ferris Wheel and the Window theory view why there should be such a level in the first place. Thus one might ask why LF is not directly connected to PF, a question that we might express by asking why we do not "speak in LF?" Why does the PF of our sentences correspond more closely to their S-structure representation than to LF? Thinking of S-structure as a "solution to a set of equations" or as a level at some intermediate point on the D-structure–LF mapping does not appear helpful in bringing us closer to an answer. On either of these theories S-structure appears to be a gratuitous complication. Since it distorts LF it makes a representation on this level more difficult to map to and to recover from PF. Given either the Ferris Wheel or the Window theory the question arises why LF and PF are not directly connected, why is PF instead connected to some intermediate point on the syntactic derivation, an arrangement that again seems non-optimally efficient.

Consider now the status of S-structure in the LLF theory. If S-structure exists, and we shall assume here that it does, it cannot be an intermediate point on the D-structure–LF derivation since such a derivation is not part of the grammar. Thus if S-structure is a non-interface level of the grammar, it can now only be an intermediate level on the LF–PF mapping, the only derivation that UG contains. Schematically then we have a theory like (3):

(3) Lexico-Logical Form theory

LF * ----------------------||----------------------- * PF
                      S-structure

Thinking of S-structure as an intermediate point on the LF–PF derivation clearly does not pose the same problem that arose in the standard alternatives. LF is mapped to PF directly via S-structure, thus no problem arises of an intermediate point on the LF–D-structure mapping providing the input to the derivation leading to PF. Our theory will have to answer another question instead: how come that S-structure could have been taken as an intermediate point on a D-structure–LF derivation, why did S-structure appear to have such a status?

In earlier work (Brody 1985, 1987, 1991) I have argued that D-structure should be characterized in terms of chains, as in (4):

(4) (of the set of positions in chains) at D-structure all and only root positions are present

(4) is not meant as an additional stipulation, but rather as an alternative to the characterization of D-structure as "pure representation of thematic structure," i.e. the level where all and only theta positions are present. It follows from (4) and the projection principle that only root positions of chains can be theta positions, since by the projection principle theta positions have to be present at every level. Since D-structure contains only chain-roots, only these can be thematic. Thus it follows that movement can land only in non-thematic positions. (4) allows chains with multiple thematic roots, as appears necessary in parasitic gap structures (cf. Browning 1987, Brody 1995).

In the framework defined by (4), it is natural and perhaps inevitable to think of movement as a chain-internal process. Thus standardly movement is taken to be free and chains are considered to recapitulate the movement history of a derivation (as e.g. in Chomsky 1986). Movement applies to D-structure and creates the derived levels, S-structure and LF on which chains are defined. But we define D-structure in terms of chains, so it does not seem natural to define chains in terms of D-structure to S-structure/LF movement, leading by transitivity to defining D-structure in terms of such movement. This would result in defining D-structure in terms of a process that takes D-structure as its input. We shall instead take LF chain construction to be free in principle and define move-α as restricted to apply chain internally.

But this solves the problem of why S-structure appears to be an intermediate level between D-structure and LF. Since all movement is chain internal and chains relate D-structure and LF and levels may differ only to the extent made possible by move-α (or affect-α) it follows that all other levels must appear to be intermediate between these two levels. But as we have argued above, this is only appearance, since D-structure is only an abstraction on LF, and no derivation links the two.

References

Brody, M. (1985) On the Complementary Distribution of Empty Categories, *Linguistic Inquiry* Vol. 16.4.

Brody, M. (1987) On 'Chomsky's Knowledge of Language', *Mind and Language*, 2.

Brody, M. (1991) Economy, Earliness and LF-based Syntax, *UCLWP in Linguistics* Vol. 3.
Brody, M. (1995) *Lexico-Logical Form*, ms. UCL, Cambridge, Mass.: MIT Press.
Browning, M. A. (1987) *Null Operator Constructions*, Doctoral dissertation, MIT.
Chomsky, N. (1986) *Knowledge of Language: Its Nature, Origin, and Use*, Praeger.
Chomsky, N. (1989) Some Notes on the Economy of Derivation and Representation, ms. MIT.

6

Θ-THEORY AND ARGUMENTS

1. The LF θ-Criterion

1.1. Some problems

In standard Government-Binding Theory there are several well-known unresolved problems concerning the θ-Criterion and the notion of arguments. One typical problem is that different elements function as arguments for the θ-Criterion at different levels. If the θ-Criterion holds at D-Structure, then heads of Ā-chains (i.e. elements like *wh*-phrases and quantifier/operator phrases) will have to count as arguments for it, since these are in θ-positions at this level:

(1) θ-*Criterion (at D-Structure)*
    a. Each argument is in a θ-position.
    b. Each θ-position contains an argument.

Given standard assumptions, at LF these elements are not arguments; the θ-role assigned to them at D-Structure is taken up by the associated variable. Since the θ-Criterion also holds at LF, the condition appears to need two concepts or one concept with two different extensions: argument-at-LF and argument-at-D-Structure.[1]

A second characteristic problem concerns the uniqueness requirements of the θ-Criterion. If we are to avoid a chain composition mechanism, then in a parasitic gap structure like (2a) we will have a chain that contains multiple θ-positions: here both the real gap and the parasitic one must be thematic. Conversely, adjectival complement structures of the *easy to please* type seem to have only one θ-role for two arguments (in (2b) the matrix subject *John* and the variable in the embedded object position).

(2) a. Which book did you criticize t without reading e?
    b. John is easy Op to please t.

A third, somewhat different type of problem concerns PRO. Sentences like (3a–b) where PRO would have to be expletive are impossible.

(3) a. *It's impossible PRO to be so obvious that IP.
   (cf. It's impossible for it to be so obvious that IP.)
   b. *PRO being likely that IP, we didn't go.
   (cf. It being likely that IP, we didn't go.)

This fact creates the sole but rather serious difficulty for what appears to be the optimal theory of empty category classification with respect to argumenthood: that empty categories are taken to be arguments optionally. Why is PRO always an argument?

I shall argue that there is in fact no syntactic θ-Criterion either at LF or at D-Structure. In section 1.2, I argue against stating the LF θ-Criterion on chains. I drop the LF uniqueness requirement on the mapping between θ-positions and arguments in section 1.3, and claim that the θ-Criterion holds at LF only to the extent required for meaningful interpretation. Eliminating the uniqueness requirement in turn opens up the possibility of a new analysis of the *easy to please*-type adjectival complement constructions in section 1.4. I argue for a derivation of these structures that would standardly be taken to involve "improper movement" – hence, in section 1.5, I examine how the relevant distinction between ungrammatical improper movement structures and *easy to please*–type constructions could be made.

Section 2 starts with a discussion of the D-Structure θ-Criterion. I suggest that the rather limited evidence for it should also be accounted for in other ways and dispense with this condition. In section 2.3, I return to the question of why chains generally have a unique θ-position. Instead of attributing this to the θ-Criterion, I argue that it should be taken to follow directly from the Projection Principle (as in Brody 1985, 1987). For the Projection Principle to have this consequence, it is necessary to define D-Structure in terms of chains. I show that this entails that chains are not defined on S-Structure/LF but are formed presyntactically. I propose that (head) chains and not simply heads project syntactic representations and that (nonhead) chains instead of (nonhead) categories insert into these.[2]

In section 3.1, I propose a theory that ensures that PRO is necessarily an argument. In section 3.2 Rizzi's (1986) arb-assignment rule is extended to PRO. Finally, in section 3.3 the effects of the PRO Theorem are attributed to a version of Rizzi's pro licensing principle and I discuss what appears to be an important problem of the interpretation of empty chain-initial elements. There is a general similarity, but also a curious discrepancy, between the interpretation of PRO and the type of pro element that, like PRO, is not capable of independent reference – the Italian object pro discussed by Rizzi. Unlike PRO, this type of pro cannot have a fully referential antecedent. The proposed theory will explain this and will thus make possible a unified theory of empty categories with arbitrary interpretation.

1.2. *The LF θ-Criterion for chains*

In the standard Government-Binding framework, we can think of the LF θ-Criterion in two ways. We may take it to ensure a one-to-one relationship between θ-positions and chains as in (4), and/or as requiring a biunique relation between θ-positions and arguments as in (5).

(4) θ-*Criterion*$_1$ *(at LF)*
   a. Each θ-position is in a unique chain.
   b. Each chain contains a unique θ-position.
(5) θ-*Criterion*$_2$ *(at LF)*
   a. Each θ-position is (chain-)related to a unique argument.
   b. Each argument is (chain-)related to a unique θ-position.

Consider first the condition in (4). I shall argue that the first part of this condition, (4a), is redundant, and that the second half, (4b), is both too weak and too strong. Thus, (4) should not be part of the grammar.

Starting with the second half of the condition, (4b) appears useful, since it entails that movement cannot occur between two θ-positions. Such movement would result in a chain having more than one θ-position:

(6) *John believed t to like Mary.
(7) *John BELIEVED t to like Mary.

(6) contains an example of an ungrammatical structure with movement between two θ-positions. The relevance of this example for θ-theory is unclear, however, since it can also be excluded by the requirement that NP-trace must not be in a Case position, probably a consequence of the assumption that movement is possible only if necessary (see Chomsky 1986b).

But we can avoid the interference of this assumption if we pose the problem in a different way – that is, we can ask why there are no verbs with the thematic structure of *believe* that assign no Case to their complements. (See Chomsky 1981 for this way of stating the problem and also Chomsky 1986b for relevant discussion.) This is of course the same as asking why the part of Burzio's Generalization that requires heads with a complement and a thematic subject to assign Case to their complement holds. Clearly Burzio's Generalization, linking two modules through the lexicon in a stipulative way, is not a plausible primitive of the theory.

In (7) *BELIEVE* is to be taken as such a lexical item, with a thematic subject and a Caseless complement position. The ungrammatically of (7) is ensured by the principle prohibiting movement between two θ-positions. Since movement in (7) is forced (by the fact that the complement position is Caseless), but cannot take place (by (4b)), (4b) appears to entail that a verb like *BELIEVE* cannot exist.[3]

However, as Chomsky's (1981) discussion already makes clear, in order to exclude a verb like *BELIEVE*, we must also prevent structures like (8), where the movement originated from a non-θ-position.

(8) *John BELIEVED t to seem that IP.

Thus, the relevant generalization is not that movement cannot link two θ-positions but rather that the landing site cannot be a θ-position:

(9) Only the root position of a chain can be a θ-position (where x is a root position iff it does not c-command any other member of the chain).

We see that a condition like (4b) is too weak to ensure the exclusion of thematically improper movement. It remains of course to account for (9) – a problem to which we return in section 2.3.

Not only is (4b) too weak; there are reasons to think that it is also too strong. As argued by Chomsky (1982) and Browning (1987), the optimal theory should take parasitic gap structures like (10a) to involve only one chain, which includes both the primary and the parasitic gap. We shall represent this chain as a "forking" chain – a chain-tree, in effect – as in (10b).

(10) a. Which book did you criticize t without e [PRO reading t]?
           t}
     b. [which book
                    e t}

But this chain violates the θ-Criterion in (4): both gap positions are thematic, in contravention of (4b). It appears that all root positions in a chain can be θ-positions:

(11) A chain can have as many θ-positions as it has root positions.

This generalization shows (4b) to be incorrect.[4] Again, it remains to explain why only chains with multiple roots have multiple θ-positions; we shall address this problem in section 2.3 as well.

Let us also briefly consider (4a), the condition requiring that each θ-position be in some chain and furthermore that this chain be unique. There appears to be no evidence to contradict what is a minimal assumption once chains are postulated: all positions in a tree are in some chain. In any case there is no reason to think that there is a distinction between θ- and non-θ-positions with respect to whether they need to belong to a chain. As for uniqueness, the same considerations apply: we may again take the stronger and therefore more desirable position that all positions must be in a unique chain, irrespective of their thematic or nonthematic nature.[5]

To summarize this section, the LF θ-Criterion in (4) that requires biuniqueness between chains and θ-positions is partly redundant (4a) and partly incorrect and insufficiently general (4b). (4) does not account for the generalizations that no nonroot position in a chain can be thematic (9) and that any root position may be thematic (11). We therefore dispense with (4). This highlights the necessity of explaining (9) and (11), as will be done in section 2.3.

1.3. The LF θ-Criterion for arguments

Let us turn to the other LF θ-Criterion, the one in (5), which refers to arguments:

(5) θ-Criterion$_2$ (at LF)
  a. Each θ-position is (chain-)related to a unique argument.
  b. Each argument is (chain-)related to a unique θ-position.

I shall argue that (5) is unnecessary and partly incorrect. Chomsky (1981) notes that at LF the θ-Criterion is true almost by definition, by virtue of the fact that it appears to be a necessary prerequisite to meaningful interpretation. This claim would not be correct for the principle in (4) and some of the details in (5), but it still should hold for the central idea. We can identify this central idea of the LF θ-Criterion as (5').

(5') a. Each θ-position/role is related to some argument.
  b. Each argument is related to some θ-position/role.

We may assume then that – as much as (5') does not need to be and therefore should not be ensured by syntactic means – if (5') is violated, the sentence is uninterpretable.[6] Some further evidence for this is provided by the fact that (5)/(5') as stated could not even ensure that an argument receives the kind of θ-role that licenses its referential nature.

Thus, consider quasi θ-roles, the kind assigned to quasi arguments, such as weather-*it*. This element must be taken as a (special type of) argument since, as is well known, it can control PRO, as exemplified in (12a). As this element is an argument, it receives a θ-role. But then what prevents the quasi θ-role from being assigned to a fully referential argument like the one in (12b)? – in other words, why is (12b) ungrammatical?

(12) a. It often rains without PRO snowing.
  b. *This rains.
  c. ?Sincerity kissed Mary.
  d. *What t rains?
  e. What t kissed Mary?
(13) a. *It rains too fast Op to consider t likely t to stop.
  b. (?)The train was running too fast Op PRO to consider t likely t to stop.
     (example attributed to Barry Schein by Rizzi (1986:528))

This is not only a matter of selection in the general sense in which an agent θ-role, for example, cannot be properly assigned to an abstract noun argument as in (12c). The problem has to do with selection of referential properties, the type of selection the θ-Criterion is designed to capture. As the contrast between (12d) and (12e) and between (13a) and (13b) indicates, the problem with (12b) (and (12d), (13a)) is that the quasi θ-role does not license a fully referential argument – in the case of (12d) and (13a) a variable.

The empty trace associated with the *wh*-operator in (12d) and (13a) can be taken either as a quasi argument or as a fully referential one. We have an account of why a quasi argument cannot be questioned: this may be due to the special restrictions on its reference – perhaps a designated element, as proposed by Chomsky (1981). But what prevents the quasi θ-role in (12b,d) and (13a) from being assigned to a real argument, a variable? Apparently we need a supplementary principle that ensures that a quasi θ-role cannot license an element that is referential in a stronger sense.[7] Thus, we need to assume that some statement like (14) is true.

(14)   A θ-role that is referential to a degree X can license only an element that is referential to the same degree X.

The LF θ-Criterion should ensure a correspondence between referential categories and θ-roles. Presumably, then, (14) should follow from/be part of this condition. Now whatever sense we give to the notion of argument, a θ-Criterion like (5) could not capture the generalization in (14). Hence, if we take (5) to be a syntactic condition, (14) will have to be a stipulated rider on it. On the other hand, it is plausible to view (14) in the same light as (5'), as a necessary prerequisite to a meaningful interpretation.

Let us assume then that (5') and (14) are not to be stated as syntactic conditions and ask what remains of (5), the θ-Criterion that concerns the relationship between arguments and θ-positions at LF. The only consequence of the θ-Criterion in (5) that would not be entailed by principles like (5') and (14) – ultimately, by the requirement of meaningful interpretation – is the uniqueness restriction. Let us temporarily (until section 2.1) attribute the uniqueness restriction on the relation between arguments and θ-positions to the D-Structure θ-Criterion in (1). This can be taken to ensure the one-to-oneness of the mapping between θ-positions and arguments simply by virtue of the topology of the trees: one position can contain only one argument, one argument can be in only one position.

At LF, where θ-positions can be related to arguments through chains, uniqueness does not follow, and if we drop the LF θ-Criterion in (5), we expect to see cases where a chain contains more than one argument. I shall argue in the next section that such cases indeed exist. If this is correct, then the only effect of (5) that does not follow from independent considerations is incorrect, and (5) is not part of the grammar.

1.4. *Easy to please*

Let us then consider a case where a θ-role is shared by two arguments: adjectival complement constructions of the *easy to please* type. In these constructions the matrix subject position is nonthematic, as shown by (15a). But an argument can appear in it, as exemplified in (15b).

(15)   a. It's easy [to please John].
       b. John is easy [to please t].
       c. *John is easy [to please Mary].
       d. It's easy [to please t]. (*it* not pleonastic)

As (15c–d) show, the argument appears in the matrix subject position of this type of adjective-with-sentential-complement construction iff the complement contains an appropriate gap related to the argument. Thus, this appears to be a movement structure. The fact that both the position of the gap and that of the moved element are A-positions makes the movement similar to NP-movement. In other respects, this is unlike NP-movement: the gap is in the object position of an ordinary nonpassivized transitive verb, the movement does not obey the strict locality characteristic of NP-movement, and there is even an intervening subject (that of the embedded clause). Since Chomsky (1977) pointed out that the *easy to please* construction exhibits all major features of *wh*-movement, it has generally been assumed that examples like (15b) involve the movement of an empty operator; that is, they have the structure indicated in (16).

(16) John is easy [Op [to please t]].

This construction has been an outstanding problem for GB Theory since Chomsky 1981, where the θ-Criterion and the assumption that variables are arguments were introduced. Given this assumption, (16) contains two arguments at LF. Both the matrix subject and the variable are arguments, violating the θ-Criterion, if this is construed to entail a one-to-one relation between arguments and θ-positions at LF. The problem dissolves given the framework outlined in the previous section: there is no uniqueness requirement on arguments at LF; in fact, there is no θ-Criterion at this level at all. Only such restrictions hold on the correlation between various θ-roles and various referential categories as are required to make meaningful interpretation possible. All that we need to conclude on the basis of (16), then, is that it is quite compatible with meaningful interpretation for the θ-role of a particular θ-position to be shared between two associated arguments, where we can analyze one of them as the subject of a predication and the other as the associated predicate variable. Presumably a similar analysis is appropriate for topicalized referential NPs and possibly also for clefting, relativization, and so on.

A residual problem for the *easy to please* construction in (16) is created by another standard assumption of GB Theory: the prohibition against so-called improper movement derivations. Thus, we must answer the question, How is the argument in the matrix subject position related to the operator and the variable? Since the argument is in a non-θ-position, it must have moved there. But the only potential candidate for the D-Structure position of this element is that of the variable, which appears to be the launching position of the empty operator. So we have a rather curious and otherwise unattested peculiarity: an argument materializing in a non-thematic A-position with no proper D-Structure source. The argument must also somehow be connected to the operator variable chain, if for no other reason than to ensure correct interpretation. If we take this to be accomplished by some construal rule, then we also have an otherwise unattested construal rule relating an argument in a non-θ-position to a θ-position.

But of course we have a rule with precisely these properties, namely, movement. So the problem appears to be located in the assumption that improper movement is generally prohibited. Suppose that it is not. We can now assume that (16) is derived from the D-Structure representation in (17) with two applications of Move α, which moves *John* first to Spec of CP and then to Spec of IP.

(17)　np is easy [[to please John]]

It remains to ensure that improper movement derivations that need to be excluded, like (18), are ruled out.[8]

(18)　*John [seems [t [Mary [saw t']]]].

1.5. Improper movement

Suppose that in (18) the most deeply embedded trace, t', is an R-expression and the intermediate traces are not operators. We can then attribute the ungrammaticality of the structure to Principle C, formulated in the standard way as in (19).

(19)　An R-expression must be A-free up to the domain of its associated operator.

We understand (19) as usual: an R-expression must be A-free in the domain of its operator if it has one; otherwise, it must be A-free throughout. Given the assumption that in (18) t' is an R-expression variable and that (18) contains no operator, (19) straightforwardly excludes the structure: t' is A-bound by the matrix subject *John*.

How can it be ensured that the intermediate traces in (18) are not operators? Let us assume that empty operators need to be licensed. We can leave open whether this licensing is due to the operator's being selected by a lexical category, to its being in an appropriate predication relation with some element, or to some combination of these two considerations. In any case the contrast between (20a) and (20b) or (21a) and (21b) shows the lexically governed nature of this licensing.

(20)　a.　John is easy [Op [to please t]].
　　　b.　*John is feasible [Op [to please t]].
(21)　a.　John is impossible [Op [to please t]].
　　　b.　*John is not possible [Op [to please t]].

Thus, we can take (18) to be on a par with (20b) and (21b): no operator is licensed, and (18) is excluded by Principle C.

Next consider what happens if the most deeply embedded trace, t', in (18) is not an R-expression. We could say the following. NP-movement and adjunct movement chains are uniform in the sense that they involve only A- and Ā-positions, respectively. These chains clearly do not have a root R-expression. Perhaps, then, we could require chains that contain no R-expressions to be uniform in this sense.[9] We must be somewhat more careful: the relevant chain in (18) contains an R-expression (*John*), even if we do not consider the most deeply embedded trace t' to be one. It seems that what we need to say is that those subchains of a chain must be uniform that do not c-command an R-expression within the same chain:

(22) *The Chain Uniformity Principle* (CUP)
The (sub)chain $\{\alpha_1, ..., \alpha_i\}$ of $\{\alpha_1, ..., \alpha_i, ..., \alpha_n\}$ must be uniform unless $\{\alpha_i, ..., \alpha_n\}$ contains an R-expression (where a (sub)chain is uniform iff it involves only A- or only Ā-positions).

(22) will now prevent improper movement in both (18) and (23a), the latter the improper NP-movement structure, whether or not the most deeply embedded trace is taken to be an R-expression. If it is, then the structure violates Principle C in (19); if it is not, then the structure violates the CUP in (22). In general, A-Ā-A chains are now possible only when the lower A-position is potentially an R-expression and the Ā-position is licensed to contain an operator: the *easy to please*-type case.

(23) a. *John [seems [t [it [appears [t' to VP]]]]].
b. Himself, John likes t.
c. Him, John (said Mary) likes t.

This approach will have to be revised or supplemented to allow for reconstruction effects of the kind exemplified in (23b–c), where the trace appears to behave like an anaphor or a pronoun with respect to the binding theory. Thus, in (23b) the trace can apparently be bound by the NP *John*, since this category and the antecedent of the trace, *himself*, are coreferential.

Suppose that we take a different approach and make the relevant distinction in terms of Case: that is, we take (22) to refer to Case-bearing categories instead of R-expressions. This immediately excludes the improper NP-movement in (23a): t' is Caseless. Instead of attributing the impossibility of improper movement from a Case position as in (18) to Principle C, we can now appeal to a chain-theoretic requirement. (See Barss 1986 for arguments that the binding theory does not apply chain-internally.) Let us assume that intermediate nonoperator empty categories in Ā-position are not taken to break A-chains. Thus, (18) contains an A-chain [John, t, t'] with two Case-marked categories, an ill-formed configuration. The approach in terms of Case has the advantage of predicting that syntactic variables in A-positions must have Case:

(24) a. *Who did it seem [t' to VP]?
b. *Who was it illegal [t [t' to VP]]?

The Caseless variables in (24) are excluded by the CUP under the suggested revision. Since the trace in A-position t' is Caseless, the chains [who, t'] in (24a) and [who, t, t'] in (24b) are excluded as violations of the uniformity requirement.[10]

2. Chains and levels

2.1. The D-structure θ-Criterion

I have argued so far that the θ-Criterion does not require a one-to-one mapping between arguments and θ-positions at LF. However, we still need to ensure a biunique relation between arguments and θ-positions to exclude structures like (25) and (26).

(25)   *This seems that IP.
(26)   *It proved that IP. (with pleonastic *it*)

On the relevant analysis of (25), the available θ-position is taken to license two arguments; and on the relevant analysis of (26), the argument is associated with two θ-positions. As noted earlier, we can exclude such possibilities at D-Structure, where biuniqueness of θ-positions and arguments follows from the more general biuniqueness of positions and categories occupying them.

But the D-Structure θ-Criterion is suspect, since it appears to duplicate the LF interpretive requirement. In my view, it does not appear particularly plausible to attribute this duplication to the Projection Principle, whose clear effects have to do with lexical requirements. Thus, the requirement of the θ-Criterion that each θ-position must be occupied by some argument could conceivably be thought of as a lexical contextual condition, but it seems impossible to put such a construal on the requirement that each argument must be in a θ-position. Furthermore, if it is correct to claim that the θ-Criterion holds at LF not as a syntactic principle but only as an interpretive one, then there would seem to be nothing for the Projection Principle to project.

Looking at (25) and (26) more closely, we notice that we only need to exclude the analysis where the two positions involved form a chain: [this, CP] in (25) and [it, CP] in (26). If no chain is formed, then the subject arguments in (25) and the subject θ-role in (26) will violate the interpretive condition in (5'). The former is not related to any θ-role; the latter is not linked to any argument.

Consider then the structure where the chains indicated in the previous paragraph have been formed. (5') is now not violated since all arguments are chain-linked to some θ-role and all θ-roles are chain-linked to some argument. But (26) violates the condition in (9): a nonroot position of the chain [it, CP] is thematic. The remaining problem is (25), where one θ-role is assigned to both arguments in the chain. However, this appears to be too narrow to warrant the postulation of a D-Structure θ-Criterion. We can assume, following Chomsky (1986b), that A-chains are abstract representations of arguments. Hence, no A-chain can be formed that includes two arguments.

We shall assume, then, that no θ-Criterion holds at D-Structure either. This immediately eliminates the problem of multiple characterization of quantifier/operator phrases with respect to argumenthood – they are simply not arguments as expected. (See in this connection May's (1985) tentative proposal to explain the obligatoriness of quantifier raising, namely, that the θ-Criterion holds only at LF.)

2.2. Condition (9)

Let us now try to explain the generalization in (9) that only root positions in chains can be thematic, a question we left open in section 1.2. Recall that the problem was to exclude the possibility of the nonexistent verb *BELIEVE* that assigns no Case to its complement but provides a θ-role for its subject, as in (7) and (8) (reproduced here as (27) and (28)).

(27) *John BELIEVED t to like Mary.
(28) *John BELIEVED t to seem that IP.

Movement of the NP *John* from the Caseless complement position is forced by the Case Filter (see also footnote 3) but is ruled out by the principle in (9) that prohibits movement into θ-positions.

Let us first consider the explanation proposed by Chomsky (1986b). Chomsky assumes a characterization of chains that takes them to recapitulate at S-Structure and LF the "movement history" of the derivation. Chains are thus defined in terms of movement: a chain contains a moved element and its traces. The requirement of (9) that nonroot positions of chains cannot be thematic then follows from (29).

(29) Move α cannot land in a θ-position.

(29) is derived in the following way. Assume that all chains contain some argument. By the D-Structure θ-Criterion, the D-Structure position of this argument is a θ-position. Movement to another θ-position is prohibited by the uniqueness restriction of the LF θ-Criterion.

It should be clear by now that both main assumptions of this chain of reasoning are problematic. The D-Structure θ-Criterion and the uniqueness requirement on the LF θ-Criterion are crucially used, yet neither appears to have independent motivation; moreover, as parasitic gap structures show, the latter appears to be factually incorrect.

Another explanation that has been suggested for (9) uses the D-Structure θ-Criterion together with a principle of recoverability. Thus, the θ-Criterion requires that there be an argument in the thematic subject position at D-Structure. Movement of *John* in (28) and (29) into the same position presumably results in the deletion of this argument, violating recoverability. But again the explanation crucially assumes a D-Structure θ-Criterion, which we have argued is not part of the grammar.

The recoverability approach has other problematic aspects. Consider what happens if the thematic landing position of movement has indeed contained an argument at D-Structure, but one that has moved away from that position. (30) and (31) are two different cases that instantiate this situation.

(30) a. D-Structure: the man who BELIEVED he to like Mary
     b. S-Structure: the man who he BELIEVED t to like Mary
(31) a. D-Structure: John BELIEVED t to seem that IP
     b. S-Structure: John BELIEVED t to seem that IP

In (30) the *wh*-phrase is moved from its D-Structure θ-position to an Ā-position and the pronoun moves up to take its place. (31) could be derived by lowering and then raising the subject *John*.

Consider the matrix subject position, a movement landing position in both cases. In (30) and (31) the element that occupied this position at D-Structure has not been deleted, but moved away. Derivations like these thus cannot be excluded by a simple appeal to recoverability and the D-Structure θ-Criterion. Let us ask, then, whether the movement of the D-Structure argument from the matrix subject position violates other principles. In (30) the *wh*-phrase moves to an Ā-position, where it does not need a θ-role. Since the element that takes its place is a pronoun that can serve as a variable in resumptive pronoun constructions, the principle prohibiting vacuous quantification is not violated. Compare a marginal resumptive pronoun construction like *The man who the fact that he met no one at the party upset you* with the completely impossible **The man that the fact that he believed t to have met no one at the party upset you*. In (31) the argument that moves away is the same as the one that moves into the position; hence, this category will have the θ-role it needs for interpretive reasons at LF.[11]

2.3. Presyntactic chains

Let us then consider a different explanation for the fact that movement always lands in a non-θ-position. Adopting a suggestion made in Brody 1985, 1987, I should like to propose that the effects of (9) follow from an alternative characterization of D-Structure. Standardly this level is thought of as a pure representation of thematic structure, as the level where we abstract away from the nonthematic structure of the sentence. Let us instead think of D-Structure as a level where we abstract away from the chain structure of the sentence, as the level where there are no chains:

(32) Of the set of positions in chains, at the level of D-Structure only the root positions are present.

Notice that (32) is not meant as an additional stipulation. If D-Structure exists, we must characterize/define what it is in some way. According to the present proposal, instead of characterizing it as a level where all and only θ-positions are present, we should think of it as the level where all and only chain root positions are present.

This characterization of D-Structure presupposes a prior characterization of chains; thus, it makes sense only if the concept of chains is prior to that of D-Structure. If chains are defined at S-Structure/LF, then this means that D-Structure is a level derived from one or the other of these levels.

Now, given the Projection Principle, all θ-positions must be present at all levels, hence also at D-Structure. In other words, only root positions may be thematic; otherwise, given (32), the Projection Principle will be violated. Thus, I claim that the prohibition against movement into a θ-position is due not to some version of the θ-Criterion but to the Projection Principle. Looking at the concrete cases (29) through (31), we have the following chain structures:

(33) a. [John, t]   for (29) and (31)
     b. [who] [he, t]   for (30)

All these examples have a chain that has a nonroot θ-position, namely, the matrix subject position. Since by (32) this position, not being a chain root, is not present at D-Structure, the Projection Principle excludes these structures: all θ-positions must be present at every syntactic level, hence at D-Structure.

It immediately follows as well that a chain can have as many θ-positions as it has root positions. The root position does not have to be unique, as parasitic gap structures such as (10) show. By (32), chain roots are all present at D-Structure; hence, the Projection Principle, which requires θ-positions to be present at every syntactic level, will not be violated.

We should generalize the requirement of the Projection Principle that θ-positions must be present at all levels, since this is true not only of positions projected by θ-roles but also of (head) positions that assign these θ-roles. So we shall say that the Projection Principle requires all positions involved in thematic projection to be present at every level – hence also at D-Structure.

But we have now created a problem. Chains are usually thought of as being defined at S-Structure and/or LF. We now define D-Structure in terms of chains. But S-Structure/LF are a function of D-Structure if we assume that D-Structure is the level where syntactic structures are projected from the lexicon. Hence, we have a "near contradiction" or rather a "near circularity." In order to know what the S-Structure/LF representation in a given derivation is, we need to know what D-Structure representation has been projected from the lexicon. But because we define D-Structure in terms of chains, as chain roots, in order to know what positions a sentence's D-Structure representation contains, we need to know the chain structure of the sentence. But chain structures can be read only off of LF/S-Structure; we have come full circle.

We need the definition in (32) to give us (9), the condition that only chain roots can be thematic. We also need the assumption that D-Structure is the level at which syntactic structure is projected from the lexicon since dispensing with this assumption would leave us without any substantive concept of how syntactic structures can be projected. Thus, we must resolve the problem by dropping the assumption that chains are defined on syntactic representations.

Suppose that chains are formed independently of syntax. Then, a head coming out of the lexicon does not project a syntactic representation (a subtree) directly; rather, it forms a chain first with whatever empty categories will be its traces at LF or S-Structure. It is this head chain, then, that will project the syntactic structure. Projection will take place through the root position of the head chain, in accordance with the characterization of D-Structure in (32).

Consider next a nonhead element, a maximal projection. Suppose this is the head of a nontrivial chain; that is, there are traces associated with it. Again, this maximal projection will not be inserted directly into the syntactic tree that will dominate it. When its head has projected it and its Spec and complement positions are filled, the chain of which it is the head will be formed – through the addition of empty categories. It is this chain that will finally be inserted into the tree, rather than a maximal projection by itself.[12]

In principle, this approach leaves open the question of whether derivations are real objects or whether D-Structure is only an abstraction on chain structure. However, once we dispense with the D-Structure θ-Criterion, there remains little reason to assume that derivations between S-Structure/LF and D-Structure exist – that the heads of chains in fact move into the root position at some level. I shall assume, then, that D-Structure is abstracted from chains in the way indicated and that no movement derivation links it to S-Structure/LF. (I take the question of the existence of a derivation between LF and S-Structure to be an independent issue.)

This means that we no longer need to think of D-Structure as a representational level: there is no θ-Criterion here, and other D-Structure conditions that have been suggested can easily be restated at S-Structure or LF in terms of chain roots. Under this proposal, then, D-Structure is simply a set of positions constrained by the Projection Principle: the set must contain all positions involved in thematic projection. Let us call this set of positions the *D-set* of a sentence. Instead of saying that D-Structure is projected from the lexicon, we now assume that S-Structure/LF is projected directly through the D-set of the sentence – this includes the root positions of head(X^0)-chains.

It remains to determine at which syntactic level chains project: S-Structure or LF. I shall leave this matter open here; but see Brody 1987, 1991 for some suggestions that the relevant level is LF.[13]

3. Arguments and "Arb"-interpretation

3.1. *A condition on arguments*

In section 2.1, following Chomsky (1986b), we took A-chains to be abstract representations of arguments to account for the fact that these elements can contain only one argument. Chomsky also proposes that only the head position of an A-chain can be visible for θ-role assignment. Given the view that Case makes a position visible, this predicts that all A-chain heads and no other members of A-chains have Case. As Chomsky notes, the assumption that Case is a necessary condition of visibility is problematic because PRO can also head an A-chain, as in (34).

(34)   It is illegal PRO to be seen t here.

The proposal also leaves open the question of why it is the head of an A-chain rather than its root or some other position that must be visible/Case-marked.

Let us attempt to formulate the visibility requirement in a different way. Suppose that we think of Case as a mechanism for addressing categories. Suppose further that we think of governors as anchors for this addressing: Case addresses relative to a given governor. The notion of governor relevant here is head government. For concreteness, I assume the following definition of government (essentially the definition of head government given by Rizzi (1990)):[14]

(35) x governs y iff
x = N, V, A, P, [+ Agr] Infl;
x m-commands y;
there is no barrier separating x and y.

If governors serve as anchors for addressing, then each Case-marked category will have an associated governor to anchor its Case. But it would be natural to require also that if there is a governor of a category x to anchor the address of x, then x must have such an address, that is, Case. This address would link the category to its governor.

(36) If a category x is governed, then x has Case.

(36) says that all governed categories are Case-marked. This is of course incorrect: NP-traces are governed and Caseless. Suppose that we take (36) to refer to arguments:[15]

(37) (At LF) x is an argument iff Case-linked (where x is Case-linked iff if x is governed, then x has Case).

We can think of (37) as an LF thematic visibility condition. By (37), ungoverned categories and those that are governed and also have Case are arguments. This seems generally right: PRO is an argument and it is ungoverned, syntactic variables and lexical arguments are governed and Case-marked. NP-traces are governed but Caseless; therefore, they are not Case-linked and thus are predicted to be nonarguments. What about governed and Case-marked expletives in examples like (38)?

(38) There arrived a man.

We can assume that these elements are not present where the constraint applies. Chomsky proposes that as a consequence of the principle of Full Interpretation the postverbal argument replaces (Chomsky 1986b) or adjoins to (Chomsky 1991) the associated expletive at LF, where it becomes the head of the A-chain.[16,17]

It follows from the visibility condition in (37) that PRO (i.e. the ungoverned empty head of A-chains) is invariably an argument. Consider the examples in (39), where PRO appears in an expletive-associate structure.

(39) a. *PRO to arrive a man would be marvelous.
(cf. For there to arrive a man would be marvelous.)
b. *PRO being likely that IP, we didn't go.
(cf. It being likely that IP, we didn't go.)

In (39) the ungoverned empty subject NP is Case-linked, hence an argument. Thus, these structures have two arguments: PRO and the postverbal associate. These structures are then excluded in the same way as (25) (*This seems that IP). The two arguments cannot form an A-chain, but if they are not linked by a chain, then the structure violates (5′) – one of the two arguments will not be associated with any θ-role.

The CUP of section 1.5 stated that a nonuniform chain is possible only if it contains a Case-marked element in the appropriate position. This meant that a locally Ā-bound category in an A-position must be Case-marked; otherwise, the Ā-A operator-variable chain violates the CUP. Thus, locally Ā-bound categories in A-position will always be Case-linked, and the visibility principle in (37) will entail that they must be arguments in the sense relevant for θ-role assignment. Note that locally Ā-bound categories do not need to be arguments in general (those created by adjuncts in fact must not be), and the fact that locally Ā-bound elements in A-position are arguments thematically is not a logical necessity.

Reconsider finally the "improper movement" structures (18) and (23a), reproduced here as (40).

(40) a. *John seems t that Mary saw t′.
b. *John seems t that it appears t′ to VP.

We assumed that these structures contain the A-chain [John, t, t′]. If no Case is assigned to t', the CUP is violated. With t' Case-marked, a possibility that arises only in (40a), we attributed the ungrammaticality to the condition prohibiting multiple Case positions in A-chains. But we no longer need to refer to such a condition. If t' is Case-marked, it is also Case-linked and therefore an argument. Thus, it cannot be part of the A-chain that is the abstract representation of the argument *John*. If *John* is in a separate chain, then (5′) excludes it since this argument is not linked to any θ-role. Thus, (40a), with t' Case-marked, is ruled out in the same way as (25), *This seems that IP*.[18]

3.2. PRO and "Arb"-assignment

As we have seen, the visibility condition in (37) ensures that an ungoverned element (i.e. PRO) is invariably an argument. PRO has further interpretive properties, however: either it is coreferential with an antecedent – obligatorily as in (41b) or optionally as in (41a) – or it is free and has its special arbitrary human generic interpretation as in (41c–d).

(41) a. John$_x$ thought it'd be impossible PRO$_x$ to leave.
b. John$_x$ tried PRO$_x$ to leave.
c. John told Mary how PRO to wash oneself.
d. John wondered how PRO to wash oneself.

It has been suggested (see, e.g. Epstein 1984) that the arbitrary interpretation of the free PRO is in fact due to control by an arbitrary implicit argument. As is well known, examples like (41c–d), where there is no potential implicit argument controller, argue against this view. The contrast between (42a) and (42b), discussed by Brody and Manzini (1988), reinforces the conclusion that antecedentless PRO with arbitrary interpretation in fact exists: without such a PRO the lack of a disjointness effect in (42b) would be difficult to explain.

(42) a. *PRO to teach them$_x$ math is easy for the children$_x$.
      b. PRO to teach them$_x$ math is useful for the children$_x$.

In (42a) *them* and *the children* cannot be coreferential since the latter NP controls PRO obligatorily and Principle B prevents the pronoun from being coreferential with PRO. Since no disjointness effect obtains in (42b), we must conclude that the *for*-complement does not control PRO – but there is no other potential controller around either syntactically realized or implicit argument. Hence, PRO has no antecedent. (See also the discussion of Epstein's proposals, and similar ones, in Browning 1987.)

As Rizzi (1986) points out, the interpretive properties of antecedentless PRO are shared by the Italian arbitrary pro complement construction. Thus, for example, (43a) and (43b) (= Rizzi's (39b)) must both be taken to involve a [+ human] interpretation for the null element even though the predicates carry no such requirement.

(43) a. John told Mary how PRO to roll down the hill.
      b. Certe innovazioni tecniche rendono pro più efficienti.
         'Certain technical innovations render (one) more efficient.'

Within Rizzi's theory there is a principle of formal licensing that makes an empty pro possible in the object position in Italian but not in English:

(44) "*pro* is governed by X_y^0 [,which] means that *pro* is licensed by a governing head of type y, where the class of licensing heads can vary from language to language." (1986:519)

(45) a. Questo conduce pro a [PRO concludere quanto segue].
         this   leads   to   conclude   as follows
      b. *This leads PRO to conclude as follows.
      c. This leads to the following conclusion.
         ($\Rightarrow$ This leads one$_{arb}$ to the following conclusion.)

Thus, assuming that in object control structures the controller must be structurally represented, Rizzi attributes the contrast between (45a) and (45b) to a different setting of the formal pro licensing parameter in (44). In Italian pro is licensed in object position by the verb; in English it is not.

Rizzi proposes a convention to the effect that the content of a pro must be recovered through the relevant features of its licensing head:

(46)   Let X be the licensing head of an occurrence of pro; then pro has the grammatical specification of the features on X coindexed with it. (1986:520)

He proposes further a rule of arb-assignment that applies to certain types of internal θ-roles, either in the lexicon or in the syntax. Thus, in (45a) the direct object θ-role of the verb *conduce* projects a position in which pro is licensed by this verb. Its internal θ-role is assigned the arb specification: since arb counts as an argument, this satisfies the θ-Criterion and furthermore accounts for the interpretation. Since pro objects are not licensed in English by (44), arb-assignment in this language has no opportunity to apply to empty categories in the syntax. The rule will be able to apply in the lexicon, however — hence the possibility of (45c), with the interpretation indicated.

Clearly it would be preferable not to have to restrict arb-assignment to internal θ-roles. Suppose it applies freely to both internal and external θ-roles.[19] Consider now free, antecedentless PRO. We would like to account for the fact that it has essentially the same kind of interpretation universally as arbitrary pro objects in Italian. Since we assume that arb-assignment can also apply to subjects, we can attribute the interpretation of antecedentless PRO to this rule. This accounts for the fact that free PRO and arbitrary object pro have essentially the same type of interpretation: both are due to arb-assignment, the major, presumably default, process by which a θ-role to which no lexical material is related can be saturated.

3.3. *PRO and identification*

If indeed the arbitrary interpretation of free PRO is due to arb-assignment, then how is the recovery convention (44), which requires content to be determined through the licenser, satisfied in the case of PRO? Moreover, how is the formal licensing requirement (46) met for PRO? One possibility would be to restrict these requirements to governed empty categories. Alternatively, we could understand the formal licensing and the content recovery conditions in such a way that an ungoverned element will meet them vacuously. First consider formal licensing. Instead of requiring that a pro be licensed by its governor, we can require the governor of an empty nontrace element, pro or PRO, to license this category. If the governor does not exist, the condition is met vacuously. Similarly, instead of requiring that the content of a pro be provided by its formal licenser, we can say that the formal licenser (if it exists) of a nontrace empty element must provide the content of the empty category it licenses.

Let us then generalize Rizzi's licensing condition to all empty heads of chains. These must be licensed, and they can be licensed only by their governor. Thus, both pro and PRO must be licensed, although the latter always satisfies the condition vacuously. This generalization also gives us the effects of the PRO Theorem. Consider a nontrace (head of chain) governed empty category. This must be licensed by its governor. Hence, in English such a governed nontrace will never occur: English has no licensing heads.[20]

PRO and the Italian object pro are now similar in that both are arguments for the θ-Criterion and both can have arbitrary interpretation. But an important difference remains. Arb-assignment is obligatory for the nonexpletive Italian object pro, but optional for PRO: the latter but not the former can also participate in referential dependencies. Structures like (41a–b), with a definite nonarbitrary referent antecedent, are impossible with the Italian object pro.

Suppose that an empty category can have Case at LF only if it is identified. This is natural within the general framework of Case visibility: we assume that Case can make a category visible for θ-role assignment only if it already has the features necessary to function as an argument.[21] Thus, identification by the arb features makes it possible for the Italian object pro to have Case and to qualify as an argument by (37). In the case of Infl and clitic-associated pro it is Infl or the clitic that identifies the features of the associated empty category in A-position, making it possible for it to retain Case and serve as an argument.

Our theory now predicts that arb-assignment is obligatory for the Italian object pro but optional for PRO – in other words, that PRO can have an antecedent with a non-arbitrary reference. PRO is an argument by virtue of satisfying (37); no arb-assignment is necessary. We assume that antecedentless PRO needs arb only for interpretive reasons: an argument whose content is not determined in any other way by the structure must receive the default interpretation. Thus, PRO can be an argument with a non-arbitrary interpretation and can enter referential dependencies as in (41a–b). In contrast, a governed pro is a visible argument by (37) only if it has Case, which in turn is only possible if it has other grammatical features recovered from its licenser. For arbitrary pro the only features the element can recover are the features of the arbitrary specification, without which it cannot have Case and therefore could not be an argument. This will result in a violation of the interpretive θ-Criterion (5′). Thus, for arbitrary pro objects but not for PRO, arb-assignment is required to take place obligatorily in the lexicon or in the syntax. This element therefore cannot participate in (41a–b)-type dependencies, except with arbitrary antecedents, since it is necessarily identified and interpreted with the arb features.[22]

We have, then, the following theory of empty arguments in A-positions. An empty maximal projection is either governed or ungoverned. If the empty category is ungoverned, it is an argument by (37) and will need a θ-role. This element is PRO. If the empty category is governed, the governing head might provide it with features and thereby enable it to have Case at LF. This element is pro, the empty category associated with clitics, Infl, or Rizzi's arb-assigned θ-role. If the governed empty category is to be an argument, it must be Case-linked at LF by (37), and it can be Case-linked only if it has Case. Given the assumption that at LF only empty categories that are identified can have Case, all governed empty arguments must be identified. We follow Rizzi in assuming that empty categories that are not heads of chains will be identified by their antecedents. Chain-internal empty syntactic variables will thus be identified. Hence, they can be Case-marked and thus Case-linked; and as a result they will be able to serve as arguments.

4. Summary

To summarize, in sections 1 and 2, I argued that there is no syntactic θ-Criterion either at LF or at S- or D-Structure. Dispensing with the uniqueness requirement on the mapping between arguments and θ-positions made it possible to reintegrate *easy to please* constructions into GB Theory. It followed that there should be no general prohibition against so-called improper movement structures. I took these to be legitimate, subject to the Chain Uniformity Principle and other conditions. I argued that the fact that only root positions of chains can be thematic motivates defining D-sets on chains. This entailed the conclusions that chain formation must be presyntactic, head chains rather than heads project syntactic structures, and nonhead chains rather than nonhead categories insert into them. I also proposed a theory of visibility that entailed that PRO is necessarily an argument. I reformulated Rizzi's (1986) licensing condition slightly so that the effects of the PRO Theorem also follow from it. Finally, the theory accounted for the fact that PRO but not Italian object pro can have a fully referential antecedent.

Acknowledgments

Early versions of this article were presented as part of a graduate course at University College London and at the 1990 GLOW conference in Cambridge, UK. I am grateful to both of these audiences for comments and to two *LI* readers for very helpful reviews that influenced considerably the final shape of the article.

References

Aoun, Joseph. 1979. On government, Case-marking and clitic placement, ms., MIT, Cambridge, Mass.

Barss, Andrew. 1986. Chains and anaphoric dependencies. Doctoral dissertation, MIT, Cambridge, Mass.

Belletti, Adriana. 1988. The Case of unaccusatives. *Linguistic Inquiry* 19:1–34.

Borer, Hagit. 1986. I-subjects. *Linguistic Inquiry* 17:375–416.

Brody, Michael. 1985. On the complementary distribution of empty categories. *Linguistic Inquiry* 16:505–546.

Brody, Michael. 1987. On Chomsky's *Knowledge of language. Mind and Language* 2:165–177.

Brody, Michael. 1991. Economy, earliness and LF-based syntax. In *UCL working papers in linguistics 3*. Department of Phonetics and Linguistics, University College London.

Brody, Michael. 1992. Lexico-logical form, ms., University College London.

Brody, Michael, and Maria Rita Manzini. 1988. On implicit arguments. In *Mental representations*, ed. Ruth Kempson, 105–130. Cambridge: Cambridge University Press.

Browning, M. A. 1987. Null operator constructions. Doctoral dissertation, MIT, Cambridge, Mass.

Burzio, Luigi. 1986. *Italian syntax*. Dordrecht: Reidel.
Chomsky, Noam. 1977. On *wh*-movement. In *Formal syntax*, ed. Peter Culicover, Thomas Wasow, and Adrian Akmajian, 71–132. New York: Academic Press.
Chomsky, Noam. 1981. *Lectures on government and binding*. Dordrecht: Foris.
Chomsky, Noam. 1982. *Some concepts and consequences of the theory of government and binding*. Cambridge, Mass.: MIT Press.
Chomsky, Noam. 1986a. *Barriers*. Cambridge, Mass.: MIT Press.
Chomsky, Noam. 1986b. *Knowledge of language: Its nature, origin, and use*. New York: Praeger.
Chomsky, Noam. 1991. Some notes on economy of derivation and representation. In *Principles and parameters in comparative grammar*, ed. Robert Freidin, 417–454. Cambridge, Mass.: MIT Press.
Chomsky, Noam. 1992. A minimalist program for linguistic theory, ms., MIT, Cambridge, Mass.
Cinque, Guglielmo. 1991. *Types of Ā-dependencies*. Cambridge, Mass.: MIT Press.
Epstein, Samuel David. 1984. Quantifier-pro and the LF representation of PRO_{arb}. *Linguistic Inquiry* 15:499–505.
Epstein, Samuel David. 1987. Empty categories and their antecedents. Doctoral dissertation, MIT, Cambridge, Mass.
Manzini, Maria Rita. 1992. *Locality*. Cambridge, Mass.: MIT Press.
May, Robert. 1985. *Logical Form*. Cambridge, Mass.: MIT Press.
Rizzi, Luigi. 1986. Null objects in Italian and the theory of *pro*. *Linguistic Inquiry* 17:501–557.
Rizzi, Luigi. 1990. *Relativized Minimality*. Cambridge, Mass.: MIT Press.
Sportiche, Dominique. 1983. Structural invariance and symmetry in syntax. Doctoral dissertation, MIT, Cambridge, Mass.

TOWARDS AN ELEGANT SYNTAX

7

PROJECTION AND PHRASE STRUCTURE

Perfect Syntax dispenses with the idea of externally forced imperfections in syntax. This article presents a system of principles relating (L)LF representations and lexical items that aims to be compatible with this assumption. The core of this theory is that phrase structures are viewed as projection lines (lexical items and their projections) linked by an Insert relation. This explains uniqueness and locality of projection, the fact that phrases and nonphrasal elements can immediately dominate each other only when they are part of the same projection line, and most effects of the "target projects" requirement. I attribute a residue to the Generalized Projection Principle, for which I also provide an explanation. In addition, I explore various consequences of the present approach for the Move/Chain relation.

1. Perfect syntax

Consider a rather standard system of grammar in which the relationship between meaning and sound is mediated by two interpretive systems applying to some interface representation(s) generated by syntax. Suppose that these apply to the same representation (say, the level Lexico-Logical Form (LLF) of Brody 1995a), clearly a desirable additional assumption. Such a view takes the Spell-Out component of the minimalist framework to correspond in the relevant respect to the post-LF semantic interpretation processes. The syntactic computation can then be viewed as having the task of determining certain basic properties of this interface representation, in particular those having to do with the relation between such representations and the elements provided by the lexicon, from which these are composed. Syntax generates (L)LF representations, either in a representational mode, putting interface constraints on possible relations between lexical items and (L)LF structures, or in a derivational idiom, assembling these structures from lexical items.[1]

Given this background, consider a strong version of the minimalist hypothesis according to which (L)LF interface conditions reduce to "bare output conditions," that is, conditions forced on (L)LF representations by the interpretive systems applying to them. The conjunction of this hypothesis with the assumption that the relations between lexical items and (L)LF structures are stated as interface conditions entails that there is no syntax at all that is part of human grammatical competence.

An alternative hypothesis might hold that there exists a separate component of syntax, a set of conditions that do not follow from the nature of the interacting interpretive systems. These conditions, relating lexical items and (L)LF representations, could largely, and perhaps completely, follow from the necessity of relating lexically stored elements and the representations that contain them.

Suppose that syntax, in the sense just characterized, exists. There is then an empirical issue regarding the nature of this system, which relates lexical items creating the (L)LF representation. Optimally, this system should be nearly trivial: we would hope that apparent complexities are indeed only apparent and are due either to independently motivated properties of the interpretive components or to the interaction of these with the syntactic module. The general methodological point is further reinforced by the expectation that the properties of this system are consequences of the need to relate lexical and (L)LF representations. We might thus expect to find a system that is significantly more perfect than the assembly system of the standard minimalist framework.

Even if the Chain/Move relation is taken to be part of this system, there should be no *syntax-internal* conditions on it (e.g. uniformity, Minimal Link Condition, C-Command, Last Resort); see Brody 1995b and the discussion of uniformity below. Furthermore, there should be no representational-derivational duplications of (nearly) identical concepts (e.g. Chain and Move or the representational definitions of well-formed syntactic objects in addition to actual derivations); see Brody 1995a and section 6 below, respectively. A more restrictive framework such as this also eliminates the possibility of using representational-derivational distinctions like deletion (interface invisibility) versus erasure (invisibility for the syntactic computation) that build on such duplications. Additionally, we will expect to be able to dispense with economy conditions and the serious computational complexity that some of these create. Restrictions like these are consequences of the assumption that apparent imperfections in the system relating (L)LF to its alphabet, the lexicon, result from syntax-external considerations. Let us call the theory meeting them *Perfect Syntax (PS)*. In the light of recent advances in the minimalist framework, the apparently ambitious program of PS seems quite reasonable. (See Brody 1995b for more discussion of this approach.)

In this article I discuss a system that could be part of such a theory of PS, and I empirically justify some of its restrictive aspects. I provide a set of necessary conditions on categorial projections (i.e. a theory of phrase structure) in section 2. In section 3, I derive basic conditions of this system from a theory of the assembly of syntactic structures or, more neutrally, from a theory of the relation between lexical items and (L)LF representations. I compare certain salient aspects of this theory with the corresponding properties of the standard minimalist framework (especially in section 5), arguing that the theory defended here is not only simpler but also more adequate in other ways.

In section 4, I turn to explaining the Generalized Projection Principle, the condition that entails that categorial projection, like selectional requirements, must involve the root position of chains. I discuss an explanation that I argue (in section 6) is superior to other recent accounts that give only partial solutions and assume the accidental conspiracy of unrelated principles.

2. A minimal theory of phrase structure

2.1. The principle of categorial projection

Phrases (XPs), words (X^0s), and their heads (X^{min}s) in an X-bar projection appear to share properties – for example, being a nominal or a verbal element. It is often assumed that the shared properties of the phrase and the word are inherited from the head: category labels arise through projection, ultimately from a lexical element dominated by the labeled categories. It seems that every phrase and more generally every non-X^{min} category must share properties with some lexical X^{min} head; there are no "pure" phrases.[2] In other words, phrases and non-X^{min} words can only arise through projection.

(1) *Principle of Categorial Projection (PCP)*
 Every (non-X^{min}) word and phrase is projected by a category that it immediately dominates.

The step from "Some phrases and non-X^{min} words are projected" to "All phrases and non-X^{min} words are projected" seems highly natural, although obviously it is not logically necessary. But given Chomsky's (1995) general condition of inclusiveness (which entails that the interface levels consist only of arrangements of lexical features), the additional assumption in (1) seems unavoidable: all phrases, like everything else at the interface, must consist of lexical features.

Let us understand the term *projected* in (1) as "is a partial copy of." Take phrases and non-X^{min} words to be copies of features of lexical items. Presumably non-X^{min} words are copies of syntactic and morphological features whereas phrases are copies of syntactic features only. X^{min} itself is a full copy of a lexical item. (It is not the lexical item itself since it was copied from the lexicon into the syntactic structure rather than "moved" there.) A non-X^{min} word or a phrase is directly or indirectly projected by an X^{min}; it is a partial copy that immediately or nonimmediately dominates X^{min}. The PCP requires a category (word or phrase) to be directly projected by (be a partial or full copy of) the element that it immediately dominates. Since sentences are finite structures, only a finite set of copies can be created by reapplying the copy relation in this way. It follows that ultimately all non-X^{min} categories are copies of the X^{min} head ("head" in the X-bar-theoretical sense) of the construction, which is itself a copy of a lexical item.[3]

It seems to be an advantage of the PCP that it relates the fact that phrases have nonphrasal heads and the fact that phrases and their (phrasal or nonphrasal) heads share features. Compare the PCP with Kayne's (1994) approach, where the Linear Correspondence Axiom (LCA) entails that in certain configurations phrases have nonphrasal heads,[4] but does not entail that phrases and their heads share properties.

That the PCP is stated in terms of immediate domination ensures the locality of the projection relation. We can state this requirement separately as in (2).

(2) *Locality*
If X^{min} directly or indirectly projects an X^0 or an XP, then there is no category C such that X^0/XP dominates C, C dominates X^{min}, and C is not a projection of X^{min}.

(2) excludes configurations like (3a). (3b), where the lower YP may be interpreted as an intermediate-level projection or as a segment of adjunction, exemplifies (3a).

(3) a. [$_{XP}$[$_C$ X^{min}]]
     b. [$_{XP}$[$_{YP}$ X^{min} [$_{YP}$ Y^{min}]]]

Locality is again not ensured by the LCA: there is an asymmetric c-command relation between X^{min} and Y^{min} in (3b). This orders the terminals as required by this condition.

As in Chomsky 1995, we can consider a phrase maximal if it is not immediately dominated by its copy, nonmaximal otherwise. Could the whole theory of phrase structure reduce to the PCP? It is clear that this well-formedness condition does not suffice; additional assumptions are necessary.

First of all we need to distinguish words (X^0s) and phrases (XPs). It seems incorrect to consider all X^0s to be lexical items given open-class incorporation phenomena showing syntactic movement properties. Let us proceed differently. Call the object headed by an X^{min} and licensed by the PCP (i.e. the X^{min}, the copy of X^{min}, the copy of the copy, etc. – each related by the immediate domination relation to the next) a *projection line (PL)*. Assume that there is a word-phrase boundary on the PL at some random point. Some corresponding additional assumption distinguishing words and phrases is also needed in the framework of Chomsky 1995, at least if we do not make the implausible move of considering all X^0s to be lexical items. The relational definitions of this theory classify both a non-X^{min} X^0 and a nonmaximal XP as intermediate projections. (They are both neither maximal phrases nor lexical items.) But they apparently must be distinguished somehow. To avoid violating inclusivity, let us assume that the word-phrase boundary is marked by the fact that words but not phrases carry morphological features. (Note that I do not adopt the view that a category may be classified in more than one way with respect to its projectional status; see section 5.)

Second, it must be ensured also that all and only non-word-internal heads project a phrase. Let us call this the *extended structure preservation restriction*.

(4) *Extended structure preservation restriction*
    a. Every non-word-internal head projects some phrase.
    b. No word-internal head projects a phrase.

Chomsky (1995) assumes that (4b) is due to a morphological condition: morphology does not tolerate phrases. Adopting a relational definition of projection levels, he rejects the assumption in (4a) and assumes instead that a non-word-internal head that has not projected is both minimal and maximal. Such elements can thus occupy specifier, complement, and X^{max}-adjoined positions, which are reserved for maximal projections. He then rules out the presence of a "moved" nonroot X^{min} or X^0 in such positions using the principle of uniformity, which disallows chains whose members do not all have all the same projection-level characteristics. However, such an approach to (4) fails to capture the suggestive symmetry of this condition. (The same is true of Kayne's (1994) LCA account of (4).) I shall provide additional arguments against the uniformity condition in section 5.

Third, the uniqueness of the relation between a phrase and a head needs to be ensured – say, as in (5).

(5) *Uniqueness*
Every phrase is projected by a unique category.

The uniqueness requirement ensures that a phrase cannot be projected by two heads. Thus, (5) excludes cases like (6a–b).

(6) a. *[$_{X/YP}$ X Y]
    b. *[$_{X/ZP}$ Z [$_{XP}$ X]]

In (6a–b) *X/YP* indicates a phrase that both X and Y have projected, that is, a phrase that shares properties with both. Notice that the LCA predicts this result only for the special case when the two heads are both immediately dominated by the phrase, as in (6a). The LCA rules out this structure since contrary to its requirement there is no pair (C, C′) of constituents related by asymmetric c-command such that C dominates X and C′ dominates Y. (According to Kayne's theory, the terminals dominated by X and Y will therefore violate the requirement that all terminals need to be ordered by an asymmetric c-command relation between categories dominating them.)

The LCA will remain silent, however, about cases where multiple categorial projection does not occur in a configuration where more than one head is immediately dominated by the offending phrase. For example, it allows (6b), a head-complement structure, where XP is the complement of Z. (Z asymmetrically c-commands X in (6b), ordering the terminals appropriately as required by Kayne's condition.) The uniqueness requirement on projection thus does not follow from the LCA in general.

The PCP includes the locality requirement and also entails that every non-X^{min} X^0 and XP have an X^{min} head, namely, the one that ultimately projected it. Together with the uniqueness and the extended structure preservation conditions, the PCP also entails that every phrase must have a unique head.

(7) *X, when X is not phrasal and is immediately dominated by a word-external projection of Y, Y^n, unless $X = Y^m$.

In other words, a nonphrasal X, X^{min} or X^0, cannot be the complement or specifier/adjunct of some other projecting head Y. We note first that this $X^{min/0}$ cannot be properly word-internal since by hypothesis it is dominated by a word-external projection of Y. A non-word-internal $X^{min/0}$ distinct from Y cannot be immediately dominated by Y'', since if $X^{min/0}$ is not properly word-internal, then it must project some phrase XP by extended structure preservation, and this XP can be shown to intervene between Y'' and $X^{min/0}$. We know that Y'' cannot intervene between XP and $X^{min/0}$ by the locality requirement in (2)/the PCP. Furthermore, XP is distinct from Y'', the phrase projected by Y, by uniqueness. Hence, Y'' cannot immediately dominate $X^{min/0}$ – it can only immediately dominate an XP, which may in turn dominate $X^{min/0}$.

To sum up so far: The PCP expresses the idea that syntactic categorial structure is projected from the lexicon. The PCP states that all syntactic categories are related to the lexicon: they are partial copies of (full copies of) lexical items (i.e. of X^{min}s). That phrases and words must have an X^{min} head follows from the PCP, given the independently necessary assumption that PLs must be of finite length. The extended structure preservation requirement ensures that a not properly word-internal lexical element must and that a word-internal element cannot project a phrase. That a phrase must not have more than one head will follow from extended structure preservation and the PCP together with the (subsumed) locality and (additional) uniqueness assumptions.

Of course, like uniqueness and locality, extended structure preservation is so far only stipulated, and all three are in need of an explanation. Before going further in trying to understand why these conditions on phrase structure should hold (section 3), I would like to comment on several concepts that current theories generally assume, the discussion of which I have so far avoided.

2.2. Speculations on adjunction and intermediate projections

Notice first of all that the theory of phrase structure outlined in section 2.1 is neutral with respect to the question of binary branching and universal SVO order. A condition ensuring this (like the LCA) may or may not apply in addition to the PCP and related principles.

Current theories of phrase structure diverge in two major but related respects from a simple configuration where a phrase dominates a head and a number of other phrases. First, an intermediate X' level is assumed between the head and the phrasal node; and second, the configuration of adjunction is allowed in addition. What is the status of adjunction and of intermediate projection levels given the theory of section 2.1?

These two configurations can be reduced to one if, as proposed by Kayne (1994), the intermediate X' level is treated as the lower segment of adjunction. It would be straightforward to graft a segment-category distinction, and with it a theory of adjunction, onto the theory of phrase structure as developed so far. But a simpler alternative might be to assume that there is no special adjunction configuration.

Various arguments have been put forward that adjectives and adverbials, which have typically been treated as adjoined elements, must in fact occupy either the head or the specifier position of some higher projection (Sportiche 1994, Cinque 1993, 1995). Under this option, instead of left-adjunction of XP to YP as in (8a), we will have the configuration in (8b) with the higher head Z. Z may or may not be invisible and/or transparent for selection. (Selectional requirements may be satisfied here by the lower head Y.)

(8) a. b.

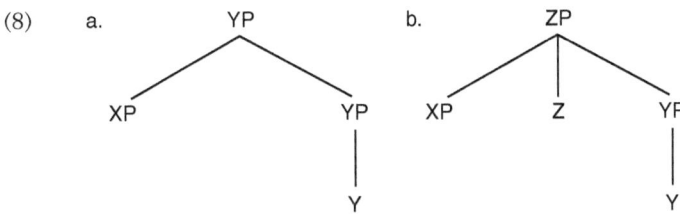

Consider next the question of intermediate projection levels. As noted, one possibility is to follow Kayne in treating the intermediate projection as a segment of adjunction. However, if adjunction does not exist, a different account is necessary. The PCP, as it stands, allows a PL to be composed of more than one phrasal node. A phrase does not have to immediately dominate the X^{min} (or X^0) element of the PL that (indirectly) projected it; they can be separated by phrasal (and also nonphrasal) nodes of the same type. The system outlined above allows nonmaximal projections.

But let us consider an alternative theory. It is widely assumed that intermediate phrasal projections are not visible for the grammar; in particular, they cannot participate in chain formation. If correct, this fact could best be explained if intermediate phrasal projections did not exist at all. Let us suppose that they do not. A word can then project only a single phrase; at the phrasal level the PCP cannot reapply.

The corresponding restriction may be justified in the word-internal domain as well, given Kayne's (1994) arguments that only a single element can adjoin to a word. This leads to the assumption that a lexical X^{min} can project only a single X^0 and a single XP. Suppose that this is correct. The PL of a lexical item X^{min} may then consist of (a) only X^{min}, (b) X^{min} immediately dominated by X^0 or XP, or (c) X^{min} immediately dominated by X^0 immediately dominated by XP. The relational definition distinguishing maximal and nonmaximal projections can be dispensed with; only the independently necessary distinction between words and phrases is needed.

The question then arises how specifiers and complements can be distinguished. For many cases the checking configuration will provide the answer: the specifier is the element that undergoes checking. This will need to be extended to specifiers of those projections that instantiate adjunction in the impoverished system tentatively suggested above. But the specifiers of lexical categories may not participate in a checking relation with the lexical head. If so, then here a different solution is necessary.

We can differentiate specifiers and complements of lexical heads without postulating either adjunction structures or the existence of categories that are neither word-level nor maximal projections by an analysis partly in the spirit of Larson's (1988) work. Suppose that we take a phrase to consist of an internal XP that includes the head and its complements and an external XP shell that contains an empty head and the specifier or specifiers of X as in (9). The empty head X^1 and the lexical head X^2 are then taken to be related – suppose first as a head chain, (X^1, X^2).

(9)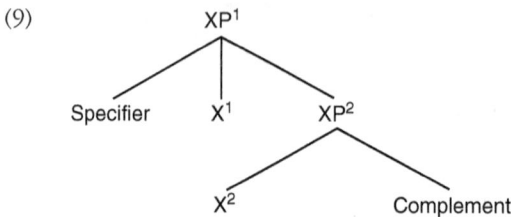

We could then take the specifier to be the sister of the higher head that does not contain the lower head; the complement(s) would be simply the sister(s) of the lower head. Notice that the tree in (9) is only partly Larsonian, since although it involves a higher shell, it is not binary branching.

The solution, as it stands, inherits a general problem of Larson's empty shell approach – namely, that it is incompatible with the Generalized Projection Principle (GPP; see Brody 1995a and section 4 below for discussion), which requires that the selectional properties of a head must be satisfied in the root position of its chain. In the case of (9), the problem is that the subject is not in the same phrase (XP^2) that contains the root position of the head chain. The specifier in (9) would therefore have to be selected from the position of X^1, not the root position X^2 of the (X^1, X^2) chain. Furthermore, the higher head X^1 projects an XP, again in spite of not being in the root position of its chain, in violation of the "target projects" requirement.

One possible solution is to assume that the higher head creating the "empty shell" is in fact not empty but is itself an abstract lexical element, one that carries the appropriate categorial features and selectional requirements of the lexical item whose features are shared between a number of head positions. (This modification of Larson's approach is suggested in Brody 1993a, 1995a; see also Koizumi 1993, Collins and Thráinsson 1993, and Chomsky 1994, 1995 for similar proposals and additional argument.) Multiple-argument verbs under a Larsonian analysis would all require such a decomposition treatment.

Let us apply this analysis to the present problem of eliminating the intermediate X' level in terms of a structure like (9). If X is decomposed into X^1 and X^2, then the head chain that relates X^1 and X^2 would not be (X^1, X^2), but presumably a (covert) (X^2, X^2) chain, where the higher member is in the word-internal checking domain of X^1. If categories standardly taken as sisters of X' and sisters of X are distinguished as sisters of X^1 and sisters of X^2, then simple transitive and intransitive heads must also decompose into two heads. For example, the verb *kick* would have to be composed of an agent-selecting segment and a nonagentive KICK, something like the passive *was kicked*.[5]

It is interesting to observe that ternary structures like (8b) and (9) are compatible with the LCA if (a) instead of adjunction segments (intermediate projections) the complements themselves are taken not to be able to c-command and (b) the LCA is taken to apply only to nonempty terminals as proposed by Chomsky (1995) and Koopman (1996). (Perhaps (a) can be eliminated if there are no nonempty complements as suggested by Koopman.) Such an LCA would entail that in (8b), where the adjunct XP in specifier position is overt, the head Z must be empty. Similarly in (9), if the specifier is overt, then a phonologically realized head must appear in the lower X^2 position.

On the other hand, as we have seen, the LCA would create some redundancy with the phrase structure principles motivated above. Additional problems arise from structures usually analyzed as involving right-adjunction. This configuration cannot exist in a strictly binary-branching theory, where complements of embedded heads correspond to right-adjoined elements. As is well known, various tests suggest strongly that right-adjoined constituents are in fact higher than a general condition like the LCA allows them to be (see, e.g., Williams 1994, Brody 1994). Without the LCA these problems will not arise.

A treatment of right-adjunction compatible with the present framework might view the element A adjoined to constituent B as an additional complement of a *higher* head (rather than of a lower one as in the binary-branching account) whose preceding complement is B. Instead of structures like (10a), this treatment will produce ones like (10b).

(10) a.   b.

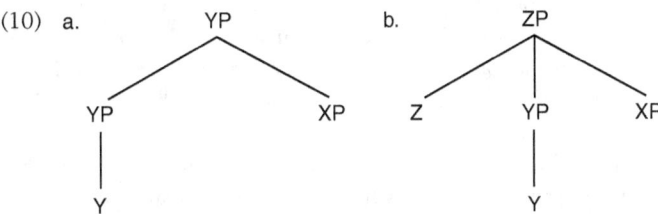

As in the case of "left-adjunction," the higher head Z may be invisible and transparent for selection.

If structures like (10b) exist, then the LCA cannot be a general condition on syntactic structures. The major residual effect of the LCA that we may need to find an alternative account for will be the universal word order restriction. Suppose that the hypothesis of underlying universal specifier-head-complement order is correct. This follows from the LCA, given some additional assumption that ensures that universally the specifier asymmetrically c-commands the head, which in turn asymmetrically c-commands elements embedded in the complement. To ensure this, we could stipulate (11), for example.[6]

(11) A word-external element in the minimal domain of a head H can asymmetrically c-command H iff it is the specifier of H.

In the framework put forward here, specifier, head, and complement are sisters; hence, (11) must be rejected or modified. To ensure the specifier-head-complement word order, we can retain (11) but substitute *precede* for *asymmetrically c-command*. The stipulation appears to be necessary in some form whether or not the LCA is adopted. Formulated in linear terms, it is also sufficient to ensure – to state, in effect – the universal word order restriction.

3. Assembly of syntactic structures

3.1. Chain, project, and insert

The discussion of phrasal projection in section 2.1 has raised several questions. I would like to show that a version of the theory regarding assembly of syntactic ((L)LF) structures proposed in earlier work (Brody 1995a) provides straightforward answers.

This theory postulated three operations: Project, Chain, and Insert. Some additional operation selects a lexical item (LI) from the lexicon and creates a copy (LIC) for syntactic use. *Project* creates another copy of a subset of the features of this copy, F(LIC), and establishes the relation "immediately dominates(F(LIC), LIC)." Project can apply only once to any category, and it can create only one copy in any application. As we have seen, this ensures that there are no "upward-branching" PLs. However, Project can reapply to the F(LIC) it creates, thus creating a further copy. Single or multiple applications of Project that involve copies of features of a given LI result in a PL: a set of copies, originally of an X^{min} (the LIC created by the selection operation), each related to the next by immediate domination. If the speculations in section 2.2 are correct, then the longest possible PL consists of three categories: an X^{min} LIC, an F(LIC) with morphological and syntactic features (X^0), and an F(LIC) with syntactic features only (XP).

Chain creates a copy of a PL (multiple copies in the case of chains with more than two elements). This is either a copy of the whole PL (XP chains are *always* of this type, and if there is no excorporation of incorporated material, then *only* XP chains are) or a copy of the lower "morphological" part of the PL, up to the word-phrase boundary (X^{min} and X^0 chains).

Chain and Project create the (syntactic) *input list* – a concept different from but related to the notion of "numeration." The input list consists of a set of PLs. (Notice that a chain is not a member of the input list, but members of the chain – that is, the PLs – *are* members of the input list.) Although the objects in the input list (PLs) can be complex, they all involve copies of a single X^{min}; they are all copies of a single lexical item. The input list thus can be taken as the normal form in which LIs are presented to syntax.

Insert then applies to PLs, the elements of the input list. Insert establishes immediate dominance relations between members of distinct PLs. Relations created by

Project remain fixed, however; they cannot be modified by Insert. Insert establishes a relation between two PLs and, like Project, it can apply only once to any given PL: a PL can be inserted into one PL only. "Upward-branching" structures are therefore impossible both PL-internally and PL-externally.

For a concrete example consider (12a), with the simplified structure in (12b).

(12) a. Marie embrasse Pierre.
  Marie kisses   Pierre
  b. [$_{IP}$ NP$^{1'}$ V' + I [$_{VP}$ (NP^1) (V) NP^2]
(13) a. Project: NP^1 > N^1, NP^2 > N^2, VP > V, IP > I* > I
  b. Chain: NP$^{1'}$ > N$^{1'}$, V'
  c. Insert all
(14) a. V', VP > V NP^2 > N^2, NP$^{1'}$ > N$^{1'}$, NP^1 > N^1, IP > I* > I
  b. IP > NP$^{1'}$, I* > V', IP > VP, VP > NP^1, VP > NP^2
  (where $X > Y$ means 'X immediately dominates Y')

(Superscripts and stars in (12) through (14) are meant only as presentational aids.) Project creates the PLs in (13a), and Chain adds two more as in (13b): the higher members of the (V', V) X$^{min/0}$ chain and of the phrasal XP chain (NP$^{1'}$ > N$^{1'}$, NP^1 > N^1). Chain and Project in (13a–b) create the input list, an unordered set of PLs, shown in (14a). Finally Insert (13c) applies, relating elements in the input list by simultaneously establishing the further immediate dominance relations in (14b).

The theory is built on two core concepts: the concept of copy and the structural concept of immediate domination. Both concepts are involved in projection: a projection of an element is a (partial) copy that immediately dominates this element. Only the notion of copy is involved in lexical item selection and Chain, and only the notion of immediate domination is involved in Insert. As discussed in Brody 1995a, a major advantage of such a system is that the structure is built in one step; there are no intermediate syntactic structures (i.e. no structures distinct from LF where lexical items are related to each other). Notice that although the input list consists of structured objects (PLs), it is not a syntactic structure: all members of the input list and all (immediate dominance and copy) relations involve only a single lexical item. The theory is thus able to explain the basic minimalist generalization that no conditions can hold on noninterface structures: the generalization holds because noninterface structures do not exist.[7]

A question that is only partly specific to this framework has to do with the notion of copy. Since XP chains are formed by copying a PL with a phrasal element, there must be a nondistinctness requirement on copies in chains to ensure that the same argument and selectional structure is inserted in all copies/members of this PL. (The problem arises also with non-X^{min} X^0 chains.) For example, we need to ensure that the Principle C violation indicated in (15) can be ruled out at or beyond LF. This cannot be done if the chain member in the lower (bracketed) position is simply the PL projected by the highest head of the antecedent: that is, the PL DP > D^{min} projected by *which* in (15a) and the PL PP > P^{min} projected by *to* in (15b).

(15) a. *which claim that John$_x$ was asleep did he$_x$ deny (which claim that John$_x$ was asleep)
b. *to John$_x$ he$_x$ gave a snake (to John$_x$)

The information that two (or more) elements are copies of each other must be available to the post-LF interpretive systems: copies that are members of the same chain must be distinguished at least at LF from accidentally identical categories that are not so related. Suppose, then, that structures in which two copies/chain members dominate distinct elements cannot be interpreted – in other words, that these are not proper copies. This nondistinctness condition will thus constrain the selectional requirements, and therefore both chain members in both (15a) and (15b) will dominate the same elements.[8] Take for example (15b). Here the chain is formed on the PL that was projected by the preposition *to* – that is, on $PP > P^{min}$. The preposition in both copies selects a complement that must be the same in both copies by the nondistinctness condition. The same account holds for (15a), with the selectional requirements of heads applying recursively. The head of the highest DP in the copy selects an NP, which must have been projected by the noun *claim*, given nondistinctness. This noun then selects a CP; and so on.[9]

3.2. Predictions for phrase structure

Let us return to the questions raised by the theory of phrase structure set out in section 2.

(16) a. Why do all and only not properly word-internal categories project a phrase (extended structure preservation)?
b. Why is projection local (no "foreign" elements may intervene between X^{min} and any category it directly or indirectly projects)?
c. Why is projection unique (each category is projected by a unique head)?

(16b) and (16c) receive an immediate answer, given the above theory of (L)LF assembly. Project applies before the syntactic structure is created (by Insert), and it applies separately to each LIC. Hence, two LIs cannot be involved in projecting a given phrase, and no "foreign" projection can ever intervene between an X^{min} head and its projections in the input list. Since Insert cannot modify the relations established by Project, the conclusion carries over to fully formed syntactic representations.

As for extended structure preservation, recall that the impossibility of word-internal phrases, (4b), has been attributed to the fact that morphology does not tolerate such constituents. The symmetry of the extended structure preservation condition in (4) suggests an extension of this restriction to (4a). Consider the claim that parallel to (4b), (4a) holds because syntax does not tolerate nonphrasal elements. This would be an elegant modular solution, but the condition would clearly be incorrect: both phrases and nonphrasal elements (X^{min}s and X^0s/words) appear to play a role in syntax. But let us reconsider this idea in the context of the system of (L)LF assembly outlined above. The modular solution is made available here by the separation of Project, where words play a syntactic role, and Insert, where they do not. So let us assume that Insert is modular in the relevant sense.

(17) Insert relates words to words (morphological application) and phrases to phrases (syntactic application).

(17) entails that all non-word-internal heads must project a phrase. If an X^{min} projects only an X^0 and does not project a phrase (i.e. if the whole of the PL is subject to morphology), then only morphological Insert can apply to it; hence, it will be word-internal. It also follows from (17) that there can be no word-internal phrases; again, these could arise only if Insert were to combine words and phrases in a nonmodular fashion.

The theory of (L)LF assembly involving Chain, Project, and Insert was originally constructed as a system that can build syntactic structures in one step from input lists. Since it does not create intermediate syntactic structures, it explains their nonavailability. As I have just shown, the theory also explains three basic properties of the theory of phrase structure: extended structure preservation, uniqueness, and locality.

3.3. F-Movement and pied-piping

The account of chain formation proposed in Brody 1993a, 1995a, summarized and in some respects modified above, incorporates what is in effect a "pied-piping" hypothesis. Both X^0 and XP chains involve linking elements (PLs) that were created (copied) from a single lexical item. "Pied-piping" of the rest of the chain – that is, filling out all the copies with material additional to this highest head – occurs, as we have seen, because the selectional requirements apply recursively, subject to the nondistinctness condition on chain members.

Chomsky (1995) presents a different theory of movement and chain formation that shares the general idea of pied-piping with this account. He proposes that movement can only take place to establish a checking relation, and for this only a feature F needs to move. Movement of categories occurs only in the overt component of the grammar, and it occurs because F-movement pied-pipes the whole category. Such pied-piping in overt movement is forced by PF considerations. (It is assumed in addition that certain features (formal features, FFs) are mechanically pied-piped in both overt and covert movement.)

For example, in *Whose book did you read?* the *wh*-feature must move to establish a checking relation with the corresponding feature on the C node. It must pied-pipe the word *who*; otherwise, the PF features of this word would be scattered at PF, a state of affairs naturally taken as resulting in an ill-formed representation. The genitive *'s* must also be pied-piped because of its affixal nature; thus, *whose* must move as a unit. But *whose* is not a syntactic object; it is not a constituent. Hence, the whole phrase *whose book* must move together.

Abstracting away from the difference between movement and chain formation (see Brody 1995a for discussion), we see that the two theories have much in common. Both assume that chains are formed on a single element of the head or phrase that ultimately is the member of the chain. In the account I proposed, this element is the head of the chain member; in Chomsky's account, it is the checking feature. The crucial difference appears to be that in the account defended here, pied-piping is a consequence of LF requirements, whereas in Chomsky's account, it is a consequence of PF conditions.

There are reasons to prefer the LF pied-piping approach. In the PF pied-piping theory, the question arises why pied-piping does not take place only in the Spell-Out component. Given a minimalist perspective, it is particularly difficult to understand why a PF requirement should force complications in the syntactic computation. But a theory according to which pied-piping takes place only in the Spell-Out component does not seem to be correct. The position of the "moved" phrase has syntactic and semantic effects. As an example, consider the contrast in (18).

(18) a. Mary wondered which picture of herself John saw.
b. *Mary wondered when John saw a/which picture of herself.

If anything beyond the *wh*-feature (or the formal features of the *wh*-word) remained in situ in syntax, then we would expect (18a) to behave syntactically and semantically in a way parallel to (18b). However, it does not. Thus, the contrast between (18a) and (18b) would be near-impossible to account for on the assumption that pied-piping takes place in the Spell-Out component. But this is the assumption that the PF-driven pied-piping hypothesis would naturally lead us to make.

On the other hand, there is evidence that pied-piping is LF-driven. The adjunct-argument asymmetry in reconstruction (Lebeaux 1989) follows from the nondistinctness requirement and projectional requirements discussed earlier.

(19) which claim that John$_x$ made did he$_x$ later deny (which claim)
(20) *which claim that John$_x$ was asleep did he$_x$ deny (which claim that John$_x$ was asleep)

The Principle C violation in (19), where the relevant name, *John*, is inside an adjunct (the relative clause), is weaker than the one in (20) (= (15a)), where the name is inside a complement clause. As we have seen, selectional properties together with the nondistinctness requirement force the name in the complement to be present in the parenthesized copy in (20), and a Principle C violation results. In contrast, in (19) no selectional requirement forces the presence of the relative clause, and the nondistinctness condition also allows its absence in the (parenthesized) copy. Hence, this sentence has a structure on which no Principle C configuration obtains. Clearly, the PF-triggered pied-piping account cannot capture such a distinction, but an appropriately constructed LF-triggered pied-piping account can.

Chomsky (1995) brings up another consideration: "The computation 'looks at' only F ..., though it 'sees' more. The elementary procedure for determining the relevant features of the raised element α is another reflection of the strictly derivational approach to computation" (p. 269). For example, in (21) there is no question of determining where the *wh*-feature is located inside the complex *wh*-phrase *pictures of whose mother* since the computation looks at such features directly: pied-piping of the rest of the phrase is only an additional matter.

(21) Pictures of whose mother did you think were on the mantelpiece?

In reality, however, the elementary procedure for determining the relevant checking features is a property of the pied-piping theory. As we have seen, a representational pied-piping account is feasible (and also quite well motivated); hence, the question of derivationality does not seem relevant. Note, furthermore, that in any case the pied-piping account does not seem to achieve a genuine result here. This is because on this account also the relation between the XP (in (21) the *wh*-phrase) and the checking feature F (in (21) the *wh*) remains mysterious. This is of course true of both the LF- and the PF-triggered versions.

On the other hand, the PF-triggered pied-piping theory appears to create an additional problem within the standard minimalist framework in that it gives rise to a duplicate mechanism that appears conceptually and empirically unjustified. Consider a grammatical structure where movement without pied-piping has taken place. This could in principle be due not only to the covert nature of the movement but also, as Chomsky (1995:264) notes, to the failure of overt movement to pied-pipe, for whatever reason, as for example in Watanabe's (1991) theory. There is no genuine evidence for making the theory more permissive in this way. See Brody 1995a for a critical discussion of Watanabe's theory. (The problem is in fact more general, which strongly suggests that the covert component of syntax is superfluous. In the versions of the minimalist theory that allow the Spell-Out point to be distinct from (L)LF, empty categories can also be inserted both overtly and covertly.)

3.4. "Covert movement" structures

Let us also consider briefly how overt and covert "movement" structures can be distinguished in the present framework. The simplest assumption is that the distinction does not pertain to syntax at all, that it is only a matter of Spell-Out positions: in overt movement a higher copy, in covert movement a lower copy is subject to Spell-Out. It seems to me that in a framework that assumes that there are no covert Ā-movement relations, there is little reason to depart from this simple hypothesis. If, however, there exist chains at LF corresponding to what used to be treated as covert Ā-movement (see Brody 1995a,b), then the simple Spell-Out hypothesis will run into problems. For example, if the relation between the *wh*-in-situ and the [Spec, CP] where it is interpreted is a chain relation, then [Spec, CP] must not contain a full copy of the *wh*-in-situ at LF.

(22) a. John wondered which pictures of himself Mary bought (which pictures of himself)
b. *John wondered which girl (which girl) bought which pictures of himself

If the [Spec, CP] of the embedded clause contained a full copy of the *wh*-in-situ *which pictures of himself*, then we would expect (22b) to be on a par with (22a); the anaphoric element should be appropriately bound by the matrix subject. But this is incorrect, strongly suggesting that the higher position in the chain of the *wh*-in-situ must not contain a copy. In earlier work (Brody 1993a, 1995a), I treated these structures in terms of what I called "expletive-associate chains." Such chains expressed relations standardly treated in terms of LF movement. In expletive-associate chains the chain-forming associate always remains in situ and the higher positions in the chain are occupied, not by copies, but by an expletive element (or copies of this expletive). The expletive can carry features of the associate; this accounted for various "agreement" effects (e.g. checking of the *wh*-feature in covert *wh*-structures, or subject-verb agreement in *there*-associate structures).

Chomsky's (1995) theory of covert movement as movement of only formal features (FF-movement) is very similar to this proposal. If we again abstract away from the representational/derivational difference, the major difference we find is that FF-movement is essentially head movement, whereas expletive-associate chains may be either head chains or XP chains. Without attempting to resolve the issue, I note that what evidence currently exists appears to favor the hypothesis that chains corresponding to covert movement relations can be phrasal.

(23) There arrived three men.

Raising of FF(three men) in (23) to T violates the Head Movement Constraint, as Chomsky notes. The assumption that FF can be phrasal would avoid this problem. There are then two options: either FF is an additional specifier of T, or FF is identical to features of *there*. (The second option is equivalent to the expletive-associate chain solution modulo the representational/derivational issue.)

3.5. A fully representational version

Given that the nondistinctness of chain members must be ensured by an interpretive condition, the Chain operation of the assembly system in section 3.1 appears to be partly redundant. The identity of the top PLs of chain members appears to be forced both by Chain and by the interpretive nondistinctness condition. But in fact the nondistinctness condition is not strong enough to ensure the identity of the top PLs of chain members. The nondistinctness condition ensures that the corresponding PLs in all chain members must be identical (i.e. based on the same LI). But as observed in section 3.3, it allows nonselected PLs (adjuncts) to be omitted. Now the highest PL in a chain member must be present in all chain members, but it is often not a selected element. Hence, the nondistinctness condition will not require this PL to be present in all chain members, and some additional principle that has the effect of Chain remains necessary.

A different problem with the assembly system proposed above is that the concept of "input list" – like that of "numeration" – is essentially a residue of D-Structure. If Chain could be eliminated from syntax, then the theory of (L)LF assembly could be stated as a fully representational condition along the lines of (24).

(24) *Structural licensing*
(L)LFs partition into PLs (quasi-lexical units). PLs are linked to each other by the modular immediate domination relation between their member categories.

The Chain operation (a) creates additional PLs, (b) links the additional PLs to other PLs created by Project, (c) ensures that the linked PLs involve the same LI, and (d) ensures that they contain an identical set of copies of the features of this LI. (The effect of the operation in (d) rules out nonuniform chains in which for example one member is an XP and another an X^0.)

As for (a), Chain is of course not necessary to create additional PLs; this can be achieved by reselecting the relevant LI and, where necessary, reapplying Project. Linking elements that belong to the same chain (i.e. (b)) could be achieved by simply randomly marking elements at LF; in fact, Chain can be taken to reduce to this random marking. Notice though that both Chain and the LF random marking proposal still violate the inclusiveness principle according to which LF representations consist of nothing other than lexical features. A preferable option might be to assume that chains are not marked at LF and that they are constructed randomly, subject to nondistinctness and other conditions, by the interpretive principles applying to LF representations. This view will necessitate a global recoverability link between post-LF interpretation and PF, since the latter component needs the chain structure information to operate properly (e.g. for "trace-copy" deletion).

This leaves (c) and (d). As for (c), in addition to the nondistinctness condition that refers to chain-member-internal elements, we need (as noted above) a full identity requirement on the highest PL of the chain members. This full identity condition will ensure (d) as well. (As we will see in section 5, in the context of the proposed theory of phrase structure, it entails the major effects of the chain uniformity condition.)[10]

4. A nonsyntactic explanation of the Generalized Projection Principle

The discussion of categorial projection would remain incomplete without considering the Generalized Projection Principle (GPP), a major and pervasive condition, one effect of which is that categorial projection is restricted to root positions of chains. Although the existence of D-Structure as a distinct level of representation is quite dubious, there are few reasons to doubt the existence of the major generalization it expressed (Brody 1993b, 1995a; see also Chomsky 1993, 1994, 1995 for relevant discussion). This generalization, captured by the GPP, constrains the relation of chain members to their chain-external environment. It refers not only to categorial projection but also to thematic selectional requirements, and in fact to syntactic and semantic selection in general. I assume therefore that the GPP is a principle of the interpretive component. All these requirements hold in the root positions of chains.

Thus, for example, a verb V^0 raised to some higher functional projection – say, C^0 – never projects a VP here: categorial projection holds only in the root positions of chains. Furthermore, a V in C never forces the specifier and the complements of C to satisfy the selectional requirements of V: selectional requirements hold only in chain roots. I argued in earlier work (Brody 1995a) that an appropriately formulated projection principle is both compatible with and necessary in a minimalist framework. I also attributed to the GPP the restriction against movement into a θ-position on the assumption that the GPP requires that selectional, including thematic, features not only must hold in but also must be satisfied by root positions. The statement of the GPP in (25) makes explicit that the principle refers to relations that link a chain member to elements external to its chain.[11]

(25) *Generalized Projection Principle*
Projectional (categorial, thematic, selectional) features that link a member of chain C to its C-external environment must hold in and be satisfied by the root position of C.

In the rest of this section I would like to provide an explanation of the GPP, based on the account given in Brody 1995a. I will concentrate on selectional features first. Consider two chains that are to be related by a selectional feature F. It is natural to assume that F must identify all positions of the chain to which it is assigned. Assume, in addition, that all positions of the chain whose member assigns F must be marked as having assigned F. This second requirement is also natural in a framework like the present one, where chains consist of copies: all members of the chain of some X^0 element H are copies of H. Thus, if H has some selectional feature F, then all copies of H are naturally taken to have F, and in all these copies F must somehow be satisfied. In other words, I assume that the two chains will be properly related iff all members of both chains are appropriately identified as being related in this way.[12]

(26) If a selectional (more generally, projectional) feature F of a member of chain C_1 selects (a member of) chain C_2, then
a. all members of C_2 must be identified as being selected by F and
b. all copies of F on members of C_1 must be identified as having been assigned.

Assume further that a projectional feature F, even if present on all chain members of C, can be assigned only from one position of C_1 and can be received only in one position of C_2. Notice that projectional features behave differently in this respect from checking features. Unlike a projectional feature, a checking feature in a given chain can be multiply linked. Suppose finally that information can be transmitted in chains, or perhaps more generally in syntactic ((L)LF) representations, only bottom to top, from a position P to positions c-commanding P. It now follows from this general principle of information transmission that projectional features must link root positions of chains, as required by the GPP; if they linked a higher position, then the information that linking has been successful could not reach chain members that are located lower.

A particular implementation of this approach could take the interpretive process of information transmission to correspond to feature percolation. Let us say that an assignee position is selectionally identified if it has the appropriate selectional feature F, and the assigner position is selectionally identified if it has some feature S indicating that proper assignment[13] has taken place. Like all features, F and S can percolate only to c-commanding positions. It follows, then, that the selectional feature F must be assigned to the most deeply embedded position in the assignee chain; otherwise, lower positions in this chain will not be selectionally identified. Similarly, F must be assigned from the most deeply embedded position of the assigner chain; otherwise, the feature S indicating that the selectional requirement F has been satisfied cannot percolate to all members of the assigner chain. All members (copies) of the assigner chain carry the selectional feature, which can only be satisfied through percolation of S under the assumption that a selectional feature can only be assigned[14] once in any given chain.

Chains in which a nonroot position is selected (including "movement" to θ-positions) are now impossible: the selectional feature cannot percolate to the lower position of the chain, which thus fails to be identified. Conversely, no selection can take place from a nonroot position either. For example, a V raised to I or C now cannot select from the higher position of its chain since the information that this feature is satisfied could not reach the lower position of the chain.

The requirement that information transmission/feature percolation in chains is constrained by c-command corresponds to and extends the derivational principle excluding lowering applications of Move. In a framework that assumes the operation Move, a representation where the assignment of some projectional feature involves a nonroot chain position in violation of the GPP could have arisen in two ways: either through raising, in violation of the derivational equivalent of the GPP prohibiting movement into a position that involves selectional features, or through lowering from this position. Downward percolation of the selectional features corresponds to lowering in a system incorporating Move. This needs to be excluded in both frameworks. If it is, then in the present theory the GPP reduces to the principle in (26), namely, that all positions in a chain need to be selectionally (projectionally) identified. Thus, although the GPP follows from fairly simple chain-theoretical assumptions once the equivalent of lowering is excluded, the same explanation could not be translated into derivational terms in a system that assumes the operation Move. Excluding lowering rules would not help to explain why raising into a selected position is impossible.

Since feature percolation is restricted by c-command, the assumptions that entail the GPP also entail, as a side effect, the c-command requirement on chains. Consider first an XP chain in which not all members of the chain are ordered by c-command. Any element that does not c-command the root of the chain C will not receive the selectional feature(s) that are assigned to the root element; hence, the non-c-commanding nonroot member of C will violate the identification condition in (26a). Similarly, in the case of an X^0 chain, the selectional feature(s) of the element that does not c-command the root element will not be satisfied, violating (26b).

Let us return to the effects of the GPP for categorial projection. Recall that the "target projects" generalization states that categorial projection is invariably initiated in the root positions of assigner chains. Categorial projection is thus similar to selection in this respect. Given the assumptions made in section 2.2, only a residue of the "target projects" problem remains. Given an XP or X^0 chain, a nonroot XP or X^0 cannot be dominated by a further XP or X^0 projection since a PL cannot consist of more than one XP/X^0. Since only X^0 and XP chains exist, the only residue of the problem is the case where the nonroot element of an X^0 chain is illegitimately dominated by an XP that this X^0 projected further.

The explanation of the GPP will immediately exclude this configuration if it is generalized from selectional features to cover categorial features as well – that is, features involved in categorial projection. Selectional features appear to be inherited from X^{min} categories by X^0 elements, which in turn assign these to other categories. Let us assume that categorial projection works similarly: the categorial feature inherited from X^{min} by X^0 is assigned/projected by X^0 to the category immediately dominating it. Like selectional features, categorial features licensing phrases can then be assigned only in a unique position of a given chain; this must be the most deeply embedded position, given (26) and the assumption concerning the direction of (chain-internal) information transmission.

The similar behavior of selection and categorial projection suggests that we should distinguish both of these features from the features usually referred to as checking features. As mentioned in footnote 13, projectional features can also be treated in terms of the checking technology – the real distinction is a different one. But I shall continue to call the two types projectional and checking features. Both checking and projectional features relate chains, rather than categories, but they appear to do so in different ways. Checking features are properties of chains. If such a feature is checked, then it is automatically taken to be checked in all copies (chain members) in the chain, independently of whether the copies are in a higher or lower position. A natural way of capturing this is to say that the checking feature is a property of the chain in syntax, rather than a property of the category from which it originates. By contrast, although a projectional feature also relates chains, it does not become a chain property but remains the property of the category that is lexically specified to carry it.[15]

Consider finally an aspect of the interaction of the GPP with the theory of (L)LF relations presented earlier. Take a "moved" non-chain-root word-external head H. Given the modularity of the Insert relation, H must project a phrasal node HP; Insert can only combine a phrase with a phrase. There are two options to consider: either the projected phrase HP may be internal to the phrase into which H was inserted, or it may force the category label of this phrase to be HP. Both options must be excluded, and indeed the GPP excludes them both: projection is restricted to root positions. Thus, the GPP and the modularity of the Insert relation together ensure that "moved" non-chain-root heads must invariably be head-internal. There is no contradiction here between modular Insert and the GPP. These principles only create a contradiction for word-external heads in non-chain-root positions. Insert requires all word-external heads to project a phrase, and the GPP restricts all projection to originate in root positions of chains. Hence, word-external heads that are not in root positions can neither project nor not project: they cannot exist.

5. Uniformity, relational definition(s) of projection levels, and the X^0/XP distinction

The system of phrase structure defended here assumes a nonrelationally defined distinction between X^0s and XPs – that is, between words and phrases. Recall that I take words and phrases to be inherently different: only the former carry morphological features. It might appear that this assumption is in addition to those that the phrase structure theory of the standard minimalist framework has to make, where projection levels are defined relationally. But as noted in section 2.1, this is not the case. Consider the relevant definitions from Chomsky 1994, 1995.[16]

(27) a. A maximal projection (X^{max}) is one that does not project further.
 b. Minimal projections (X^{min}) are the lexical items themselves.
 c. Intermediate projections (X') are elements that are neither maximal nor minimal.

Given a substructure S that is an intermediate projection (i.e. neither an X^{min} nor an X^{max}), (27) does not specify whether S is an X^0 or an X' (i.e. a nonmaximal XP). In all standard frameworks, however, a distinction is necessary: syntax and morphology appear to treat X^0s and phrases differently. To take a relevant case, X^0s but not intermediate phrasal projections are generally assumed to be available for chain formation (movement).

Let us next turn to the uniformity condition on chains, (28).

(28) A chain is uniform with respect to phrase structure status.

Here the "phrase structure status" of an element is its (relational) property of being maximal, minimal, or neither. Since only X^0 and maximal XP projections are assumed to be accessible to the syntactic computational system, and hence for chain formation, the uniformity condition in (28) predicts that only (X^{max}, X^{max}) and (X^0, X^0) chains exist.[17]

Given definitions like those in (27), it is easy to construct nonuniform chains. In (29) an $X^{min/0}$ forms a chain with a copy that adjoined to or substituted into a word(X^0)-external Y^n, $Y \neq X$. Given (27a), this $X^{min/0}$ will form a chain with an X^{max}: here the first X_i of the chain is an X^{max} and the second an $X^{min/0}$.

(29)
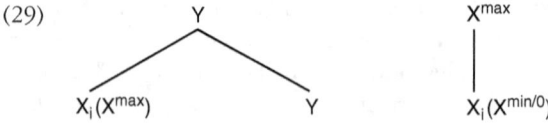

In (30) a non-chain-root ("moved") element X merges with some category Y, and then X (rather than the target of the operation) projects further, violating the "target projects" generalization and resulting in a nonuniform chain. In (30) the second X_i of the chain is an x^{max}; the first is not.

(30)

On usual assumptions, the structures in (29) and (30) are ill formed: minimal projections cannot move to (form chains with) positions that are not word(X^0)-internal, and it is always the target of movement that projects (only chain-root positions can project). The impossibility of configurations like (29) and (30) has been considered to provide evidence for the uniformity condition.

The behavior of clitics has been cited as additional empirical evidence for this system. According to the definitions in (27), a category can be both a minimal and a maximal projection: a lexical item that does not project further. Clitics appear to transparently instantiate this option, since they exhibit properties of both minimal and maximal projections. As X^{min}s, they show up word-internally; but they seem to be linked to argument positions that are maximal. Furthermore, they can often form chains that ignore intervening heads, again suggesting (in the context of the Head Movement Constraint) that they are maximal. Thus, given the relational definitions in (27), clitics might be treated as both X^{max} and $X^{min/0}$ at the same time, accounting for their apparent dual nature.

The uniformity solution to the problems raised by the structures in (29) and (30) and by clitics faces numerous problems itself. Let us look at some of these before considering the alternative account that the present theory provides.

1. Ordinary X^0 head movement chains that target word-internal positions are nonuniform by the definitions in (27). Consider a chain where the root is a lexical item ($X^{min/0}$) that projects further, whereas the nonroot word-internal member does not (hence X^{max}). Such chains must be allowed, but they violate uniformity. Chomsky (1994, 1995) suggests that there is a special component "WI" at LF, where "independent word interpretation processes" apply. This then ensures that word(X^0)-internally the

principles in (27) and (28) do not apply. WI is "a covert analogue of Morphology" (1995:322). But the reason for the existence of such a covert analogue of Morphology, and thus the status of WI, is unclear. Given the lack of evidence for such an additional module, the WI hypothesis appears to amount to little more than a statement that head movement targeting a word-internal position is exempt from the uniformity requirement. But if so, then we cannot say that uniformity explains the impossibility of head chains like (29) where a nonroot member is word-external. The crucial distinction between good and bad cases here is the word-external versus word-internal contrast. Uniformity says nothing about this distinction, which is simply stipulated.[18]

2. If relational definitions do not apply word-internally, then the evidence clitics appeared to provide for them (namely, that clitics appear to have a different projectional-level status word-internally and word-externally) disappears. Since grammatical cases of head movement make it necessary to exempt word-internal structure from these definitions, the word-internal status of clitics becomes irrelevant and thus cannot be used to support the system.

3. The assumption that the relational definitions do not apply word-internally creates further problems. Consider the assumption that word-internal XP-adjunction is excluded in Morphology: "The morphological component gives no output (so the derivation crashes) if presented with an element that is not an X^0 or a feature" (Chomsky 1995:319). The question arises how Morphology will be able to tell what is an XP inside a word if contextual definitions do not apply inside a word. Clearly, some other characterization of minimal and maximal projections will be necessary. But the resulting system seems quite undesirable: why should we need two systems (one relational, one presumably not) to define projection levels? Differently put, why do we need contextual definitions of projection levels in addition to the apparently independently necessary inherent characterization?

4. An additional curious feature of the relational-definitions-plus-uniformity theory is that according to this system, chains but not categories have to be uniform (recall that a nonprojecting lexical item is both an X^{min} and an X^{max}). This is of course logically possible: a chain member may be multiply characterized, but all chain members must have the same characterizations. But once we recall that characterizing an element as both minimal and maximal does not necessarily lead to contradiction and ungrammaticality, the uniformity assumption seems to lose much of its intuitive appeal.

5. As we saw in connection with the structure in (30), uniformity can be used in certain cases to ensure that the target rather than the "moved" (non-chain-root) category projects. (30) could also be excluded by noting that here the contextual definition of $+/-$ maximal projection makes the higher chain member in (30) a nonmaximal intermediate projection, which cannot be a chain member (Nunes 1995). But here uniformity captures only a small part of a much larger generalization. First, it cannot ensure generally that categorial projection always takes place in the root positions of chains. The generalization holds also for X^0 chains that involve word-internal positions. But uniformity is relevant only for phrasal movement.

Given the system in (27) and (28), word-internally different principles must apply. Furthermore, if the extension of the GPP to categorial projection in section 4 is correct, then the condition that categorial projection always holds in the root positions of chains is only one aspect of a much larger generalization. Since the relevant general principle also constrains semantic properties like nongrammaticalized selection, it does not appear to be fully reducible to syntax.[19]

6. The violations in (29) and (30) can be combined, in which case the system incorrectly accepts the double infringement. Thus, if a "moved" X^0, merged with some word-external element Y (as in (29)), happens to project further (as in (30)), then the chain can be uniform (X^0, X^0), even though the structure involves both a word-external nonroot element of an X^0 chain and a "target projects" violation.

(31)

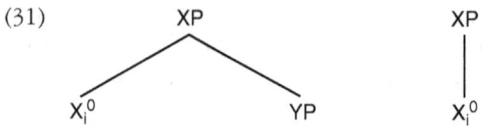

7. In my view, a further serious objection to the uniformity condition is that one would expect an optimally designed theory of syntactic computation simply not to make it possible to violate this condition: the theory should not provide devices that can create nonuniform chains. Relational definitions of projection levels seem dubious, since without them uniformity is also unnecessary in general. Chains are copies.[20] Given an intrinsic characterization of projectional status, the copy of an X^{max} is an X^{max}, the copy of an X^0 is an X^0.[21] This suggests that the grammar should contain no contextual definitions of projection levels. Since chains consist of copies, uniformity is unnecessary in general since there are no means to violate it – the optimal situation.

Consider the desirable effects attributed to uniformity. In the theory put forward here, these are entailed by independent principles. A structure like (29) is a special instance of illegitimate structures where a nonphrasal X^0 element is immediately dominated by some YP, not projected by it. This is ruled out by the modularity of the Insert relation. As for (30), this structure cannot arise under the present theory since a given PL can include only a single XP level, whether or not this belongs to a root or nonroot chain member.[22] Finally, (31) is ruled out by the GPP: a nonroot $X^{min/0}$ can neither select nor project an XP.[23]

6. Conspiracy theories of the "target projects" condition and the GPP

6.1. "Target projects" in Chomsky 1994, 1995

In section 4 I considered (a) the requirement that categorial projection always takes place in chain-root position and (b) the restriction that selectional – in particular, thematic – properties must hold in and be satisfied by chain-root positions. As discussed, both generalizations may be effects of the GPP, itself a consequence of the principle restricting information transmission in syntactic structures.

Chomsky 1994 and Chomsky 1995 provide different explanations. In this section I discuss the approaches taken in these works.

I shall focus on the issue in (a) first and start with the solution proposed in Chomsky 1994. Here the generalization that categorial projection always takes place in root position results from conditions answering four distinct questions:

(32) a. Why can a head in a substituted non-chain-root position not project?
b. Why can a head in an adjoined non-chain-root position not project?
c. Why can an XP in a substituted non-chain-root position not project further?
d. Why can an XP in an adjoined non-chain-root position not project further?

Heads in nonroot position cannot project (32a–b) because the Head Movement Constraint would force such a raised head α to substitute into or adjoin to the αP, the phrase α itself projected. This is prohibited by the fact that such "self-attachment" would create an ambiguity: in such structures, the category/segment (αP) that dominates α in the nonroot position can be taken to have inherited its label from α in the nonroot position or from the αP that α projected in its root position. However, it is not clear why the ambiguity of "self-attachment" cases of adjoined and substituted projecting heads should create a violation.

In another case of adjoined nonroot heads, the prohibition concerning self-attachment is not relevant – namely, the case in which the head α in the nonroot position is adjoined to another head. This is the usual configuration of head chains and thus cannot be excluded in general. α in this adjoined nonroot position of course cannot project either. But it is not clear what excludes the configuration where the moved element projects instead of the head to which it adjoined.

Turning to the question of why nonheads (i.e. phrases) cannot project further in non-chain-root positions, the substitution case (32c) is ruled out by the principle known as Greed: "Move raises α only if morphological properties of α itself would not otherwise be satisfied in the derivation" (Chomsky 1994:43). In a configuration like (33), if XP* raises to K and projects XP+, then XP* ceases to be a maximal projection, given the relational definition of projectional status.

(33) *[$_{XP+}$ XP$_x$* [$_K$ t$_x$]]

XP* then will be "invisible for the computational system," which sees only nonprojected elements and maximal projections, and therefore cannot "enter into a checking relation."

But the raised XP in (33) could satisfy Greed before it projects (compare: "Adjunction to X′ by merger does not conflict with the conclusion that X′ is invisible to [the computational system of the grammar]; at the point of adjunction, the target is an XP, not X';" Chomsky 1994:32). At the "point of substitution," then, the raised element is a maximal projection, not an X'.

Another reason is given in Chomsky 1994 for the ungrammaticality of (33), namely, the uniformity condition. This also rules out (33) since here the trace of XP* is maximal (by hypothesis) but XP* is not. But as we saw in section 5, there are strong reasons to reject the uniformity condition.

Finally, consider the facts that adjoined heads cannot project and nonheads (phrases) cannot project further (32b,d). An adjoined element that projects would create the following configuration:

(34)   *$[_\alpha\ \alpha_x\ [_K\ t_x]]$

Chomsky assumes that the two-segment category in adjunction involves two elements that each have the status of a category: the lower segment and the two segments together. On this assumption, Full Interpretation (FI) is violated in (34). Whichever of the two categories, α or the two-segment element $\{\alpha, \alpha\}$, is taken to be the head of the chain whose root is t_x, the other element receives no interpretation at LF and thus violates FI. Chomsky concludes that the target must have projected. Taking $\{\alpha, \alpha\}$ to be the head of the chain is ruled out additionally by the uniformity condition. (This seems to work only where α is nonmaximal; if α is maximal, then so is $\{\alpha, \alpha\}$, and uniformity is not violated.)

However, whichever category projects, the fact that in adjunction structures there is only one LF role for the two-segment category, $\{K, K\}$, and the category corresponding to the lower segment, K, is a general problem in adjunction. (This appears to be recognized in Chomsky 1995.) To allow adjunction to heads, Chomsky invokes WI: the relevant restrictions again do not hold word-internally. For nonheads he suggests that this fact essentially restricts adjunction to non-thematic categories (plus some other restricted cases; see the appendix below). But if WI can neutralize the problem when a minimal projection α adjoins to X and X projects, it will also neutralize the problem if α projects. Hence, the conclusion that the nonroot element cannot project does not follow.

Similar comments hold for nonminimal projections. If a configuration in which the target of adjunction is in a nonthematic position is permitted because no problem arises with FI, then in the same kind of position the adjoined element should be able to project without violating this principle. This again is probably an incorrect result.

Additionally, the assumption that there are exactly three elements in adjunction structures with categorial status seems somewhat stipulative. Even granting that assumption, further questions arise. For example, it is not clear why α and $\{\alpha, \alpha\}$ could not jointly serve as the antecedent of the trace.

Later Chomsky approaches the generalization that phrasal projection always takes place from chain-root positions somewhat differently (see Chomsky 1995). He rejects earlier formulations of Greed and tentatively assumes that word-external adjunction does not exist (also see Brody 1994 and above). He bases much of the argument on the hypothesis that movement can take place only to "immediately" establish a checking configuration. This hypothesis is somewhat dubious since it conflicts with apparently well-established cases of successive-cyclic movement where intermediate landing sites appear to involve no checking (e.g. adjunct *wh*-movement in English). Given this assumption, however, word-external head movement cases will obey generalization (a), since if a moved head α projects, it necessarily establishes a head-complement relation with its target K: [$_\alpha$ α K]. Checking relations can only be established in specifier-head configurations. (Notice, though, that it is only because nonbranching projections do not exist in this system – in contrast to the theory of assembly adopted earlier, where they do exist – that the conclusion that K is the complement of α follows. In [$_\alpha$[$_\alpha$ α] K], K would be a specifier.)

As before, the account does not extend to the word-internal domain. But the generalization (a) that a moved head does not project of course does. In the word-internal domain it is necessary to distinguish two cases: structures where the moved head H′ adjoins to some other head H that projects a phrase HP, and structures where H′ adjoins to some head H″, where H″ itself is adjoined to H or to some other head adjoined to H. In the former case, if H′ projects, the structure in (35) results since HP must have been projected before H′ raised and projected.

(35) [$_{HP}$[$_{H'}$ H′ H]]

Chomsky proposes that the resulting structure is not well formed: HP has no appropriate head. In effect, he proposes a recursive filter (his (5)) that defines well-formed syntactic objects and rejects (35). This seems to be a dubious move. In a derivational theory the derivation necessarily provides a recursive definition of well-formed syntactic objects; no filter should duplicate this function.

Further conditions are required, as Chomsky notes, if H′ illegitimately projects after raising and adjoining to some head H″ that is itself adjoined to a projecting head H. Here we get a structure like (36), where the considerations just reviewed are not relevant.

(36) [$_H$[$_{H'}$ H′ H″] H]

Turning to the question of why a moved XP cannot project further, Chomsky rejects the formulation of Greed that he earlier took to be relevant, and he attributes the impossibility of (33) to the uniformity condition, which I found numerous reasons to question in section 5.

Chomsky tentatively considers another approach as well, according to which the checking relation is asymmetrical and requires the checked element to be in the specifier position of the checking head. This would not be satisfied in (33). Here the head of K is taken to be the checking head and XP the checked element, but XP is not a specifier since its head projects the phrase; instead, K is the specifier of XP. Chomsky notes several problems with this approach, but in any case it would seem to contribute little to a solution: if checking is asymmetric in the way suggested, then the question still remains: why can a checking relation not be established in (33)? K cannot be checking XP now, but X could in principle check K, unless we stipulate that the target of movement must be the checker. But that is barely different from the original problem to be explained: the target must project.

6.2. GPP effects in Chomsky 1994, 1995

Next let us consider the solutions for the other GPP effect: that thematic properties must hold in and be satisfied by chain roots. In his 1994 paper Chomsky does not discuss the problem of why the selectional (thematic, etc.) requirements of heads must hold in the root position of their chain, so I shall put this aside for the moment. He does, however, provide an account of the fact that thematic requirements must be satisfied by chain roots.

Consider the hypothetical verbs HIT and BELIEVE that assign a θ-role to their subject but no Case to their object. The GPP explains why such verbs cannot exist, given the independently motivated assumption that the Caseless object position in structures like (37) must form a chain with the subject position: such a chain involves a nonroot θ-position.

(37) a. *John [$_{VP}$ t' [HIT t]]
      b. *John [$_{VP}$ t' [BELIEVE [t to VP]]]

In derivational terms the generalization translates as a ban on movement to thematic positions. Chomsky attributes this also to the principle of Greed. The DP *John* in (37) cannot raise to [Spec, VP] to pick up the unassigned θ-role, since it does not need to do so to satisfy its own requirements.

Even if the DP originates in a non-θ-position, Greed would prevent raising to a θ-position on the assumption that "the need for a theta role is not a formal property, like Case, that permits 'last resort' movement" (Chomsky 1994:38). This explanation may not be general enough. First, the prohibition against movement to θ-positions holds also for θ-positions that are at the same time Case positions. As an illustration, consider the hypothetical preposition IN, which is like *in* except that it does not assign Case. This should allow a structure like (38a) (compare (38b)).

(38) a. I gave John the study IN t.
      b. I gave John a book in the study.

The GPP predicts that structures like (38a) are ungrammatical. The explanation based on Greed does not have this consequence, unless not only structural Case positions but indeed all Case positions are taken to be systematically distinct from θ-positions.

Second, the Greed-based account allows movement to a θ-position when this is made necessary by some other principle. This again seems to be an incorrect prediction. For example, Relativized Minimality/the Minimal Link Condition (MLC) can force movement through a θ-position in a derivation in which a later step satisfies Greed. To see this, consider first Chomsky's analysis of the ungrammaticality of (39).

(39) *John reads often books.
(40) [$_{VP}$ John [$_{V'}$ v [$_{VP_2}$ often [$_{V'}$ reads books]]]]

He suggests that (39) has the structure in (40), and this is ruled out since the adverbial in [Spec, VP$_2$] prevents raising of the object *books* to [Spec, Agr$_O$]. He writes, "Note the crucial assumption that the subject *John* is in [SPEC, VP] ... otherwise that position would be an 'escape hatch' for the raising of *books*" (p. 33).

Consider in this light (41), containing the verb HIT that assigns no accusative but is otherwise like *hit*. In (41) movement lands in a θ-position.

(41) John [$_{VP}$ t [$_{VP_2}$ often HITs t]]

Here the DP *John* must raise outside the VP in order to get Case. But then, as in the case of (39), Relativized Minimality/the MLC forces it through [Spec, VP], where it can pick up the subject θ-role. Thus, the nonexistence of a verb like HIT is not predicted.

As noted, in chapter 4 of his 1995 book Chomsky assumes that every application of Move must establish a checking relation, and he rejects the earlier formulation of Greed. Here he provides a different account of why movement cannot land in thematic positions, one that is meant to generalize to also answer the question why all thematic selection holds in chain-root positions:

> With regard to assignment of θ-roles, the conclusion is natural in Hale and Keyser's [1993] theory. A θ-role is assigned in a certain structural configuration; β assigns that θ-role only in the sense that it is the head of that configuration.... Suppose β raises, forming the chain CH = (β, ... ,t) ....[T]he chain CH is not in a configuration at all, so cannot assign a θ-role. In its raised position, β can function insofar as it has internal formal features: as a Case assigner or a binder. But in a configurational theory of θ-relations, it makes little sense to think of the head of a chain as assigning a θ-role.
>
> (Chomsky 1995, p. 313)

First of all, it is not clear that it is any more natural (and it is certainly not independently motivated) to assume that a chain is "not in a configuration at all," rather than taking it to be in multiple configurations. More important perhaps is the question why "it makes little sense" to think of the head of a nontrivial chain as a θ-role assigner. In particular, why does it make little sense to think of the head of the chain as a θ-role assigner when apparently the root of the chain can be a θ-role assigner? "The trace *t* remains in the structural configuration that determines a θ-role and can therefore function as a θ-role assigner ..." (p. 313). It is true that in its raised position β cannot assign a θ-role – or, more generally, activate any of its selectional features. But surely β is in *some* configuration in its raised position.

145

What we in fact need, then, is a characterization of configurations where selection is possible and those where it is impossible. An obvious suggestion is to assume that only categorially projecting heads can select. This will work once categorial projection itself is restricted to chain roots. Although perhaps not unnatural, it is clearly an additional stipulation that should be unnecessary. It is, if categorial projection and selection are both cases of semantic (nonformal) feature assignment constrained directly by the GPP, as argued in section 4.

Chomsky writes, "With regard to receipt of θ-roles, similar reasoning applies. If α raises to a θ-position Th, forming the chain CH = (α, t), the argument that must bear a θ-role is CH, not α. But CH is not in any configuration, and α is not an argument that can receive a θ-role" (p. 313). Again it is not clear why the chain is not in any configuration. But independently of this, the paragraph is difficult to interpret. If the chain and not α must bear the θ-role and the chain cannot, then the θ-Criterion is violated also in the grammatical cases where the chain would receive the θ-role in its root position. Given minimalist assumptions, α cannot receive the θ-role before it moves; to say that it did so would be to resurrect D-Structure (on the reasons for rejecting D-Structure, see Brody 1993b, 1995a, Chomsky 1993). Thus, we seem to be left here without any account of the selectional effects of the GPP.

Appendix

Chomsky (1994, 1995) suggests a theory that radically restricts word-external adjunction but (in 1995 tentatively and partially only) retains this configuration in cases where the target has no θ-role (expletive-associate chains) or where in his derivational system the adjunct is not present at LF (intermediate traces deleted by LF and "semantically vacuous" scrambling where LF reconstruction eliminates the scrambled element). These cases do not seem to provide strong motivation for retaining the configuration. LF adjunction of the associate to its expletive chain-mate is a problematic and probably unnecessary operation. The agreement facts, which constitute the main evidence for this operation, can be accounted for without actual displacement of the associate (see Brody 1993a, 1995a). This is also recognized in Chomsky 1995; see section 4.2 above.

The necessity of adjoined intermediate traces in nonuniform chains is equally moot (see, e.g., Manzini 1992). Notice that the best and perhaps only strong evidence for their existence involves reconstruction effects (Lebeaux 1989, Barss 1986). For example, in (42) binding of the anaphor appears to be licensed from the position that is internal to the intermediate trace/copy.

(42) Which picture of herself did John think [t [Mary told Bill to buy t]]?

But in the minimalist framework such evidence supports the copy theory of movement. Given the basic assumption of this framework that conditions (like the binding theory) hold only at and/or beyond the interface levels, evidence like (42) shows that contrary to Chomsky's suggestion in this context, intermediate traces/copies must be present at LF (see Chomsky 1993, Brody 1995a).

As for scrambling, an alternative treatment of radical reconstruction may be to consider it to be stylistic displacement – that is, to consider that it takes place in the Spell-Out component (see Aoun 1995). Chomsky suggests that LF reconstruction will provide an account of the contrast he finds between English topicalization cases like (43a) and (43b). Assuming that these work like examples that involve scrambling, the expectation is that (43a), the adjunct case, is worse since forced reconstruction in this example will create a configuration that violates Principle C. Since the fronted phrase *which pictures of John's brother* is not an adjunct in (43b), this example will not be similarly excluded.

(43) a. Pictures of John$_x$'s brother, he$_x$ never expected that I would buy.
b. Which pictures of John$_x$'s brother did he$_x$ expect that I would buy?

But this approach would make it difficult to account for the *wh*-chain reconstruction effects like the contrasts between (44a) and (44b) that depend precisely on forced reconstruction of the *wh*-phrase. (The selected clausal argument but not the unselected adjunct internal to the fronted phrase must be present in the reconstructed copy, as shown in section 3.3; also see Lebeaux 1989, Chomsky 1993, Brody 1995a, for different ways of instantiating this idea.)

(44) a. Which claim that John$_x$ made did he$_x$ deny?
b. ?*Whose claim that John$_x$ was asleep did he$_x$ deny?

Thus, the evidence for an account involving forced reconstruction of elements adjoined to semantically nonvacuous categories seems unconvincing. Its support for the more general claim that word-external adjunction exists in syntax (under restricted circumstances) is therefore weak.

Acknowledgments

The main ideas of this article were presented in Brody 1994, read at the GLOW Colloquium in Vienna. The article itself was then written in its present form in the spring of 1995. Various versions were presented between 1994 and 1996 at University College London, MIT, UCLA, University of Massachusetts at Amherst, at the Universities of Vienna, Tübingen, Stuttgart, Potsdam, Budapest, Florence, and Venice, at the LOT Summerschool in Amsterdam, and at the SICOGG conference in Seoul. I am grateful to the audiences at these universities and conferences, to the *LI* reviewers, and particularly to Michal Starke for detailed comments and helpful conversations. For a theory that develops further the major themes discussed here, see Brody 1997.

References

Aoun, Joseph. 1995. Interception and reconstruction. Talk presented at the Vienna Round Table Colloquium, University of Vienna.

Barss, Andrew. 1986. Chains and anaphoric dependencies. Doctoral dissertation, MIT, Cambridge, Mass.

Brody, Michael. 1993a. Lexico-Logical Form. Ms., University College London.

Brody, Michael. 1993b. θ-theory and arguments. *Linguistic Inquiry* 24:1–23.

Brody, Michael. 1994. Phrase structure and dependence. In *UCL working papers in linguistics 6*, 1–33. Department of Phonetics and Linguistics, University College London.

Brody, Michael. 1995a. *Lexico-Logical Form: A radically minimalist theory*. Cambridge, Mass.: MIT Press.

Brody, Michael. 1995b. Towards perfect chains. Ms., University College London. [Published in *Handbook of syntax*, ed. Liliane Haegeman. Dordrecht: Kluwer.]

Brody, Michael. 1997. *Mirror Theory*. Ms., University College London.

Chomsky, Noam. 1993. A minimalist program for linguistic theory. In *The view from Building 20: Essays in linguistics in honor of Sylvain Bromberger*, eds Kenneth Hale and Samuel Jay Keyser, 1–52. Cambridge, Mass.: MIT Press.

Chomsky, Noam. 1994. Bare phrase structure. Ms., MIT, Cambridge, Mass. [Appeared as MIT Occasional Papers in Linguistics 5. MITWPL, Department of Linguistics and Philosophy, MIT, Cambridge, Mass. Published in *Government and Binding Theory and the Minimalist Program*, ed. Gert Webelhuth, 383–439. Oxford: Blackwell (1995).]

Chomsky, Noam. 1995, Categories and transformations. In *The Minimalist Program*, 219–394. Cambridge, Mass.: MIT Press.

Cinque, Guglielmo. 1993. On the evidence for partial N movement in the Romance DP. Ms., University of Venice.

Cinque, Guglielmo. 1995. Adverbs and the universal hierarchy of functional projections. Abstract of paper presented at the 18th GLOW Colloquium, Tromsø.

Collins, Chris, and Höskuldur Thráinsson. 1993. Object shift in double object constructions and the theory of Case. In *MIT working papers in linguistics 19: Papers on Case and agreement II*, 131–174. MITWPL, Department of Linguistics and Philosophy, MIT, Cambridge, Mass.

Hale, Kenneth, and Samuel Jay Keyser. 1993. On argument structure and the lexical expression of syntactic relations. In *The view from Building 20: Essays in linguistics in honor of Sylvain Bromberger*, eds Kenneth Hale and Samuel Jay Keyser, 53–109. Cambridge, Mass.: MIT Press.

Kayne, Richard. 1994. *The antisymmetry of syntax*. Cambridge, Mass.: MIT Press.

Koizumi, Masatoshi. 1993. Object agreement phrases and the split VP hypothesis. In *MIT working papers in linguistics 18: Papers on Case and agreement I*, 99–148. MITWPL, Department of Linguistics and Philosophy, MIT, Cambridge, Mass.

Koopman, Hilda. 1996. The spec head configuration. Ms., UCLA, Los Angeles, Calif.

Larson, Richard. 1988. On the double object construction. *Linguistic Inquiry* 19:335–391.

Lebeaux, David. 1989. Relative clauses, licensing and the nature of the derivation. Ms., University of Maryland, College Park.

Manzini, Maria Rita. 1992. *Locality*. Cambridge, Mass.: MIT Press.

Nunes, Jairo. 1995. The copy theory of movement and linearization of chains in the Minimalist Program. Doctoral dissertation, University of Maryland, College Park.

Sportiche, Dominique. 1994. Adjuncts and adjunction. Abstract of paper presented at the 17th GLOW Colloquium, Vienna.

Watanabe, Akira. 1991. *Wh*-in-situ, Subjacency and chain formation. Ms., MIT, Cambridge, Mass.

Williams, Edwin. 1994. *Thematic structure in syntax*. Cambridge, Mass.: MIT Press.

8

PERFECT CHAINS

1. Towards perfect syntax

1.1. *Duplications, conditions on chains, economy*

In the Principles and Parameters theory representational conditions on various levels carried most of the burden of restricting syntax. In the minimalist framework representational conditions will only hold at interface levels, the only levels that exist. Let us assume the strong version of the minimalist hypothesis according to which syntactic interface conditions are "bare output conditions," that is conditions forced on syntax by the interpretive systems that are fed by the syntactic computations. Suppose furthermore that most of the effects of representational conditions of the Principles and Parameters theory turn out to be the effects of either bare output conditions or of conditions holding within the syntax-external systems. If so, then we may expect the syntactic computation, whose task is to assemble interface representations from a set of lexical items, to be near-trivial.

In any case the syntactic system may turn out to be significantly more trivial than in standard minimalist theories. One area where simplification is achievable is the derivational duplication of representational concepts. A central case is the independently motivated interface notion of Chain which captures the same relations as the derivational rule of Move, making the latter redundant and in fact untenable in a restrictive system. Notice that eliminating Move in favor of Chain does not necessarily make the theory strictly non-derivational: see the one step derivational theory of Brody (1995a,b). (This is not to say, however, that it would not be possible to construe this theory in a strictly representational fashion.) Eliminating Move will however necessarily make the architecture of the mapping system between lexical items and the two interfaces radically simpler: since there are no intermediate structures between the lexical input and the semantic interface, this level has to serve as the input to the SPELLOUT component. There is therefore only a single syntactic interface level, say the level of Lexico-logical Form (LLF) of Brody (1993a, 1995a), which is the input to both semantic interpretation and the SPELLOUT component.

There are various other related distinctions and duplications that seem equally dubious. For example, Chomsky (1995) proposes a representational definition in addition to the derivational system of interface assembly (in effect an additional definition) of what counts as a well-formed syntactic object (cf. Brody 1995b for some discussion). Or take the additional distinction he makes between deletion (interface invisibility only) and erasure (essentially invisibility also for Move), where erasure occurs only if this would not violate the representational duplicate definition of well-formed syntactic object. Such duplications, and distinctions that build on these duplications, should have no place in a restrictive system of syntax.

Another area where we might expect the system of interface assembly to be radically simplified has to do with economy conditions. Strong empirical argument is necessary to motivate the undesirable complication of the system of assembly which would make it powerful enough to compare derivations – especially in view of the attendant computational complexity. It does not seem unreasonable to think that economy conditions will be eliminable without the introduction of any additional apparatus. More recent versions of economy conditions that "compare locally" seem to represent no major improvement in computational complexity. Suppose that at any stage in the derivation only the possible continuations of the derivation already constructed are compared. But clearly, for any comparison of full derivations we can construct an equally complex comparison of "continuations," simply by embedding the appropriate structure. Notice that in order for the comparison to be meaningful, it cannot be restricted to look only at a single step in the relevant derivations. The derivations in which a step or a series of steps will be compared must all be carried out fully, if only to check that they converge, given the assumption – an inevitable one as Chomsky (1995) explains – that economy conditions select only among converging derivations.

A third set of concepts and conditions that should have no place syntax-internally in a restrictive system of interface assembly pertain to the Chain/Move relation. Assuming that the relation is part of syntax proper, various conditions specific to this relation, like Uniformity, c-command, Last Resort, Minimal Chain Link and Procrastinate, should still be attributable to the syntax external systems (either as matters internal to the interpretive components or as properties imposed by these on syntax, i.e. bare output conditions) or should be eliminable in some other way. Uniformity was discussed in this light in Brody (1995b), treatment of the other minimalist conditions on Chain/Move is the main subject of the present paper.

1.2. Interactions with the interpretive components

In Brody (1995a,b) I proposed an interface assembly system based on the notions of copy and immediate domination that complies with these restrictions. I used the term perfect syntax to refer to the theory that postulated such a near-trivial assembly system. There are two additional general constraints related to the interaction of the assembly system with the interpretive components that the standard minimalist framework does not incorporate, but we might expect perfect syntax to meet. One of these has to do with the nature of the interaction between syntax and the interpretive systems. In the standard minimalist framework it is suggested that imperfections in syntax may be due to the effect of the interpretive components. Bare output conditions will be satisfied optimally, but this may necessitate departures from perfection. In particular it is often suggested that the fact that syntax has the Chain/Move relation is an imperfection due to output conditions. Chomsky (1995) contains also the further suggestion that the optimal operation of Move is covert (feature-movement only) and overt movement of categories is again due to interpretive (PF) pressures. These pressures could have to do for example with strong checking features holding at PF (although this assumption is rejected in Chomsky 1995) or with the necessity of moved features pied piping full constituents to avoid PF crash.

The idea that the components interacting with syntax force additional imperfect operations on this system seems to raise problems. Without further assumptions, whose nature seems unclear, for the external systems to cause the addition of imperfect operations to syntax it is necessary that perfection in syntax and the demands of the external system be in conflict. But it seems difficult to think of a case where the external demands could not be met in some alternative way without sacrificing perfection. If so, then given usual methodology, we would expect the system to choose the more perfect option. To look at the actual proposals concerning Move, consider the hypothesis that the existence of this operation is forced by the bare output condition of full interpretation. This requires certain features to be checked at LF by features of lexical items generated elsewhere. But if Move is an imperfection, there are in principle many ways in which it could be avoided without violating full interpretation. For example, the checking features could freely delete or they could be generated in a position that is accessible to the lexical item without movement etc. It is not easy to see why all the alternative options should be in principle unavailable.

(Notice incidentally that the proposal that Move is forced by bare output conditions interacts only with some redundancy with Chomsky's (1995) assumption that strong features are intolerable in the derivation. Given the additional distinction between +/− Interpretable checking features, Move will sometimes be forced by full interpretation (to eliminate weak non-interpretable features of hosts) and sometimes by both derivation-technological reasons and full interpretation (to eliminate strong non-interpretable features and (non-interpretable) "strength" of interpretable features). See below in sections 2 and 4 for related discussion.)

Similar comments apply to the question of overt Move. If overtness of Move is an imperfection and the optimal way of satisfying the constraints requiring movement is covert feature-movement, then overt movement of categories within the mapping between lexical items and (L)LF could be avoided for example by eliminating strong features, or by restricting overt movement to the SPELLOUT component. (See Brody 1995b for evidence that this latter possibility is not what actually happens.) Many other options are imaginable, which seem extremely difficult to rule out on principled grounds.

Let us avoid such problems and assume that the syntax-external components cannot force imperfect additions to syntax. This is then the first general condition promised above, related to the interaction of syntax with the interpretive systems. Returning to the concrete case of Chain/Move, this is simply an instance of the copy relation. It is not necessary to take this relation to be an imperfection, indeed within the assembly system of Brody (1995b) this would not even be possible. In this theory the copy relation is involved also in categorial projection and is the only basic concept apart from the hierarchical notion of immediate domination. As for chains corresponding to "overt movement" of a full category, again this is simply the copy relation, where only the highest copy is visible for the SPELLOUT component. In the case of "expletive-associate" (Brody 1993a, 1995a) or "feature-movement" (Chomsky 1995) chains, the copy relation is not between full lexical items, but between features. See Brody (1995a,b) for some discussion of why it may not be correct to eliminate syntax internally the distinction between chains where the copy relation is between full lexical items and chains where it is between features, by treating "covert movement" relations as full copies with a lower SPELLOUT position.

Given the distinction between feature copy chains and full category copy chains, it is possible to view one of the two instances of the relation as an imperfect version of the other. For example, in the spirit of Earliness (Pesetsky 1989) or Transparency (Brody 1995a), we might take the full categorial copy to be the default operation, and consider copying a proper subset of features as a degenerate case, that occurs only where full category copy chains are not licensed by the relevant checking features. Such an assumption would still disallow the addition of imperfect syntactic properties or relations but it would countenance a special type of syntactic imperfection: the imperfect instantiation of a perfect syntactic relation, namely the copy relation.

It would clearly be better, however, to avoid even this limited kind of imperfection. Instead of viewing one of the two chain-types as an imperfect version of the other, we could assume, in the spirit of the elsewhere principle (cf. especially Williams 1995), that category copy chains, which involve more fully specified copies, take precedence over feature copy chains. Category copy chains will then block feature copy chains whenever the (strong) checking heads license the category copies.

Suppose further that the option of copying a full category is conditioned by the morphological properties of the head with which the copy will establish a checking relation. A head may or may not license a full category in its checking domain. In fact it seems necessary to distinguish heads that license a full category word (X^0)-internally, hence in principle license an "overt" X^0-chain and heads that license a full category in their word-external checking domain, hence in principle allow "overt" XP-chains. (Further, unless multiple checking of the same feature, as for example in multiple overt *wh*-movement languages, is only apparent and can be treated in some alternative way, we may in fact have to have three choices both word internally and word-externally: a head licensing zero, one or multiple full categories.)

Licensing a full category in the checking domain is, I assume, a matter of morphology, internal to the SPELLOUT component. When the relevant head is "weak" with respect to a position in the checking domain and does not license a full category there, then only a "feature movement" chain can surface. In such a case a full categorial copy chain could not be expressed by the morphology. Notice that this view not only displaces the strong/weak distinction from the syntactic component, it also eliminates the distinction, in the sense of collapsing it with an independently necessary parameter which determines the number of categorial specifiers (more precisely categories in the checking domain) of a given functional head.

I argued so far for the assumption that the interpretive components cannot directly influence the nature of the syntactic computation, although they can filter its output. In this respect the semantic/conceptual and the SPELLOUT component behave similarly. There is however also a conspicuous difference between them: syntactic elements are generally identical to elements to which the semantic/conceptual system needs to refer. Suppose that the discussion of the strong/weak distinction above is on the right track and "strength," i.e. the licensing of the "categoriality" of checking relations does not take place syntax internally. Then little reason remains to assume that syntax ever needs to make use of elements or features that have only morpho-phonological but no semantic/conceptual interpretation. This leads directly to the second general constraint pertaining to the interaction of syntax with the interpretive components. The perfect (L)LF assembly system should be constructed using only elements that the semantic/conceptual interpretive system provides. This condition, which I shall refer to as radical interpretability, is natural, and I will give some indication below that it may be tenable empirically.

Radical interpretability is related to the condition that requires syntactic representations not to contain non-interpretable features (or features without "effect" on the interpretive components) – call this interpretability. But the requirement that all features in a given structure must have either semantic or morpho-phonological content is not only weaker but may also be stronger in one respect than radical interpretability. In contrast to interpretability, radical interpretability requires all syntactic elements to be semantically interpretable, but not necessarily actually interpreted in a given structure. The latter requirement may be too strong. As just noted, in perfect syntax there can be no distinction between interface invisibility and invisibility for the computational system. But the stronger construal of radical interpretability would rule out even the concept of interface invisibility which may be necessary for checking theory. It will be crucial for the theory of checking to be presented in section 4 below, that in a checking configuration merger of checker and checked feature result in a single feature for interpretive purposes. Checking will thus presumably have to make either the checker or the checkee, or both (creating a new composite feature), invisible.

Although there seems to be no difficulty in taking the existence of the copy relation as such not to be a departure from perfection, as noted earlier the minimalist framework assumes several a priori unexpected conditions on this relation, which clearly could not be part of the perfect assembly system. In what follows I will argue that those conditons on Chain/Move that do not dissolve on closer examination should be thought of as either constraints on the interpretive components or as bare output conditions. In the next section I shall start with the c-command and the cyclic properties of Move. After critically examining two approaches in the standard minimalist framework to eliminating these stipulations (sections 2.1 and 2.2), I shall turn to an improved analysis that is made possible by the assumptions of perfect syntax (section 2.3). Section 3 will discuss the MLC and section 4 looks at checking theory.

2. Strong features, C-command and the cycle

2.1. Weak vs strong checking features

In earlier versions of the minimalist framework it was assumed that weak checking features have to be checked by a moved element by LF and strong features by PF. This ensured that both weak and strong checking features forced movement to occur and strong features furthermore forced movement to occur overtly. Chomsky (1995) makes somewhat different assumptions about strong features. He argues that strong features not only force overt movement, they also ensure the cyclicity of this operation. He suggests that strong features once Merged must be checked/eliminated "quickly" by Move or Merge. "Quickly" is defined essentially as in (1):

(1) The derivation terminates if an element H with a strong feature is in a category not headed by H

(1) entails the cycle for overt movement. Movement targeting a position in a given phrase P (and checking a strong feature of its head H there) must now precede movement targeting a higher position outside P. This is because a P-external position will necessarily be in a phrase not headed by H. Hence the strong feature of H will have survived in a phrase not headed by H, contrary to (1). (1) also ensures a form of c-command (m-command) for overt movement between the moved category and its trace. In order to overtly move α to a position that is not in the minimal domain of the head of a phrase that dominates α, to let α check a strong feature there, a structure must have been built which violates (1).

These appear to be welcome consequences: if possible we clearly do not wish to stipulate either c-command (which is only one of infinitely many possible structural relations) or the cyclic property for Move. This approach to the cycle and to c-command however does not seem promising for three reasons. First (1) appears to lack genuine independent motivation. Secondly its explanation, to be discussed below, is untenable and therefore (1) remains stipulative. Thirdly (1) would not be general enough. I shall take these points one by one, starting with the question of independent motivation. This involves mainly the question of strong features forcing overt movement.

Given the assumption that strong features cannot be inserted covertly, which Chomsky takes to be the consequence of wider considerations, (1) is taken to entail that strong features force overt movement, since the strong feature on a head H must be eliminated before the phrase H projected is merged with some other element. But covert movement will occur only after the whole structure has been assembled (after the SPELLOUT point). One problem here is that if H is the highest head in the tree then the theory predicts that its strong feature, introduced overtly, can be checked covertly. This is incorrect: a strong +wh feature on the root C for example cannot be satisfied by covert Move.

Notice that given Chomsky's (1995) assumption that strong features can only be satisfied by categories (section 2.1, p. 11), the strong +wh feature on the root C would force movement of a category rather than a feature, whether it is satisfied overtly or covertly. (The PF pied-piping theory of overt movement includes a least effort type assumption that entails that covert movement does not involve categories (section 4.4). But the least effort assumption is not strong enough to rule out category movement in this case since it requires nothing more than features to move, only when movement of nothing more is forced. Here movement of a category is forced by the strong feature under the assumption that strong features can only be satisfied by categories.)

Note also that in any case the conjunction of the assumption that strong features can only be satisfied by categories with the PF pied-piping theory creates a redundancy. The fact that overt movement must involve categories is now entailed by both, suggesting that at least one of the two ideas should be modified. Suppose we reject the PF pied-piping theory (see Brody 1995b for arguments) and assume for the sake of argument that strong features must be satisfied by categories, whereas weak ones can also be satisfied by features. This should suffice then as a strong/weak distinction, there should be no need to duplicate this in terms of a derivational property of quick elimination of the feature. The distinction does suffice in a theory where (L)LF is the input to SPELLOUT, and therefore the question of invisible (covert) movement of categories does not arise. (Recall that for reasons not strictly relevant to the discussion of (1), I suggested a somewhat different theory of the strong/weak distinction in section 1 above: strong but not weak features license categories in the checking domain, and strong features cannot be satisfied by features due to blocking.)

The direct empirical evidence for (1) is that it might allow adjuncts to intervene between the two elements of the checking relation as e.g. in (2). If adjunction does not close off a projection, then the strong feature of the inflectional head can be checked by the subject, still within the projection of this head. The dubious status of adjunction configurations in general (e.g. Chomsky 1995, Brody 1994, 1995b), and in the particular case of adverbials (Cinque 1995), weakens this point considerably. If such adjuncts are heads or specifiers, then the argument will not go through.

(2) John probably has left already

The result is quite questionable also on directly empirical grounds: many clear cases of checking configurations require adjacency that does not tolerate intervening adverbials, for example wh-checking in English or in Hungarian:

(3) a. Who (*suddenly) did Bill discover
     b. Kit (*tegnap) latott Mari
        Who+acc yesterday saw Mary

Let us next look at the question of whether (1) can be attributed to some more general consideration. In Chomsky (1995) it is claimed that (1) follows from (4), where (4) itself is claimed to be a consequence of other considerations.

(4) Nothing can join to a non-projecting category

"Non-projecting" here cannot mean a category C that is embedded in some phrase not headed by C. This is because in the standard minimalist framework under this interpretation (4) would exclude covert movement. Could "non-projecting" in (4) mean a category that does not project as a result of the joining operation, i.e. could (4) express an extension of the generalization that it is always the target of Move that projects (cf. Chomsky 1994, 1995, Brody 1995a,b for different approaches to this principle)? But this reading is irrelevant since the requirement that the target projects does not entail (1). If Move lands in an embedded position, its target could still in principle project.

It appears that we must choose the first reading of (4) and in order to distinguish weak and strong features we need to restrict it to overt movement:

(5) Nothing can overtly join to a non-projecting category

But although (5) does not refer to feature strength, it is just as much a stipulation as (1). It is simply a statement of the overt cycle which (1) therefore failed to explain.

Let us turn to the third set of problems with the explanation of the cycle and the c-command property of Move in (1): even if the principle was otherwise tenable, it would not be general enough. (1) stipulates that overt movement is cyclic. How about Merge? As Chomsky notes, "it applies at the root only." Embedded Merge would be more complex than at the root. "Any such complication (which could be quite serious) would require strong empirical motivation" (Ch. 4.3, p. 11). Of course this does not entail the extension requirement for Merge, the remark just explains why a theory that entails it would be desirable. (A problem for the standard minimalist theory is that the same consideration applies to any embedded operation, overt or covert. Thus it applies also to covert object shift which is allowed in the standard minimalist framework.)

Thus in the theory based on (1), the c-command property of Move and the cycle are ensured only partially, and by a conspiracy of stipulations. (1) entails the cyclicity of overt Move, the stipulation in (5) would entail the extension requirement for overt Merge – further conditions will be necessary to rule out covert countercyclic Move and covert Move to non c-commanding positions. If overt embedded Merge is taken to be ruled out for the same reason as overt embedded Move (as in (5)), then still further stipulations are necessary to rule out covert embedded Merge. (Recall that Uniformity entails that covert Merge is available in principle.)

Chomsky also appears to note that the explanation of cyclicity and c-command based on (1) is not a full solution. He observes that "it would be interesting to strengthen [the] conclusion: to show ... that overt targeting of an embedded category (hence lowering and non-cyclic raising) is not possible, hence *a fortiori* not necessary" (section 4.1, p. 16). But the remark seems to me to somewhat misstate the issue which does not have to do with the modality of the restriction but with its generality.

2.2. C-command by Merge

Crediting Kawashima and Kitahara (1994) and Eric Groat (p.c.), Chomsky briefly sketches a more general solution to the problems of cyclicity and c-command. This is based on the theory of Epstein (1994) where

(6) "C-command is just the relation that holds between α and elements of β when α is attached to β by Merge or Move" (section 4.1, p. 16)

Hence an embedded operation that attaches α to β will establish no c-command relation between elements in the tree higher than β and α. Given the further assumptions that all terminals must be ordered at PF and that terminals are ordered at PF only by c-command relations holding between them (or between categories dominating them) at LF (Kayne 1994), such embedded operations will be prohibited in the overt syntax. They would result in terminals preceding β and those dominated by α being unordered. Thus overt Merge and Move must be cyclic. Similarly overt Move to a non c-commanding position, whether lowering or "sideways" (i.e. where no c-command relation is established between α and its trace), is prohibited.

Again, there are a number of problems with this solution. First, the assumption that LF c-command determines PF precedence establishes an LF–PF link that might cause a PF crash. But this conflicts with what seems to be the optimal assumption, that within core grammar there are no such LF–PF interactions. (Cf: "We thus adopt the (non-obvious) hypothesis that there are no PF–LF interactions relevant to convergence ..." (section 1, p. 1).)

Secondly, since traces need not be ordered at PF (cf. Chomsky 1995, section 8), all improper overt operations will still be allowed as long as they are followed by cyclic raising. For example, lowering (from P) followed by raising (to P', not lower than P) is still allowed:

(7) * [$_{IP}$ John [$_{VP}$ t believed [$_{IP}$ t to have arrived a man yesterday]]]
      P'   P

(8) * [$_{IP}$ Who [$_{VP}$ t wondered [t+WH [Mary left]]]]
      P'   P

In (7) *John* lowered from its thematic VP-spec position into the non-thematic spec-IP position of the embedded clause. It cannot remain here since no c-command relation would hold between itself and, say, the matrix verb *believe*. If it subsequently cyclically moves to the matrix spec-IP, then no PF violation remains: *John* c-commands the rest of the sentence and its traces, invisible at PF need not be ordered. The same problem is raised by the "round trip" A'-movement derivation in (8). While one might think of various ways of ruling out such derivations, it is clear that the c-command and the cyclicity properties of overt Move do not follow fully from the approach under consideration.

There are further problems of coverage, echoing the shortcomings of the strong feature theory of cyclicity and c-command considered above. This theory allows countercyclic covert Move (like object shift) since covert operations do not feed PF, hence they need not establish a c-command based full ordering. But this means that the theory does not extend to any covert operation: countercyclic covert Merge, covert lowering and covert "sideways" Move will also be incorrectly allowed.

2.3. The cycle and C-command in perfect syntax

As a first step, observe that the problems with the solution based on c-command ordering can be largely remedied on the assumption that elements of LF rather than of PF representations are ordered by this relation. This assumption immediately eliminates the problem of linking LF and PF representations: no such link is necessary. Since traces are represented as visible copies at LF, the possibility of saving an illegitimate operation of Move which lands in a non c-commanding position or applies countercyclically by a later legitimate application disappears. The traces/copies also must be ordered at LF, hence the possibility of making an illegitimate operation avoid exclusion by turning the element in the landing position into an invisible trace ceases to exist. Furthermore, if all elements must be ordered by LF c-command then all Move and Merge operations (overt or covert) will now have to be cyclic and all applications of Move (overt or covert) will have to target a c-commanding position. Thus the problems relating to the covert applications of these rules disappear also.

A salient consequence of assuming Epstein's definition of c-command and stating the ordering requirement of Kayne's Linear Correspondence Axiom at LF is that there will be only a single cycle in the derivation of LF. This should not be problematic if covert Move does not affect PF material. That "covert Move" relations do not affect the placement of the category and its phonology anywhere in syntax was argued in Brody (1993a, 1995a), see also Chomsky (1995), Brody (1995b). Of course the assumption makes it also unnecessary to consider the SPELLOUT point in the syntactic derivation to be different from LF.

The assembly system of Brody (1995a,b) which satisfies the strictures of perfect syntax is not cyclic: the elements of the input list (a concept related to the notion of numeration) are joined simultaneously in one step. The cycle is incompatible with the requirement that the syntactic derivation create no intermediate structures between the input list and the interface level LF (Brody 1995a). But the question of how to ensure the cycle may be a pseudo-issue if the cycle in fact is unnecessary. Cyclic effects can be noticed only where the application of some constraint can be illegitimately avoided by a noncyclic derivation. But if the constraints in question in fact apply to or beyond the syntactic output representation (the expected case in perfect syntax, where they will be constraints on the interpretive components or bare output conditions) then it will generally be impossible to avoid them through changing the derivational history.

A typical case is the late insertion of intervener type cycle violations for the minimal link condition (MLC). But if the MLC (or any other condition with the relevant effect) applies to the fully formed LF representation (cf. section 3 below), then the derivational history of the structure will be irrelevant: the effect of the MLC cannot be avoided at LF where the intervening elements are necessarily present. In (9) for example the intervening subject *it* will necessarily occur between *John* and its trace at LF.

(9) *John seems it is certain t to go
(10) *Who were [pictures of t] bought [pictures of t]

Similarly, the subject island violation of (10) cannot be voided by first applying *wh*-movement and then passive if the presence of a subject-internal trace is determined on the basis of the output representation.

Thus no cycle should be necessary in perfect syntax given the general architecture of the theory, where constraints apply to the output of the assembly system. There will be then nothing to explain: the optimal case. The question of excluding lowering operations may similarly turn out to be a pseudo-issue due to the minimalist duplication of the concept of Chain by Move. In perfect syntax lowering and raising cannot be distinguished: chains are neutral with respect to this dimension. Again the situation is optimal: the theory is designed in such a way that there is nothing to explain. (The question of hierarchical directionality does arise in the treatment of the Generalized Projection Principle, but this is demonstrably a matter for the interpretive component since this principle constrains also nonsyntactic features. Cf. Brody 1995a,b.)

All that remains then is the question of chains connecting positions that are not related by c-command. One possibility would be to exclude such chains by adopting a version of the Epsteinian solution to the assembly system of perfect syntax. We could require that there must be a syntactic relation at LF between the members of a given chain and assume that the only syntactic relation that exists is the one created by the operation of Insert (cf. Brody 1995a,b). Thus c-command is just the relation that holds between α and elements of β on one hand and (irrelevantly for the present problem) the head of β and elements of α (including α) on the other, when the operation Insert joins α and β by making β immediately dominate α. Alternatively, if ellipsis involves chains, as suggested by Chomsky (1995), then chains whose members are not in a c-command relation in fact exist. The question then shifts to differentiating ellipsis chains from others in terms of c-command – presumably a problem in the interpretive component and not in the assembly system.

This raises a different though related issue of whether all relations involving c-command reduce to the chain relation or whether the interpretive component will need to refer additionally to c-command. I will not attempt here to go beyond noting the issue. Thus one possibility is to resurrect the early Principles and Parameters theory view that the c-command requirement on chains is due to the anaphoric nature of traces/non-head elements (copies) of chains. Then chain-members are not forced to be in a c-command relation by syntax, and the interpretive system has access to this relation. On the other hand the obvious counter-example of anaphora to the alternative hypothesis, according to which all c-command relations reduce to chain-relations can be fairly straightforwardly accommodated. Thus ordinary anaphors have been treated as involving a chain/move relation, while bound (variable) anaphora, a less plausible candidate for a chain analysis, has been argued to require precedence rather than c-command (Williams 1994, Brody 1994, see also Hornstein 1994 for a contrary view and some discussion in section 3 below).

3. The minimal link condition (MLC) and covert A'-chains

The MLC in Chomsky (1995) restricts elements moving to a given target K to the closest one among those that have the property that they can enter into a checking relation with K. This version of the MLC covers cases like superraising (11b), superiority (12b) and *wh*-island violations (13b).

(11) a. **It seems t(it) is certain John to meet Mary
     b. **John seems it is certain t(John) to meet Mary
(12) a.   Who t(who) saw what
     b. ?*What who saw t(what)
(13) a. *Who did you wonder [CP t(who) [IP t(who) gave this book to whom]]
     b. ?To whom did you wonder who gave this book t(to whom)

The MLC does not allow these derivations since in each case there is a nearer element to the target of movement that has appropriate checking features. In (11b) this is the expletive subject *it*, in (12b) and (13b) the *wh*-phrase *who* in subject and spec-CP position respectively. The MLC would therefore allow the derivations in the a. examples in (11) through (13). Such a derivation happens to give a grammatical result in (12), but crashes in (11) and (13). Chomsky points out that under such a formulation the MLC could not be an economy condition: if crashing derivations could block a converging one then presumably no operation would ever take place. So he takes the MLC to be part of the definition of Move.

The restrictive assembly system of perfect syntax aims to avoid both economy conditions and stipulated conditions on chains/movement like the MLC. There are also empirical reasons for questioning the generalization the MLC expresses. Superraising, Superiority, *Wh*-island violations appear to have very different (un)grammaticality status, raising initial doubts about a principle that treats them uniformly. Judgements range from the completely hopeless superraising case through the intermediate superiority effects to the only mildly deviant and sometimes fully grammatical *wh*-island violations. As is well known, the *wh*-island cases improve probably to full grammaticality with infinitival complements, as for example in (14). Since the MLC cannot be made sensitive to the presence or absence of tense in any obvious way, it will rule out also such cases.

(14)   Which crimes does the FBI know how to solve

Another problem with the MLC is that it is not compatible with covert A'-movement: covert A'-movement of *wh-in-situ* and similar elements would regularly violate the MLC, as exemplified in (15) where the *wh-in-situ* should be understood with matrix scope.

(15) Who wondered who t bought what

Chomsky (1994, 1995) assumes that A'-movement can take place only in the overt derivation, but it is not clear why A- and A'-movement/chains should differ in this way. Furthermore the assumption makes some of the standard evidence for covert A'-movement/chains puzzling. *In-situ* neg-phrases are sensitive to complement non-complement divide as was first observed by Kayne (1981) (see also Jaeggli 1981, Rizzi 1982, Longobardi 1991 for the same effects in other Romance languages). This is parallel to overt A'- chains as exemplified in (16) and (17):

(16) a. Who did you say that Mary saw
      b. *Who did you say that saw Mary
(17) a. Jean n'exige que Pierre voit personne
          J not requires that P has seen no one
      b. *Jean n'exige que Pierre soit arrêté
          J not requires that P be arrested

Or as argued first by Longobardi, the relation between the *in-situ* neg-phrase and its scope (marked by *non*) shows subjacency effects:

(18) Complex NP Constraint
      * Non approverei la tua proposta di vedere nessuno
      "I would not approve of your proposal of seeing anybody"
(19) Sentential Subject Condition:
      ?* Chiamare nessuno sarà possible
         "To call no one will be possible"
(20) Adjunct Condition:
      a. *Non fa il suo dovere per aiutare nessuno
         "He does not do his duty in order to help anyone"
      b. *Per ottenere nulla ha fatto il suo dovere
         "In order to obtain nothing has he done his duty"

As observed by Watanabe (1991), *wh-in-situ* in Japanese type languages also has properties that parallel those of overt movement/chains. (21) is an example, where the *wh-in-situ* within the *wh*-island creates a degraded grammaticality status:

(21) ??John-wa [Mary-ga nani-o   katta   [ka dooka]] Tom-ni
           top   nom what-acc bought whether   dat
         tazuneta no
         asked   Q
         "What did John ask Tom whether Mary bought t?"

Hornstein (1994), who assumes the MLC and rejects covert A'-movement, attempts to neutralize Longobardi's examples by assuming that they involve A-movement. This does not appear to lead to an easily tenable position however for two reasons. First, as Longobardi made clear, the relation has typical A'-chain locality properties, in particular it can escape from embedded tensed clauses:

(22)   Non approverei che tu gli consentissi di vedere nessuno
       "I would not approve that you allow him to see anybody"

Second, as (21) shows, covert *wh*-relations show similar effects. But *wh*-chains are prototypical A'-relations.

A different theory that would neutralize the evidence of the examples in (18) through (21) might claim that all syntactic A'-movement is subject to the MLC and that syntactic A'-movement occurs only to satisfy some checking feature of a +wh/+Neg head. This point is neutral with respect to whether the movement of the *in-situ* neg-phrase in (18)–(20) and the *wh*-phrase in (21) involves overt movement (of, say, an empty operator as in Watanabe 1991) or covertly (say, as movement of formal features, as in Chomsky 1995). The crucial distinction would be between *in-situ* elements that need to move to satisfy some checking feature and *in-situ* elements that do not have similar motivation to move. The two groups correspond to the primary and the secondary or parasitic wh/neg-chains respectively of Brody (1995a). The *wh-in-situ* not constrained by the MLC in (15) would belong to the group of secondary relations, while the *in-situ* elements exhibiting movement characteristics in (18) through (21) would be primary ones. Could it be claimed then that only primary relations involve syntactic movement/chains, and hence only these show movement/chain characteristics including the MLC?

Such a claim would be incompatible with the checking theory to be discussed in section 4 below, in which no distinction can be made between primary and secondary chains with respect to their behavior in checking relations. There is also direct empirical evidence that appears to show that the claim that only primary relations involve syntactic movement/chains would not be correct: secondary relations also show island effects. Neg-phrases participating in secondary relations show parallel locality behavior to parasitic gaps. As Kayne (1983) showed, although parasitic gaps can be separated from the primary gap by an island, within this island they show movement diagnostics with respect to further islands. As pointed out by Longobardi (1991), secondary neg-phrases appear to do likewise. Some of his examples are reproduced in (23)–(24).

(23)   Parasitic neg-phrases:
       a. (In a Sentential Subject)
          (?) Chiamare nessuno [secondary neg-phrase] servirà a niente, ormai
          "To call nobody will do any good now"
       b. (In an Adjunct)
          Non fa niente per aiutare nessuno [secondary neg-phrase]
          "He does not do anything in order to help anyone"

(24) a. Adjunct island inside Subject island:
   * Partire per incontrare nessuno [secondary neg-phrase] servirà a niente
   "To leave in order to meet no one will do any good"
   b. Adjunct island inside another:
   * Non fa niente per scoprire la verita indagando su nessuno [secondary neg-phrase]
   "He doesn't do anything in order to discover the truth by investigating anyone"

In Brody (1995a) I argued for extending the analysis in terms of parasitic chains to *wh*-relations. Chomsky (1986) drew the conclusion about parasitic gaps on the basis of such locality evidence that they must involve movement. If we draw the same conclusion here about secondary neg-and *wh*-relations, then the relation of the *in-situ wh*-phrase in (15) to its scope position must involve a chain/Move relation. The analysis creates difficulties then for the MLC, since in examples like (15) with matrix scope for the *wh-in-situ*, this condition will be violated.

Various further problems for the MLC arise from properties of superiority effects. These can be alleviated in several types of constructions including (25), where the *wh-in-situ* is associated with the matrix *wh*-phrase (cf. Lasnik and Saito 1992) and (26) where the *wh-in-situ* is d-linked (cf. Pesetsky 1987):

(25) Who wondered what who bought
(26) Which book did which girl buy

From the perspective of the MLC, such cases are difficult to understand and therefore they raise doubts about this condition. The alternative quasi-semantic treatment of superiority based on work by Chierchia (1991), put forward independently by Williams (1994) and Hornstein (1994), on the other hand is able to make sense of such apparent counterexamples.

The analysis, which relates the phenomenon to weak crossover, claims that a *wh-in-situ* is or contains an element whose interpretation is dependent on the A-position copy of the *wh*-phrase in spec-CP. Superiority violations arise when this dependency is illegitimate. For present purposes it does not matter if this is because the antecedent of the dependent element D must precede D (Williams 1994, Brody 1994) or because it must "almost c-command" (Hornstein 1994) D. Such an analysis captures the three way parallel between the crossover and the superiority violations in (28) and (29) and the lack of pair-list interpretation in (30) (cf. especially Hornstein 1994 for details and much additional argument):

(28) What did who buy (what)
(29) Who did his father meet (who)
(30) What did everyone say (what)

In none of the three cases does the trace of the *wh*-phrase in spec-CP c-command or precede the dependent element (*who*, *his* and *everyone* respectively). Furthermore in

(25) the trace of the matrix *wh*-phrase does c-command and precede the *wh-in-situ*, thus the latter element can be associated with the matrix *wh*-phrase without incurring a superiority violation. (26) also becomes understandable on the assumption that a d-linked *wh*-phrase need not be a dependent element. (Notice that we cannot meaningfully make a similar exemption from the MLC for d-linked *wh*-phrases by allowing these to be crossed. The MLC is a formal no-crossing requirement not directly sensitive to the interpretive status of the elements involved.)

To summarize so far, the island behavior of neither overt nor covert A'-movement conforms to that predicted by the MLC. Furthermore the condition incorrectly predicts superiority violations in various cases and is incapable of capturing the similar behavior of weak crossover, pair-list reading and superiority constructions. Discounting superiority and *wh*-islands, the major remaining effect of the MLC is the exclusion of superraising. Here again there are alternatives. One possibility might be to restrict theta role percolation in the spirit of Williams (1994). Brody (1995a,b) argues for an interpretive mechanism of feature percolation in chains, that involves thematic roles alongside non-syntactic selectional features. Suppose that NP-traces can receive but cannot directly percolate (transmit) theta roles to higher chain members: they can do this only via the subject–predicate relation under a stricter locality condition. Let us assume for concreteness that the theta role can be inherited from the NP-trace vertically by the smallest predicate VP that includes the trace, and which can in turn assign it to its subject via the predication relation. Vertical transmission is possible only from (Caseless) NP-traces. This may be a subject trace as in raising or an object trace, as in passives and ergatives. This will allow successive cyclic chains but no superraising in English.

In (11b) for example the theta role of the most deeply embedded verb, *meet*, will be assigned to the VP-internal NP-trace from which it will percolate to the predicate VP *t meet Mary*. This assigns the theta role to the subject, again a Caseless trace that allows further percolation to the next predicate. The subject of this predicate is the expletive *it*, however, so this receives the theta role. No further percolation can take place and the matrix subject *John* will remain without a theta role. The account predicts also that superraising will be possible in multiple subject languages (Ura 1994) on the assumption that in these a predicate can sometimes enter multiple predication relations. (Under the theory of theta role and selectional feature percolation of Brody (1995a,b), a theta role assigned to a chain C must percolate to all members of C, regardless of their status as arguments or expletives. Given this background, a structure like "*There seems it to be certain t to be a man in the garden," in which the relation of the expletive *there* to its trace violates the superraising condition, will be ruled out by the assumptions concerning percolation just made, without the need to invoke an expletive replacement mechanism or some equivalent.)

The MLC thus largely dissolves, as perfect syntax leads us to expect it would: most of the phenomena in its scope turn out to involve interpretive relations that should be constrained within the interpretive component. Dependency, in the sense used here in the account of superiority and related phenomena, is clearly a semantic relation, and so is the mechanism of theta role percolation. This is just a particular case of percolation of selectional features, only a subset of which are syntactic – cf. Brody (1995a,b).

Numerous questions remain in the area of locality phenomena, which a fuller treatment would need to address. Let us look here at one case that might appear related to the MLC: the well-known *wh*-island effect that shows up even in constructions like (14). This is the so called scope reconstruction – in fact a dependent reading of the *wh*-phrase on a quantifier c-commanding its trace. This reading does not obtain even in otherwise grammatical *wh*-islands (on "scope reconstruction" cf. e.g. Longobardi 1984, Rizzi 1990, Williams 1994, Hornstein 1994). Thus (31a) can be construed as a question asking about each individual which book that individual read, where they all potentially read different books. Such a construal is possible also where the quantifier is in an embedded clause as in (31b). (31c) on the other hand only has a reading "which book is such that you wondered whether everyone read that book," i.e. on which everyone read the same book. Similar judgement obtains with the infinitival embedded clause in (31d).

(31) a. Which book did everyone read
      b. Which book did you believe everyone to have read
      c. Which book did you wonder whether everyone read
      d. Which book did you wonder whether to believe everyone to have read

Hornstein proposes that the MLC is responsible for this difference: it always prevents extraction from the *wh*-island. (14) and (31c,d) will then involve an island internal empty operator movement (cf. Cinque 1990) construed with the matrix *wh*-phrase. The dependent reading of the *wh*-phrase in (31c,d) will be impossible since the MLC effectively prevents "reconstruction" of the *wh*-phrase into the island: the trace in the island will be the trace/copy of the empty operator and not that of the *wh*-phrase. This account raises numerous questions. First of all, if our discussion so far is correct, the standard minimalist version of the MLC has little independent motivation, hence invoking it here would be quite stipulative. Other problems have to do with the empty operator: what is its landing site, what checking relation triggers its movement (there are no plausible candidates)? Yet others have to do with the scope of the phenomena. Since the effect shows up in other types of islands, Hornstein (1994) suggests assimilating all relevant island violations to *wh*-islands. If all islands have a filled A'-spec then crossing these will be ruled out by the MLC (note 26, p. 181). This would make it necessary to postulate a filled A'-spec (in addition to postulating a head that is necessary to check the empty operator) also in complex NP constructions and adjuncts where the same effect obtains. The marginal structures in (32) cannot have the "scope reconstruction" reading either.

(32) a. ??Which book did you deny the fact that everyone read
      b. ??Which book did you meet Mary before everyone read

But there is no evidence for any of the three empty elements that this account needs to postulate (empty blocking A'-spec, empty Operator, empty head to check the empty Operator). Thus it is unlikely that that the MLC is responsible for "scope reconstructions" effects. (This is not to say that it is inconceivable that some notion of crossing is at issue in the examples in (31), although (32) raises some doubts even about this much weaker claim. In the context of Rizzi's (1990) relativized minimality it was reasonable to put examples like (32) aside as due to some other notion of barrier, since relativized minimality captured a rich generalization in that it constrained also the behavior of adjuncts. But this is not true of the MLC. One important respect in which the MLC differs from relativized minimality is that it refers to argument-type elements. Thus if it was taken to constrain also adjuncts, it would predict the same type of violation: correctly or not, it would not capture the adjunct argument asymmetry with respect to extraction from islands.)

4. Checking theory

4.1. Bare checking theory

Let us start with subject verb agreement. The checking theory of Chomsky (1993) assumes that in addition to agreement features appearing on the verb and the subject, mediating features occur on the agreement node. In "'John hits Bill' ... The φ-features appear in three positions in the course of the derivation: internal to *John*, internal to *hits*, and in AGR$_S$." In effect the mediating features are present in duplicate: "AGR must in fact have two kinds of features: V-features that check V adjoined to AGR and NP-features that check NP in SPEC-AGR." The mediating features delete when checked, so "at PF and LF the φ-features appear only twice, not three times: in the Noun Phrase and verb that agree" (p. 42).

In Brody (1995c) I argued against such mediating features. The major objection against NP- and V-features was that at LF the φ-features of subject/object-verb agreement should only occur on the subject, they do not appear to have a consistent additional interpretive function on the verb. Additional copies of checking features would presumably be excluded by the principle of full interpretation. But under a checking theory where Agr has separate V- and NP-features, there will still be two copies of the relevant features at LF after the mediating features have deleted. One of these will be on the subject and the other on the verbal head.

Such considerations led to a theory without splitting of Agr features: The approach, which I called "bare checking theory," takes seriously one of the original intuitions behind checking theory, that "movement" or rather non-trivial chain formation is forced by bare output conditions at the LF interface. According to bare checking theory, chains are formed because of the way information is stored in the lexicon. The lexical items in a sentence duplicate certain features – the checking features – these duplications must disappear by LF through checking. Checking of a given feature F is forced by the fact that the multiple copies of F are interpretively redundant and would violate the principle of full interpretation. (We may assume that checking involves marking the redundant copies of some feature invisible, perhaps as a result of merger of features in some sense. Merger might make both checking features invisible creating a single visible LF unit.)

Given bare checking theory, checking takes place because multiple instances of what is in fact one feature are not tolerated at the interface. It is not necessary then to invoke non-interpretability of features to force a checking configuration. Bare checking theory is thus consistent with radical interpretability according to which all features have semantic content.

Dispensing with NP- and V-features leaves the further question of whether mediating features (now without the split into NP- and V-features) exist. The basic assumption of bare checking theory does not require the elimination of the mediating features in Agr, although it would not disallow this move either. This theory is not compatible with the splitting of the features of Agr into NP- and V-features since this would result in two copies of ϕ-features at LF. But if ϕ-features are present in three position, then bare checking theory will simply require all three positions to merge by LF through checking.

Nevertheless I will assume that mediating features do not exist. Apart from simplicity considerations, an argument against these in Brody (1995c) was that the evidence for the third copy of ϕ-features is missing even where it could be expected to occur. When the feature on Agr is weak we would expect it to show up at PF. It is only by stipulation (namely that unchecked weak features are invisible or delete in the PF component) that this incorrect prediction is neutralized. I assumed therefore that within bare checking theory subject verb agreement involves only a single checking relation: the ϕ-features of the verb and the subject are checked directly against each other. (On the assumption that checking must involve spec-head configurations in functional phrases, this will entail the formation of NP- and V-chains.)

Chomsky (1995) also develops a theory that is not compatible with the existence of mediating ϕ-features. He proposes to eliminate the Agr node altogether. Although he does not discuss the matter, eliminating Agr could give the result we seek: after subject verb checking there will be only a single set of ϕ-features present at LF. Chomsky rejects the Agr node for reasons that are not dissimilar to those given in Brody (1995c) for rejecting mediating features. Apart from simplicity (section 4.1, pp. 16–17), Chomsky notes that unlike other functional categories like C, T or D for example, Agr does not contain interpretable (either LF or PF) features (section 10). "We therefore have fairly direct evidence from interface relations about T, C and D but not AGR" (p. 8).

Notice, though, two differences. First the argument from PF invisibility does not distinguish between (semantically/conceptually) interpretable and non-interpretable features: it argues against triplications irrespective of this dimension. Chomsky's argument on the other hand is relevant only for features that have no interpretation at either interface.

Second, the argument in Brody (1995c) questioned only the existence of mediating features while Chomsky argues against the Agr node itself. But the question of whether the Agr node exists is in fact composed of two issues: only one of which is the question of the mediating features. Even if these do not exist, it might be that some node α above T projects a phrase which hosts both a member of the subject chain (in its spec) and a member of the verbal X^0 chain that enter into a checking relation here. One possibility is that T or perhaps all categories have the option of projecting recursively: α would then correspond to the higher T node. Thus we could retain the spec and the head positions as appears to be empirically desirable, without assuming the existence of mediating φ-features. The condition of interpretability (cf. section 1.2 above) could be satisfied jointly by the two T nodes. (Similarly, recursively projecting Vs may be a way of creating multi-layered VPs.)

Consider next English interrogatives.

(33) I wonder (what) who +WH [(who) saw what]
(34) a. I wonder who +WH Bill saw (who)
      b. Bill saw who
(35) Who did +WH Mary (did) see (who)
(36) Did +WH John see Mary

In (33) there are three instances of the *wh*-feature (two on the *wh*-phrases and one on the embedded C node). But there is only one question. So by full interpretation the *wh*-features must all merge. This is possible if both *wh*-phrases form a chain that has a member that forms a checking relation with the +wh head. Thus bare checking theory entails the existence of A'-chains that express "covert A'-movement" relations, in accordance with our earlier conclusions. As noted in section 1, a chain corresponding to an "overt movement" relation is the default case, it will occur if the relevant head (here the +wh C) is "strong" enough to license a categorial element in the checking domain in the morphological component; in the case of an XP-chain word-externally as a specifier. (On the reasons for "extended structure preservation" that prevents word-internal phrases see Brody 1995b.) Given the generalization that SPELLOUT operates only on the highest copy in a chain, the lexical item will show up in spec-CP. In English this head licenses a single spec, hence additional *wh*-phrases checked by it must remain *in-situ* forming feature-chains only.

(34b) will be possible only with a −wh C and an echo interpretation. If it had a +wh C then the two *wh*-features in the structure should merge through checking by full interpretation. This makes a chain necessary, linking the *wh*-phrase to the checking domain of the +wh C. Since this head licenses an overt specifier in morphology, the chain must be a full copy chain as in (34a).

In (35) the auxiliary *did* must have a *wh*-feature. We can analyze (35) in two ways. The choice between these depends on whether features on heads mediating spec-head relations between other elements can exist. If they do, then both C and T can have a *wh*-feature and T (together with the auxiliary) forms a chain because these must merge through checking. Additionally the *wh*-feature on *who* must also merge with this complex, hence an XP-chain is also formed. These will be chains involving copies of full categories since the relevant C licenses both a word-internal and a word-external categorial element in its checking domain. Alternatively if mediating features are dispensed with, then the T with the *wh*-feature and the *wh*-phrase both form a chain linking them to CP because this is the only way that they can establish a checking relation. (This latter alternative corresponds essentially to the account in Rizzi 1991, see also Brody 1990, 1995c.)

If yes-no questions contain an empty (*wh-*)operator in spec-CP then the analysis of (36) will not significantly differ from that of (35). If not, then (36) will be parallel to (34), modulo the difference between an X^0-chain and an XP-chain.

Notice that we must apparently allow merger of a set of checking features without all of these occupying positions in the same checking domain. In a language that exhibits the pattern in (37), this structure will contain three instances of the +plural feature, but only one plurality: that of the DP. The +plural feature of the XP-chain of *they* apparently merges with the other two in two distinct spec's. Given the independently necessary assumption that checking features are properties of the chains and not of the members of the chain (cf. Brody 1995b), this should create no problems. At LF there is only a single +plural feature in (37), that of the XP-chain.

(37)   They(pl) seem(pl) (they(pl)) clever(pl)

4.2. The minimalist checking theory and the +/−interpretable distinction

Let us next consider briefly the current version of checking theory in the minimalist framework of Chomsky (1995). He suggests that interpretable features like categorial features and φ-features on nouns do not need to be checked, whereas noninterpretable features like for example Case or φ-features on verbal heads or "strength" (presumably a feature) of an interpretable feature must be checked because this makes it possible to eliminate these, as required by full interpretation. (In fact he assumes further that once checked, these features are not visible for the remaining syntactic computation either.) Thus checking relations and indirectly movement and chain relations are forced by noninterpretable features. These must be eliminated, and they can be eliminated only when already checked.

The principle of radical interpretability is incompatible however with the existence of noninterpretable features: according to this principle all syntactic features must be potentially interpretable. As we have seen, under bare checking theory it is not necessary to make use of noninterpretable features: checking relations are forced by the duplication of interpretable features. Furthermore the checking theory based on this distinction seems to lead to less optimal analyses. Consider for example the analysis of interrogatives within this theory.

The *wh*-feature is clearly interpretable hence not in need of being checked. A +wh feature will be checked only if it is "strong" and then overtly (some of the problems with the notion of strength used here were discussed in section 2 above). Thus in English the *wh*-feature on C is strong and hence it can be checked either by (T+)*did* as in (36) or by a *wh*-phrase as in (34). Since a strong feature can be satisfied by a single element, the analysis raises the question of why (38a) is unacceptable. Here the strong *wh*-feature of C is satisfied by the hosted verbal element.

(38)   a. did John give which book to Mary
       b. +WH John gave which book to Mary

Chomsky suggests that (38a) "converges as gibberish." (Notice that (38a) would then contrast with (38b), which crashes since the strong *wh*-feature on C has not been checked.) But since Chomsky rejects covert A'-movement type syntactic relations, he needs to assume the existence of some interpretive mechanism to link *in-situ wh*-phrases to their scope. It is then unclear why (38a) is gibberish, why it cannot be interpreted with the interpretive strategy generally used for *in-situ wh*-phrases. As we have seen, under bare checking theory, where all *wh*-features must merge, the problem does not arise: *which book* in (38a) must form a chain linking it to the *wh*-feature of the auxiliary (and perhaps also of C). Further, the chain must be a full category copy chain, that is one that corresponds to overt movement of the minimalist framework, since English C is strong, i.e. it licenses a specifier in addition to an element in the word (X^0)-internal checking domain.

(Further elaboration, like for example multiple strong features are necessary to generate (35) within Chomsky's system of assumptions. Note that (35) like many other examples will also violate the MLC of the minimalist system: the *wh*-phrase moves to CP even though another element that could (and does) legitimately move there, namely the verbal complex, is nearer.)

A major prediction in the theory where noninterpretable features are crucially involved is the exclusion of movement from Case positions. On the assumption that Case is noninterpretable and that such features once checked are invisible for further computation, the derivation of (39) will crash. The Case feature of the DP *John* are checked and deleted in the embedded clause (together with the Case feature of the embedded T). Hence the noninterpretable Case feature on the matrix T cannot be checked and deleted when DP raises, and therefore the derivation will crash at LF.

(39) a. *John seems [t saw Mary]
 b. *There seems [a man was clever]

If this is the only case where noninterpretable features are needed then the explanation is less appealing. Additionally *easy-to-please* and grammatical superraising suggest that the generalization in terms of Case is too strong:

(40) John is easy [Op to please t]
(41) John seems [t' Mary liked t]

If the analysis in Brody (1993b) is correct then in (40) we have a chain [John, Op, t] that involves two Case positions. Similarly in the grammatical superraising cases, which pattern like (41) (Ura 1994), the superraising chain [John, t', t] appears to involve two Case positions. Notice that if *John* in (41) is taken not to check (accusative) Case in the position of t, then *John* in (39a) (and *a man* in (39b)) should similarly be able to avoid Case-checking in the lower clause. This would however eliminate the explanation of the ungrammaticality of (39): these DPs could check the Case feature of the matrix T and the derivation would converge. (Ura suggests that in the grammatical superraising constructions lack of Case assignment to the trace correlates with the possibility of filling the position with a *pro* element. This generalization would still incorrectly allow (39) in subject *pro* drop languages like Italian or Hungarian.)

The contrast between (39) and (40)/(41) suggests that the subject non-subject difference may be relevant. Nominative subjects correlate with and presumably check Tense. We could thus attribute the ungrammaticality of (39) to Tense conflict instead of Case-conflict: subject raising in these examples illegitimately establishes an (indirect) chain-relation between two independent tenses. If null Case of PRO is assigned by an inflection with "unrealized" Tense (Stowell 1982, Martin 1992, Bošković 1994), then the account will generalize to chains involving infinitival subject positions:

(42) a. *John is illegal t to go there
     b. *John tried PRO to be illegal t to go there

5. Conclusion, uniformity, last resort, procrastinate

Although various issues remain, the results so far seem encouraging. Stipulative conditions of the minimalist framework on the Move/chain relation, like the cycle/c-command, and the MLC appear unnecessary or attributable to the interpretive components as perfect syntax leads us to expect. Checking relations and indirectly (non-trivial) chain formation is forced by bare output conditions. Given bare checking theory this need not involve noninterpretable features that would violate radical interpretability. I have discussed in detail and rejected the remaining major stipulative condition on Move/chain, namely Uniformity, in Brody (1995b). I argued there that a well-designed theory should not make available devices that would make it possible to violate the condition, which requires that all chain members be of the same projection level. If projectional levels are not defined relationally, then the question of uniformity cannot even arise. Since chains are sets of copies the chain members necessarily share also the projection level property.

Finally let me comment briefly and incompletely on two more conditions: Last resort and Procrastinate. Last resort can be thought of as an interface condition on the assumption that all categories must be licensed by full interpretation. This licensing involves participation in either (a) a projectional relation (selectional/modificational relation or categorial projection) or (b) in a checking relation. Since by the generalized projection principle projectional relations are relevant only for chain roots (cf. Brody 1995b), non-roots of non-trivial chains (i.e. "Move" of the minimalist framework) can be licensed only by a checking relation.

I assumed that in the default case chains are formed on full categorial copies, feature chains occur only when full copies are not licensed in the checking domain of some head. This preference for "overt movement" type relations is consistent with the Transparency principle and incompatible with Procrastinate which would require feature chains as the default case. (For Transparency and arguments against Procrastinate cf. Brody 1995a).

There is a particular prediction of Procrastinate that our account so far has nothing to say about. The ungrammatically of the examples in (43) has been attributed to this principle. Procrastinate will predict this, if at the embedded subject position it prefers insertion (of the expletive *it, there*), over the raising of the associate (*a man*). Instead of the ungrammatical (43), we will then derive the grammatical (44).

(43) a. *There seems a man to have arrived
 b. *It was believed a man to have been here
(44) a. There seems (there) to have arrived a man
 b. It was believed (it) to have been a man here

Let us consider the alternative of claiming either that the embedded subject position simply does not exist, or that its inflection is weak, and licenses only a featural subject. On either of these assumptions, the embedded subject position cannot be occupied by the associate and (43) cannot arise. This entails immediately that English object shift must be overt: *him* in (45) cannot be in the embedded subject position. (For independent arguments for the overtness of English object shift see e.g. Johnson 1991, Koizumi 1993, Lasnik 1994.)

(45) John believed him to be clever.

The stronger claim that the governed and Caseless subject positions of the Principles and Parameters theory do not exist entails also giving up the successive cyclicity of A-chains since intermediate A-chain links occupy such subject positions. If A-chains are not successive cyclic, then the intermediate traces will not be present in (46a) and (47a) to act as interveners for the binding relations indicated. (The principle C violation in the b. examples shows that c-command holds between the relevant elements.)

(46) a. John seems to Mary$_x$ [(t) to appear to her$_x$//*herself$_x$ [(t) to have met me]]
 b. *John seems to her$_x$ [(t) to appear to Mary$_x$ [(t) to have met me]]
(47) a. John seems to Mary$_x$ [(t) to be considered [(t) clever] by her$_x$//herself$_x$]
 b. *John seems to her$_x$ [(t) to be considered [(t) clever] by Mary$_x$]

Hence we will presumably have to account for the binding relations in examples like (46a), (47a) along the lines of Williams' (1980) Predicate Opacity Condition (see also Reinhart and Reuland 1993 for relevant discussion): anaphors need to be bound and pronominals free within their predicate – in (46a), (47a) this is within the intermediate level of the structure.

Consider the alternative assumption: the subject positions are only weakly licensed, and intermediate traces in A-chains involve only feature copies. This will make it possible to retain the theory of feature percolation sketched in section 3 above. The feature copies can then act as interveners for the binding theory. If this analysis is correct, it would represent a case where a full copy is higher in a chain than a feature copy. The scenario would be unexpected in the minimalist theory: a "covert movement" type relation cannot be followed by an "overt movement" relation. (This is not to say of course that the configuration is not achievable through stipulation, say by deleting the intermediate copy up to its formal features.)

On the other hand given the assembly system of Brody (1995a,b), such a configuration would be expected to occur. Here copies of features or of full categories and their content can be freely made (subject to the blocking effect by full category copies, as discussed above). Unless further constraints prevent this, feature copies and full copies can be inserted in the structure in any c-command order. In particular a full categorial copy may be higher than several feature copies (which in turn may be higher than another full copy), as appears to be necessary to retain successive cyclic A-movement in the context of the above assumptions.

References

Bošković, Željko (1994) "Selection and the categorial status of infinitival complements," *NLLT*.

Brody, Michael (1990) "Some remarks on the focus field in Hungarian," *UCLWP* 2, University College, London.

Brody, Michael (1993a) *Lexico-Logical Form*. Ms., University College, London.

Brody, Michael (1993b) "Theta theory and arguments," *Linguistic Inquiry* 24, 1–23.

Brody, Michael (1994) "Dependence and phrase structure," *UCLWP* 6, University College, London.

Brody, Michael (1995a) *Lexico-Logical Form. A Radically Minimalist Theory*. MIT Press, Cambridge, Mass.

Brody, Michael (1995b) *Phrase Structure and Projection*. Ms., University College, London, to appear in *Linguistic Inquiry*.

Brody, Michael (1995c) "Hungarian focus and bare checking theory," in *Arbeitspapiere des Sonderforschungsbereichs 340*, University of Tubingen.

Chierchia, G. (1991) "Functional wh and weak crossover," *The Proceedings of the WCCFL 10*. Stanford Linguistics Association, Stanford, pp. 75–90.

Chomsky, Noam (1986) *Barriers*. MIT Press, Cambridge, Mass.

Chomsky, Noam (1993) "A minimalist program for linguistic theory," *MIT Occasional Papers in Linguistics*, MIT, Cambridge, Mass.

Chomsky, Noam (1994) *Bare Phrase Structure*, ms., MIT, Cambridge, Mass.

Chomsky, Noam (1995) "Chapter 4." ms., MIT.

Cinque, Guglielmo (1991) *Types of A'-dependencies*. MIT Press, Cambridge, Mass.

Cinque, Guglielmo (1995) "Adverbs and the universal hierarchy of functional projections," Tromso GLOW abstract.

Hornstein, Norbert (1994) *LF: The Grammar of Logical Form. From GB to Minimalism*. Ms., University of Maryland.

Jaeggli, Osvaldo (1981) *Topics in Romance Syntax*. Foris, Dordrecht.

Johnson, Kyle (1991) "Object positions," *Natural Language and Linguistic Theory* 9, 577–636.

Kawashima, R and Hisatsugu Kitahara (1995) "Strict cyclicity, linear ordering and derivational c-command," to appear in *WCCFL* 14.

Kayne, Richard (1981) "ECP extensions," *Linguistic Inquiry* 12, 93–133.

Kayne, Richard (1983) "Connectedness," *Linguistic Inquiry* 14, 223–249.
Kayne, Richard (1994) *The Antisymmetry of Syntax*. MIT Press, Cambridge, Mass.
Koizumi, Masatoshi (1993) "Object Agreement Phrases and the Split VP Hypothesis," *MITWPL* 18. MIT, Cambridge, Mass.
Lasnik, Howard (1994) Antecedent contained deletion and/or pseudo-gapping. Talk, presented at MIT.
Lasnik, Howard and Mamoru Saito (1992) *Move* α. MIT Press, Cambridge, Mass.
Longobardi, Giuseppe (1991) "In defense of the correspondence hypothesis: island effects and parasitic constructions in logical form," in: C.-T. James Huang and Robert May (eds.), *Logical Structure and Linguistic Structure*. Kluwer, Dordrecht.
Martin, Roger (1992) *On the Distribution and Case Features of PRO*. Ms., University of Connecticut.
Pesetsky, David (1987) "WH-in-situ: movement and unselective binding," in: Eric Reuland and A. ter Meulen (eds.), *The Representation of (In)definiteness*. MIT Press, Cambridge, Mass, pp. 98–129.
Pesetsky, David (1989) *Language Particular Processes and the Earliness Principle*. Ms., MIT.
Reinhart, Tanya and Eric Reuland (1993) "Reflexivity," *Linguistic Inquiry* 24, 657–720.
Rizzi, Luigi (1982) *Issues in Italian Syntax*. Foris, Dordrecht.
Rizzi, Luigi (1990) *Relativized Minimality*. MIT Press, Cambridge, Mass.
Rizzi, Luigi (1991) *Residual Verb Second and the Wh-Criterion*. Ms., Universite de Geneve.
Stowell, Timothy (1982) "The tense of infinitives," *Linguistic Inquiry* 13, 561–570.
Ura, Hiroyuki (1994) *Varieties of Raising and the Feature-based Phrase Structure Theory* (chapter 1). Ms., MIT.
Watanabe, Akira (1991) *Wh-in-situ, Subjacency and Chain Formation*. Ms., MIT.
Williams, Edwin (1980) "Predication," *Linguistic Inquiry* 11, 208–238.
Williams, Edwin (1994) *Thematic Structure in Syntax*. MIT Press, Cambridge, Mass.
Williams, Edwin (1995) *Blocking and Anaphora*. Ms., University of Princeton.

9

THE MINIMALIST PROGRAM AND A PERFECT SYNTAX

A critical notice of Noam Chomsky's
The Minimalist Program[1]

1. Introduction

The Minimalist Program (*TMP*) is comparable to many of Chomsky's earlier major linguistic contributions. This volume also powerfully integrates several strands of research into an exciting and intellectually seductive novel view of the field and proceeds to develop and elaborate, sometimes in great detail, various aspects of the resulting picture.

Chapter 1, co-authored by Howard Lasnik, is an overview of the final stages of the principles and parameters (aka government binding) theory, which already contains some hints of ideas to come. Chapter 2 (re)introduces the notion of economy, chapter 3 corresponds to the paper that originally outlined the basic ideas of the minimalist enterprise and chapter 4 contains many further developments.

Chapter 4 very thoroughly revises an earlier paper ("Bare Phrase Structure"), the other three chapters are reprints with minor revisions of published earlier articles. This state of affairs of course results in repetitions and inconsistencies. In fact it results in many fewer repetitions and many more inconsistencies than might be expected purely on the basis of the bibliographical history. Each chapter rejects and revises much of the general framework of previous chapters, sometimes, especially in the case of chapter 4, even that of earlier sections. But this is a "creative inconsistency" where each successive theory builds on and rebuilds the earlier ones. I find much of this highly inspiring, although it is well known that many find it objectionable. Detractors can justifiably note that this style of writing led in *TMP* to numerous, sometimes more, sometimes less trivial inconsistencies and other related problems, even internal to the various versions of the framework presented. But to make the point somewhat metaphorically, when I listen to a grand master piano player with a unique message, understanding and insight to communicate, it does not seem too important if he sometimes hits the wrong keys. And I wonder who would prefer the flawless alternative of the computer-generated or similar rendition.

In what follows, I will not attempt to point out such "false notes". Instead, I shall try to identify some major features of *TMP* that may not be fully justified, and concentrate on comparing this approach with an alternative that is related in spirit but leads to a rather different theory of grammar.

2. Some features of the Minimalist Program

The original paper, "A Minimalist Program for Linguistic Theory", now also chapter 3 of *TMP*, brings together at least three major lines of research. First, there is a set of ideas concerning phrase structure and in particular specifiers. One of these ideas is the project of restricting the set of possible structural relations. An important suggestion is the elimination of the notion of government, a central concept in the Principles and Parameters theory. No direct relation is taken to hold between a head (e.g. a verb) and the specifier (e.g. a DP subject) of another head. Another is checking theory: syntactic movement (the most important among the descendants of the transformations in a sixties style transformational grammar) takes place only when forced, and it can be forced only by the need to establish a specifier-head (checking) configuration between certain features of the elements involved.

The second major element of the mixture is the restriction of representational conditions to the interface levels. It is a standard assumption that syntax relates the articulatory/perceptual- and the conceptual-interpretive systems by providing instructions for these at two interface levels: Logical Form (LF) and Phonetic Form (PF) respectively. Optimally, no conditions should hold at other levels, or essentially equivalently, no additional level of syntactic analysis should be postulated. Furthermore, we might hope to show that most, or perhaps all, interface conditions reflect interpretive requirements; that is, they are consequences of the fact that syntax interacts with external systems with given independently motivated properties.

The third major ingredient is the idea of economy of derivations and representations, already reintroduced in the previous chapter. Economy of representation is simply a principle of full interpretation at the interface: "every symbol must receive an 'external' interpretation by language independent rules." Economy of derivation comprises a set of diverse conditions; for example, derivations must be as short as possible, steps in a derivation must bridge the smallest possible distance, movement takes place only if forced by some checking requirement and takes place as late as possible in the derivation.

3. Derivations and representations

Some readers of *Mind and Language* with encyclopedic memory might remember a discussion in this journal in 1987 relating to Chomsky's then recent book *Knowledge of Language*. My contribution to the discussion consisted in an argument based on the theory of thematic ("theta") roles, that the basic syntactic level is not D-structure (the standard view at the time), nor S-structure (as some have suggested) but LF. Chomsky in his answer attacked the view that all syntactic levels other than LF are dispensable and that the D-structure to LF (via S-structure) derivation is not real. These arguments were somewhat misdirected, since the proposal he criticized did not dispense with these theoretical entities, it only suggested that in place of the standard derivation we should substitute a system where S- and D-structure are abstracted from LF via some algorithm/derivation:[2] A couple of years after this debate, I did in fact start to argue for the related stronger claim that Chomsky attacked, at least with respect to D-structure.[3]

Chapter 3 of *TMP* eliminates D-structure on the same grounds as Brody 1993.[4] It also makes the further step of eliminating S-structure as a level where representational conditions can hold by successfully restating the relevant restrictions at LF. Eliminating D- and S-structure are precisely the hypotheses that Chomsky once argued against in connection with my proposal in this journal, and of course these steps entail also the (weaker) position I took at the time, that LF is the "basic" syntactic level of representation.

The theory of *TMP* does not embrace, however, a position that is different in every respect from that of Chomsky, 1987. In particular, both publications assume the existence of syntactic derivations relating the lexical input to the interface level LF. But, in my view, this is precisely one of the aspects of the overall organization of the grammar in *TMP* which is unjustified, and probably wrong. I argued in Brody, 1995a,[5] that derivations and properties of LF representations duplicate each other (for example movement and chains express the same relation) and that therefore a parsimonious theory of syntax should dispense either with representations or with derivations. I opted for the representational alternative, others have since explored the derivational approach. The representational view still seems preferable to me on general grounds partly because it is more restrictive than the derivational theory in that it does not allow reference to rule order relations. Thus it rules out in principle the so-called feeding–bleeding relations in rule application sequences. Such relations do not seem to exist in syntax at all, but we would expect them to be commonplace on the derivational theory. (Note that this issue is different from the question of how the order of rule application is determined.) Independently of the choice between the fully derivational and the fully representational theory, it is clear that the framework of *TMP*, which postulates both representations and derivations, is the least restrictive and hence in principle the least explanatory of the three approaches.

I will not look again at the main argument for derivations based on the properties of successive head-movement presented in Chomsky, 1987, which reappears also at several places in *TMP*. I have discussed in detail and rejected this in Brody, 1995a, pp. 35–40. In this work I also noted that derivational economy conditions are generally quite easily restatable in representational terms.

The Principles and Parameters theory had a characteristic forking organization, that the theory of *TMP* inherited. The derivation proceeded to S-structure, which served as an input to the phonological component and then continued to LF. The minimalist theory eliminates S-structure as a level where representational conditions hold, and allows the phonological – now "Spellout" – (sub)module to apply in principle to any point of the derivation. Like the Principles and Parameters theory, this framework incorporates a distinction between (pre-S-structure/pre-Spellout-point) operations that constitute "visible" input to phonology and (post-S-structure/

post-Spellout-point) "invisible," covert operations. The distinction was natural within the earlier framework: syntax consisted of the D- to S-structure mapping and was overt, while the two interpretive components (S-structure to LF and to PF) were inaccessible to each other. But the assumption is less natural in *TMP*.

It is less natural because *TMP* incorporates the insight that there is no stipulated difference between the overt and the covert computations – "computational procedures are uniform throughout" (p. 229). (This is not contradicted by the fact that covert operations in practice have different properties from the overt ones, due to the interaction of computation-independent assumptions, cf. also below.) Thus the Spellout point is now not the divide that S-structure was between syntax and interpretation. It is an arbitrary point on the uniform syntactic derivation between the lexical input and LF. But this is strange: the relation between PF and LF is mediated by a Spellout component, together with some arbitrary subpart (potentially different from language to language and from construction to construction) of the system of uniform computational procedures that assembles LF representations from lexical elements.

Other, perhaps more tangible, problems also arise in this setup. Less worrying are the recoverability issues. Various proposals have been made concerning the question of how lexical insertion of elements with phonological material might be prevented in the covert, post-Spellout syntax, where this would not result in any PF effects. Allowing this option, "John left" could mean for example "Mary said John left" with covert insertion of the elements of the matrix clause "Mary said ..." *TMP* excludes this possibility by assuming that PF features must not be present at LF. This makes it necessary to stipulate that the Spellout operation, in addition to copying PF features (the minimal assumption), also deletes – "strips" – these from the covert part of the lexicon to LF computation. In the case of post-Spellout-point lexical insertion, PF features cannot be deleted and will illegitimately reach LF.

It is not clear, however, why PF features could not be ignored by the interpretive component at LF, after all in the framework of *TMP* the syntactic computation must be able to ignore them. (There is a more general issue in the background here: namely, what are the units for the principle of "full interpretation.") Furthermore, even if PF features must be deleted from the syntactic computation, optimally we would expect this to happen freely. Restricting the option to the Spellout point seems to exchange the stipulation against covert lexical insertion for another.

A universal global recoverability condition that relates PF and LF may well be an acceptable alternative answer to the issue of covert lexical insertion. A more serious problem is again the looseness in the theory. Empty category (i.e. category without phonological material) insertion for example is now possible both overtly and covertly, but the additional freedom allowed here is not justified by any arguments in the literature establishing its necessity. Similarly, if properties of movement in fact differ in the overt and covert part of the syntactic derivation, then covert type movement (feature movement) can in principle occur both before (cf. Watanabe 1991, quoted approvingly in *TMP*, p. 264) and of course also after the Spellout point.

In the fully representational theory, these problems do not arise. Since there is only a single syntactic representation, LF, and no derivations, Spellout can only apply to this level. This creates, however, a different problem: LF was standardly taken to be a level that is different from S-structure: in both the principles and parameters and the minimalist theory movement rules operate between S-structure/Spellout point and LF, just as they do between D-structure/lexical input and S-structure/Spellout point. If movement rules make LF different from S-structure, then LF can be the Spellout point only if Spellout contains an (inverse) movement algorithm. But given the fact noted above that movement rules duplicate LF chains, the inverse movement approach seems equally incorrect: it simply places the duplication into a different component of the grammar.

To resolve this difficulty, without denying that covert movement relations in crucial respects form a natural class with overt movement relations, I argued that covert movement relations correspond to LF chains just like overt movement relations, but LF and S-structure/Spellout point do not differ with respect to the placement of phonological material. (Others argued against the standard position of the principles and parameters theory that overt and covert movement relations have enough properties in common to consider them a natural class, now also *TMP* partly rejects the claim – for A-relations – but I believe incorrectly.[6]) I referred to the relevant type of chains as "expletive-associate" chains, where a lexical or empty expletive element carries the features of its associate chain-mate. Interestingly, chapter 4 of *TMP* proposes a characterization of covert movement, "feature movement," that corresponds exactly (apart from certain fairly technical differences and the choice of the derivational idiom) to the expletive-associate chain proposal. Under the feature movement hypothesis, like under the expletive-associate chain account there is no covert deplacement of phonological material in the grammar. It becomes then particularly difficult to see, why the Spellout point should be distinct from LF, since with respect to the topology of the phonological material the two structures cannot differ. And of course if the Spellout point is in fact LF then it becomes even more difficult to assign a role and a raison d'être to syntactic derivations.

4. Perfection

According to *TMP* then, a computational system, part of linguistic competence puts together from lexical items the interface representation LF. All representational conditions hold at the interface levels and beyond. Syntax is taken to be a near perfect system where the only imperfections are those that the external interacting systems force on syntax.

For example *TMP* takes the existence of the rule of "Move" (i.e. movement transformation) to be such an imperfection. It assumes that optimally lexical items would be assembled into syntactic structures by the relatively simple operation of "Merge." Move is due to "'extraneous' conditions ... conditions imposed on [the computational system] by the ways it interacts with external systems. That is where we would hope the source of 'imperfections' to lie, on minimalist assumptions" (p. 317).

Similarly, once we have Move, *TMP* takes covert post-Spellout-point movement of features (in my terminology expletive-associate chains) to be the optimal case. *TMP* introduces two (I believe) alternative hypotheses concerning pre-Spellout-point movement of more than the grammatical features involved in checking relations (i.e. movement of full categories together with their phonological material). One of these is that such movement is due to a special checking feature. Another assumption is that it is due to PF requirements. "... only PF-convergence forces anything beyond features to raise. If that turns out to be true or to the extent that it does, we have further reasons to suspect that language 'imperfections' arise from the external requirement that the computational principles must adapt to the sensory-motor apparatus, which is in a certain sense "extraneous" to the core systems of language as revealed in the [lexical input to LF] computation" (p. 265).

The view that external systems force imperfections on syntax is rather surprising. I think the desirability of this idea fades when it is compared with an alternative that is based on more standard methodology. According to this alternative picture, the observed imperfections are only apparent, and the fact that they show up is due to the interaction of otherwise "perfect" subsystems. This view is of course more restrictive and therefore preferable if facts allow us to maintain it. Let me refer to the framework that rejects the idea of (externally forced) syntactic imperfections as "perfect syntax."[7] I take syntax to be perfect in the sense in which for example the propositional calculus is perfect: a system with a simple set of primitives and axioms. Of course the nature of syntax remains an empirical question: syntax is one module of a larger system of our mind-brain.

In the setting of *TMP*, arguments based on general considerations similar to those in the physical sciences, like simplicity, symmetry, nonredundancy etc. are at last wholeheartedly accepted. Provisos that these features may be surprising properties in biological systems are not taken to weaken the force of such arguments any more and the issue such provisos raise is placed where it appears to belong: it is "a problem for biology and the brain sciences, which, as currently understood, do not provide any basis for what appear to be fairly well established conclusions about language" (p. 2). But this background, it seems to me, removes any remaining general motivation to deviate from the standard methodology, according to which "data imperfections" do not point to imperfections in the underlying systems, but rather result either from the interplay of perfect systems or simply from our incomplete understanding of these.

Furthermore, in order to deviate from the optimal assumption of syntactic perfection, it would be necessary to demonstrate that this is in conflict with external requirements. But not only has this not been demonstrated, it is very unlikely (without of course being logically impossible), given the current state of our knowledge, that anything of the sort could be convincingly shown. This is because the system of perfect syntax is not a priori given; whenever a perfect system is in conflict with external requirements, there is always a possibility that a different perfect system would not create the conflict.

For concreteness, let us look at the assumption in *TMP* that Move is an imperfection forced by LF checking requirements. If Move was really an imperfection, we would like to know why it cannot be avoided by, say, freely deleting checking features or by checking features being always generated in a position that is accessible without Move, etc. Further possibilities are easily imaginable and numerous: in order to demonstrate conflict between external requirements and Move-less perfection all would need to be excluded on principled grounds. Nothing like this has been established, or looks demonstrable. Remember also that although the result would in some sense be interesting, it would not be a desirable one. (Similar comments apply in the case of the idea that overt Move of categories and phonological material is a forced imperfection. How do we rule out overt movement restricted to the Spellout component, how do we rule out free deletion of strong features, etc.)

Perfect syntax can be thought of as a theory that attempts to take the minimalist program at least in certain respects to its logical conclusion. It is therefore interesting to observe, that already at this early stage it is clear that the outlines of this approach will look completely different from the picture *TMP* draws. The step of disallowing the remaining (forced) syntactic imperfections of *TMP* might seem to be minor, but it naturally leads to the rejection of many of the central differentiating features of this theory. Let me try to indicate very sketchily and without any attempt at justification some major differences (cf. Brody 1998, 1995b, for more discussion and initial arguments).

First, since perfect syntax does not allow imperfections, Move cannot be one. It is therefore necessary to find a different conceptualization for this relation. Given the representational nature of perfect syntax, one obvious alternative is the copy relation. Move creates LF copies in *TMP*, properties of Move can in principle be taken to be properties of the relevant copy relation. Importantly, unlike Move, the copy relation does not seem to be an imperfection: it appears to be a necessary feature in syntax, given its relation to the lexicon. Lexical items must be in a copy relation with their correspondents in a syntactic structure. An entry does not disappear from the lexicon when used syntactically.

Another approach might be to eliminate the Move relation from syntax. Although the point must of course be substantiated, which I cannot undertake here, I find this possibility worth exploring. Suppose that the conceptual-semantic interpretive system optionally takes two identical elements to be in the relevant "Move" relation (abstractly understood, not involving movement). In most, and perhaps all cases, there will be independently motivated principles violated if the wrong choice is made. It is generally assumed that the Spellout rule needs to know about the movement history of a derivation, since it needs to distinguish copies that are traces of Move from others. If the abstract "Move" relation is established only at a post-syntactical level L, then L and PF will need to be linked by a global recoverability condition. But such a recoverability condition between PF and some non-phonological level may be necessary anyway, given the natural inclusiveness condition of *TMP*, that prevents lexicon-extraneous marking of elements as having participated in a Move relation.

Second, the strategy of *TMP* appears to be to attribute non-optimal syntactic properties to the Move relation, presumably on the assumption that Move is an imperfection in any case, hence the fact that it shows non-optimal properties is not surprising. The more restrictive framework of perfect syntax cannot proceed this way. There are reasons to think that some of the putative properties of Move (e.g. c-command, last resort) may be more general and not Move-specific properties; others like "chain-uniformity" dissolve given an improved theory of phrase structure. Thus perfection in the domain of chain theory does not appear to be obviously out of reach either. True, a number of issues, mostly having to do with questions of locality, remain.

A third difference between perfect syntax and *TMP* concerns economy conditions. In the system of *TMP* interface conditions will be satisfied "as well as possible," as measured and ensured by economy conditions. But if there are no (externally forced) imperfections, no economy conditions may be necessary to ensure that the conditions are satisfied optimally. If there are no imperfections, there is no need to measure and compare degrees of imperfection. Such a conclusion is consistent with the fact that even within *TMP*, the role of economy conditions seems to shrink considerably by the end of the book. Chomsky argues forcefully in chapter 4 that one of the paradigm cases of economy in chapter 3, the shortest derivational steps restriction is in fact not an economy condition. It is often easy to restate many of the other global economy conditions as computationally simpler "default" or licensing conditions, preventing optionality. (Perhaps the only unexplained residue once the derivational economy principles of *TMP* are eliminated in this fashion will then be a small empirical advantage for the shortest derivation – representationally: "minimize number of chain-links" – condition, generated by some highly controversial assumptions that Chomsky makes (p. 357).)

The fourth major difference I already touched on earlier: perfect syntax cannot assume the redundant and much looser derivational-representational system of *TMP*. This leads to a necessary rejection of various theoretical innovations. I mention here just one, which seems to be important enough to merit being considered to be a fifth central difference between the two theories. In chapter 4 of *TMP* Chomsky introduces a difference between interpretable and non-interpretable checking features. Non-interpretable features are visible for the derivation, but cannot be tolerated at LF, given the principle of full interpretation. Interpretable features can be present both during the derivation and at the interface. Interesting consequences follow from this distinction.

But a distinction in such terms is natural only in the nonrestrictive framework, where both representations and derivations are postulated. Non-interpretable features are derivational in the sense of not being allowed to be present at the (sole) syntactic representation LF, while interpretable features can exist both derivationally and representationally. Since interpretable features presumably cannot be eliminated from the theory, perfect syntax must dispense with non-interpretable ones. This more restrictive framework has the nontrivial task of accounting for the predictions achieved through this distinction, but without assuming it. Furthermore, the assumption that all syntactic features must be semantically interpretable is a natural further restriction on syntactic primitives and as such it is desirable independently of the derivational/representational duplication issue. Note the hypothesis that there are no solely

PF motivated syntactic features takes seriously the spirit of the remark in *TMP* quoted earlier, according to which the "core systems of language" involve the lexicon–LF interaction, with an extraneous Spellout system.

In sum, Perfect syntax, in contrast to *TMP*, makes the optimal assumption and aims to eliminate forced and unforced imperfections from syntax as a matter of principle. When the consequences of this more restrictive approach are examined, it quickly turns out to lead to a picture of the syntactic competence that is rather different from the one presented in *TMP*.

There are at least two central features of Chomsky's syntactic theories that either remained constant through the various framework metamorphoses or had a tendency to reincarnate and which I believe are empirically unjustified as part of syntactic theory. The first is the mixed, partly derivational nature of the system, and the second a notion of measurement and comparison, once an aspect of the long abandoned "evaluation metric," now resurfacing in the rather different shape of economy conditions, part of a particular interpretation of syntactic perfection. These ideas are central, and establishing their truth or falsity is important for the field, and quite probably beyond it. But these and the other related issues I tried to sketch should be set against the background of Chomsky's major and ongoing contribution of creating a scientific field of linguistics. To this enterprise *TMP*, whatever its imperfections, added perhaps more than any of his other works since *The Logical Structure of Linguistic Theory*.

References

Brody, M. 1993: Theta Theory and arguments. *Linguistic Inquiry*, 24, 1–23.
Brody, M. 1995a: *Lexico-Logical form. A Radically Minimalist Theory*. Cambridge, MA: MIT Press.
Brody, M. 1995b: Towards Perfect Chains. MS, University College London, to appear in Liliane Haegeman (ed.), *Handbook of Syntax*, Kluwer.
Brody, M. 1998: Projection and Phrase Structure. *Linguistic Inquiry*, 29, 367–398.
Watanabe, A. 1991: Wh-in-situ, Subjacency and Chain Formation. MS, MIT.

10

ON THE STATUS OF REPRESENTATIONS AND DERIVATIONS

1. Representations and derivations – the status of the mixed theory

1.1. Restrictiveness and duplication

As set out in earlier work, elegant syntax (ES) differs from the minimalist framework in several important respects.[1] I shall elaborate here some remarks made earlier on those features of this approach that relate to the so-called representational – derivational issue. I argued that since chain and move express the same type of relation, a theory that contains both concepts is redundant, and, therefore, at least in the setting of ES, wrong.[2] As has been also noted repeatedly, the issue is more general: there is a redundancy built into the architecture of theories that assume that both representations and derivations play a role in the competence theory of narrow syntax.[3]

Let us note first that a general conceptual argument from simplicity in favour of a pure (representational or derivational) theory against a mixed one is weak or nonexistent. This is because it is in principle possible that derivational and representational principles are both necessary in syntax and that they hold in different domains, and/or are distinguished also by other independently needed principles and properties – i.e. cluster in a modular fashion. Such clustering of properties with chains in one module and move in another does not seem to obtain in narrow syntax (the lexicon to LF-interface mapping), but this does not seem to be a necessary state of affairs, but rather an empirical fact about language. It may be that in wider domains, like the theory of mind, for example, both derivational and representational components will be necessary. The important point here is that the argument from redundancy against mixed theories of narrow syntax, to be discussed below, is not purely conceptual but is ultimately empirically based.[4]

Consider then representations and derivations in narrow syntax.[5] In principle there are two possibilities here (ignoring now logically possible but apparently nonexistent mixed situations that involve both possibilities in a modular fashion). Either derivational and representational accounts of the lexicon to LF relation are (a) empirically distinguishable, or (b) they are not. Although it may have been sometimes

185

argued that both of these situations obtain, it is obvious that these two states of affairs are incompatible.

I return to (b) in the next subsection. Let us consider first the situation where we take (I think correctly, see section 1.2 below) the representational and the derivational theory to be empirically distinguishable. When the argument against the mixed theory was initially put forward there were essentially no attempts to construct analyses that relied on the existence of both derivations and representations. Given the lack of such arguments one obviously opts for either a fully derivational or a fully representational theory on general grounds of restrictiveness.

While there may now be some contributions in the literature that postulate both representations/chains and derivations/move and exploit one or another assumed (typically stipulated) difference between these pairs, as far as I am aware there are essentially no strong arguments for postulating both concept-pairs as part of narrow syntax.[6] Nobody has attempted to show that the results achieved in the less restrictive framework, that apparently involves systematic duplications (a property that is strange even in a minimalist setting, let alone ES), cannot be restated in a nonmixed system that avoids redundancy and lack of restrictiveness. There are also no attempts to argue that the assumed advantages outweigh the considerable burden of weakening the grammar. It is clear that even if focused arguments existed for the claim that both derivations and representations must exist side by side within the competence system of the language faculty and largely duplicate each other, these would have to be treated with extreme caution, since they would amount to a proposal to adopt a less restrictive grammar.[7] Everything else being equal, there are clearly more analytical possibilities in a theory that has both representations and derivations with differing properties than in a system that only has one of these concepts.

I shall refer to these considerations as the argument from restrictiveness against the mixed theory of narrow syntax. Let me summarize this argument. Suppose that representations/chains on the one hand and derivations/move on the other have different properties. (This seems to be the case.) Then it's an empirical question which notion(-sets) are the right ones. Having both would weaken the theory in the sense of increasing the analytic options available (see note 7), hence very strong arguments would be needed to maintain that both concept-sets are part of the competence theory of syntax. No strong argument appears to exist. Further, in addition to the problem of the unmotivated lack of restrictiveness, we would also have the problem of the unmotivated systematic (representational–derivational) duplications.

1.2. Principles of I-language

Suppose then, as is sometimes suggested, that arguments for a mixed theory are lacking because the issue they would address is effectively meaningless. Representations and derivations are just notational variants, they are simply different approaches to expressing the same notions and the same generalizations. Suppose that there were no empirical differences to distinguish the derivational and the representational views.

But on such an assumption a mixed theory like standard minimalism only becomes more strange. Putting aside the uninteresting case where notational variance means synonymy – two names for the same concept – let us look at the situation where we take derivation/move and representation/chain to be two different aspects of, or two different ways of looking at, the same phenomena. Consider first a situation in physics that might be somewhat similar. The famous double slit experiment of quantum theory can be interpreted either in terms of probability waves or in terms of a particle being able to traverse multiple trajectories before hitting a target.[8] The two interpretations apparently do not result in distinguishable empirical predictions. (This is the case now, and may or may not remain so in the future.) Assuming this fact, it would be a strange theory that postulates both multiple trajectories and probability waves, say mapping one into the other. It would be much like a theory whose ontology is committed to two entities, the evening star and the morning star, in the context of the assumption that ultimately they are empirically indistinguishable. The standard minimalist framework mapping derivations into representations appears to be equally curious – especially so when viewed from the perspective of ES, which rules out in principle the option of attributing syntactic redundancy to the effect of selection or to evolutionary accidents.[9]

To repeat, on the assumption that representation/chain and derivation/move are just notational variants (i.e. no empirical evidence distinguishes them), they are either just different names for the same notions or perhaps different but (at least currently) not empirically distinguishable notions. So one could suggest that the choice between them is not real, that one of them is just a way of looking at the other. In such a situation it may be reasonable to look for some deeper notions that subsume the two competing ones. But it seems mistaken to conclude from the assumption that, say, move captures the properties of chain, that both chain and move are part of the grammar. If we talk about (some module of) I-language, and say that y is part of it, hence a real object and furthermore that x is just an aspect of y, a way of looking at or treating y, this does not then seem to entail postulating x as a distinct element of the mind. Further evidence would be necessary for that, but by hypothesis this would be unavailable if the two notions cannot be distinguished empirically. I shall refer to this consideration below as the argument from I-language ontology. So this argument is meant to establish that the mixed theory cannot be defended even on the (empirically dubious) grounds of derivations and representations being notational variants. But the main argument against mixed theories remains the consideration based on restrictiveness and duplication: there is relatively little evidence for distinguishing derivations and representations, and not surprisingly there is essentially no serious evidence for adopting both.

2. Representations or derivations

2.1. Derivational theories and weak representationality

Suppose then that the rejection of mixed derivational–representational theories, mainly on grounds of empirically and conceptually unmotivated lack of restrictiveness, is correct. Next comes the related but distinct and secondary issue of whether syntactic theory is better thought of as purely derivational (PDT) or purely representational (PRT). By a PRT of narrow syntax (or LF) I understand a system that generates the interface level in the mathematical sense of generation. This consists of a set of constraints or principles that determine well-formedness. We could assume that, essentially as in the standard minimalist framework, these constraints can only include bare output conditions and a definition of possible LF structures (that bare output conditions constrain further).

Such a structural definition could, for example, run along the following lines: a representation (tree) consists exclusively of nodes ($n_1, \ldots, n_n$) and the immediate domination relation such that each node (except the root) must be immediately dominated by some other unique node (ensuring the connectedness of the tree). (This sketchy definition is not intended as an actual proposal, but simply as an indication of the form a representational definition of LF could take. Under various theories, various elaborations will be necessary and various aspects of this definition may follow from elsewhere. See for example Brody (1997b, 2000a) and Abels (2000) for more extensive discussions of two versions of a particular approach along the above lines.)

We could proceed further by defining constituents recursively in terms of immediate domination. Alternatively, as suggested in note 5, we could take domination as the primitive notion and assume that x immediately dominates y iff x dominates y and there is no z such that x dominates z and z dominates y. A constituent will then be a subtree that contains every node a given node n reflexively dominates. (Note, however, that in the context of the theory in the works just cited, it may not be necessary to define constituents for the purposes of narrow syntax at all. If linking of chain members, binding, etc. are taken to be matters of interpretation – a natural and empirically motivated assumption – then constituents might be visible/created only in the interpretive components.)

I assume further, though not crucially, that the question of how to assemble as opposed to constrain (or generate, in the sense of "specify") the representation falls outside of the competence theory of grammar and is part of how the linguistic competence system is used – most plausibly it pertains to the theory of parsing and sentence production.

A PDT is an ordered series of operations with input and output, where the input may only consist of terminals and the outputs of some other operations.[10] The following three-way distinction will be useful: (i) a derivational theory is nonrepresentational if the derivational operations create opaque objects whose internal elements and composition is not accessible to any further rule or operation; (ii) a derivational theory is weakly representational if derivational stages are transparent in the sense that material already assembled can be accessed by later principles (i.e. the derivational stages are representations); finally (iii) a derivational theory is strongly representational if it is weakly representational and there are constraints on the representations (weak sense) generated.

It is clear that derivational theories must be at least weakly representational. Take an object z, the result of merging x and y. At some later step move can only apply to y if z is a transparent rather than an opaque object since otherwise y would not be accessible or even visible for this operation. Notice that even if move is reduced to merge and an interpretive linking operation (as in the theory of distributed chains, Brody 1998b, 1999a), the same conclusion would still hold: the interpretive link between x and y could not be established if z was opaque. The derivational theory therefore is at the same time a (weakly) representational theory with multiple (weakly) representational stages instead of just one at the interface.[11]

So there can be no derivational theories that are fully nonrepresentational. The derivational theory will always be a mixed one to some extent. It would also seem to be almost necessarily a multirepresentational theory. One might think that this sort of weak representationality does not matter, since the spirit of the theory remains derivational. I can see two problems with this sort of skepticism about the argument. First, weakly representational derivational theories are clearly mixed theories and the I-language ontology argument above in section 1.2 applies to them just as much as to any other empirically unmotivated mixed theory. The fact that all derivational theories must be mixed then appears to already provide a good reason for rejecting derivational theories of all kinds.

Second, consider the suggestion that weak representationality does not matter, because the crucial difference between the representational and derivational view is that the latter is not strongly representational, there are no representational constraints on the structures that the derivation assembles, hence these structures (although weakly representational) are still not levels of representation in some more important sense. But given that derivational theories are at least weakly representational, a derivational operation must have an input and an output both of which are at least weakly representational. Hence a derivational operation involves, or is equivalent to, a set of representation-pairs: a set of possible input–output pairs (in fact, representation n-tuples in the general case, since in principle there can be more than one input or output). The operation can thus equivalently be thought of as a member of a (partially?) ordered set of multirepresentational constraints. We can understand a weakly representational derivational theory as having an ordered set of such multi-representational constraints.

It should be clear then, that the distinction between weakly and strongly representational derivational theory, despite appearances, does not really have to do with the derivational–representational distinction. What the distinction between weakly and strongly derivational theory really concerns is the question of whether there are constraints that are additional to those captured by the postulated derivational steps (whether we view these latter as representational or derivational constraints) and bare output conditions. Currently the restrictive working hypothesis of many linguists working in this domain is that there are no such additional constraints. But the answer to this question may be either negative or positive, both on the representational and on the derivational view.

Consider current "derivational" theory with the operation merge, some applications of which are a suboperation of move. The input of merge is any two well-formed representations WR and WR′ (built from terminals and subtrees by merge) and the output WR″ is WR augmented by WR′ in a way that merge specifies. Thus in general merge is a tri-representational constraint. Where merge is a subpart of move, it applies to an element WR′ of a tree WR and augments WR with a proper subpart of WR, WR′. What merge specifies is that WR and WR′ will be sisters in WR″ and furthermore WR″ inherits its label from WR or WR′ (in the case of move, always from WR for reasons independent of merge).

Thinking of the derivational approach as a multilevel representational theory, we see that this constraint is essentially equivalent to the requirement that at every level L a (sub)tree ST″ is well formed iff (a) it immediately dominates two well-formed subtrees ST and ST′ [whose correspondents are present at L-1] each composed of terminals and other subtrees (in the case of move, ST′ is properly dominated by ST [at L-1]); and (b) ST″ carries the label of ST or ST′ (always ST in the case of move). Given this background, the question of whether there are any syntactic constraints that are additional to the structural definition of possible LF representations (whether in terms of merge and move or their representational equivalents, or in terms of different notions) has little to do with representationality or derivationality of the system. We expect, mostly on the grounds of the (at least partial) empirical explanatory success of theories heading in this direction, and on the basis of considerations of theoretical elegance, that there aren't any. But if there are, they can be stated either in derivational or representational terms. Note in particular that a constraint on a single representation can always be phrased as a bi- or tri-representational constraint with no restriction on the input(s), or with placing parts of the condition on the input as in fact happens in the case of merge and move. (Note in this connection also, that the square bracketed level statements above seem unnecessary, as expected from the viewpoint of the single level representational theory.)

Thus the essence of representationality appears to be weak representationality. Strong representationality does not seem to add a property that genuinely distinguishes between derivational and representational approaches. The distinction between weak and strong representationality in fact pertains only to the irrelevant, though otherwise important, issue of whether the elegant theory that assumes only a (hopefully trivial) structural statement and bare output conditions can be maintained. If it is true that the core concept of representationality is weak representationality, then of course, having shown that derivational theories must be weakly representational, the question of whether we should adopt derivational theories of narrow syntax again reduces to whether we should adopt mixed theories in this domain. As we have seen in the previous section, this we should probably not do.

2.2. *Restrictiveness again*

So current (apparently pure) derivational theory is equivalent to a restricted multi-representational theory that has only such conditions on representations that can be stated as conditions that hold on two adjacent levels. As we have seen, it is in fact not clear that this really is a restriction with respect to a multilevel representational theory, since a single-level condition could be equivalent to a bi-level condition where the input may be any structure. The real difference between derivational and representational approaches is different. The representational theory is a single-level theory: all representations/derivations except the "final" representation, LF, are eliminated – so conditions can only hold here. This is clearly one obvious way to constrain the multirepresentational theory: assume the existence of only a single representation, the one corresponding to the final output of the derivational system. Henceforth I refer by representational theory unambiguously to the single-level representational approach. To emphasize the representational properties of derivational theories I shall use the term "multirepresentational."

The derivational approach constrains the multirepresentational theory differently, in a way that does not resolve the problems of the mixed theory. The derivational representational duplication now translates as the duplication between the final representation and the relevant aspects of all representations generated that carry the same information. Sisterhood and projection is duplicated at multiple levels by the effects of merge and chain by those of move.[12] The derivational theory ignores the problems of duplication and lack of restrictiveness, but suggests a different restriction. In this approach constraints like merge and move (which, as we have seen, are effectively equivalent to multilevel representational constraints) are individuated and are crucially required to operate in a sequential manner.

Perhaps there are aspects in which the sequential derivational theory is more restrictive than the unilevel representational theory in an empirically motivated way. As far as I know, this has never been argued and there is little to indicate that this might be the case. On the other hand, there is immediate evidence of this type for the unilevel representational theory. It is more restrictive than existing derivational approaches since it disallows bleeding relations, which do not seem to occur in narrow syntax. In particular the effects of the cycle follow automatically from the representational nature of the theory. But the cycle (unlike an inviolable extension condition that current derivational approaches reject) is just an additional stipulation under the derivational system.

If there really were derivational components in syntax we would expect bleeding relations to occur with some regularity, and if syntax was fully derivational, as is frequently suggested, bleeding relations should be commonplace. Derivational systems are eminently suitable to express the situation where one operation bleeds another rule or constraint. Consider cases where lack of bleeding of some constraint C can be detected as the fact that ungrammatical sentences (ruled out by C on one derivation) do not become grammatical on a different one where the context for C would not arise. Take for example the well-known fact that the wh-island or the subject island constraint cannot be bled by a derivation that involves movement before the relevant configuration is created, as e.g. in (1) and (2):

(1) a. What did you wonder Mary bought (what) when ⇒
    b. *What did you wonder when Mary bought (what) (when)
(2) a. Who was bought [a picture of (who)] ⇒
    b. *Who was [a picture of (who)] bought ([a picture of (who)])

To deal with the descriptive problems, the usual restrictive assumption added to derivational framework has for a long time been the idea of the cycle in various incarnations. The derivations in (1) and (2) do not obey the cycle: cyclic application of all rules and constraints removes this empirical problem together with other similar ones. The solution is less than satisfactory if proposed as an explanation of the lack of bleeding in derivational frameworks. While the cycle may be a simple and attractive construct, nevertheless it is an additional stipulation that (as first observed in a somewhat different framework by Freidin 1978) appears to be unnecessary on the representational view. Until the cycle is independently motivated, the representational theory has the advantage of being more restrictive than the derivational theory in an empirically motivated way. The derivational approach can achieve the same degree of restrictiveness and empirical adequacy only by invoking an additional descriptive stipulation.[13]

Epstein *et al.* (1998) proposed that the cycle is a consequence of an appropriately defined notion of c-command together with a PF ordering requirement. The intuitive idea is that a relation based on c-command must be defined between all terminals of the tree – to make possible the exhaustive ordering of the terminals at PF by Kayne's (1994) Linear Correspondence Axiom (LCA) – and c-command is defined in terms of merge (as holding in a particular way between the merged categories, see section 3.1 below). In a countercyclic operation applying to A, A will not therefore have this c-command-based relation established with higher nodes in the tree. Such operations will thus be impossible.

As noted in Brody (1997a), the account based on PF ordering does not rule out, however, all violations of the cycle. Since traces are invisible at PF and therefore do not need to be ordered, countercyclic movement or merger of A followed by cyclic raising of A is still incorrectly allowed. The approach allows also lowering rules if followed by cyclic raising – highlighting another aspect in which the derivational theory is less restrictive than the representational.

In the representational theory chains are neutral with respect to lowering, raising, and round trip (lowering followed by raising into the same position) derivations. These distinctions by now rather clearly seem empirically unmotivated. Although they could be stipulatively grafted onto a representational theory, the basic concepts of this approach, unlike that of the derivational theory, do not naturally provide for these unnecessary distinctions.

The reliance of Epstein *et al*.s' explanation of the cycle on the LCA is also questionable. The status of the LCA as an external stipulation on an otherwise overgenerating derivational system raises the same issues as the cycle. Surely we should prefer a theory in which the basic building blocks of hierarchical relations simply did not permit the types of structures that in standard frameworks we need the LCA to rule out? Brody (1997b, 2000a) presents a theory with this property, and recently Kayne also discussed the problematic nature of the externally stipulated LCA and argued for a partly similar approach (Kayne 2000).

In addition to these considerations there is an even more crucial problem with deriving the cycle from (an appropriately constructed) c-command: the notion of c-command has a complexity presented by its asymmetrical nature, so it is probably even more problematic than the cycle that it is called for to explain. See Brody (1997b, 2000a) and below, especially note 18.

3. C-command

3.1. Derivational definition

Epstein pointed out in an influential paper (1995) – see also Epstein *et al.* (1998) – that in the cyclic derivational framework of the minimalist approach, c-command can be defined as in (3):[14]

(3) x c-commands all and only the terms of a category y with which x was paired by merge or by move in the course of the derivation

He compared (3) with Reinhart's representational definition, which I restate in (4):

(4) x c-commands y iff
   a. the first branching node dominating x dominates y; and
   b. x does not dominate y; and
   c. x does not equal y.

Epstein claimed that the derivational definition in (3) answers certain questions concerning properties of the relation that are "unanswerable given the representational definition of c-command" (p. 185). Before looking at this claim, notice that (4) can be made more easily comparable to (3) if it is restated as (5) in a form parallel to (3):[15]

(5) x c-commands all and only the terms of its sister

He suggests that (3) explains that (a) x appears to c-command whatever the *first* (and not fifth, nth etc.) branching node dominating x dominates, since "this is the projected node created by pairing of x and y ... " Furthermore x does not c-command (b) the first branching node dominating x, (c) nodes dominated by x and (d) x itself – in each case the reason being that x was not paired with the category in question by merge or move during the derivation.

But the derivational definition in (3) appears to give us neither more nor less insight into why these properties characterize c-command than the representational definition in (5). We can say without any loss (or gain) in understanding that x appears to c-command whatever the *first* (and not fifth, nth etc.) branching node dominating x dominates, since "this is the node that dominates (all and only) the terms of x and those of its sister y." Similarly instead of saying that x does not c-command itself, the nodes dominating it and the nodes it dominates because x was not paired with these, we can say without any apparent loss of insight that x does not c-command these because these are not its sisters (since all and only sisters are paired).

The insight these alternative definitions give is limited. In the case of the representational version we might ask why sisterhood is relevant. Additionally we

193

don't know why x c-commands the terms of its sister rather than, conversely x's terms c-command x's sister. Or why does not x only c-command its sister or why all x's terms don't c-command all the terms of x's sister. The same questions arise for the derivational statement: here we may ask why derivational pairing is relevant – notice that pairing is not identical to c-command but only enters its definition. The other questions just asked in connection with the representational version also arise here: why a paired category c-commands the terms of its pair rather than conversely, or symmetrically (i.e. why x does not only c-command its pair or why terms of x do not c-command terms of x's pair).

It is important to see that if the derivational account of c-command is to be taken as evidence in a strict sense for a derivational view, then the question of why derivational pairing is relevant to c-command cannot be answered by saying that derivational pairing is the only mechanism that establishes (purely) syntactic relations. The existence of derivations cannot be presupposed in an argument that wishes to establish precisely that. So this way of answering would beg the question: does the pairing relation have to be derivational?

Epstein suggests also that the fact that c-command makes reference to branching can be explained in a framework where "Structure Building (Merge and Move) consists of Pairing, hence it invariably generates binary *branching*." Again, this point is in fact neutral with respect to the issue of whether syntax should be constructed as a representational or derivational system. The assumption that pairing by merge and move is always binary is an additional assumption – there is nothing in the notion of concatenation that would force this operation to always be binary. The syntactic concatenation could in principle operate on any number of elements. This would allow also the unary operation alongside the binary, ternary etc. options. But just as the concatenation operation can be restricted to be binary, correspondingly, the branching of trees can be restricted to the binary option, ensuring the same result in representational terms: the elimination of nonbranching nodes (along with the elimination of other n-ary branching for n not = 2).

Additionally, Epstein argues that the representational definition of c-command is inconsistent with the independently motivated hypothesis of the invisibility of intermediate projections.[16] He considers the example of the category that is the sister to a VP-internal VP-spec subject – I will refer to this as V'. If V' is invisible for the computation of c-command relations then the elements contained in it (the verb and its complement) will c-command the subject and also the categories the subject contains. This is undesirable. On the other hand, Epstein suggests that the situation is different if c-command relations are determined derivationally by (3). Then even under the assumption that the intermediate projection V' can ultimately neither c-command nor be c-commanded (i.e. if its c-command relations established by (3) are eventually eliminated), the subject will still asymmetrically c-command the verb and its complement as required by Kayne's LCA. Notice that if V' is fully visible to c-command relations then the subject and V' will symmetrically c-command each other, creating problems for the antisymmetry hypothesis.

Given the assumption of antisymmetry, it seems necessary to assume that V' or more generally intermediate projections (or lower adjunction segments) are visible for the computation of c-command relations, but cannot themselves c-command or be commanded. There is nothing, however, in this state of affairs that would be "incompatible" with a representational view.

Consider instead the weaker claim that this behavior of intermediate projections can be naturally attributed to the assumption that at the point in the derivation where a category becomes an intermediate projection (i.e. once it projects further), its c-command relations become invisible (it neither c-commands nor can it be c-commanded) but nevertheless during the earlier stage of the derivation it has already participated in determining c-command by other nodes (it counts for the calculation of c-command by these).

The problem with this line of argument is that the interpretation of "becoming invisible" is not antecedently given, it is not any more natural to understand invisibility as entailing only the loss of ability to c-command and be c-commanded than to understand it as the loss of any c-command related role (including the role in the calculation of c-command relations between other nodes). Thus again the advantage of the derivational approach is only apparent. The statement that intermediate nodes participate in the calculation of c-command relations by other nodes but they do not participate in c-command relations themselves is not improved upon by saying that this latter property arises at a point in a derivation where the nodes become intermediate nodes/project further.[17]

3.2. Derivational explanation?

The various definitions of c-command — as Epstein notes in connection with his cyclic derivational version — do not explain why c-command exists, they just state its properties. The question remains why certain — or perhaps all — syntactic relations are restricted by c-command. Why cannot categories establish the relation with any other category in the tree? And if the set categories with which a given element can establish a (relevant) relation is to be restricted, why is it restricted precisely in the way the definition of c-command states, rather than in one of the infinitely many other imaginable ways?

Epstein offered an explanation within the cyclic derivational framework he adopted. This is based on two assumptions, which he refers to as (a) the first law/the unconnected tree law and (b) the law of pre-existence. The unconnected tree law states that a syntactic relation can only hold between elements that are members of the same tree and excludes relations between elements of unconnected trees. "Derivationally construed," as in (6), it disallows relations between elements that at any point in the derivation were members of different unconnected subtrees.

(6) [Epstein's (27)] T_1 can enter into c-command (perhaps more generally, *syntactic*) relation with T_2 only if there exists *no derivational point* at which:
  (i) T_1 is a term of K_1 (not $= T_1$) and
  (ii) T_2 is a term of K_2 (not $= T_2$) and
  (iii) there is no K_3 such that K_1 and K_2 are terms of K_3.

Given the cycle, the condition in (6) prevents sideways c-command between two elements x and y. In all such configurations cyclicity allows only derivations in which two unconnected subtrees have been formed at some stage that properly contain x and y respectively.[18]

Notice that "derivationally construed" actually adds another assumption to the unconnected tree law, namely that lack of (c-command) relation at any derivational level freezes and cannot be overridden later:

(7) If there was no (c-command) relation at any given point in the derivation between terms x, y (both already merged into some subtree) there cannot be a relation later.

Statement (7) still allows x to have a relation to (c-command) y where y c-commands x, since in such a configuration no unconnected subtrees that contain both x and y have been formed.[19] Epstein excludes this configuration by his principle of derivational "pre-existence" (8), which disallows x c-commanding y on the grounds that y was not present when x was introduced.

(8) x cannot bear a relation to y when y is nonexistent.

Given the assumption that the lack of a relation at a derivational point cannot be remedied at a later stage, i.e. (7), (8) entails the exclusion of what we might call upward or reverse c-command.

On closer examination, the condition in (6) does not actually explain, however, the impossibility of sideways relations. The intuitive content of the condition is that two categories unconnected at any point in the derivation cannot enter into a (c-command) relation. But in fact all merged/moved categories were unconnected before merger, all can still c-command the appropriate nodes. In order to allow categories to c-command at all, it is necessary to add the stipulation in (6i,ii) that "K not = T," i.e. that the top node of an unconnected tree does not count as an unconnected element. But this means that "K not = T" in fact just encodes the difference between c-command and lack of it. In other words, it encodes the difference between the c-command domain of x being the local dominating node of x (K = T) and a nonlocal dominating node of x (K not = T) not constituting such a domain. So instead of an explanation we have only another way of stating the c-command configuration.

Epstein comments on the "K not = T" restriction by noting about the top nodes (to be related by merge/move) of the unconnected trees, i.e. about K_1 and K_2, that "each equals a root node, neither has undergone Merge or Move, hence each is (like a lexical entry) not 'yet' a participant in syntactic relations."[20,21] In other words, the two instances of the "K not = T" stipulation in (6i) and (6ii) can be exchanged for an additional fourth subclause as in (6'):[22]

(6') T_1 can enter into c-command (perhaps more generally, *syntactic*) relation with T_2 only if there exists *no derivational point* at which:
  (i) T_1 is a term of K_1 and
  (ii) T_2 is a term of K_2 and
  (iii) there is no K_3 such that K_1 and K_2 are terms of K_3 and
  (iv) merge/move has already applied to T_1 and T_2.

The intuition (6′) appears to express is that two terms that are integrated into some subtree by merge/move cannot form a relation if at any point in the derivation *after they have been so integrated* they are unconnected, i.e. they are members of distinct subtrees. With the addition of (6′iv), (6′) states that if applying merge/move to two elements x, y does not result in a subtree of which both are terms, then x does not c-command y, that is, either x or y must have been merged with some tree that included the other. (Invert the conditional: if x c-commands y then merge/move applying to x and y must have resulted in a subtree that includes both.)

The explanation of the definition in (3) involves then breaking it up into two parts: x c-commands y if neither of the following two situations obtains: (a) there is no derivational point at which x, y have been integrated into unconnected structures and (b) there is no derivational point at which x is present/integrated but y is not. Clearly, we can bring the two parts of the account (6′) and (8) together again, since in both cases what is crucial is that there is a derivational point at which a (sub)tree exists into which x is integrated but y is not. But whether or not we make this improvement, the account provides no evidence for derivations, since it can again be easily restated in representational terms.

Instead of referring to a derivational point at which there is a (sub)tree into which x is integrated but y is not, we can say that x cannot c-command y if in the single syntactic representation there is a subtree which properly contains (i.e. contains but is not equal to) x but not y. Instead of rationalizing that all derivational stages must be checked for x–y connection and, where no c-command holds, there was one at which x was in a (sub)tree that did not contain y, we can presume that all subtrees in the representation must be checked for x–y connection and we have no c-command where we find one in which they are unconnected. (Note also that the representational version is in fact preferable, if the bottom-to-top derivation and the cycle have no independent motivation (see Brody 1997a and the text above), since the derivational account needs to assume these. Furthermore, the easy translatability of the account into noncyclic representational terms provides some additional evidence against these constructs.) But until we have an explanation of why a relation cannot be established at a later derivational stage that connects the relevant subtrees that were unconnected earlier (or, in representational terms, why the connection must hold in all subtrees), it will remain at the very least debatable for both the representational and the derivational versions to what extent the account explains and not just rephrases Reinhart's definition.

In contrast to the clear exposition of the nonexplanatory nature of the definition in (3) in Epstein's paper, this definition is itself sometimes taken to provide a sufficient explanation of c-command. Thus, for example, Groat (1995) states that while c-command is arbitrary as a representational definition, "it is explainable as a property of the derivation." Take a configuration like (9), where Z c-commands A, B, C, but A, B do not c-command Z:

(9)   Z+[$_C$ A B]

According to Groat this "follows straightforwardly if the relations formed by [merge] are in fact properties of the operation. Z is merged, hence Z is in relation with [$_C$ A B]. A B were not merged with Z, hence they are not in relation with Z."

But again, we need to decide if merge/move applies to trees or to categories. If the former, then in (9) Z merges with C, hence Z does not c-command A and B. If the latter, then say [$_Z$ D E] merges with [$_C$ A B], and D and E are incorrectly predicted to c-command A and B. In neither case do we get the desired result. We can, of course, stipulate c-command again, by saying, for example, that it is always a category that merges with a tree.

3.3. Domination

The core of the c-command problem is the arbitrary asymmetric conjunction in its definition: x c-commands y iff the following two conditions of somewhat different nature obtain: (a) there is a z that immediately dominates x, and (b) z dominates y. It is crucial, but unexplained, that the two subclauses make use of different notions of domination. None of the attempted explanations, some of which I reviewed in the previous section, are able to explain this asymmetry.[23] Consider a different approach (Brody 1997b, 1999a). Instead of trying to explain the strange properties of c-command, let us assume that no such strange properties exist because, despite appearances, no notion of c-command is part of syntax or more generally of the grammar. Cases where c-command appears to be useful are cases of accidental interplay between two (in principle unrelated) notions, one of which is domination.

How about the other notion? In standard frameworks this must sometimes be the specifier–head relation and sometimes the head–complement relation. I shall only consider here the specifier–head relation because in the ES representation provided by mirror theory (Brody 1997b, 1999b, 2000a) the head–complement relation reduces to domination. (In mirror theory heads and the associated "projected" phrases are not distinguished in the syntactic representation, hence c-command by a head H reduces to domination by H.)

Consider a typical condition that refers to c-command like, for example, principle C of the binding theory. Suppose that spec–head agreement has the effect of the head inheriting/sharing the referential/thematic features of its specifier. Then instead of requiring that an R-expression not be c-commanded by a coreferential category we can prohibit the configuration where the R-expression is dominated by an Agr node carrying the same reference.

Similarly, the requirement that each chain member c-command the next can be straightforwardly restated in terms of domination. Again I ignore head chains here, since in mirror theory their members will be in a strict domination relation with each other. Consider chains that are constructed on potentially larger structures (phrasal chains in standard terms). Assume that the members of these chains always occupy spec positions. Let us think of the heads associated via spec–head relations with the spec positions occupied by the chain members as themselves constituting a chain, call it r(estricted)-chain. (Note that an r-chain is a chain whose members are heads, but it has nothing to do with the head chains expressing the head–chain/movement relation. In mirror theory head chains in this latter sense reduce to morphology and do not exist narrow syntax internally.) It is the domination relation that must hold then between members of r-chains. Additionally and independently we require that r-chain members must have identical or nondistinct specifiers. This is natural since the heads participating in the chain are by virtue of that fact at least in some respects identical, so they will naturally require identical, or at least nondistinct (see Brody 1997b, 1998b), specs.[24]

4. Summary

The representational framework seems more restricted than the derivational one in that there are many derivations for a single representation, but not conversely. I argued on the empirical grounds of bleeding relations that some of the derivations need to be eliminated to reach descriptive adequacy. Additional asumptions are necessary in the derivational framework, which are not entailed by the hypothesis that syntax is derivational. As we have seen, the corresponding problems do not arise in the representational framework where the correct consequences follow directly from the representational nature of the system. Additionally I provided arguments against mixed derivational–representational theories of the kind where derivations and representations essentially duplicate each other's work. I showed that no observationally adequate pure derivational theory can exist, that on closer examination derivational theories are mixed theories with derivational–representational duplications, hence arguments against mixed theories hold also against apparently pure derivational theories.

In the second part of the chapter I argued that the derivational explanation of the asymmetry in c-command is unsuccessful, hence no argument for a derivational approach can be based on it. I suggested that the explanation may be so difficult to find because this complex notion is epiphenomenal only and does not exist within the grammar. I put forward an alternative approach, developed in more detail elsewhere,[25] according to which syntactic principles thought to refer to c-command refer to simple domination instead. Other independently necessary principles of spec–head agreement ensure that reference to domination, instead of c-command, is sufficient.

Note finally that derivational explanations tend to assume that merge is a conceptually necessary part of the competence theory of syntax, and argue that given its inevitability, it should be taken as a basic concept that makes various other assumptions unnecessary. All that seems really unavoidable, however, is that consequence of merge, that lexical items must be related in some way, so that they form a (connected) syntactic representation. Other properties of merge, like its derivational (sequential) nature, the fact that it relates sisters directly, and also its projection and labeling properties, seem to be stipulative and arbitrary. Although many linguists are used to the notion of merge as an unanalyzed primitive, at least sequentiality, projection and labeling are curious additions to some basic relation R between lexical items, and together they appear to form a strange and arbitrary package. Furthermore these properties of R seem to be unnecessary and eliminable. They are in fact eliminated in mirror theory, the approach to LF hierarchical structure that ES subsumes.

Acknowledgments

I am grateful to Noam Chomsky for a series of detailed and helpful e-mail exchanges relating to some of the points discussed. I'd like to thank also Klaus Abels, David Pesetsky, Sam Epstein, Daniel Seely, and Michal Starke for comments that I hope resulted in clarifications. As usual, no agreement on anything or transfer of responsibility is implied. Earlier prepublication versions of this manuscript appeared in University College London Working Papers (UCLWP), 12 and in Israel Association of Theoretical Linguistics (IATL), 8 (Tel Aviv University).

References

Abels, Klaus. 2000. "Move?" MS, University of Connecticut.
Brody, Michael. 1995. *Lexico-Logical Form: A Radically Minimalist Theory*. Cambridge, MA: MIT Press.
Brody, Michael. 1997a. "Perfect chains." In Liliane Haegeman (ed.), *Elements of Grammar*. Dordrecht: Kluwer, pp. 139–67.
Brody, Michael. 1997b. "Mirror theory." MS, University College London. (Still earlier short version in *UCL Working Papers in Linguistics*, 9, University College London.)
Brody, Michael. 1998a. "Projection and phrase structure." *Linguistic Inquiry* 29, 367–98.
Brody, Michael. 1998b. "The minimalist program and a perfect syntax." *Mind and Language* 13, 205–14.
Brody, Michael. 1999a. "Chains in perfect syntax." Paper presented at the GLOW workshop on "Technical aspects of movement," Potsdam, April 1999.
Brody, Michael. 1999b. "Word order, restructuring and mirror theory." In Peter Svenonious (ed.), *Proceedings of the Tromso VO-OV Workshop*. 27–43. Amsterdam: John Benjamins.
Brody, Michael. 2000a. "Mirror theory: syntactic representation in perfect syntax." *Linguistic Inquiry* 31.1.
Brody, Michael. 2000b. "Relating syntactic elements." *Syntax* 2, 210–26.
Brody, Michael. 2000c. One more time to appear in *Syntax* 4, 126–38.
Brody, Michael and Anna, Szabolcsi. 2000. "Overt scope: a case study in Hungarian." MS, New York University and University College London to appear in *Linguistic Inquiry*.
Chomsky, Noam. 1995. *The Minimalist Program*. Cambridge, MA: MIT Press.
Chomsky, Noam. 1999. "Derivation by phase." MS, Cambridge, MA: MIT Press.
Chomsky, Noam. 2000. "Minimalist inquiries: The framework." In Roger Martin *et al.*, eds, *Step-by-step: Essays on Minimalist Syntax in Honor of Howard Lasnik*. Cambridge, MA: MIT Press.
Epstein, Samuel. 1995. "Un-principled syntax and the derivation of syntactic relations." MS, Harvard University. Published version in *Working Minimalism*. 1999. Cambridge, MA: MIT Press.
Epstein, Samuel, *et al.* 1998. *A Derivational Approach to Syntactic Relations*. Oxford: OUP.
Fiengo, Robert and Robert, May. 1994. *Indices and Identity*. Cambridge, MA: MIT Press.
Fox, Daniel. 1999. "Reconstruction, binding theory and the interpretation of chains." *Linguistic Inquiry* 30, 157–96.

Freidin, Robert. 1978. "Cyclicity and the theory of grammar." *Linguistic Inquiry* 9, 519–49.
Groat, Eric. 1995. GLOW abstract.
Heycock, Caroline. 1995. "Asymmetries in reconstruction." *Linguistic Inquiry* 26, 547–70.
Hornstein, Norbert. 1999. "Movement and chains." *Syntax* 1, 99–127.
Hornstein, Norbert. 2000. "On A-chains: A reply to Brody." *Syntax* 3, 129–43.
Kayne, Richard. 1994. *Antisymmetry of Syntax*. Cambridge, MA: MIT Press.
Kayne, Richard. 2000. "Recent thoughts on antisymmetry." Paper presented at the Cortona Workshop on Antisymmetry, May 2000.
Kuno, Susumo. 1998. "Binding theory in the minimalist program." MS, Harvard University.
Lechner, Winfried. 2000. Class handouts, Blago Summer School, July–August 2000.
Nunes, Jairo. 2000. "Sideward movement." MS, University of Maryland.
Pesetsky, David and Esther Torrego. 2000. "T-to-C movement: Causes and consequences." In M. Kenstowicz, ed., *Ken Hale: A Life in Language*. Cambridge, MA: MIT Press.
Reuland, Eric. 1997. "Primitives of binding." Utrecht Institute of Linguistics, working paper.
Richards, Norwin. 1997. "What moves where in which language." Doctoral dissertation. Cambridge MA: MIT.
Safir, Ken. 1998. "Vehicle change and reconstruction in A'-chains." MS, Rutgers University, NJ.
Starke, Michal. 2000. GLOW abstract.

ASPECTS OF MIRROR THEORY

11

MIRROR THEORY

Syntactic representation in perfect syntax

In the better-developed sciences it is the departures from symmetry rather than the symmetries that are typically taken to be in need of explanation. Mirror theory is an attempt to look at some of the central properties of syntactic representations in this spirit.

The core hypothesis of this theory is that in syntactic representations complementation expresses morphological structure: X is the complement of Y only if Y-X form a morphological unit – a word. A second central assumption is the elimination of phrasal projection: a head X in a syntactic tree should be taken to ambiguously represent both the zero-level head(s) and its (their) associated phrasal node(s).

1. Introduction

It has been known since Mark Baker's work in the 1980s that there is a pervasive symmetry between aspects of morphological and syntactic structures. Baker and others attempted to explain this symmetry in terms of conspiracies of other syntactic principles. I shall argue that these explanations are not successful. But even on general grounds, it seems to me that a different approach is needed. In the better-developed sciences it is the departures from symmetry rather than the symmetries that are typically taken to be in need of explanation. The approach to be presented here, mirror theory, is an attempt to look at some of the central properties of syntactic representations in this spirit.[1]

The core hypothesis of this theory is that in syntactic representations complementation expresses morphological structure: X is the complement of Y only if Y-X form a morphological unit – a word. Call this the mirror hypothesis, or just Mirror for short.

A second central assumption is Telescope. As in Brody 1998b I refer to the set of nodes that are usually considered to be the projections of some head X (X^{min}), X's *projection line* (PL). The PL is usually taken to include a set of zero-level and a set of phrasal nodes. Kayne (1994) argued that a head has only a single zero-level projection, and in Brody 1998b I argued that it has only a single phrasal projection. According to Telescope, however, none of these projections exist. A head X in a syntactic tree should be taken to ambiguously represent both the X^{min} and zero-level head and the phrasal node of the PL.

Mirror reduces the basic structure of the sentence in (1), where (V + *v* + I) under V indicates the checking theory assumption that words enter syntax as preassembled units, to (2).

(1)
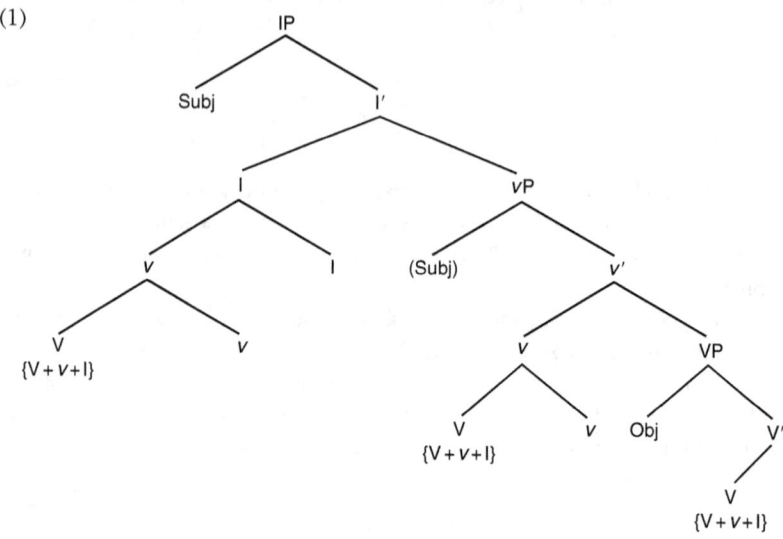

(2)
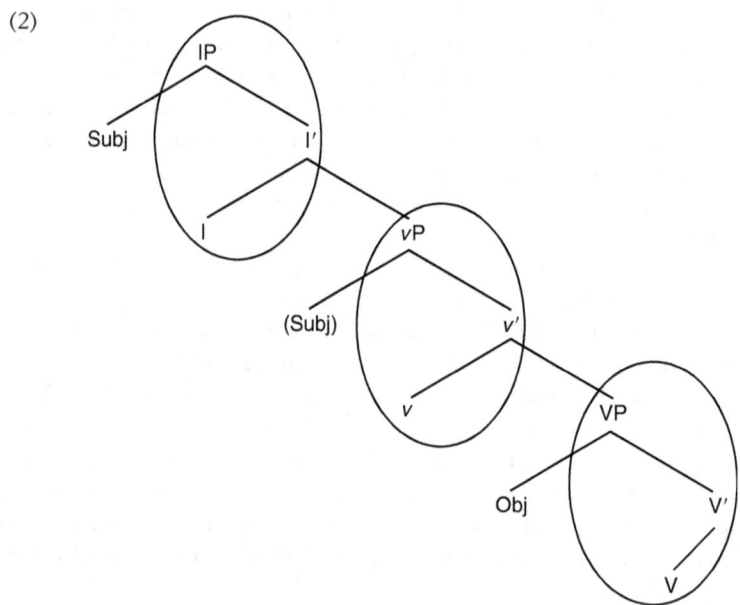

The three circled sets of nodes (series of PLs, each except the first the complement of the next) are taken to express the morphological $V + v + I$ unit that head chains are usually taken to create. Just as in the standard approach, we can assume that this unit is spelled out in the highest "strong" position involved – say, in I in French but in v in English.

Once Mirror is adopted, there appears to be no reason to retain the $(X^{min}/)X^0/XP$ distinction(s). In the context of multiple functional heads and shell structures the main remaining justification for these distinctions is that they make head chains possible. Given Mirror, this is now unnecessary. (2) is then further reduced to (3), where the structure of the word "V-v-I" is syntactically expressed directly by the (inverse order of the boxed) complementation line. The morphological unit (V-v-I), which I shall call a *morphological word* (MW), is then not interrupted by irrelevant phrasal nodes.

(3)

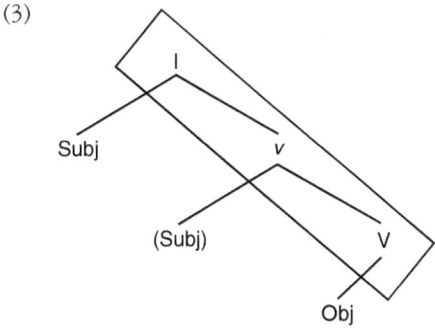

Thus, although Telescope is in principle independent from Mirror, assuming the latter leads directly and naturally to adopting the former. The converse also holds: in the context of Telescope the most immediate way to solve the question of how head chain – type relations are to be expressed is to adopt Mirror.

In mirror theory the only primitive relation between elements in syntax and morphology will be the specifier → head relation, where the specifier (and its constituents) are ordered to precede the head. Mirror licenses the syntactic head-complement relation as a (geometrically mirrored) morphological specifier-head relation. Thus, the head-complement relation is just a reverse order (morphological) specifier-head relation. This gives specifier-head-complement order as well.

MWs consist of elements (heads) in morphological specifier-head relations, and all syntactic head-complement relations correspond to (are identical with) such morphological specifier-head relations. Furthermore, members of MWs (heads) can form specifier-head relations with other MWs. For example, in (3) Subj (which abbreviates a set of MWs) is the specifier of I, and I is a head, a member of the MW V-v-I. Finally, an MW is then spelled out (in the morphological specifier-head order) in the position of the highest strong head (or, lacking a strong head, in the lowest position).

In section 2, I enumerate some problems with the standard explanation of the mirror generalization (often, somewhat misleadingly, referred to as the "mirror principle") based on head movement and the Head Movement Constraint. In section 3, I present mirror theory, in which there is no syntactic distinction between words and phrases and where Mirror provides explanations and is not taken to be in need of one. I also outline the advantages of the mirror theory view. Owing primarily to its restrictiveness (there is only one primitive configurational relation), the theory explains generalizations ranging from locality of head chains to various additional properties of "phrase" structures having to do (in standard terms) with phrasal projections.

In the version of mirror theory to be defended here, complementation is restricted to mirrored MWs. If X and its argument Y do not form an MW, then Y cannot be the complement of X: hence, Y must be a specifier of X or the specifier of some element of (a decomposed) X. In section 4, I discuss some (apparently inferior) alternatives to this version of the theory and some consequences and advantages of this view.

In section 5, I present an additional advantage of mirror theory. This theory makes it possible to eliminate c-command as a term of the grammar by systematically factoring it into its two constituent relations: the specifier-head relation and domination (in fact also an extended specifier-head relation in the proposed system). I present independent evidence for this approach. I also show that mirror theory entails the main effects of Kayne's (1994) Linear Correspondence Axiom: the structures that would violate this principle cannot arise.

In section 6, I summarize the major general characteristics and advantages of mirror theory.

2. The standard explanation of the mirror generalization

2.1. *The mirror generalization, locality, and "no excorporation"*

Cinque (1999) develops a strong empirical case for the claim that there is a correspondence in Universal Grammar between the hierarchy of specifier positions that he argues adverbs occupy and the hierarchy of clausal functional projections. In the process he provides much additional support for the mirror generalization. According to one version of this generalization, where words syntactically move to a host with which they form a unit, the order of morphological affixes mirrors the syntactic order of the relevant heads. For example, the syntactic order of T, permissive suffix, and V mirrors their overt morphological order in Hungarian.

(4) olvas-hat-om
     read-PERMISSIVE-1 SG,PRESENT

(5)

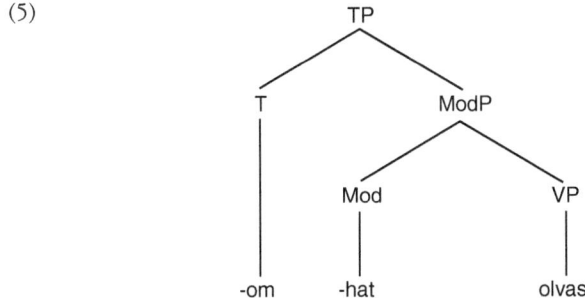

The importance of the mirror generalization is enhanced by work that argues explicitly or suggests strongly that languages and constructions choose elements and segments from a universal and universally ordered series of functional projections (e.g. Starke 1994, Rizzi 1995, Cinque 1999).

The mirror generalization is often attributed to the strict locality of head movement/chains (Baker 1988). This involves two assumptions. One is that in a head chain the top element of the chain (left-) adjoins to a host that is the nearest c-commanding head – essentially the Head Movement Constraint (HMC). The other is that excorporation is prohibited, so head chains must be of the "roll-up" type, where a head X rolls up into Y, the resulting X-Y unit rolls up into Z, and so on. There is no non-roll-up successive-step head chain.[2] For example, there cannot be a three-membered head chain (X^1, X^2, X^3) where X^1 has a host Y, and X^2 has another host Z. X can only "move" further together with its host. The partial structure in (5) cannot be completed with a chain as in (6); it can only be completed with the chain structure in (7). (Phonologically unexpressed traces – that is, chain members that are not the top of the chain – are in square brackets; top members of nontrivial chains are in curly brackets.)

(6)

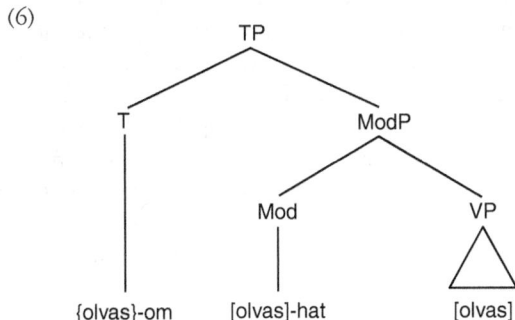

(7)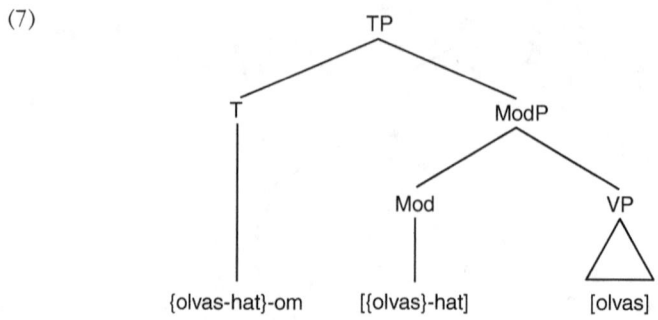

It is easy to see how these assumptions can entail the mirror generalization. If successive heads roll up, the last element and each unit so created subsequently moving to the left of the immediately higher one (i.e. respecting the HMC), the resulting order of the heads will be the exact inverse of the original (syntactic/complement) order.

Various empirical questions have been raised concerning the strict locality requirement of the HMC. For example, it has been argued in connection with Romance and Slavic languages that head chains can sometimes cross more than one head. I will assume here that an analysis in terms of phrasal movement can ultimately be given for such cases.[3] Koopman (1994) proposes that host heads can excorporate. Again, I will tentatively assume that they cannot. The relevant structures might involve phrasal chains (cf. Koopman and Szabolcsi 1998), with a phrase in the host's specifier position rather than a word adjoined to the host, in which case no complex head is created from which the head would excorporate. (Another logical possibility is that there is no excorporation because incorporation into the apparently excorporating host in the relevant cases has never taken place: the highest member of the chain of the apparently incorporating element is in fact in a lower position.)

Another issue has to do with the fact that considerations pertaining to head chains, the HMC, and the mirror generalization do not seem to exhaust the set of ordering requirements of the Spell-Out component. Prefixes in general (e.g. Romance clitics) and certain types of compounding (e.g. French *ouvre-boîte* "can opener") quite clearly do not fall under these principles, at least not in the same way as suffixes like the ones discussed so far do. It would be incorrect to take the mirror generalization to require that Spell-Out systematically mirror the syntactic order in all cases. The appropriate domain of application for the mirror generalization needs to be defined. The characterization above restricted the generalization to applying to just those affixes that form head chains linking their word-internal and their syntactic, complement-internal positions. I will offer a somewhat different characterization in the context of the theory to be developed below.

But even after the directly empirical issues are set aside, questions remain about the HMC-based derivation of the mirror generalization. First of all, in syntax the information that explicates the structure of words is expressed both word-internally (i.e. X^0-internally) and by the phrasal order given by the (inverse) structure of complementation. For example, given a word consisting of a V and an I morpheme, in that order, the associated complementation structure will be constructed from a projection of I, IP, and a lower projection of V, VP. It is not obvious that the account of this duplication, based on the conspiracy of the HMC and the No Excorporation Condition, qualifies as a genuine explanation of this pervasive parallelism. Relating the phrasal and the word-internal orders in this way makes the correlation somewhat accidental and invites the following question: why should it be the case that these two in principle unrelated conditions force grammar to express the same ordering twice, both in terms of the phrasal complementation structure and morphologically, in terms of word structure? If both the HMC and the No Excorporation Condition could convincingly be reduced to a simple theory of locality, then this point would become weaker, but still not all of its force would be taken away. (Inverse) phrasal order and morphological order seem to be just two sides of the same coin. The question still remains, if locality is not used here to ensure the correspondence of some order with itself. In other words, we might expect that a better account would somehow capture the identity of the two orders, and in this way explain their correspondence by in fact making an explanation unnecessary.

2.2. Checking theory

Further problems arise from checking theory. The explanation of the mirror generalization at least in the crude form given above predicts that a complex word composed from a host suffix and a chain-forming guest (with a lower trace) will appear in the syntactic position of the host suffix. Thus, in (3) *olvas* will surface in TP and not in VP. But, as is well known especially since Emonds's (1978) and Pollock's (1989) analysis of the verbal complex in French and English, the phonological position of a word often does not correspond to the syntactic pre-suffix position. For example, the verb in English precedes its inflection(s); hence, on the account of the mirror generalization just outlined, it should form a chain whose top member is the guest of the higher host inflection. Pre-VP adverbs and negation show that the verb in English remains in the VP (cf. e.g. Pollock 1989, Chomsky 1995).

The most popular resolution of this problem is checking theory (Chomsky 1995). According to checking theory, the verb is introduced into the syntactic tree together with inflection, and remains in place in syntax.[4] The V + I unit forms a chain with the guest-of-inflection position(s),[5] and through this chain the V + I unit can check the specifications of the I node(s), ensuring that they are identical to its own. A necessary additional assumption is that a checked duplicate (functional) head deletes at some point in syntax or phonology.

Thus, checking theory introduces yet another duplication of the word structure. The information is now reproduced three times in syntax: in the structure of complements, on the lexical item that is to check functional heads, and on the heads that are to be checked. The duplication involved in checking theory can perhaps be defended by reference to checking in other chain types. For example, in the case of *wh*-movement such duplications (*wh*-features on both the host C node and the *wh*-phrase) were characteristic of the standard analysis long before checking theory and can indeed be argued for on independent grounds.

But checking theory raises at least two apparently serious questions. First, this theory does not in fact resolve the problem that configurations where the phonological position of a head is lower than the syntactic position of its suffix raise for the locality-based explanation of the mirror generalization. This is because given the duplication that this theory introduces, we now need an auxiliary assumption to ensure the mirror generalization effect. Given the checking approach, the structure of (3) will be along the lines of (8). (Traces and deleted functional heads are in square brackets.)

(8)

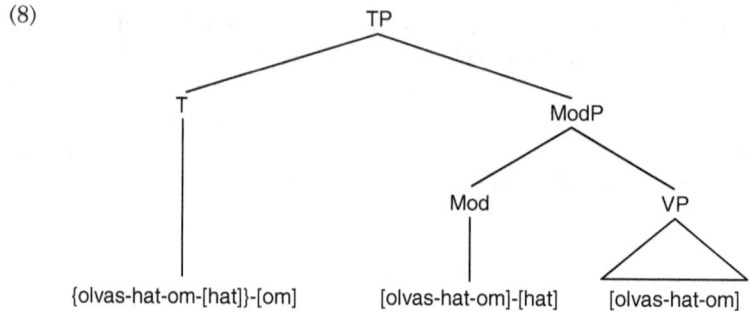

Let us think of this structure in derivational terms for a moment. Given checking theory, to get all and only the correct suffix orders it is necessary to stipulate additionally that checking must proceed in strict order, starting from the innermost suffix on the complex lexical element. The impossible *olvas-om-hat* could also arise from the syntactic structure in (8) if the external suffix could be checked when this unit moves to the lower functional head and then the internal suffix could be checked in the second movement step. Let us put aside the problem that starting from the innermost element is rather unexpected for a quasi-morphological operation (Pollock 1993) and concentrate on the requirement that checking order must respect the order of suffixes. That this requirement is distinct from the question of whether checking starts with the innermost or the outermost suffix is transparent with three or more suffixal elements. But the ordering requirement amounts to a stipulation that is not obviously better than stipulating the mirror generalization itself: the mirror generalization is also just an ordering statement that refers to suffix order.

The point becomes perhaps even more obvious if we return to the representational framework. The ordering statement in the representational approach cannot refer to earlier and later applications. The statement that the innermost suffix must be checked first will have to be translated as saying that the innermost head must be checked by the lowest head among those that host a member of the chain of the lexical head + suffixes unit. The requirement that checking order must respect the order of suffixes becomes the condition that the inverse order of the syntactic heads that host a member of the head + suffixes unit must correspond to the order of suffixes — in other words, the residue of the mirror generalization itself with locality for the chain stated separately.[6]

The second problem with checking theory concerns the fact that it inherits the duplication problem noted in section 2.1. Checking theory ensures (in conspiracy with the X-bar theory of phrasal projection, the HMC, and the No Excorporation Condition) that word structure and (inverse) phrasal complementation structure match. The order of host suffixes must match (the inverse of) the word-internal order of suffixes. If each suffix projects a phrase and each phrase is projected by a suffix, then this order of host suffixes corresponds to the order of phrasal complements.

The problem here is reminiscent of the duplication that phrase structure rules created in theories antedating the principles-and-parameters approach. In these theories the number and type of arguments of a lexical head were specified in the lexicon and also by the appropriate phrase structure rules, which were then required to match. The assumption that phrase structure is projected from lexical properties resolved this duplication by eliminating phrase structure rules. Similarly, we seem to need a theory that makes it possible for the complementation structure and the morphological structure encapsulated in the structure of words not to be generated independently. Notice that this problem is not just that, given the lack of independent evidence for the duplication, it might be better to avoid syntactically representing the ordering information twice, both word-internally and by the structure of complementation. There is also a different (and stronger) point here, namely, that under checking theory a different set of principles will generate each incarnation of the duplicate information.

2.3. Head chains

An additional difficulty for the head-chain-based explanation of the mirror generalization arises from the fact that the guest and the host head must form a unit. In phrase structure grammars this must be a labeled constituent, necessarily labeled by the host. These assumptions introduce a further systematic set of otherwise unmotivated duplications. A fuller structure for (5), for example, will be (9). The checking operation will result in deletion of the square-bracketed functional heads, and neither the V head of VP nor the Mod head of ModP surfaces, since these are traces. We need not worry about duplications introduced by traces and the checking heads, as we may consider these to be motivated on independent grounds. But there is another duplication in the structure that appears more difficult to defend, namely, the repetition of the V + Mod + T series in the set of heads dominating this unit in its chain top position in T. This duplication may appear to be a technical issue of little consequence. However, there is no evidence for this additional duplication, which, given the triplication of this information that checking theory creates, makes the analysis quadruplicate the features in question. Furthermore, again, the problem is not just that (unlike in the case of trace copies) presence of the duplicate (quadruplicate) information in the syntactic representation is not independently motivated. The additional and more serious issue is that three distinct sets of principles generate the same structure. The duplication created by the series of word-internal dominating nodes appears unavoidable in standard approaches, as it is the consequence of certain basic assumptions that are distinct both from those that determine word-internal morphological order and from those that define the complement series/extended projection. These assumptions are that (a) words and chain members are constituent nodes, (b) nodes are labeled by one of their constituents, and (c) elements that are not chain tails cannot label (attributed to the Generalized Projection Principle in Brody 1994, 1995, and also in part in 1998b. Also see Brody 1998b for a discussion of the "target projects" requirement of Chomsky 1995).

(9)

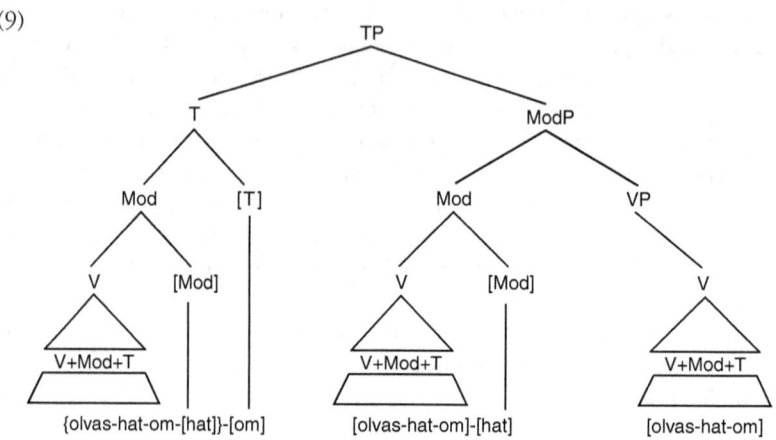

There are additional issues that have to do directly with properties of head chains and therefore are problematic for the explanation of the mirror generalization, which crucially involves such chains.

The first of these is that the mirror generalization will follow from locality only if excorporation is impossible, but it is not clear why in general it should be impossible. Wh- and NP- "movement" XP chains can be successive in a non-roll-up fashion (see note 5 regarding the notion of roll-up). Why should head movement be different? Although various technical and partial answers exist,[7] we seem to have no clear understanding of the reasons for this prohibition that needs to hold for all head chains if the mirror generalization is to be attributed to locality, but appears to hold *only* for head chains.

The second problem here is the one we encountered in a different connection in section 2.2: assuming that c-command must hold between chain members, head chains necessitate the introduction of a more complicated and more stipulative definition of c-command. In particular, it is necessary to allow for c-command "out of" certain types of constituents, namely, the constituent created by the host and the top of the chain of the guest head. Kayne (1994) defines c-command in such a way that c-command out of adjunction is allowed, but the evidence for this modification that does not involve head chains remains inconclusive (see Brody 1997b). (It is perhaps suggestive also that none of the theories, reviewed in Brody 1997b, that attempt to reduce c-command to more basic notions appear to be able to allow for c-command out of adjunction.)

The third problem concerns the somewhat idiosyncratic nature of locality involved in head movement. A- and Ā-chains cannot cross A- and Ā-positions that may be occupied by a potential antecedent – Rizzi's (1990) Relativized Minimality. But head chains typically cross a head: namely, the host of the chain top. There are various ways to make XP and X^0 chains more similar here. Rizzi, for example, appears to assume that the host does not count as an intervener for the chain of the guest because it c-commands the guest: a category is a potential intervener for a chain link only if it c-commands the lower chain member but not the higher. It is interesting to observe that the solution is incompatible with the adjunction structure of words and Kayne's (1994) definition of c-command: it is crucial in Kayne's theory that neither the lower nor the higher segment of an adjunction host c-command the adjoined element.

Other approaches are imaginable that would make it possible to ignore certain head positions for Relativized Minimality. For example, one could try to define interveners as XP- or X^0-internal specifiers, where an X^0-internal specifier would be a head that did not project. But I shall instead take the facts at face value, as another difference between head chains and XP chains.[8]

3. Mirror theory

3.1. Telescope

I shall take the problems listed in the previous section to motivate the search for an alternative view of the mirror generalization and of head chains. I shall now present such a theory, which expresses the "head chain" relation differently. This theory takes the mirror generalization to be a more basic generalization than the HMC and derives from it certain properties having to do with excorporation, c-command, and locality, currently attributed to head chains and constraints on them.

Let us approach this framework by looking first at the distinction between words and phrases in the theory of phrase structure proposed in Brody (1998b). Phrases in this theory were created from lexical items by the rule Project, which forms PLs. Some elements on the PL are phrases, other (lower) elements are words (X^0s), and the lowest element is the lexical item (X^{min}).

I argued that a PL should contain only one phrasal node, an assumption that led to the postulation of a tripartite shell structure for specifier-head-complement structures. Similarly, I adopted the view (Kayne 1994) that there is only one X^0 node on a PL, eliminating the nonmaximal phrasal and the intermediate (nonhighest among the X^0 projections) X^0 levels. Let us now ask the more radical question: are the remaining distinctions among XP, X^0, and X^{min} really necessary? In other words, do PLs exist? Is the postulation of the PL structure justified?

Focusing first on the distinction between words and phrases, consider the basic structure in (10).

(10)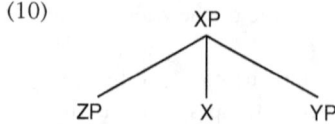

Here X projects a phrase, XP, creating a (partial) PL consisting of an XP immediately dominating X. In the theory developed in Brody (1998b) the principle called Insert licensed the phrase-to-phrase immediate domination relations between XP and ZP on the one hand and XP and YP on the other. As noted in Brody (1997b, 1998b) specifier-head-complement order follows from Kayne's Linear Correspondence Axiom (LCA) only if the relevant structural asymmetries are stated: the specifier asymmetrically c-commands the head, which asymmetrically c-commands material in the complement. One alternative I discussed was to state specifier-head-complement order directly. Let us accordingly assume specifier-head-complement order as a primitive (subject to some simplification later), with a view to eventually deriving the major effects of the LCA from the theory. More precisely, the assumption is that the specifier and its constituents precede the head, whereas the complement and its constituents follow it.[9]

Given this approach to specifier-head-complement order, there seems to be no compelling reason to distinguish XP and X syntactically – in other words, to retain the PL of X in (10). A single node can just as well serve as the syntactic representation of both a phrasal category and its head. Applying the argument also to ZP and YP, (10) reduces to (11).

(11)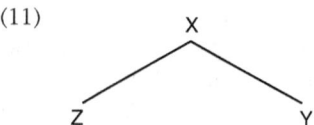

Thus, as far as the word/phrase distinction is concerned, there is no need for the ultimately somewhat strange operation Project or its counterparts (i.e. the set-forming and -labeling effects of Merge and Move) in the minimalist framework. As far as the word/phrase distinction is concerned, there is no need to create copies of a lexical item and establish an immediate domination relation between these copies. I refer to the assumption that a single copy of a lexical item can serve both as a head and as a phrase as Telescope.

Telescope can be viewed as eliminating the apparent conflict between the long tradition of dependency theories (see, e.g. Hudson 1990 and references cited there) and phrase structure theories of syntactic representations.[10] Taking X to stand for a phrase, the lines connecting nodes can stand for immediate dominance relations. Taking X to stand for a head, the lines express dependencies.[11]

Consider next the distinction between X^{min} and X^0. If X^{min}s are lexical elements, then this distinction captures the difference between words that are assembled in syntax and those that are assembled in the lexicon. Two questions arise. First, does the distinction really exist? It does not if either all words are assembled syntactically or all words are assembled in the lexicon. Second, even if the distinction exists, it does not follow that it must be made explicit in syntactic representations. Take V + I as a simplified example. Instead of retaining the two different guest positions indicated in (12), we now adopt the simpler structure (13), where X^0 and X^{min} levels are not distinguished.

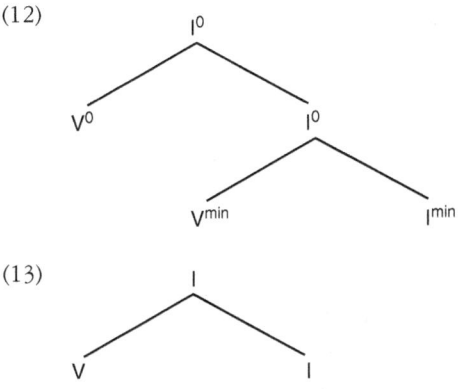

(12)

(13)

3.2. *Mirror*

But even without looking at empirical phenomena that might be taken to motivate the X^0/X^{min} distinction (like the distinction between inflectional morphology and the incorporation of elements that are members of open classes, a matter to which I shall return), an immediate problem arises. Although neither the word/phrase nor the lexical item/word distinction seems necessary at least in the elementary cases, abolishing both appears to make it difficult to provide a structure for complex words. Given a genuinely minimal analysis of the specifier-head-complement structure like (11), there appears to be no place in syntax to express word-internal structure.

But this is not quite true. In fact, the impossibility of expressing word-internal structure in syntax in the traditional X^0-internal format is an advantage, since it eliminates a redundancy. As noted in section 2, this syntactic configuration duplicates morphological information that is duplicated in syntax in another way as well: in the (inverse) order of functional and nonfunctional projections. Given standard phrase structure trees, phrasal nodes intervene between segments of the word in the representation the inverse order of projections provides, making these relations perhaps less suited to express word-internal structure. But the impoverished theory expressed in (11) presents no such problems. For example, the lexical V + v + I structure will be expressed in syntax as I taking a v and v in turn taking a V complement.

At the same time each of these nodes can as usual have its own specifier. In (14), for example, these specifiers are the subject, its trace, and the object.

(14)

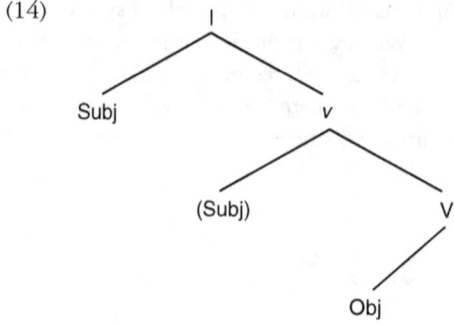

Given representations like (14), the fact that two elements X, Y are part of a single morphological word (MW) is in general still made explicit in the syntactic structure. Although X and Y need not collect under a special type of syntactic node, the X^0, their morphological relation is typically signaled by the fact that one is the complement of the other. (But see also note 12.)

Let us ask next what licenses the syntactic complement structure in (14), where V is the complement of v and v is the complement of I. Here the MW consists of a V that is the specifier of a v, which in turn is the specifier of an I node. The answer of course has to do with the mirror generalization. Suppose that the single primitive relation of the morphological and the syntactic representations is the specifier-head relation. In this relation the specifier precedes the head. The principle I refer to as Mirror ensures that the complement relation is nothing but a topologically mirrored morphological specifier-head relation; that is, it is an ordinary specifier-head relation in inverse order. Head-complement relations in syntax express morphological specifier-head relations.

As exemplified in (14), additional specifier-head relations (here Subj-I, (Subj)-v, and Obj-V) can then be licensed in syntax between elements of MWs that have free specifier valences (are not morphologically specified as being the specifier of anything) and elements of (syntactically mirrored) MWs.

I state Mirror, the principle that inverts the morphological specifier-head order, in (15).

(15) *Mirror*
   The syntactic relation "X complement of Y" is identical to an inverse-order morphological relation "X specifier of Y."

(Universal) specifier-head-complement order does not need to be specifically stipulated: it follows from the primitive specifier-head order (specifier precedes head) and from the (equally axiomatic) Mirror, which reverses this order in syntax in some of those cases where it exists also morphologically.

So, given Mirror, the morphological and therefore the Spell-Out order of two elements X, Y in the syntactic complement relation (hence co-members of an MW) is the inverse of their syntactic order. There is no need to postulate two symmetrical representations, one syntactic and the other morphological. The morphological representation is simply the inverse-order mirrored construal of the syntactic complement line. Notice that in (15) Mirror is not stated as a biconditional; it does not require that all MWs be expressed in the mirrored syntactic form.[12]

Consider next the Spell-Out question regarding mirrored MWs: which element of the MW represents the Spell-Out position? Here I adopt the standard account. Spell-Out takes place in the position of the deepest unit of the mirrored MW if none of its other elements has a "strong feature." If some do, then Spell-Out takes place in the highest strong position. Thus, both "overt" and "covert" head chains correspond to MWs. In (14), for example, take a VP adverbial like *often* to be in the specifier of some head F, between I and *v* (Cinque 1999). V-*v*-F-I is then spelled out in the position of I in French and in the position of *v* in English, preceding and following the adverbial, respectively.

In the standard framework the mirror generalization follows from the HMC and the No Excorporation Condition only with numerous major difficulties, as we have, seen. In the proposed system Mirror trivially entails the effects of the HMC and the No Excorporation Condition. Crossing over an intermediate head by means of a non-local step or excorporation would correspond to a structure where, say, a head H with a suffix S is spelled out in the position of S but where the complement structure is S-X-H, that is, where S is separated from the complement that mirrors (syntactically represents) H by another head, X. This is impossible by hypothesis (i.e. by Mirror): no such complement structure could have been created, since the complement structure must mirror the morphological structure – here H + S.

Now that we have eliminated head chains in favor of MWs, the c-command and locality problems relating to head chains cease to be problems. In the present theory only chains corresponding to XP chains in standard frameworks can exist; these link syntactic specifier positions. Head chains correspond to MWs, which are not chains; hence, they do not need to share properties like c-command and locality with ("phrasal") chains.[13]

The theory has other advantages. Certain questions that arise in the minimalist and earlier phrase structure systems, and that the theory in Brody 1998b makes some headway in solving, simply do not arise – the optimal situation. Since there is no phrasal projection and no PLs – or, in minimalist terms, Merge does not create sets distinct from the elements merged and therefore does not label any such units – the issues of uniqueness and locality of projection do not arise.

The extended structure preservation problem also disappears from syntax: there is no syntactic distinction between XPs and X^0s, hence no possibility that one type will dominate the other in an illegitimate configuration. (For a discussion of uniqueness and locality of phrasal projections and the extended structure preservation condition, see Brody 1998b.)

Recall also that when a category is interpreted as a word, all specifier-head relations, mirrored (i.e. complement) or not, express dependencies. But the categories can also be interpreted as constituents, in which case morphological and syntactic specifier-head links are accordingly understood to express immediate domination or constituency relations. Since head chains reduce to a Spell-Out issue of the mirrored MWs, all chains remaining in mirror theory target syntactic specifier positions and correspond to the phrasal chains of the minimalist framework and its predecessors.

Such chain construction is possible, because categories and relations between them can also be interpreted as expressing constituency. In what follows I shall use terms like *VP* to refer to the V node together with its constituents (i.e. the nodes it dominates). This use of the term *phrase* should of course not be taken to imply the existence of a V projection (i.e. of a phrasal category distinct from the V head).[14]

4. Specifiers and complements

4.1. Mirror and morphological words

Without any auxiliary assumption, the hypothesis that the syntactic head-complement relation corresponds to a morphological specifier-head relation entails that all standard complements that do not form an MW with the element on which they depend must be reanalyzed as syntactic specifiers. This conclusion does not appear to create major problems for arguments of lexical heads, such as direct objects of verbs. These must now be specifiers not only in their chain top but also in their chain tail position. Some theories of aspect (e.g. that proposed in Borer 1993) allow the assignment of semantic roles in Case-checking specifier positions. In the context of the Generalized Projection Principle (Brody 1995) this leads directly to the conclusion that objects must be "base-generated" in their Case-checking specifier positions (i.e. that they do not have a lower (complement) chain tail). (See Arad 1996 for a theory of aspect related to Borer's that embraces this conclusion.) If on the other hand objects have a lower "VP-internal" chain tail, that tail can still be a specifier in a structure that would correspond to a multiple-layer VP (with a decomposed verb interpretation of the Larsonian shell structure; on this matter see Brody 1995, 1998b, and references cited there).

(16)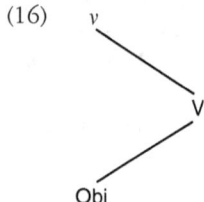

In (16) Obj is the specifier of V and a member (constituent/dependent) of the complement of *v*; hence, it follows *v* and precedes V. This may be an appropriate structure for a sentential complement, for example, if this does not form a Case-checking chain. Further decomposition of the verb may be necessary to accommodate additional complements like datives, obliques, and adverbials, but this is no different from the situation in other binary-branching theories.

What about those complements of functional categories that neither are arguments of lexical heads nor appear to form an MW with the selecting head? Take the English complementizer nodes C and I, ignoring their internal composition for present purposes. It may be possible to say that when the C node is empty, as in *C Mary has left*, the element in I forms an MW (corresponding to a covert head chain) with the C node that is spelled out in I. Mirroring this MW makes I the syntactic complement of C. However, I and C can also be spelled out independently, as in *that Mary should leave*. In order to treat *should* as the syntactic complement of *that* here, it would be necessary in present terms to postulate an MW that includes both. This would correspond to the standard covert head chain linking these two elements. In principle, in the standard framework nothing prevents us from referring to the less restricted notion of covert head chain. But if we allowed such a unit to be spelled out as two nonadjacent, independent, and morphologically noninteracting segments, the notion of MW would seem to be emptied of most of its content.

We are thus led to assume that contrary to the generally held view, I must be a specifier of C, rather than its complement. Similarly, assuming that in the above example the main verb *leave* does not form an MW with the auxiliary *should*, the verb must be analyzed as a specifier rather than the complement of *should*. (Again, for the sake of the example I ignore decomposition of these elements and other potentially intervening heads.) Note that from the point of view of the validity of this conclusion it is immaterial whether the auxiliary is a higher verb or whether it fills a position in the extended projection of *leave* (see, e.g., Cinque 1999 for discussion of these possibilities).

The conclusion that those complements that constitute separate MWs are in fact always specifiers is a very natural one in mirror theory although not strictly speaking forced. But I shall accept it, essentially because it appears to be preferable to the alternatives that would avoid it. Before we explore the consequences of this conclusion further, consider the following alternative approach, which I shall call the *extended-word theory*. The complement relation between two functional heads or a functional and a lexical head has long been assumed to be somehow different in kind from ordinary complement relations (see Grimshaw 1991 for a theory that is explicit on this point). It is widely accepted that such projections and their complements form larger units, which Grimshaw refers to as extended projections and which, as noted above, recent research suggests have a universal structure. One could assume that it is in fact "extended words" corresponding to extended projections, rather than MWs, that complement relations mirror.[15]

4.2. Mirror and extended words

This theory of extended-word mirroring could then have two different versions with respect to the status of MWs. One possibility would be to create MWs along the usual lines by creating chains. Given the antisymmetric nature of the structures, this would regularly involve remnant "movement" chains. Alternatively an extended word could be thought of as an abstract MW, larger than the unit that morphology can submit to phonology/Spell-Out. This larger unit would be related to the pronounceable MW via the same specifier-head relation that relates elements of the smaller pronounceable units – specifier-head being the only configurational relation. In this version the (rightmost) element E_n of an MW L_1 (e.g. *-en* of *eaten*) that is not the specifier of anything internal to L_1 can become the specifier of the (leftmost) element E_1 of another MW L_2 (e.g. *have* of *have* + *s* = *has*), that is, of the element that has no specifier internal to its own MW L_2. If the links that create extended words are taken to be morphological, then the whole of the extended word (*eat-en-have-s*) will be mirrored in syntax (*s-have-en-eat*) since each morphological specifier-head relation corresponds to a syntactic head-complement relation.

Both versions of the extended-word theory seem dubious. If MWs are assembled via syntactic chain construction, then in addition to Mirror, which would then ensure that extended words are mirrored as complement series, the HMC and the No Excorporation Condition need to be reintroduced to constrain the structure of MWs. But as we have seen (recall the discussion following (15)), these conditions are redundant in the context of Mirror in a theory based on the mirroring of MWs.

The second version of the extended-word theory, according to which extended words are abstract morphological units, does not improve matters either. This is because whatever initial plausibility the idea that morphology allows larger units than it can submit to phonology/Spell-Out might have, incorporation phenomena tell us that extended words are no larger than what can phonologically present itself as an MW. N- and V-incorporation involve MWs that can span several extended words (see, e.g., Baker 1988 or Brody 1997b for examples). Hence, on this version of the extended-word theory we would be left without any principled reasons for why extended words do not necessarily form phonologically observable MWs.

This argument against the second version of the extended-word theory might be taken to be weakened by the fact that the present framework in principle provides the usual two major options for the treatment of open-class incorporation structures, which can be assimilated either to syntactic chains (which correspond to XP chains in standard theories) or to MWs (which occupy the place of head chains). If open-class incorporation involves chains, then the incorporated element will be in a syntactic specifier position. If incorporation involves MWs, then a unit consisting of an incorporated element and its host will normally involve two "extended words."

Consider then another variant of the second version of the extended-word theory in which extended words are created nonsyntactically and mirrored as before, and thus inflectional morphology is treated in terms of MWs but open-class incorporation is analyzed differently, as involving syntactic chains and thus syntactic specifier positions. This theory is also unlikely to be correct, however. Recall that head chain-type relations like inflection and incorporation obey a stricter locality requirement than XP chains. (See Brody 1997b, to appear, for additional evidence in the context of mirror theory.) Lacking the successive-step option, an antecedent in the former relation must surface in a position that is strictly local to its trace. This property is shared by inflectional morphology and open-class incorporation, but not by other (XP) chains. If inflection but not open-class incorporation is treated in terms of MWs, their similar strict locality behavior will not be captured. On the other hand, if both phenomena are expressed in terms of MWs, then their strict locality will immediately follow in the present theory from Mirror.[16]

Given the foregoing considerations, I conclude that the mirror theory should hold in its strong form: a category C can be the syntactic complement of another, C', only if C is the morphological specifier of C'; that is, C and C' form an MW. (See note 12 on the question of whether the relation between MWs and complementation can be strengthened further to a biconditional.)

4.3. Mirror and specifiers

The relation between the syntactic specifier and the head is biunique. Hence, if the category C that would standardly be treated as the complement is analyzed as the specifier of C' (where C' is a functional category or a (decomposed) lexical category (segment)), C' cannot have another syntactic specifier. An element that standardly would have been taken as its specifier will now have to occupy the specifier position of some higher (functional or lexical category segment) head. This, perhaps radical, conclusion is corroborated by an increasing amount of independent evidence.

Cinque (1999) argues that there exists an Agr-type "DP-related" head that dominates each functional element (cf. Kayne's (1998a,b) W nodes). There is also evidence (Koizumi 1993, Bobaljik 1995) for an Agr_O position lower than the v head associated with the base position of the subject and similarly for an Agr_{IO} position lower than the θ-position of the object. Thus, there are independent reasons to make the assumption, essentially forced by the restrictive nature of mirror theory, that lexical and functional heads are alike in being at least potentially dominated by an Agr-type (whatever that exactly means) head. This head can host specifiers standardly associated with the functional or lexical head that the Agr-type element immediately dominates.

Note that the fact that a head C' cannot have a second syntactic specifier does not entail that all categories that are standardly treated as specifiers (i.e. sisters of some intermediate projection level) will now necessarily be specifiers of an Agr-type node. All that follows from mirror theory is that if a category C' has standard specifier and complement C" and C, respectively, and under mirror theory C is now the syntactic specifier of C' (in the case where C and C" do not form an MW, so C cannot be the complement of C'), C" cannot also be the specifier of C'. But it may be not only the specifier of the Agr-type head associated with C', but also the specifier of some other higher head. One such case may be instantiated by subjects in VPs if these are indeed in the specifier position of a v head dominating V.

Thus, the standard phrasal structure in (17) will generally correspond to the structure in (18) under mirror theory.

(17)

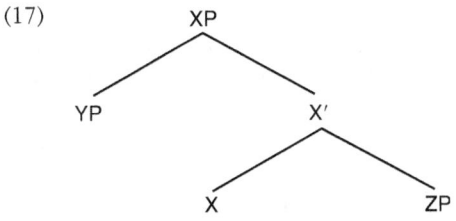

(18)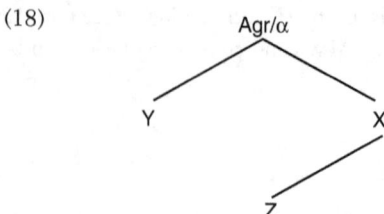

Agr/α and X must form an MW here, which on the assumption that Agr/α is strong will be spelled out in Agr/α, giving specifier-head-complement order.[17] Even though not strictly speaking incorrect, it is somewhat misleading to relate (17) to (18). (18) does indeed express the specifier-head-complement structure that has been expressed standardly as (17), but (18) expresses the claim that the specifier and the complement are specifiers of two related but distinct heads. Thus, it in fact corresponds more closely to a structure that in standard terms would look like (19).

(19)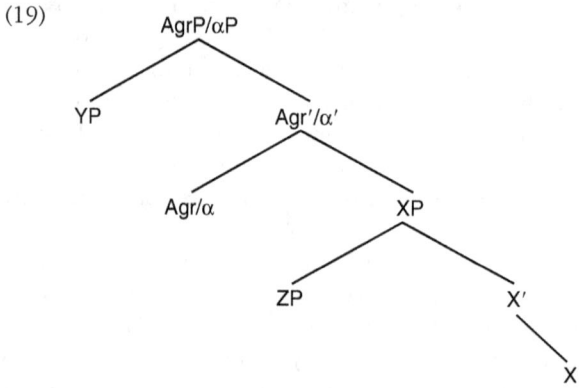

4.4. "Wiggly" extended words

Let us return finally to the concept of extended projections. Recall that these correspond to extended words in the present theory, which eliminates phrasal projection altogether. In mirror theory a category can be a complement only if it forms an MW with the element it is the complement of. Extended words cannot generally be thought of as a series of heads, each the complement of the next. It will remain true, however, that extended words must correspond to a series of heads where each dominates the next (each depends on the previous one), but the dominance/dependency relation can now involve not only a morphological specifier-head relation that corresponds syntactically to a head-complement link but also a syntactic specifier-head relation. Extended words can be "wiggly."

This has an immediate advantage in the analysis of those structures that under Kayne's (1994) antisymmetry hypothesis have to be treated in terms of a "phrasal" roll-up chain structure. For example, Kayne (in derivational terminology) suggests

(20) as one possible structure for sequences of inflectional morphemes in head-final languages. (The other alternative is leftward head raising with complements shifted across the Spell-Out position of the head + suffixes unit, a configuration that in terms of mirror theory is analyzable as an MW; see Brody 1997b for more detail and analyses of related constructions.)

(20)   ... [$_{XP}$[$_{YP}$ ZP Y (ZP)] X (YP)] U (XP)

In (20) the complement of Y, ZP, is shifted to Y's specifier position, and YP, a complement of X, is rolled up as a whole into the specifier position of X. Similarly XP, U's complement, which contains all the elements so far described, turns up in the specifier of U. If Y is a verb and X and U are inflectional suffixes, then the verb will follow its complement, ZP, but it will precede the suffixes, with which it will not form a constituent. Cinque (1999) observes that the fact that in Hindi the sentence-final sequence of verbs carrying the functional suffixes does not form a constituent is expected under Kayne's suggested analysis of this language. This appears to also rule out the alternative of a simple leftward head movement analysis.

Cinque observes further that in Hindi the order of the V + functional suffix series combinations is the mirror image of what he argues is the universal order of these elements, shown in (21). This order, exhibited directly by English and Spanish, for instance, is exemplified in (22a) and (22b) (from Cinque 1999).

(21)   tense > perfect aspect > progressive aspect > voice > V
(22)   a. These books have been being read all year.
       b. Esos libros han estado siendo leídos todo el año.

Compare the Hindi examples in (23) (from Cinque 1999, citing Mahajan 1990).

(23)   a. Kis-ko Raam-ne socaa   ki Siitaa-ne dekhaa thaa?
          who   Raam   thought that Sita   see-ANT be-PAST
          "Who did Raam think that Sita had seen?"
       b. Raam rotii   khgaataa rahtaa thaa.
          Raam bread eat   PROG   be-PAST
          "Raam used to keep on eating bread."

Cinque's point, that the inverse order of the series of main V + functional suffixes follows directly from Kayne's roll-up structure, may be taken as further evidence for the "phrasal" roll-up analysis (i.e. roll-up into syntactic specifier positions of constituents that correspond to heads together with whatever these heads dominate). Similar nonhead roll-up structures have been proposed also for various configurations, such as sentence-final adverbial clauses and VP-final stacked adverbials and PPs in head-initial languages (for more detailed discussion, see, e.g. Kayne 1994, Cinque 1999, Barbiers 1995, Brody 1997b, 2000).

As is widely acknowledged, however, this approach is quite problematic, for three reasons. First, the chain structures it postulates have no independent motivation. In particular, no systematic set of "triggers" for these movements has been found.

In representational terminology: we have no principled account of what licenses the nontail positions of these chains. Second, often there appears to be no genuine independent evidence for the presence of the tail positions of these chains in the relevant structures. Finally, it is not clear how it can be ensured that these roll-up structures never involve successive-step non-roll-up movement, which would destroy the desired predictions (e.g. the inverse order of PROG and PAST in (23b)).

In other words, (at least in some of the relevant cases) it would be preferable to generate the roll-up structures directly, with the complements starting out in specifier positions and eliminating the chains linking specifiers and complements. We can then take whatever selectional relation was taken to license the complement to in fact license the same element in the specifier position. This eliminates not only the "movement trigger" problem, but also the successive-step chain problem and the problem of lack of direct evidence for the chain tail in complement position. In order to represent the roll-up structures without the roll-up chains, it is necessary to reject the assumption that each element of an extended projection must be the complement of the previous one. But this is exactly the proposal I arrived at above on independent grounds in the more restrictive framework of mirror theory: that in the series of elements corresponding to an extended word, where each dominates the next, both morphological specifier-head (i.e. syntactic head-complement) and syntactic specifier-head relations are legitimate. The restrictions of the theory thus again force an apparently empirically justified analysis.[18]

5. C-command and antisymmetry

5.1. C-command

The relation of c-command ceases to be necessary as it has applied to head chains: elements of MWs are in a dependency/domination relation with respect to each other. The remaining conditions that involve c-command can also be restated to refer to the simple dependency/domination relation – the structural "equivalent" of precedence. Suppose that as a consequence of the specifier-head relation, an Agr-type node can carry the referential/thematic features of its specifier. Principle C can then be taken to prohibit an R-expression from having an antecedent that dominates it (or equivalently, on which it depends). If the syntactic specifier of this Agr is taken to pick up the reference of the head, then this specifier in turn cannot corefer with the R-expression.[19]

In mirror theory the structural requirement on chain construction might similarly reduce to the simple notion of dependence/domination. In a *wh*-chain, for example, the Q head associated with the *wh*-phrase can be taken to form a chain with the (*wh*-feature of the) trace/copy *wh*-phrase that it dominates. The antecedent *wh*-phrase will then not be a member of the chain itself, but a constituent (whose highest category is) in a syntactic specifier-head relation with the chain.[20]

The central problem of c-command is the strange asymmetric stipulation in the definition of this relation: X c-commands Y iff the category immediately dominating X dominates, [± immediately], Y. This fact is not explained by any of the approaches that attempt to reduce c-command to simpler notions.[21] If the approach suggested in the previous paragraph proves feasible, then the conclusion will be that the strange asymmetry was an artifact of coalescing two distinct relations to which in fact different constraints refer: the domination/dependency relation and the syntactic specifier-head relation. As indicated, this conclusion is made possible by the mirror-theoretical analysis of head chains as MWs.[22]

Some evidence for factoring the notion of c-command into the domination and specifier-head relations is provided by the properties of the nondistinctness requirement that chain members are subject to. Lower members of a chain may sometimes omit information present in the highest member of an "overt" chain. For example, the "reconstructed" trace/copy position triggers no Principle C violation at least in cases like (24) in contrast with (25). This can be accounted for if – for whatever reason – the R-expression *John* is not present in the lower chain copy (see Lebeaux 1989, Brody 1995, 1997b, 1999, Safir 1998, Kuno 1998 for discussion and somewhat different analyses).

(24)   Which claim that John made do you think he later denied?
(25)   ?*Which claim that John was asleep do you think he later denied?

On the other hand, it has been proposed that "covert" chains involve only a subset of the features of the contentive element (i.e. argument, *wh*-, or other quantificational category) in the tail of the chain (see Brody 1995, Chomsky 1995). Thus, in "covert" chains the lowest element must be the most fully specified one and higher members are feature sets, whereas in "overt" chains the highest member must carry the full specification and lower members are (potentially) less fully specified categories.

We can make sense of this situation in terms of the assumption that the concept of chain refers to the relation between a constituent and one or more sets of features that dominate this constituent. So in a chain it is always the lowest element that is the most fully specified one. This approach instantiates the idea that "covert" chains only have certain features of the contentive element in their nontail positions in a way that is different from the approach in Brody 1995, 1998b (and also from the related one in Chomsky 1995). Cases standardly treated as "overt" chains will involve additional specifier-head relations with the feature sets in the chain. Presumably for reasons of recoverability, the highest, normally phonologically overt, specifier constituent must be more fully specified than either the other lower specifiers of the same chain or the contentive element of the chain itself.[23]

5.2. Antisymmetry

Finally, the antisymmetric property of representations is also ensured by mirror theory. Although this is intuitively clear, Kayne's LCA, which relates (asymmetric) c-command and precedence, cannot be adopted here. Given mirror-theoretical structures, neither the standard definition of c-command, nor the domination relation that I have proposed as an improved alternative, can be straightforwardly mapped to precedence relations between terminals. But mirror theory simply provides no means with which non-antisymmetric structures can be built. Hence, no external condition like the LCA is necessary to ensure the antisymmetry effects. As in the case of the structure of crystals, the properties of the basic building blocks determine the limits of variability of the composed larger structures.

More specifically, (given some additional assumptions; see Brody 1997b, 1998b) the LCA ensures that specifier and complement are on different sides of the head. This follows here directly from Mirror. A stipulation/axiom to the effect that the specifier precedes the head is necessary in both frameworks (see Brody 1997c: sec. 2.3). The LCA entails binary branching; mirror theory does not provide a means to violate this restriction. For each head only one specifier-head and one mirrored morphological specifier-head (i.e. complement) are possible as syntactic relations. The LCA ensures that PLs always branch rightward – in other words, that only the complement can be on the right of the head, and that specifiers and adjuncts must be on the left. Furthermore, it rules out multiple adjunction to the same element. In the present theory adjunction is eliminated (see, e.g., Sportiche 1994, Brody 1994, 1998b, Cinque 1999 for arguments); hence, the issue of multiple adjunction does not arise. Similarly, given Telescope, PLs are also dispensed with; hence, rightward branching reduces to specifier-head-complement order, which, as just noted, mirror theory ensures.

6. Summary

I recapitulate the major general characteristics and advantages of mirror theory.

General characteristics of mirror theory

1   The only primitive relation between elements in syntax and morphology is specifier → head, where the specifier (and its constituents) precede the head.
2   By Mirror (some or all) morphological specifier → head orders can be (geometrically) mirrored in syntax. The head-complement relation is just a reverse order (morphological) specifier-head relation.
3   Members (heads) of MWs can form specifier-head relations with other MWs.
4   An MW is spelled out (by Mirror, in the morphological specifier-head order) in the position of the highest strong head (or, in the absence of a strong head, in the lowest position).

Advantages of mirror theory

1   There is a single primitive configurational relation: specifier-head.
2   Locality and no-excorporation properties of head chain – type relations follow. All head-complement links must match (are identical to) a(n inverse) specifier-head link in the word structure: structures corresponding to excorporation or nonlocal head chains cannot be created.
3   C-command problems of head chains do not arise: MWs involve domination.

4 Antisymmetry effects are guaranteed (there are no means for violating LCA requirements; hence, there is no need for the LCA).
5 There is no categorial projection; hence, uniqueness and locality issues of categorial projection (Chomsky 1995, Brody 1998b) do not arise.
6 There is no word/phrase difference in syntax, hence no extended structure preservation (Chomsky 1995, Brody 1998b) question.
7 There is a single expression of word structure in syntax (in the case of suffixes, the complementation structure). All duplications (listed in section 2) are eliminated.
8 The apparent conflict between dependency and constituent structure frameworks is resolved. (Structures are interpretable as a dependency diagram or as a constituent structure.)
9 The theory forces the independently motivated (e.g. Larson 1988, Cinque 1999) presence of additional heads dominating each head H with a specifier and also a complement with which H does not form an MW. (The complement must be the syntactic specifier of H; hence, the "standard" specifier of H must in fact be the specifier of a higher head.)
10 The theory forces a weaker characterization of extended "projections" (i.e. extended words), where these must correspond to a set of nodes each dominating the next, but not necessarily in the "complement of" relation. Given the evidence from "phrasal" roll-up structures, this is again apparently a correct conclusion – reached on principled grounds.
11 Given the sharing of features between specifier and head, c-command may be unnecessary in general; no principle of grammar may need to make use of this notion. In mirror theory, where heads dominate their complements, the conditions that refer to the domination and specifier-head relations suffice.

Acknowledgments

The essential parts of this material formed part of invited presentations from spring 1997 – at the Universities of Vienna, Tübingen, Budapest, Stuttgart, and London, and at conferences and workshops in Jena, Tromsø, Budapest (Collegium Budapest), Szeged (JATE), Wassenaar (NIAS), and Potsdam (GLOW workshop). I am grateful to the audiences at these presentations. I would particularly like to thank Michal Starke and Peter Svenonius for detailed correspondence and helpful conversations. Thanks also to Collegium Budapest, where Brody 1997b, which contains the prefinal version of this article, was written up during the tenure of my Fellowship.

References

Arad, Maya. 1996. A bi-directional view of the syntax-lexicon interface. Ms., University College London.
Baker, Mark. 1988. *Incorporation: A theory of grammatical function changing*. Chicago: University of Chicago Press.
Barbiers, Sjeff. 1995. Extraposition and the interpretation of X-bar structure. *GLOW Newsletter* 34.

Bobaljik, Jonathan. 1995. Morphosyntax: The syntax of verbal inflection. Doctoral dissertation, MIT, Cambridge, Mass.

Borer, Hagit. 1993. The projection of arguments. In *University of Massachusetts occasional papers in linguistics 17*. GLSA, University of Massachusetts, Amherst.

Bošković, Željko. 1997. *The syntax of nonfinite complementation: An economy approach*. Cambridge, Mass.: MIT Press.

Brody, Michael. 1994. Phrase structure and dependence. In *UCL working papers in linguistics 6*, 1–33. Department of Phonetics and Linguistics, University College London.

Brody, Michael. 1995. *Lexico-Logical Form: A radically minimalist theory*. Cambridge, Mass.: MIT Press.

Brody, Michael. 1997a. Mirror theory. In *UCL working papers in linguistics 9*, 179–223. Department of Phonetics and Linguistics, University College London.

Brody, Michael. 1997b. Mirror theory. Ms., University College London.

Brody, Michael. 1997c. Towards perfect chains. In *Elements of grammar*, ed. Liliane Haegeman, 139–167. Dordrecht: Kluwer.

Brody, Michael. 1998a. The Minimalist Program and a perfect syntax. *Mind and Language* 13:205–214.

Brody, Michael. 1998b. Projection and phrase structure. *Linguistic Inquiry* 29:367–398.

Brody, Michael. 1999. Chains in Perfect Syntax. Paper presented at the GLOW workshop "Technical Aspects of Movement," Potsdam.

Brody, Michael. 2000. Word order, restructuring and mirror theory. In *The Derivation of VO and OV*, ed. Peter Suenonius, pp. 27–43.

Cardinaletti, Anna, and Michal Starke. 1994. The typology of structural deficiency. Ms., University of Venice and University of Geneva/Max Planck Institute, Berlin.

Chomsky, Noam. 1995. *The Minimalist Program*. Cambridge, Mass.: MIT Press.

Cinque, Guglielmo. 1999. *Adverbs and functional heads: A cross-linguistic perspective*. Oxford: Oxford University Press.

Emonds, Joseph. 1978. The verbal complex V'-V in French. *Linguistic Inquiry* 9:151–175.

Epstein, Samuel David. 1995. Un-principled syntax and the derivation of syntactic relations. Ms., Harvard University, Cambridge, Mass.

Epstein, Samuel David, Erich M. Groat, Ruriko Kawashima, and Hisatsugu Kitahara. 1998. *A derivational approach to syntactic relations*. Oxford: Oxford University Press.

Grimshaw, Jane. 1991. Extended projections. Ms., Brandeis University, Waltham, Mass.

Hudson, Richard. 1990. *English word grammar*. Oxford: Blackwell.

Kayne, Richard. 1994. *The antisymmetry of syntax*. Cambridge, Mass.: MIT Press.

Kayne, Richard. 1998a. A note on prepositions and complementizers. WWW document, http://mitpress.mit.edu/celebration.

Kayne, Richard. 1998b. Overt vs. covert movement. *Syntax* 1:128–191.

Koizumi, Masatoshi. 1993. Object agreement phrases and the split VP hypothesis. In *MIT working papers in linguistics 18: Papers on case and agreement I*, 99–148. MITWPL, Department of Linguistics and Philosophy, MIT, Cambridge, Mass.

Koopman, Hilda. 1994. Licensing heads. In *Verb movement*, ed. David Lightfoot and Norbert Hornstein, 261–295. Cambridge: Cambridge University Press.

Koopman, Hilda, and Anna Szabolcsi. 1998. The Hungarian verbal complex: Complex verb formation as XP-movement. Ms., UCLA, Los Angeles, Calif.

Kuno, Susumu. 1998. Binding theory in the Minimalist Program. Ms., Harvard University, Cambridge, Mass.

Larson, Richard. 1988. On the double object construction. *Linguistic Inquiry* 19:335–391.

Lebeaux, David. 1989. Relative clauses, licensing and the nature of the derivation. Ms., University of Maryland, College Park.

Mahajan, Anoop. 1990. The A/A' distinction and movement theory. Doctoral dissertation, MIT, Cambridge, Mass.

Manzini, M. Rita. 1995. From Merge and Move to form dependency. In *UCL working papers in linguistics* 7. Department of Phonetics and Linguistics, University College London.

Neeleman, Ad, and Hans van de Koot. 1999. The configurational matrix. Ms., University College London.

Phillips, Colin. 1996. Order and structure. Doctoral dissertation, MIT, Cambridge, Mass.

Pollock, Jean-Yves. 1989. Verb movement, Universal Grammar, and the structure of IP. *Linguistic Inquiry* 20:365–424.

Pollock, Jean-Yves. 1993. Notes on clause structure. Ms., University of Picardie, Amiens.

Rizzi, Luigi. 1990. *Relativized Minimality*. Cambridge, Mass.: MIT Press.

Rizzi, Luigi. 1995. The fine structure of the left periphery. Ms., University of Geneva.

Roberts, Ian. 1997. Restructuring, head movement, and locality. *Linguistic Inquiry* 28:423–460.

Safir, Ken. 1998. Vehicle change and reconstruction in A'-chains. Ms., Rutgers University, New Brunswick, N.J.

Sportiche, Dominique. 1992. Clitic constructions. Ms., UCLA, Los Angeles, Calif.

Sportiche, Dominique. 1994. Adjuncts and adjunction. Ms., UCLA, Los Angeles, Calif.

Starke, Michal. 1994. On the format for small clauses. Ms., University of Geneva.

Williams, Edwin. 1994. *Thematic structure in syntax*. Cambridge, Mass.: MIT Press.

12

"ROLL-UP" STRUCTURES AND MORPHOLOGICAL WORDS[1]

1. Introduction

This chapter contains two case studies. The first one in section 2 elaborates the analysis of phrasal roll-up structures suggested towards the end of Brody (2000). The solution is applied to the case of sentence final adverbials which are shown to provide further evidence for the analysis and hence indirectly for the strict version of mirror theory that forces it. Section 3 looks at Hungarian prefix chains, and argues that some of these involve syntactic spec-targeting chains and others are better treated in terms of morphological words. Mirror theory, in which morphological words are necessarily local in a much stricter sense than the one in which syntactic chains are, provides a framework where apparently central aspects of the rather complex behavior of these prefixal elements can be understood.

2. Adverbials on the right

Recall the distinction between Kayne (1994) Linear Correspondence Axiom (LCA) and the antisymmetry hypothesis. That phrase structures conform to the requirements of the LCA, the antisymmetry hypothesis, is distinct from the claim that this is due to the LCA, an additional issue. As noted in Brody (1998), the LCA creates some redundancies given the theory of phrase structure outlined there. For example uniqueness of projection does not follow in general from the LCA but this condition predicts the effects of uniqueness for the special case when two heads X and Y are both immediately dominated by a phrase. (There will be no pair (C, C') of constituents then, related by asymmetric c-command, such that C dominates X and C' dominates Y.) Similarly, extended structure preservation, another consequence of mirror theory, follows from the LCA only in part. A phrase P dominated by (adjoined to) a word that has a complement C violates the condition, since categories embedded in the complement would be asymmetrically c-commanded by P but categories in P would also be asymmetrically c-commanded by C.[2] Auxiliary stipulations are necessary however to derive the other half of extended structure preservation, i.e. the fact that words cannot be immediately dominated by a phrase that they did not project.[3]

As we have seen, problems relating to projections, like uniqueness and structure preservation, disappear in the more restricted framework of mirror theory, which dispenses with categorial projection completely. As discussed in Brody 2000, this theory furthermore enforces the antisymmetric effects of the LCA by not providing elements and relations with which a non-antisymmetric structure could be built. The theory thus directly inherits certain problems that Kayne's antisymmetry hypothesis faces. In what follows I would like to look at one particular area, that appears to have caused difficulties for the antisymmetry approach, – namely the position of English sentence final adverbial clauses (cf. Williams 1994, Brody 1994, Manzini 1995, Hornstein 1995). I shall go through a number of arguments that all seem to suggest that contrary to what might be expected from mechanically applying the antisymmetry hypothesis, these adjuncts must be higher than preceeding VP-internal elements. I will argue that earlier suggestions and partial solutions to these problems are not fully adequate. I will provide further evidence that the particular member of this family of analyses that mirror theoretical considerations lead to is in fact the correct solution.

As is well known principle C tests show that adverbials like in (1) are not c-commanded by V-complements:

(1) We sent him$_x$ there in order to please John$_x$'s mother

Faced with such examples one logically possible approach is to deny that principle C tests for c-command. Haider (1993) took such a position arguing that the hypothesis that principle C operates under c-command leads to contradiction. In his example reproduced below as (2) the pronoun *her* must be disjoint from the name *Mary* in the complement clause but not from *Mary* in the extraposed relative.

(2) Someone has told her$_x$ [who Mary$_x$ met] [that Mary*$_x$ will inherit the castle]

Haider argues that no standard phrase structure could ensure lack of c-command of the extraposed clause at the same time as c-command of the more peripheral complement. But in fact there are a number of analyses compatible with the observation in (2) and a c-command dependent principle C. For example the relevant structure could be (3), with a Right Node Raising (RNR) derivation for the complement clause:

(3) Someone has told {her$_x$ (that *Mary$_x$ will ...)} [who Mary$_x$ met] [that Mary will inherit the castle]
(4) *[Which claim that John$_x$ was asleep] do you think he$_x$ denied t(which claim that John$_x$ was asleep)

Since principle C is sensitive to elements in A'-trace positions, as exemplified by the standard wh-movement case in (4), disjointness from the name in the complement clause can be determined in the trace position and the extraposed and complement clause could be stacked higher than and on the right of V and its complements.

A different Kaynean intraposition analysis that respects antisymmetry is indicated in (5). Kayne (1994 p. 122–123) considers a different example without a complement that includes a potentially coreferential category but his analysis carries over essentially unchanged. He argues that in a structure like (5) the pronoun *her* is in an A'-position and has a trace position to the right of the extraposed (in Kayne's theory: stranded) clause. He points out that principle C holds in the reconstructed positions of A'-chains and we may add that principle C does not see elements in A'-position. Hence it is this trace rather than the overt position of the pronoun that counts for principle C, and therefore disjointness is predicted from the name in the complement but not from that in the stranded ("extraposed") clause.

(5) Someone has told {her [who Mary$_x$ met] (her$_x$)[that *Mary$_x$ will inherit the castle]

Haider's example thus does not show that the assumption that principle C is sensitive to c-command leads to contradiction, even within an antisymmetry framework. Let us continue with the standard assumption concerning the relation of principle C and c-command which entails that the adverbial in (1) is not c-commanded by the object of the VP. The standard solution of adjoining the adverbial higher, while not available in the antisymmetry framework, appears to be corroborated by much other evidence. I shall next consider briefly some of this evidence.

The anti c-command requirement of parasitic gaps also diagnoses the complement-adjunct distinction.

(6) a. Who did you hire t after you talked to pg
    b. *Who t went home after you talked to pg

In (6a) the object trace appears not to c-command the parasitic gap in the adjunct, while in (6b) it c-commands the parasitic gap in the complement, resulting in ungrammaticality.

Kayne's (1994) suggestions concerning the apparent discrepancy between the parasitic gap data and the antisymmetry hypothesis are problematic. One of his suggestions is to return to the 0-subjacency account of parasitic gaps, but as noted by Manzini (1995), 0-subjacency accounts seem problematic in general, since they would allow extraction from adjuncts. Another suggestion of Kayne's is that the parasitic gap related operator should be taken as an object-oriented pronominal that moves to matrix AgrO and is disjoint from the subject in (6a) due to the effect of principle B of the binding theory. In addition to being rather stipulative, this suffers from the same problem as the 0-subjacency account: it involves movement out of the adjunct. Kayne's third suggestion is intraposition of the adjunct around the primary wh-trace, parallel to intraposition of a second complement around a "heavy" XP in "inverse heavy shift" constructions. As noted again by Manzini (1995), the problem here is that the trace is not heavy in any sense, hence a focusing/defocusing rule like (inverse) heavy shift is inappropriate and should be inapplicable.

Quantifier scope data is also sensitive to the difference between complements and adjuncts. Hornstein (1995) observes that (7) and (8) where the existential quantifier is taken to bind the pronoun in the adjunct and in the complement respectively, different scope relations can obtain. In (7) the existential unambiguously takes wide scope over the universal, but (8) is scopally ambiguous, here the universal can also take wide scope/distribute over the existential. Thus under the construal where the existential binds the pronoun, for example in (8a) a different person might have asked each attendant, but in (7a) there must be a single person who danced with every woman, not a different one for each.

(7) a. Someone$_x$ danced with every woman before he$_x$ left the party
    b. I got someone$_x$ to review every brief without PRO$_X$ leaving the office
(8) a. Someone$_x$ asked every attendant if he$_x$ could park near the gate
    b. John got someone$_x$/at least one patron$_x$ to tell every critic that he$_x$ hated the play

Hornstein explains this in terms of his A-movement theory of quantifier scope. We can abstract away here from the details of this theory, since the observations suggest that the adjunct must have a different position from the complement under any theory that achieves inverse scope in such examples via reconstruction of the existential to a lower position under the universal. As long as the adjunct is higher but the complement is lower than this reconstructed position, the contrast between (7) and (8) will follow: the existential in the reconstructed position will be able to bind the pronoun in the complement but not in the adjunct.

Additional related problems for the antisymmetry hypothesis arise from structures with multiple adverbials (cf. Andrews 1983, Pesetsky 1989, Cinque 1999). On the assumption that when these are sentence final each c-commands the one that precedes it, the scope relations among these adverbials appear to be straightforwardly determined by c-command in both pre-V and sentence-final position. In both (9) and (10) the interpretation is unambiguous, with *twice* having higher scope in (9) and *intentionally* in (10). Thus the sentences in (9) describe two cases of intentional knocking while those in (10) refer to an intention involving two knocks.

(9) a. John knocked on the door intentionally twice
     b. John twice intentionally knocked on the door
(10) a. John knocked on the door twice intentionally
     b. (??) John intentionally twice knocked on the door

The last set of data in the present inventory that shows that adjuncts and complements cannot be in the same position has to do with movement and deletion tests for constituent structure. On the assumption that complements but not final adjunct clauses are lower than V, there will be a constituent that excludes the adjunct but includes the complement. The existence of a constituent that includes V and its complements but excludes the adjunct clause appears to be confirmed by VP-deletion

(11), (12) and fronting (13). (Recall that in mirror theory there are no phrasal projections, we now take the term VP to refer to V and all categories it dominates.)

(11) Mary sent him there in order to please John's mother and Klara did in order to upset her.
(12) Although Mary did in order to upset John's mother, Klara sent him there in order to please her.
(13) ... and send him there Klara did, in order to please John's mother

Examples parallel to (11)–(13) can be constructed also with complement remnants, but the acceptability status of such examples appears to be different. (In the case of deletion (14), (15) we get "pseudo-gapping" structures):

(14) ? Mary sent John and Klara did Bill
(15) ? Although Mary gave the book to John, Klara did to Bill
(16) ? ... and give the book Mary did to John

All these examples might be analyzed as involving shifting of remnants to the front of the V followed by remnant VP-fronting/deletion. But whatever the analysis is that makes deletion and fronting of what appear to be VP subparts in (14), (15) and (16) possible, these structures are somewhat marked. A configurational difference between adjuncts and arguments can explain why VP fronting/deletion is not similarly marked with non-complement remnants.[4]

The combined evidence from principle C, parasitic gaps, quantifier and adverb scope, VP fronting/deletion clearly shows that sentence final adverbials and adverbial clauses are not in the same position as complements. Let us consider the type of solution to the antisymmetry problem this fact creates that many have proposed. This involves creating the difference between complements and adjuncts via placing some part of the structure that includes the VP-internal material into a spec position higher than the adverbial.

For the result clause structures in (17) Kayne suggests such a structure:

(17) a. She$_x$ has so much money now that Mary$_x$ is the envy of all her classmates
b. [[$_y$She$_x$ has so much money now] [$_C$ that] Mary$_x$ is the envy of all her classmates t$_y$

Kayne proposes that there is no disjointness effect in (17) because the string "she has so much money now" is in fact an embedded clause that surfaces in spec-C (as indicated). The pronoun *she* then does not c-command *Mary*; – and this is true both for its surface and trace-internal position.

Putting aside for the moment[5] the question of what triggers movement to spec-C, a problem that would be relevant for both the adverbial clause in (1) and (17), it is easy to see that an analysis along these lines, which would take the main clause to be in the spec-C (or spec-P) of the *in order to* clause as in (18) could not work for the case in (1).

(18) a. in order to please John's mother [we sent him there]
b. [we sent him there] in order to please John's mother

The analysis looks perhaps dubious to start with since it inverts the intuitively clear main and subordinate clause status in the structure and provides no plausible source for the main clause. The incorrectness of the inversion of the main/subordinate status can be shown in cases where the structure is embedded further. In (19a) selectional properties of the main predicate (*wonder*) show that the main clause of (1) is in fact the main clause. If this was in the highest spec (spec-C or spec-P) of the adverbial clause, then we would expect the adverbial clause and not the clause in its spec-C to be interrogative. The clause in spec-C would clearly be too far from the matrix predicate for wh-selection.

(19) a. John wondered who we sent there in order to please him
b. John believes him to have been sent in order to ...

Similar comments apply in the case of a matrix ECM predicate as in (19b). If the main clause was in spec position, its own spec would be too far from the matrix Case assigner to end up accusative, whether ECM applies via government or movement to spec-AgrO.

These problems will not arise under a different version of the hypothesis (essentially following the proposals of Barbiers 1995, and Cinque 1999 among others), according to which in (1) it is the VP and not the CP (i.e. in mirror theory the V and not C, together with the nodes it dominates) of the main clause that occurs in a spec position. This spec position would be lower than the subject of the main clause, and thus lower than C and I and their spec's which take their ususal place. The problems just raised in connection with the CP shift to spec-C of the *in order to* clause then would not arise, as the spec-C and the subject of the main clause would occupy their standard position, making wh-selection and ECM structures feasible. To solve the problem of lack of source for the VP assume that the *in order to* clause is in a spec position of some functional head. This is natural, given Cinque's (1999) theory in which all adverbials that precede the thematic position of V are in the spec position of their own dedicated functional head.[6] In the spirit of Barbiers and Cinque take then the VP to raise in order to serve as a subject of the adjunct clause, understood as a predicate.

Moving the VP to a spec position above the adverbial answers all the problems listed above in connection with clausal adverbials. The object of the V will not c-command then the adverbial clause, hence there will be no c-command violation in (1) and the anti c-command requirement in the parasitic gap structure (6a) is respected. (6b) will continue to violate the requirement since the subject trace in spec-I will c-command the adverbial. Assuming that the universal can distribute over the existential quantifier only if this latter is reconstructed into its theta position under V entails that in examples like (7) under inverse scope the existential cannot bind a pronoun in the adjunct: the reconstructed existential is now embedded in a spec node. In other words, if the existential binds the adverbial clause internal pronoun then it is too high to be reconstructed under V for inverse scope. There is no problem with binding the pronoun in the complement in (8) under reconstruction since the complement is dominated by V (in standard terms: internal to the VP) in spec-Pred. (The same account of the complement adjunct contrast will work also if reconstruction targets a position higher than V, say the "share" head of Beghelli and Stowell (1996), as long as instead of V this higher head (and therefore everything this head dominates) is taken to occupy the relevant spec position.)

Furthermore since the VP in spec-Pred is a constituent that includes the complements but not the adverbial clause, the analysis can straightforwardly distinguish the fully grammatical VP deletion/fronting cases in (13) and (14) that leave the adverbial clause behind and which involve deletion/fronting of a constituent from the semi-grammatical cases in (15) and (16) which either do not operate with constituents, or more likely, act on remnant constituents but involve markedness.

The analysis raises other questions however. Manzini (1995) objects to this kind of approach on the grounds that it would create a unique case where a nontrivial chain is created for the sake of satisfying a checking requirement involving predication. It is not obvious how strong this objection is. One might imagine that the presence of clausal subjects in spec-I is triggered by predication, especially in a framework like that of bare checking theory (Brody 1997a), in which all syntactic features must be semantically interpretable, and therefore heads of A-chains cannot be licensed by uninterpretable Case. At least one other likely candidate for a treatment in terms of predication would be the head of the relative under the raising analysis of relatives forced in the antisymmetry framework (Kayne 1994). On the other hand taking Tns to be the trigger for Nominative, as in Brody 1997a, may well be a more preferable option.

Notice that the adverbials must apparently sit in spec position contrary to the suggestion that the V(P) originates as (or in) the complement of the adverb (e.g. Sportiche 1994). Cinque provides evidence against this latter assumption based on the existence of head positions in Romance in between adverbials. But, in any case, the proposal of considering adverbs as heads would not generalize to clausal adverbials. The analysis could not take the adverbial clause to be the complement of the adverbial, as it assigns this position to the VP-trace (i.e. to the copy of the V which together with the nodes it dominates occupies the theta-related chain-tail position). Given that adverbials must be in spec positions, it is natural to take the V(P) to be the spec of a higher node, perhaps Pred. The complement of Pred is the adverbial suffix in the spec of which the free morpheme adverb sits. In turn the complement of this adverbial suffix includes the V(P) trace position. The heads Pred and F are empty here.

(20)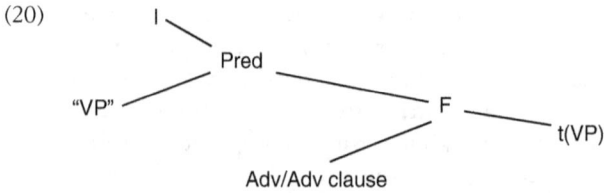

Note further the case of adverbials apparently stacked on the right periphery of the sentence as in (9a) and (10a). In the antisymmetry framework examples like (9a) and (10a) are usually treated in terms of roll-up structures, that is in terms of successive incremental intraposition. Thus, it is assumed that the adverbials are stacked on the left of the V and the VP raises first to the left of the lower adverbial A and then the constituent it forms with A raises to the left of the second adverbial. This ensures that the underlying scope order is the same in the (a) and (b) examples in (9) and (10) in spite of the surface word order difference.

In the successive incremental intraposition analysis the only likely candidate for triggering the intrapositions in the roll-up structure is Pred: the raised category must serve as a subject for the adverbial predicate. Thus the lower adverbial is taken to be predicated of the VP and the higher one of the constituent that includes the VP and the lower adverbial. This means that a Pred head must be present on top of each adverb.

This consequence cannot be avoided by assuming that stacked adverbs as opposed to adverbial clauses are in head position (and thus establish a spec-head predication relation with the VP directly). As exemplified by constructions like (21), the adverbial can have its own complement distinct from the VP also when there is more than one adverbial stacked at the sentence periphery.

(21) John kissed Mary recently more quickly than/before Bill

And there may be more than one adverbial on the right periphery, with inverse scope order even when one or more of these are clausal:

(22) John kicked the door twice (intentionally) in order to irritate Mary
(23) John left when Mary arrived in order to please her

The interpretation of (22) is that "It was in order to irritate Mary, that John intentionally kicked the door twice," i.e. "in order to > intentionally > twice." In (23) again, the rightmost *in order to* clause takes scope over the temporal adjunct clause.

Hence the analysis that takes the VP-trace to be the complement of the adverbial is unlikely to be helpful and we can assume that the analysis in (20), with the adverbial in spec position, is essentially correct also for structures that contain adverbials without complements.

The problem that this analysis of multiple adverbials creates is that we seem to be without means to rule out the case where both adverbials are predicated of the same VP, i.e. to rule out successive step non-incremental VP-intraposition. (Note that a single subject can in general have more than one predicate as for example in structures with NP-chains.) If successive non-incremental VP-intraposition was allowed, then it should be possible for example in (9a) for the VP to "move" to a spec-Pred above *twice*, and then "move" further to the spec-Pred above *intentionally*, resulting in the interpretation on which *intentionally* has higher scope than *twice*, which is unavailable in (9a).

In other words, the postulated mechanism of successive incremental VP-intraposition is quite unlike other known cases of XP-"movement." Unlike other known cases of XP-chains, it is not allowed to be multiple membered (no "successive non-incremental movement" is possible, but it can have the incremental movement structure that other well-established cases of XP-chains cannot have. In fact incremental VP-intraposition is more similar to head-movement in the standard minimalist framework than to XP-movement. It is far from clear, how such a similarity could be expressed and motivated. In Brody (2000) I argued against the existence of head-chains. If this is correct, then there remains no likely candidate in syntax to assimilate incremental intraposition to.

These considerations lead to the hypothesis, that structures involving adverbials on the right periphery should involve no chains at all. In mirror theory a "VP" (i.e. the V and whatever it dominates, – the V-family) can continue its extended word independently of whether it is structurally in a spec or a comp position. The choice will be based on morphology (see the analysis of "John comes" vs "John has come" in Brody 2000). In the V-family final adverbial construction I'll take the V-family to be "base generated" in a spec position. More precisely the tail of a (normally trivial, one-member) V-family chain can be in a spec-position. Suppose that the VP is in the spec of a higher head and the adverb occupies the spec position of the associated and dedicated functional head, as in (24). This higher head may in principle be Cinque's Agr node that may appear between any two functional heads or a copy of the empty functional head.

(24)

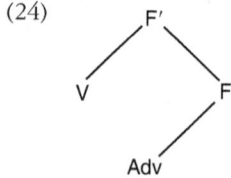

In fact the latter approach to the higher F node seems more appropriate, since this node must be of the same type as the lower F so that V can continue its extended word uninterrupted, as desired. I assume that in this structure the Adv c-commands the V, – see Brody (2000). The structure in (24) corresponds to the more standard (24'):

(24')

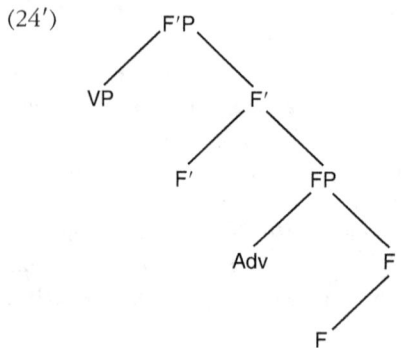

The problems of the successive incremental intraposition account do not carry over to this analysis. No triggering feature for V(P) like Pred needs to be postulated, since as we have just seen, the V-family can be in the spec of the associated adverbial. There is no issue of excluding non-incremental intraposition, V-familes do not "move" to spec-Adv at all. Perhaps such a movement/chain is always illegitimate. If so, this may be due to the fact that the adverb and the V-family are in some predication or modification relation in (24/24'), and such a relation should be governed, along with more standard selectional relations, by the Generalized Projection Principle (Brody 1995a, 1998). This principle does disallow chains whose non-root member is in a semantically selected position.

The structure of a clause with more than one sentence final adverbial will then be (25) where Adv* c-commands Adv which in turn c-commands V:

(25)

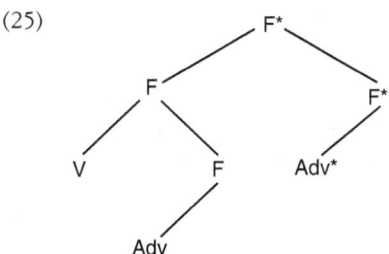

A structure like (26), corresponding to the successive non-incremental intraposition case cannot arise: this would violate universal constraints on possible extended projections. Here V is dominated by F*, but the universal (domination) order is (27) by hypothesis.

(26)

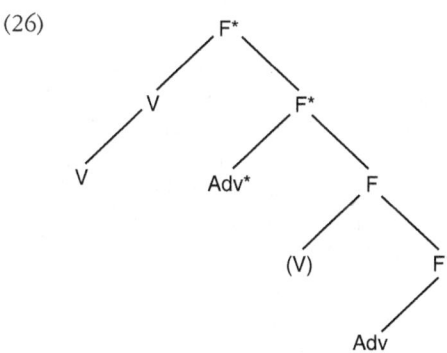

(27)   F*...>...F...>...V

To summarize: Independently of mirror theoretical considerations, theories of right-peripheral adverbials that assume that the VP forms a chain with a position on the right of these adverb(s) are problematic. In particular the solution that assumes VP shift to a spec position raises the issues of what triggers the movement (what licences the higher chain-member), why no successive non-incremental step

VP-chains can be constructed and what makes successive incremental chains possible. The possibility of successive roll up chains and the impossibility of non-incremental successive step structure are properties that are not shared by better established phrasal chains (family chains in mirror theory). If the VP/V-family originates in a spec position on the left of the right peripheral adverb(s) then the universal order of functional heads must be defined on a series of nodes where each immediately dominates the next, but without the additional requirement that each must be a complement of the previous one. This is exactly the conclusion that the strict version (where structural complements must form morphological units with their dominating node) of the mirror theory in Brody 2000 lead to. The behavior of right peripheral adverbials therefore appears to provide some further evidence for mirror theory, and in particular for its most principled variant.

3. V-raising in Hungarian

The version of the mirror theory outlined in Brody (2000) entails the traditional generalization in its strict form: head "movement" type relations are highly local. This generalization is stipulated by the HMC, and follows from relativized minimality only with some difficulty, as set out in earlier work. Strict locality follows from the general idea of relativized minimality only weakly in any case, – as witnessed by the proposals to modify relativized minimality in various ways to allow various types of apparent HMC violations. Evidence for the local nature of head-chain relations/ morphological words therefore constitutes evidence for the theory in which complementation structures mirror extended/morphological words and morphology spells out continuous subparts (lexical/morphological words) of such complementation structures. This theory dispenses with head chains but entails strict locality of head-chain type relations.

Hungarian verbal modifier and more generally prefix incorporation presents a challenge to the assumption of HMC locality, which at least superficially looks sharper than the relatively minor violations of the HMC in certain slavic and romance constructions. Unlike these structures, Hungarian prefix incorporation presents itself as an apparently long distance head-chain phenomenon, although with various peculiarities. Recently Szabolcsi (1996), and Koopman and Szabolcsi (2000) have argued for treating the relevant structures in terms of XP-chains. In what follows, I shall propose an alternative analysis that makes use of both family-chains and head-chain type relations. Recall that under mirror theory family-chains are the equivalent of standard XP-chains. These are the only type of chains under this theory, head-chain type relations correspond to morphological words. I shall argue that the Hungarian data becomes understandable, once these two relations are separated and the traditional assumption concerning strict locality of head-chains type relations is made.[7]

Hungarian has a class of verb-associated elements, usually referred to as verbal modifers (VMs) that includes verbal particles, small clause predicates, bare nouns etc, that appear to be able to form long distance chains.

(28) Szét fogom akarni kezdeni szedni [szét] a rádiót
Apart will-I want-INF begin-INF take-INF [apart] the radio
"I will want to begin to take apart the radio"

The verbal particle *szét* ("apart") in (28) belongs to the verb *szedni* ("take-INF"), but surfaces separated from it by a string of verbs. As noted in Szabolcsi 1996 these verbs do not form a reanalyzed complex, additional nonverbal material can intervene between them. The question therefore arises: Are these VM-chains long distance head-chains? Or are they pied piped XP-chains? (Given antisymmetric structures, such phrasal chains will necessarily involve remnant movement) Szabolcsi assumes the latter on the basis of the non-local nature of the relation. One might argue, however, that examples like (28) indicate precisely the untenability of the assumption that head-chains must be strictly local, and the necessity of allowing non-local chains (either via long steps or via excorporation).

I shall provide some evidence below that (28) indeed involves XP-chains (i.e. chains and not morphological words under mirror theory). But potential impressionistic support for the contrary position might be examples like (29), which show that the successive roll-up chain structure characteristic of head-chains is also sometimes an acceptable alternative option. In (29) there is a focussed element (capitalized) in the preverbal focus position characteristic of Hungarian. In (29a) the VM *szét* ("apart") appears to incorporate into the the verb *szedni* ("take-INF") creating the unit *szétszedni* ("apart-take-INF"). In (29b), this unit incorporates further into *kezdeni* ("begin"). The unit *szétszedni kezdeni* ("apart-take-INF-begin-INF") then appears to incorporate into *akarni* ("want-INF") in (29c):

(29) a. MOST fogom akarni kezdeni {szét} szedni [szét] a rádiót
NOW will-I want-INF begin-INF {apart} take [apart] the radio-ACC
b. MOST fogom akarni {szétszedni} kezdeni [szétszedni] [szét]
a rádiót
c. MOST fogom {szétszedni kezdeni} akarni [szétszedni kezdeni]
[szétszedni] [szét] a rádiót
"I will want to start to take apart the radio NOW"

The option of roll-up chain structure is not one that standard wh/NP-movement chains have. As noted in the previous section in analyses with successive cascading XP intraposition, noncascading successive intraposition must be sharply prohibited. This is in contrast to the situation here, as (28) appears to indicate.

Szabolcsi (1996) and Koopman and Szabolcsi (2000) take both (28) and (29) to involve phrasal chains. The prediction of mirror theory is that the non-local chain in (28) cannot be head-chain type: MWs cannot skip heads. The roll-up structures of (29) however can be treated in terms of MWs since the chains here (which MWs will replace under mirror theory) exhibit strictly local links. I shall provide evidence below that the prediction is correct: nonlocal relations like (28) are (syntactic-spec targeting) chains and not MWs. Furthermore I shall argue that the Hungarian verb raising paradigm can be understood only if the roll-up structures in (29) are treated in terms of head-chain type relations, – as MWs.

Before proceeding, we need to take account of some data that apparently complicate the situation further. The VM, like the phrase in successive step wh/NP-chains, cannot stop in most intermediate positions. But unlike these, it can stop in the lowest of these:

(30) MOST fogom (?*szét) akarni (?*szét) kezdeni szét szedni [szét] a rádiót
NOW will-I apart want-INF begin-INF take-INF [apart] the radio
"I will want to begin to take apart the radio NOW"

Let us start by asking why the VM appears in front of the finite verb in (28)? Verbs in Hungarian fall into two types, some like *fog* ("will") require a VM in a neutral (i.e. without a focus type operator) sentence, others like *utál* ("hate") do not allow one. Thus taking an example with *fog*, (31a) is grammatical but (31b), where no VM precedes this finite verb is not. This is in contrast to the next example with *utál*, here (32a) where the VM precedes the verb is ungrammatical, but (32b) is fine. This consideration exludes also (32c), but both (31c) and (32c) are ruled out additionally, because a nontrivial roll-up structure is too large to qualify as a VM. (33) shows that infinivals can also serve as VMs.

(31) a. Haza fogok menni
Home will-I go-INF
"I will go home"
b. *Fogok haza menni
c. *Hazamenni fogok
(32) a. *Haza utálok menni
Home hate-I go-INF
"I hate to go home"
b. Utálok hazamenni
c. *Hazamenni utálok
(33) Úszni fogok menni
swim-INF will-I go-INF
"I will go swimming"

Let us refer to verbs of the class to which *fog* belongs as deficient verbs. It appears then, that when a deficient V is tensed, it needs a VM like *haza* ("home") or the infinitive *úszni* ("swim-INF"):

(34) A tensed deficient V needs to be immediately proceeded by a VM

It is necessary to refer to tense in (34), since all the verbs in (30) belong to the deficient class. (34) clearly cannot be allowed to refer also to infinivals in general, since then a VM would not only be allowed in intermediate positions, but would actually have to occur in all intermediate positions, – an incorrect prediction.[8]

Consider next the question of why the VM can show up in the position nearest to the lowest of its chain? Notice that the VM can surface in the lowest position of its chain only if it is an infinitive:

(35) a. MOST fogok akarni kezdeni hazamenni\úszni menni
       NOW will-I want-INF start-INF home-go-INF\swim-INF go-INF
       "I will want to start to go home\to go swimming NOW"
    b. MOST fogok kezdeni akarni *menni haza\menni úszni

We can make sense of this data if we assume first that infinitives are optionally taken to be VMs and secondly that there is a requirement also on VMs that requires them to be supported:[9]

(36) A VM must be supported by a verb on its right.

It is clear that the requirement to occur in the antepenultimate position cannot be due to a requirement of the host verb. As the bad cases of (30) show, deficient infinitivals do not require a VM to precede them. But the VM cannot remain in situ. Note additionally, that when the VM shows up to the left of a verb, even if it is to satisfy its own requirement, the host verb must be of a type that licences the VM:

(37) a. MOST fogok akarni utálni\habozni\elkezdeni úszni
       NOW will-I want-INF hate-INF\hesitate-INF\away-start-INF swim-INF
       "I will want to hate\hesitate\start to swim NOW"
    b. *MOST fogok akarni úszni utálni\habozni\elkezdeni

Verbs like *utálni\habozni\elkezdeni* ("hate-INF\hesitate-INF\away-start-INF") are not deficient, they not just don't require but do not even allow a VM to immediately precede them. (So the deficient V that obtained a VM like *el-kezdeni*, ceases to be deficient, it licenses no additional VM.) In mirror theoretical terms, this means that they can neither form an MW with a VM, nor do they license them as their spec (in V or T or any other associated functional head).

The assumptions so far cover (28) and (30). In the good version of (30) where the VM is to the left of lowest infinitive, the MW or the degenerate (one element) family-chain was constructed to satisfy the requirement of the VM, i.e. (36). Given some version of last resort,[10] the VM can surface higher only if some requirement forces it to do so. The infinitivals in (30) carry no such requirement. In the sentence without focus in (28) the matrix tensed deficient verb has its own requirement (34), that justifies the presence of the VM proceeding it.

can then assume that it is this +prefix feature that percolates (optionally) to higher elements making them subject to the same requirement. The larger units created in this way do not qualify however as VMs, and only VMs are licensed in the tensed preverbal position of deficient verbs.

(42) a. +VM → +prefix
b. +prefix can percolate up MW-internally (optional)

We need accordingly to modify the licensing conditions: nondeficient infinitivals not only do not license a VM but more generally do not license a +prefix category on their left:

(43) *MOST fogok hazamenni kezdeni utálni
NOW will-I home-go-INF begin-INF hate-INF
"I will begin to hate to go home NOW"

Similarly, as (29) shows, licensing of a VM by verbs on their left is in fact more generally a question of licensing a +prefix marked element.

Given this much background, (44) provides the evidence that roll-up structures indeed involve MWs and not chains (head-chains and not XP-chains in standard terms).

(44) a. MOST fogok hazamenni kezdeni akarni
NOW will-I home-go begin-INF want-INF
"I will want to begin to go home NOW"
NOT: "I will begin to want to go home NOW"
b. MOST fogok hazamenni kezdeni akarni [hazamenni kezdeni]
[hazamenni] [haza]
c. *MOST fogok hazamenni kezdeni akarni [hazamenni] [haza]

As we have seen in (28) the VM can move long distance (presumably in successive steps) in a non roll-up fashion. But once a roll-up structure is formed as in (29), the top element of the roll-up structure can only form nontrivial chains by further roll-up, it is generally not allowed to form chains in successive non roll-up steps. For example (44a) can only be interpreted with *akarni* (want-INF) having scope over *kezdeni* ("begin-INF"), i.e. the structure must be the fully roll-up (44b) and not the partially roll-up (44c) where *haza* ("home") appears to incorporate into *menni* ("go-INF") and then *hazamenni* forms a chain that crosses the two heads *kezdeni* and *akarni*.

If these roll-up structures can only involve head-chain type relations, i.e. MWs, then the facts of (44) will automatically fall out, since MWs cannot exhibit non-local relations. The mirror theory analysis of (44) is then like (45), where again @ indicates spellout positions of complex morphological words.[12]

(45)

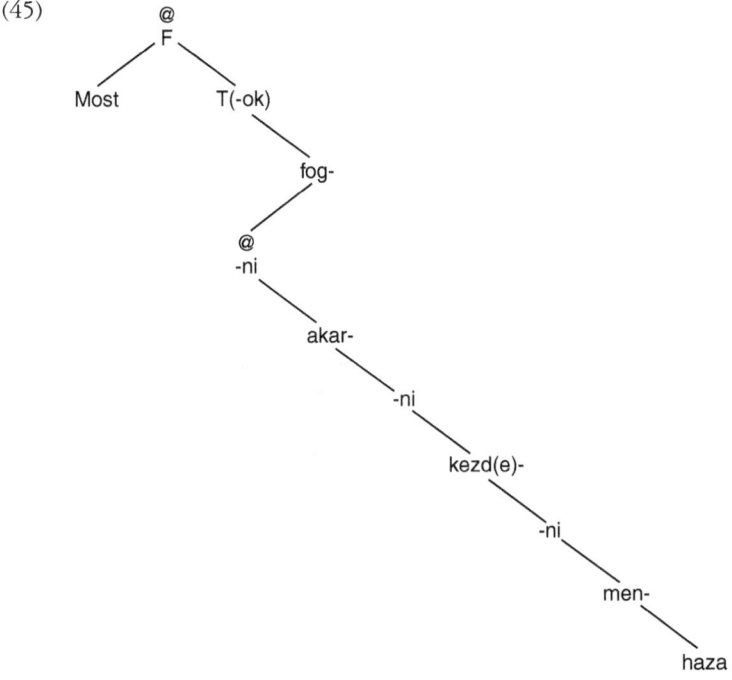

References

Andrews, Avery. 1983. A note on the constituent structure of modifiers. *Linguistic Inquiry* 13:313–317.

Barbiers, Sjeff. 1995. Extraposition and the interpretation of X-bar structure. GLOW newsletter 34.

Beghelli, Filippo and Tim Stowell. 1996. Distributivity and negation: the syntax of "each" and "every." In Anna Szabolcsi ed. *Ways of scope taking*. Kluwer, Dordrecht.

Brody, Michael. 1990. Some Remarks on the Focus Field in Hungarian UCL Working Papers in Linguistics Vol. 2, University College London.

Brody, Michael. 1994. Phrase Structure and Dependence. Ms., University College London.

Brody, Michael. 1995a. *Lexico-Logical Form: A radically minimalist theory*. Cambridge, Mass.: MIT Press.

Brody, Michael. 1995b. Hungarian focus and bare checking theory. In Arbeitspapiere des Sonderforschungsbereichs 340, University of Tubingen.

Brody, Michael. 1997a. Towards Perfect Chains. In Liliane Haegeman ed. *Elements of Syntax*, Kluwer.

Brody, Michael. 1997b. Mirror Theory. Ms. University College London, at http://www.phon.ucl.ac.uk

Brody, Michael. 1998. Phrase Structure and projection. *Linguistic Inquiry* 29.

Brody, Michael 2000. Mirror Theory, syntactic representation in perfect syntax. *Linguistic Inquiry* 31.1.

Brody, Michael and Anna Szabolcsi, to appear. In *Syntax* 2003 Overt Scope in Hungarian.
Cinque, Guglielmo. 1999. Adverbs and functional projections: A cross-linguistic perspective. New York: OUP.
Haider, Hubert. 1993. Detached clauses – the later the deeper. Ms. University of Stuttgart.
Hornstein, Norbert. 1995. *LF: The grammar of logical form. From GB to minimalism*. Oxford: Blackwell.
Kayne, Richard. 1994. The asymmetry of syntax. Cambridge, Mass.: MIT Press.
Koopman, Hilda and Anna Szabolcsi. 2000. Verbal Complexes. MIT Press.
Manzini, Maria Rita. 1992. *Locality*. Cambridge, Mass.: MIT Press.
Manzini, Maria Rita. 1995. Adjuncts and the theory of phrase structure. Ms., University College London.
Pesetsky, David. 1989. Language particular processes and the earliness principle. Ms., MIT.
Phillips, Colin. 1996. *Order and Structure*. Doctoral dissertation. MIT.
Sportiche, Dominique. 1994. Adjuncts and Adjunction. Ms., UCLA.
Szabolcsi, Anna. 1996. Verb and particle movement in Hungarian. Ms., UCLA.
Williams, Edwin. 1994. *Thematic Structure in Syntax*. Cambridge, Mass.: MIT Press.

13

WORD ORDER, RESTRUCTURING AND MIRROR THEORY

Sections 1 and 2 briefly outline some central features of mirror theory (Brody 1997) and discuss consequences with respect to "basic" word order. In sections 3 and 4 I note that mirror theory is incompatible with covert roll-up head chain type relations and argue that contrary to recent claims the analysis of Romance restructuring need not involve such structures. In section 5, I note that Kayne's correlation between null subjects and clitic climbing may be better captured under the proposed analysis than it has been in earlier approaches. I argue that both phenomena involve licensing of a Spec by an element of Infl. In section 6, I discuss some aspects of the behavior of Hungarian restructuring infinitives and their treatment in mirror theory. Section 7 looks at some similarities and differences between the "climbing" options of Hungarian verbal modifiers and Romance clitics. Finally in section 8, I argue that to understand Hungarian restructuring constructions it is necessary to distinguish (strictly local) head chain and (successive step) phrasal chain type relations, – a fact that constitutes further evidence for some core assumptions of mirror theory.

1. Mirror theory, a brief sketch

In mirror theory (Brody 1997), the morphological structure of words is expressed syntactically as complementation structure. The mirror principle of this theory ensures that if x is the complement of y then x is taken to be the morphological specifier of y. For a large set of morphemes (generally suffixes) it is also typically (though probably not always) true that if x is the morphological specifier of y, then x is the complement of y syntactically. As a simplified example, V is (part of the) the morphological Spec of Infl and V is also typically (part of the) the syntactic complement of Infl.

In mirror theory, complementation structure is taken to be the default expression of the morphological structure – the mirror hypothesis. According to this hypothesis the syntactic head-complement relation expresses the morphological specifier-head relation in inverse topological order: complements follow while specifiers (whether syntactic or morphological) precede the head. Thus no separate X^0-internal representation needs to be assumed that matches and duplicates the complement series. Consider for example the simplified structure in (1) of, say, *Mary loves John*. Here (*Mary*) is the trace of the subject in Spec*v*, so *Mary* and (*Mary*) form a chain; the object *John* is taken for the sake of presentation, probably counterfactually, not to form a chain with a position higher than Spec*v*; and Infl, v and V represent, again in a simplified fashion, the morphemes (some null) from which the word *loves* is composed.

(1)

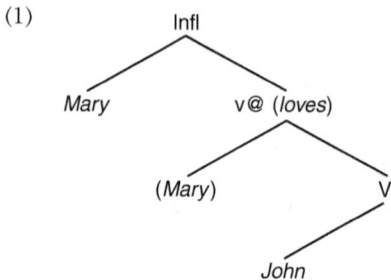

The complement series in (1), Infl + v + V serves as the syntactic representation of the morphological word (MW) V + v + Infl. Morphology spells out the syntactic representation of an MW (a) in one of the head positions, here in that of v (as indicated by "@"), from which the MW is composed and (b) in inverse order, – due to (the appropriate version of) the mirror hypothesis, an axiom of the system.

All this gives the correct morpheme order both word-internally (*love* + *s*) and also word-externally if the Spec (and whatever it dominates) precedes the head, and the complement (and whatever it dominates) follows it. The order of head and complement follows from the order of Spec-Head, given the assumption that specifiers uniformly precede the head both in syntax and in morphology and that syntactic complement relations are inverse order morphological Spec-Head relations – the mirror hypothesis again. Thus in (1) *Mary* precedes Infl, Infl precedes v where *loves* is spelt out and v precedes V and whatever V dominates, i.e. in particular *John*.

Under mirror theory the syntactic complementation relation entails morphological specifierhood: if x is the complement of y then x is the morphological specifier of y. Thus first of all the arguments of the verb that are morphologically independent of it, – (non-incorporated, non-clitic) subject or object, or clausal complement etc. – must be specifiers. Secondly if the subparts of what in standard systems are extended projections do not form an MW then these parts must also be in the specifier-head rather than in the complement-head relation. For example in "John has come" *come* cannot be the complement of *has*. The auxiliary is an element that is part of the extended word but not of the morphological word of the main verb. It must therefore be a specifier as in (2).

(2)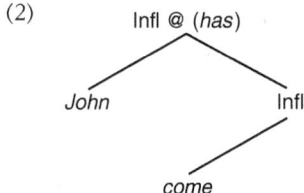

To ensure the correct word order, it must be assumed that *come* is the specifier of a head that is lower than the head in which *has* is spelt out in morphology.

The representations in (1) and (2) are simplified in several ways for presentational purposes, but there is a particular simplification that is not presentational, but is meant as a substantive restrictive hypothesis. This has to do with the elimination of phrasal nodes. The structure in (3) for example, that (1) replaces, is obviously redundant.

(3)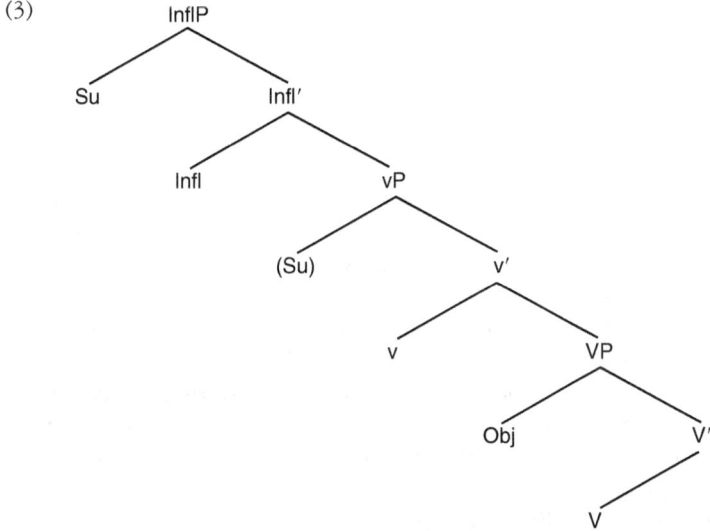

Call the claim that the set of phrasal and X^0-internal projections of a head can be systematically collapsed *the telescope hypothesis*. X^0-internal projections are unnecessary, given the treatment of MWs as (inverse order) complement lines. As for phrasal projections, the telescope hypothesis embodies the expectation that given the accumulating evidence for multiple additional heads of various types in the structure, phrasal projections will invariably be unnecessary. For example the major evidence for the V' level, based on the hierarchical subject-object asymmetry, disappears when the subject is taken to be Spec*v*. This ensures without the intermediate bar level that the subject is higher than the object. Any category can be interpreted as either a phrase or a head in mirror theory — a head by itself and a phrase together with all categories it dominates. (Notice also a terminological point: since categorial projection is eliminated, extended projections are better referred to as extended words.)

2. Mirror theory and word order

As we have seen, under mirror theory all non-clitic arguments must be specifiers. Does mirror theory therefore entail a strict "underlying" (i.e. chain-root) head final "SOV" order? While such a statement would be partly true, it would also be in part incorrect and in part misleading. There are three main reasons. First, a morphologically dependent object, like an incorporated noun for example may be the complement of the verb. Given the mirror hypothesis, it will then be spelt out preverbally as required.

Secondly, as noted above, a head like a verb for example, may form an MW with one or more higher heads like v and Infl, each of which is the syntactic complement of the next. The MW may be spelt out in any one of the complement positions that its component members (the morphemes) occupy. Now the notion of MW corresponds to the concept of head chain in standard frameworks, but it is different from this notion in that it provides no natural way of talking about "underlying" or chain root position. The set of heads, each a complement of the previous one, is a decomposed representation of the MW. So there is no clear sense in which the lowest head in the series would be an "underlying" or chain root position. Thus mirror theory consistently entails head-final structures in the sense that arguments must be specifiers, but there is no sense in which it can be said to entail underlying or chain root SOV, because the positions in which the verb may be spelt out, and which may precede or follow the object and also the subject, form an MW and not a chain.

The standard ways of creating non chain-root word orders involve not only V-raising but also VP shift. The third reason why mirror theory cannot be taken to entail chain root SOV is that it provides a treatment for the relevant VP shift operations in which the V-phrase's chain root position corresponds to what is taken to be its shifted, non-root position in other approaches. Recall the discussion preceding (2) above: a V-phrase that does not form an MW with the rest of what in standard terms is its extended projection (in mirror-theoretical terms its extended word, EW), must be in a Spec position. So in general EWs do not necessarily form a series of complements, they can also continue via specifiers. Thus we have a potential solution to the triggering problem of VP shift. When the V-phrase is in a Spec position, this need not be because it forms a chain with a root position where the V-phrase is a complement, part of its extended word. The V-phrase may simply continue its EW via the Spec position, a configuration that must be available in general if the mirror hypothesis is on the right track. Thus at least in some of the cases where non V-final order is achieved in standard terms by VP shift, under mirror theory the "underlying" chain root V(-phrase)-final order may not exist.

3. Restructuring and (covert) roll-up

Let us refer to a series of chains as a roll-up structure if it meets the following condition: each chain (except the last) takes the top of the previous chain together with the host of this top member (where this host includes the root of the previous chain) to be the root of the next chain. The term "cascade" has sometimes been used but

I shall avoid it here, since it is often employed also in a different sense. Roberts (1997) has recently suggested analysing Romance type restructuring as (in these terms) a roll-up structure that involves covert head chains. He proposed that restructuring between two verbs V1 and V2 involves head movement of V2 up to V1. The V1 V2 order in Romance is due to a filter that prevents spelling out V2 in the higher position in its chain. This filter would distinguish between morphemes and words: V can be spelt out on the left of its Infl host since both elements are morphemes, but in restructuring V2 cannot be spelt out on the left of its host V1 because both verbs are full words. V2 therefore has to surface lower, and so the V1 V2 surface order remains. Roberts assumes (a) that head movement of V2 to V1 creates an extended projection that includes both verbs and (b) that the locality or relativized minimality requirement of XP chains makes use of a principle of equidistance (in Chomsky's 1995 sense), for which positions internal to an extended projection count as equidistant.

Following Sportiche 1995, Roberts assumes that clitic climbing involves XP chains. In the clitic climbing structure in (4), for example, Roberts takes the clitic to move as XP via the lower SpecAgrO and the higher SpecAgrO. That the former position is involved is suggested by the well known participle agreement phenomenon. The involvement of the higher AgrO, as he points out, is suggested by the participial agreement in the matrix in (4).

(4) *Maria li   ha voluti   prendere.* (It)
    Maria them (MASC.PL) has wanted (MASC.PL) take

(This evidence for phrasal chains is strong only on the assumption that the notion of "checking domain" should be eliminated. Otherwise, as has been noted, agreement of the participle with a nonphrasal element adjoined to the head, i.e. still in its checking domain, is an obvious alternative. See Sportiche 1992 and Cardinaletti and Starke 1999 for additional evidence for a phrasal clitic chain.) So for Roberts, invisible movement of the verb *prendere* to a position hosted by *voluti* creates an extended projection and thus makes the SpecAgrS of the lower head and the SpecAgrO of the higher one equidistant from the lower AgrO – all three positions are in the same extended projection.

In mirror theory, roll-up structures involving heads are analyzed in terms of MWs (as opposed to "phrases", i.e. categories taken together with their constituents). Elements of MWs are morphemes and the whole MW is a word. Given this restrictive notion, it would make no sense to distinguish component elements of MWs as being either word-level or morpheme-level elements.

Another consideration that may be taken to indicate that it may be worthwhile to look for an alternative treatment of restructuring is the following. Roberts points out that his approach accounts for the possibility of (XP-)movement across restructuring predicates "without any operation deleting structure in the lower clause" (p. 432). It is not clear however if a solution based on the notion of equidistance is a priori more desirable than one based on structure deletion. The hypothesis that in restructuring contexts intervening position B is deemed not to intervene between positions A and C (whether this is due to A and B being deemed equidistant from C or to some other reason) says nothing about how B will behave under conditions or processes other than movement. On the other hand the hypothesis that in the same contexts B does not intervene because B is not present (either not present at all in the structure or present but in fact occupies a non-intervening position) entails that no principle or operation can make use of B (at all or in the intervening position). These empirical consequences are missing in the weaker equidistance approach. (For the same reason, the layered VP analyses in which AgrO is lower than the chain-root position of the subject in Spec*v* (e.g. Koizumi 1993; Bobaljik 1995) would appear to be a priori more desirable than Chomsky's (1995) equidistance solution, where the paths of subject and object cross.)

4. Restructuring as "I in C"

As is well known, there is direct empirical evidence that the complementizer level of the lower infinitive is present in restructuring. (5) is a case with *si*-passive, (6) clitic climbing and (7) an *easy to please* construction (cf. Rizzi 1982; Sportiche 1995; Kayne 1987).

(5) ?*Certe riposte non si sanno mai come dare.* (It)
 certain answers not REFL knows never how give
 "One never knows how to give certain answers."

(6) ?*Mario, non lo saprei a chi affidare.* (It)
 Mario not him know to whom entrust
 "Mario, I would not know to whom to entrust him."

(7) ?*Ce genre d'article est difficile à savoir où classer.* (Fr)
 this kind of article is difficult to know where file
 "This kind of article is hard to know where to file."

Roberts combines Sportiche's phrasal chain analysis of cliticization with the Kaynean approach to restructuring as involving movement of the lower Infl to the higher one. Apart from the suggestion already discussed, that this operation creates an extended projection spanning the two clauses, he also suggests that Infl movement is coextensive here with verb movement. Following Belletti (1990) he assumes that the infinitival verb in Italian raises to Infl. If this is so, then raising of Infl will involve raising of the verb, resulting in the incorrect word order. Hence the necessity of the * V V filter he proposes, discussed above.

The evidence that Roberts quotes from Belletti (1990) for the infinitival being in Infl comes from the observation that these must precede elements like *mai* and *piu*, naturally associated with negation:

(8) *Gianni ha deciso di non tornare mai/piu.* (It)
 Gianni has decided to not return ever/more
 "Gianni has decided not to come back ever/anymore."

(9) *Gianni ha decisio di non mai/piu tornare. (It)

However even if the polarity elements are in SpecNeg, it does not strictly follow that the verb has raised to the highest Infl position: it may still be in principle the case that Infl raising in restructuring involves a higher head in the Infl domain than the one to which the verb raises. (Cf. e.g. Cinque 1999 on multiple Neg positions.)

So this evidence in fact does not necessarily prevent a return to Kayne's Infl raising analysis. Kayne (1989) assumed that in clitic climbing the clitic raised to the lower Infl, Infl + clitic to C and the whole complex then moved to the higher Infl. It is, however, not clear why the infinitival Infl needs to move to the higher Infl of the restructuring V if clitics form XP-chains. For Kayne, movement to the higher Infl is necessary to carry the clitic up into the higher clause, which is now achieved via the XP-chain. Additionally questions arise concerning the fact that Infl movement to the higher clause appears to cross the higher V position.

Let us then dispense with the now apparently unnecessary and problematic part of Kayne's "I to C to I," namely with "C to I." The residue, "I to C," is motivated by Kayne primarily by the contrast between the restructuring constructions like in (5)–(7) and those with an overt C as in (10) and (11) (his example is (11):

(10) *Certe   riposte   non si   sanno   mai   se dare. (It)
      certain answers not REFL knows never if give
      "One never knows whether to give certain answers."
(11) *Non li   so   se fare.
      not them know if do
      "I don't know whether to do them."

As he notes it is natural to assume that "I to C," hence restructuring, is possible only where C is otherwise empty. (Currently standard assumptions about head movement as head adjunction do indeed provide a basis for expecting some correlation, although they provide no grounds for expecting exactly the observed correlation. If heads do not move through other heads, it remains accidental that only those heads to which Infl cannot adjoin happen to have overt phonological realization.)

Notice however, that the evidence pertains only to the claim that (elements of) Infl are present in C, and not to the assumption that a chain has been formed. Thus we could equally assume that restructuring involves a special type of infinitival C that is in some closer than usual relation with its Infl domain. Suppose Infl can merge with the C selected by restructuring verbs in the sense that Infl (and its Spec, if any) becomes part of the C-domain and thus will not qualify as an A-type intervener. It will thus not interfere with A-chains constructed across it. The Infl in C analysis automatically covers the case of long *si*-passive in restructuring. Lack of an A-type (Spec-)Infl in the lower clause entails that there will be no (relativized) minimality violation in long *si*-passives like (5) either. (Like others, I assume that auxiliary selection phenomena in restructuring involves long movement and thus in the relevant respect also falls under the same generalization.)

5. Null subjects and clitic climbing

The correlation conjectured by Kayne between the existence of null subjects and the option of clitic climbing is only weakly captured in Kayne (1989). His proposal was that an Infl strong enough to licence null subjects has the ability to void the barrierhood of VP, thereby enabling clitics to escape higher. It is not clear however why these two Infl properties should go together – there is no obvious intrinsic connection between licensing a particular type of Spec and voiding the barrierhood of the complement.

Under the phrasal chain analysis of cliticization, the correlation can be captured more directly. Consider Cardinaletti and Starke's (1999) hypothesis that strong and weak pronouns systematically differ from clitics in being XPs, while clitics are heads. In mirror theory terms the only natural way to translate this is to say that non-clitic pronouns are specifiers of the verb's extended word, while clitics are heads, members of the verb's extended word. We can leave it open here whether the clitic starts out as a member of this extended word (essentially as in Sportiche 1995) or as seems more likely (thanks to Michal Starke for helpful discussion) a head in the Infl domain inherits the features of its (weak) pronominal specifier via Spec–Head agreement. On these approaches syntactic cliticization in the core cases would correspond to a special type of Spec–Head agreement, possible only where the head has the ability or expressive power to carry the referential, anaphoric etc. functions of its designated Spec. Presumably the "designated" Spec is one whose every feature participates in the Spec–Head agreement relation. With the clitic option taken (the default case where possible, cf. Cardinaletti and Starke's "minimize structure"), the Spec will be typically (apart from clitic doubling) empty or null. The corresponding heads on the other hand are typically non-null, phonologically.

The similarity of VP-external, or Infl domain, cliticization to null subjects is now conspicuous. Null subjects are also licensed by a typically non-null head in the Infl domain that is able to carry the semantic functions of the subject. Thus both VP-external high cliticization and null subjects are licensed in the same way. Both will be possible in a language where clitics exist and Infl domain heads can carry the semantic functions normally carried by Specs as in Italian. In French, as Kayne (1989) points out, even though "easy to please" constructions show restructuring effects, neither null subjects nor VP-external clitics (hence no clitic climbing) are licensed.

The analysis outlined in the previous two sections assumes that the clitic's "phrasal" chain (Spec-to-Spec family chain in mirror theory terms) extends to a SpecX position higher than the matrix restructuring verb V*. In mirror theory terms this entails that x (which expresses the clitic) and V* cannot form an MW. If they did, this would result in the enclitic order: V*-x. To achieve the proclitic order, x must have a complement y with the MW of V* in the Spec of y. (The alternative on which x/clitic and V* in fact form an MW also seems worth exploring, although I will not do so here. If x-V* is an MW, then x must originate lower than V*. Hence the Spec-to-Spec constituent chain of the clitic must end lower than V*, which often (as in (5) and (6)) but not always (e.g. (4) above) means lower than the restructuring head, i.e. presumably within the Infl domain of the embedded clause. Such an analysis would be more in the spirit of Kayne's I-to-C-to-I rule, but it would not inherit the problem of I(+C) crossing the matrix V.)

6. Hungarian verbal clusters

Verbal clusters in Hungarian involving typical restructuring infinitives may appear in two orders: what we might call the straight order as in Romance (and elsewhere) and the inverted roll-up order:

(12) *Utálok [kezdeni   járni   úszni]*.   (Hu)
     hate.I   begin.INF go.INF swim.INF
     "I hate to begin to go swimming (regularly)"

(13) *Utálok [úszni   járni   kezdeni]*.   (Hu)
     hate.I swim.INF go.INF begin.INF
     – same

The infinitives in (13) are behaving as dependent bound morphemes while those in (12) behave as words. Adverbials (or other material like the matrix subject for example) may intervene between the infinitivals in (12) but not between those in (13) – cf. Koopman and Szabolcsi 1999. Thus, Hungarian restructuring verbs must apparently be intrinsically underspecified (or dually specified) for word-hood/morphemehood. The infinitives in (13) in standard terms appear to form an X^0 roll-up structure and thus in mirror theory they must be analysed as constituting a single MW – syntactically a series of complements:

(14)
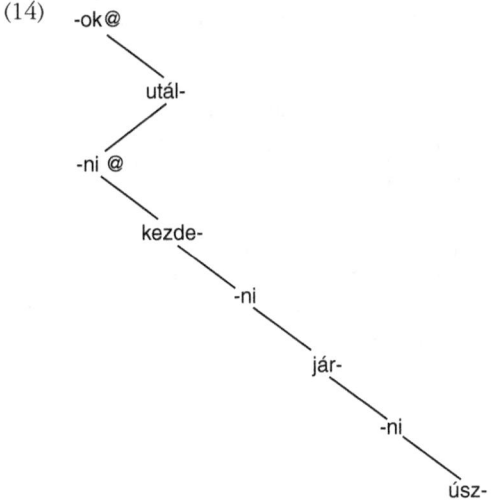

The correct word order results in (14) if the MW *utalok* is spelt out higher than the position of the verb *utal*, i.e. in some head in the Infl domain represented here by Tns + Agr -ok. *Utálok* will then precede the (specifier of) its complement the MW *úszni járni kezdeni*, a complement series spelt "backwards."

In (12) the morphologically independent infinitives cannot be each other's complements, they must therefore each be specifiers:

(15)
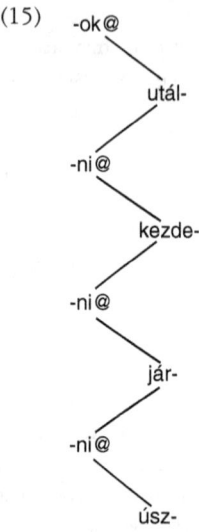

High spellout of each infinitive ensures the correct word order: each verb in (15) spelt out in the relevant inflectional head position IH will precede the (specifier of the) complement of IH.

If we did not have evidence for the infinitives in (13)–(14) constituting a single MW, the word order there could also correspond to what in standard terms we could only analyze as a phrasal roll-up structure. While that can be reproduced in mirror theory, this framework appears to provide also an additional possibility. The analysis could be the same as that of (12)/(15), but with the spellout positions of the infinitives being those of the verbs instead of the higher functional heads. Then each infinitive would be preceded by (the complement of) its specifier resulting in the roll-up order. Low spellout is apparently not an option in Hungarian, a fact perhaps connected to the language allowing null subjects (cf. Roberts 1997). (Note that in (14) and (15) "@" indicates the spellout position and not that of the strong features. These correspond to the spellout positions in (15) and may be the same in (14) on the assumption that the spellout position of an MW is its highest strong position.)

7. Verbal modifiers and clitics

As discussed in Koopman and Szabolcsi (1998) and also in Brody (1997), É. Kiss (1998), Hungarian verbal modifiers (VMs: particles, small clause predicates, bare nouns etc. that can form a single MW with the associated verb, e.g. *szét-szed*, "apart-take") can apparently also form long-distance chains across a set of restructuring infinitives (the trace of the VM is indicated by the copy in parentheses):

(16)   *Szét fogom akarni kezdeni szedni (szét) a rádiót.*   (Hu)
       apart will.I want.INF begin.INF take.INF apart the radio
       "I will want to begin to take apart the radio."

É. Kiss (1998) argues that the VMs in structures like (16) relate the verb they semantically belong to and their spellout position via a head chain type relation on the basis of the fact that the string following the VM does not appear to form a constituent and thus cannot be co-ordinated.

(17)   **Szét   [akarom próbálni válogatni a babot] es   [fogom kezdeni*
       apart   will.I try.INF sort.INF the beans and will.I begin.INF
       szedni   a rádiót].   (Hu)
       take.INF the radio
       "I will try to sort ('apart') the beans and will begin to take apart the radio."

The coordination facts however can pertain only to the question of whether the spell-out position of the VM is a head or a Spec position, they do not tell us how the relation between the VM in the matrix and the associated embedded verb is mediated by a head-chain or phrasal chain type relation. Typically the same coordination facts obtain with clitics.

(18)   **Je l'ai   vu et ai aimé.*   (Fr)
       I him.have seen and have liked

But as we have seen above there is reason to think that clitics can be involved in phrasal chain type relations. Thus Hungarian VMs can be analyzed like clitics: they involve a phrasal chain but at the top position of this phrasal chain a Spec–Head relation is established. The head participating in this Spec–Head relation is of the type that is able to express the content of its VM spec.

There is however a real difference between Romance clitics and Hungarian VMs in restructuring. While clitics can cross a filled C-Spec as (6) above shows, reproduced here as (19), VMs cannot. The infinitival with a +wh SpecC is grammatical in Hungarian as a complement of *tud* ("know") and *van* ("is"/"exists"), but no VM can cross this spec.

(19)   *?Mario, non lo saprei a chi affidare.*   (It)
       Mario not him know.I to whom entrust
       "Mario, I would not know to whom to entrust him."

(20)   *Tudok mit szétszedni.*   (Hu)
       know.I what apart.take
       "I know what to take apart."

(21) *Szét tudok mit szedni.
   apart know.I what take.INF
   – same as (20)

Given the assumption adopted here that the clitic in (19) forms a phrasal chain that spans the matrix and the embedded clause across SpecC, the solution that would attribute the contrast between (19) and (21) to the difference between the type of interveners to which head chain and phrasal chain type relations are sensitive to is not available. But a different account, still in the spirit of relativized minimality, could be adequate even if both the clitic and the VM form phrasal chains. The VM is an adverbial type element, hence it cannot cross a filled SpecC, – the ungrammaticality of (21) would then be on a par with that of (22):

(22) a. *How much did Mary wonder why John weighed?
   b. *60 kilos, Mary wondered why John weighed.

The clitic in (19) on the other hand is an argument. If the top of its phrasal chain is in an A'-position then the structure is like other A'-argument extraction, like e.g. (23).

(23) ?Who did Mary wonder why John weighed?

If the clitic is in an A-position, then A'-Specs must be taken to be irrelevant as A-chain intervenes, just like A-Specs are irrelevant for A'-chains (cf. Rizzi 1990).

As Anna Cardinaletti points out (p.c.), the present approach in terms of an argument-adjunct contrast is supported by the complete lack of idiomatic clitic climbing across filled SpecC:

(24) a. *Ce la devo fare.* (It)
   there it must.I do
   "I have to succeed."
   b. **Non ce la so come fare.*
   not there it know.I how do
   "I do not know how to succeed."

8. Straight and roll-up orders again

There is also Hungarian-internal evidence for the claim that the chain of the VM in straight order restructuring constructions is of the phrasal type (cf. Brody 1997). This is based on Szabolcsi's (1996) observation concerning the interpretation of the focussed infinitive in restructuring constructions with more than one layer of clausal embedding.

(25) a. AKARNI *fogok kezdeni úszni.* (Hu)
   want.INF will.I begin.INF swim.INF

b. "I will indeed want to begin to swim."
c. "I will WANT to begin to swim." (and not, say, TRY to begin to swim)
d. "I will begin to WANT to swim." (and not, say, TRY to swim)
e. *"I will indeed begin to want to swim."

If the focussed infinitive in (25) has scope over the others, i.e. if it is taken to be associated with the highest infinitival position, then the interpretation of the structure is ambiguous between an emphatic and an "exhaustive list" reading, as indicated in (25b) and (25c). If however the focussed infinitive has lower scope, i.e. a lower chain-root position, then the emphatic reading (25e) disappears and only the "exhaustive list" reading (25d) remains.

If head-chain and phrasal chain type relations are distinguished, then this state of affairs is straightforward to explain. There are independent reasons to assume that focussing in Hungarian involves a dedicated head, F (cf. Brody 1990, 1995) and that the emphatic reading is associated directly with this head rather than with its Spec. Only focussed heads but not focussed phrases can receive the emphatic reading. It is natural to complement this with the assumption that the exhaustive list reading is associated with the Spec position of F. If head-chain type relations are strictly local but phrasal chains can span larger distances (whether this involves the combination of strictly local links is not relevant here), only the exhaustive list reading (the phrasal chain construction) will be compatible with the lower scope reading.

The explanation is contingent on interpreting strictly the standard distinction between head chain and phrasal chain type relations: the former but not the latter are strictly local; head-chains cannot (even apparently, by combining several local steps) cross nonlocal distances. Thus, if the explanation of the correlation between scope and focus interpretation is on the right track, then head chains and phrasal chains must have different locality properties. Whatever way syntax expresses the distinction between these two types of relations, the long-distance chain of the VM in (16) must belong to the phrasal type.

Additional evidence for the existence of the need to distinguish within syntax the head chain and the phrasal chain relations is provided by the fact that the scope of the infinitives in the roll-up structure (13), reproduced here as (26), is fixed. Thus in (26) *kezdeni* ("begin") has scope over *járni* ("go regularly"), the opposite interpretation is impossible:

(26) Utálok [úszni   járni   kezdeni].   (Hu)
      hate.I swim.INF go.INF begin.INF
      "I hate to begin to go (regularly) swimming."

This is as expected if the roll-up structure involves head chain type relations, that is in mirror theory a series of complements expressing an (inverse order) MW, as in (14) above.

Suppose, however that the roll-up structure was created by phrasal chains, by the lowest infinitive (here: *úszni*) moving to a Spec above the next (here: *járni*) and then a phrase that includes both this Spec with the lower infinitive in it and the next higher infinitive (i.e. *úszni járni*) moved in front of the highest infinitive (*kezdeni*). Clearly there is nothing intrinsic in the concept of phrasal chain that would prevent the lowest infinitive phrase (*úszni*) from moving in front of the highest one (*kezdeni*), either in one or in several steps. But this would result in scope relations between the crossed infinitives that correspond to their surface order. Under such an analysis *úszni* would have crossed *járni kezdeni* and (26) would have the interpretation "I hate to go (regularly) to begin to swim" which it in fact cannot have. (Admittedly the relevant reading is slightly strange, but this is exactly what (26) would mean if the order of the last two infinitives was reversed, as in *Utálok úszni kezdeni járni*.)

The analyses reviewed in this section make it necessary to take the locality requirement on the relevant head chains to be strict and inviolable. This provides additional evidence for a basic assumption of mirror theory according to which the head chain relation corresponds simply to a local syntactic relation, typically the head-complement relation. Since in this framework no head-chains are formed either in syntax or in morphology and head chains correspond to elements in local relations spelt out in inverse order (MWs), there are no means provided to violate HMC type locality.

Acknowledgments

I am grateful to Anna Cardinaletti and Peter Svenonius for helpful correspondence relating to this material.

References

Belletti, Adriana. 1990. *Generalized verb movement: Aspects of verb syntax*. Turin: Rosenberg and Sellier.

Bobaljik, Jonathan. 1995. Morphosyntax: The syntax of verbal inflection. Ph.D. dissertation, MIT.

Brody, Michael. 1990. "Some remarks on the focus field in Hungarian." *UCL Working Papers in Linguistics* Vol. 2, 201–226. University College London.

Brody, Michael. 1995. "Hungarian focus and bare checking theory." In *Arbeitspapiere des Sonderforschungsbereichs 340*, University of Tübingen.

Brody, Michael. 1997. Mirror Theory, ms., University College London.

Cardinaletti, Anna and Starke, Michal. 1999. "The typology of structural deficiency: A Case Study of three classes of pronouns." In Henk van Riemsdijk (ed.), *Clitics in the Languages of Europe*. Berlin: Mouton de Gruyter. 145–291.

Chomsky, Noam. 1995. *The Minimalist Program*. Cambridge, MA: MIT Press.

Cinque, Guglielmo. 1999. *Adverbs and Functional Heads: A cross-linguistic perspective*. Oxford: OUP.

Kayne, Richard S. 1989. "Null subjects and clitic climbing." In Osvaldo Jaeggli and Ken Safir (eds), *The Null Subject Parameter*. Dordrecht: Kluwer. 239–261.

Kayne, Richard S. 1993. "Toward a modular theory of auxiliary selection." *Studia Linguistica* 47: 3–31.

É. Kiss, Katalin. 1998. The Hungarian verbal complex revisited. ms. Linguistic Institute, HAS.

Koizumi, Masatoshi. 1993. "Object agreement phrases and the split VP hypothesis." In Jonathan D. Bobaljik and Colin Philips (eds.). *Papers on Case and Agreement* I [*MITWPL* vol. 18]. Cambridge, MA: ITWPL. 99–149.

Koopman, Hilda, and Anna Szabolcsi. 1998. Verbal Complexes, ms., UCLA. In press, Cambridge, MA: MIT Press.

Koopman, Hilda, and Anna Szabolcsi. 1999. "Hungarian complex verbs and XP-movement." In Istvan Kenesei (ed.), *Crossing Boundaries: Current Issues in Linguistic Theory*. Amsterdam and Philadelphia: John Benjamins. 115–137.

Rizzi, Luigi. 1982. *Issues in Italian Syntax*. Dordrecht: Foris.

Rizzi, Luigi. 1990. *Relativized Minimality*. Cambridge, MA: MIT Press.

Roberts, Ian. 1997. "Restructuring, head movement and locality." *Linguistic Inquiry* 28: 423–460.

Sportiche, Dominique. 1995. "Clitic constructions." In Laurie Zaring and Johan Rooryck (eds). *Phrase Structure and the Lexicon*. Dordrecht: Kluwer.

Szabolcsi, Anna. 1996. Verb and particle movement in Hungarian, ms., UCLA.

NOTES

INTRODUCTION

1 E.g. Chomsky 1995, 2000 (the correponding ms. circulated from 1998).
2 Chomsky 2001, where "displacement is not an imperfection" any more. Here task relevant near-perfection appears to be replaced by the hope of achieving task relevant perfection – certainly a step in the right direction from the viewpoint of elegant syntax. The complication of task relevance, which weakens the general requirement of elegance remains however, together with various other apparently unnecessary complexities (see Parts 3 and 4 of this volume) of the approach.
3 Brody 1998a (written and submitted in 1996), here Chapter 9.
4 Brody 1985, here Chapter 3, see especially note 41.
5 Brody 1987, here Chapter 4.
6 Both written in 1991 before Chomsky 1992, that is chapter 2 of Chomsky 1995 became available.
7 Circulated in 1992.
8 Of Brody 1995a, the relevant chapter circulated in 1992.
9 Chomsky 1995, 2000 respectively. For some comments on this matter see Brody 1998b (here Chapter 7).
10 Brody 1995b, published in 1997.
11 Since Chomsky 1999.
12 Brody 1985, here Chapter 3.
13 Brody 1995b, 1997, here Chapter 8. See also the discussion in Chapter 10 note 7.

1 ON CIRCULAR READINGS

1 A number of such constraints have been proposed in the linguistic literature to exclude structures of this type. (For example cf. Postal 1972, Vergnaud 1974, Jacobson 1977). These proposals are conspicuously *ad hoc* and do not cover or generalize naturally to the whole range of relevant data.
2 For example cf. Williams 1977, for the distinction between sentence and "discourse" grammar rules.
3 Cf. Sag 1977, Williams 1977.
4 In an earlier version of this paper, this assumption was incorrectly attributed to HM. I am grateful to James Higginbotham and Robert May for pointing this out to me.

5 I ignore a number of interesting questions that relate to the derivation of these and similar structures since they are not directly relevant to the present discussion. I should note that HM assume that in the derivation of (15a), Quantifier Raising applies to the subject NP, and that the target of the annotation entry for *her* is not closed, not simply because it contains a pronoun, but because it contains a pronoun related to a quantifier/variable.
6 As (i)–(iii) show in HM's framework, expansion must apply *after* the level L at which the condition C that excludes (iii) is stated (in HM L = logical form).

(i) Who$_x$ x said [$_y$his$_x$ mother] thought she$_y$ liked Tom
(ii) Who$_x$ x said [$_y$his$_x$ mother] thought [$_y$his$_x$ mother] liked Tom
(iii) Who$_x$ x said Mary$_y$ thought Mary$_y$ liked Tom

The target of *she* in (i) is not closed in the sense of the Target Condition. If the predicted substitution applies not later than L producing (ii), this structure will be excluded by C. (Expansion in (i) will not be necessary in the framework I propose below.)
7 I assume along with much current work that some structural condition like c-command between antecedent and anaphor is necessary for the association to belong to sentence grammar, hence to be exempt from expansion.

Stating C of note (6) after expansion would entail that pronouns that have a c-commanding linguistic antecedent never expand; that they are related to their antecedents by a rule of sentence grammar. This would have certain advantages: it would eliminate the possibility of assigning an infinite number of representations to structures like (15a). Strict ordering here leads to a paradox however. Quantifier Raising has to be able to apply before expansion for (7a) to be derivable. But as pointed out in Brody (1979), in order to exclude "she$_x$ liked [some of the boys Mary$_x$ met]," C must apply before Quantifier Raising which might convert this structure into "[$_y$some of the boys Mary$_y$ met] she$_x$ liked y." This will not violate C any more, as the grammaticality of "[$_y$Which of the boys Mary$_x$ met] did she$_x$ like y" shows.
8 It is not clear how and whether this should be extended to anaphors whose antecedents are non-linguistic. In the same way, no position is taken here on the treatment of anaphors with antecedents that are inferred on the basis of some linguistic segment as for example in the case of "Every man who owns a donkey beats it."

2 ON CONTEXTUAL DEFINITIONS AND THE ROLE OF CHAINS

1 In LGB the right side of the definition of variables also contains the proviso "and in an A-position." This appears to be superfluous, however, since the whole theory in (5) should be understood only as a theory of A-positions; it would give incorrect results for categories in Ā-positions. For example, if (5c) is taken to be relevant for Ā-positions as well, then it predicts the empty category in Comp in (i) to be an anaphor.

(i) Who$_x$ did Mary say t_x t_x liked Tom

Principle (A) of the binding theory ((6a) in the text) would then exclude (i) and Comp-to-Comp movement in general since traces in Comp in this construction are not A-bound by definition.
2 I adopt here the LGB definition of chains (though I assume that most, if not all, of this definition should follow from independent principles. See Brody (forthcoming).) In LGB it is assumed that α and β are in the same chain only if either β is the trace of α or β is a postverbal argument related to an expletive subject, α, in a construction like (i).

(i) It seems that S

In (i) *it* and the postverbal S′ are taken to be cosuperscripted and the NP *it* is said to BIND, though not to bind, the S′. Therefore, the S′ in (i) is free and BOUND. The definition of chains is then as follows:

(ii) $C = (\alpha_1, \ldots, \alpha_n)$ is a chain iff
  a. α_1 is an NP
  b. α_i locally A-BINDs α_{i+1}
  c. For $i > 1$, either α_i is a nonpronominal empty category or α_i is A-free
  d. C is maximal; that is, it is not a proper subsequence of a chain meeting (a)–(c)

A minor technical problem is that a cosuperscripted postverbal argument, when this is an (emphatic) pronoun, can be A-bound by a category outside the chain, as for example in (iii):

(iii) La gente$_x$ dice che arrivano loro$_x$
  the people say that arrive they
  "The people say that they arrive."

We might replace A-*free* in (iic) by A-*BOUND*.

3 In LGB (Chapter 6) Chomsky states the θ-Criterion essentially as follows:

(i) Each argument is in some chain that has a unique θ-position.
(ii) Each θ-role is assigned to some chain that contains a unique argument.

(In LGB Chomsky argues that there are arguments that are not in chains. To have a consistent description, we might distinguish XP-chains and NP-chains. An NP-chain is defined as in note 2; an XP-chain differs in that condition (a) is changed to "α is an XP," with appropriate restrictions on X. The θ-Criterion refers to XP-chains; other conditions (e.g. the visibility requirement) may refer to NP-chains.)

4 One might argue that (2b) does not provide independent motivation for the claim that pronominal empty categories *necessarily* break the chain – (2b) only necessitates the assumption that pronominal empty categories *may* do so. Suppose that pronominal empty categories optionally break the chain. Then in (2b) the chain [Tom, e] will not satisfy the θ-Criterion, but the chains [Tom] and [e] will. This assumption does not suffice to rule out (1a), however, where the chain [Tom,e] would satisfy the θ-Criterion although the chains [Tom], [e] would not.

Similarly, the assumption that nonpronominals may optionally be heads of A-chains allows both (3a) and (1b); thus, (3a) appears to provide no independent motivation for the claim that nonpronominal empty categories are obligatorily nonheads of A-chains.

In Brody (forthcoming) I shall argue that the stronger conditions in fact hold, and that they are consequences of a modified version of Case- and θ-theory.

5 The identification requirement of Chomsky (1982) restricts pro to positions associated with "strong" (Italian-type) agreement and (possibly) to ones associated with clitics.

6 The formulation of principle (C) in (6) makes explicit the suggestion of LGB that it is an elsewhere condition: "Other NPs are A-free."

For present purposes we may assume the following definition of *governing category*: α is the governing category of β iff α is the minimal S/NP node that dominates the governor of β. Note that β has a governing category iff it is governed, hence the theorem that pronominal anaphors must be ungoverned (cf. LGB).

7 Chomsky has noted this (MIT lectures, Fall 1982). Both he and Rizzi (1983) have noted independently that contextual definitions are redundant in general and have made the claim, which I will substantiate here, that they do not exist.

8 Parasitic gap structures (e.g. (i)) and inverted constructions in pro-drop languages (e.g. (ii)) are suggested examples of this.

NOTES

(i) Which book did John criticize e without reading e'
(ii) e telefonano molti studenti
 telephone many students
 "Many students telephone."

In (ii) the trace left by the rightward movement of the subject appears to turn into a pronominal. It must be a pronominal at S-structure, since it is free. In (i) the parasitic gap e' is a pronominal at D-structure, where it is free, but a nonpronominal variable at S-structure.

As Chomsky has noted (MIT class lectures), it is far from clear whether these examples motivate the assumption that categories may change status during the derivation. To say that in (ii) a trace has changed into a pronominal is only an unnatural way of stating that in this case the movement has left behind a pronominal empty category. As for (i), one may assume for instance that the empty category is also a nonpronominal at D-structure, where the principle(s) that would prevent this do not apply. In terms of the analysis proposed here this means that the VEC does not apply at this level.

9 In LGB Chomsky suggests that nonempty locally $\bar{A}$-bound categories exist – in structures employing the resumptive pronoun strategy (see also Koopman and Sportiche (1981)). I assume that this is not the case for the reasons to be given in note 12.

10 Examples like (18) are discussed in Higginbotham (1980). They are also cited by Rizzi (1983) and Safir (1983), both of whom point out that they cause difficulties for the LGB contextual definitions.

11 I shall not pursue here the consequences of this conclusion for the analysis of weak crossover and parasitic gap constructions.

12 It is natural to attribute this property of PRO (that if it has an antecedent, it is referential only if the antecedent is) to its anaphoric nature. Alternatively, this might be due to its status as a pronominal. Consider the contrast between (i) and (ii):

(i) ?This is the man who the fact that someone denied that he left upset everyone
(ii) *Who did the fact that someone denied that he left upset everyone

Chomsky (1982) points out that constructions employing the resumptive pronoun strategy rarely involve a relative operator and suggests that resumptive pronouns are linked to the head of the relative directly. Suppose then (contrary to the assumption in LGB) that locally $\bar{A}$-bound pronominals do not exist. This excludes (ii). If the generalization is true, we might try to account for it by extending the assumption that PRO is nonreferential when it has a nonreferential antecedent to nonanaphoric pronominals. (ii) will then be excluded in the same way as (17b). (i) is grammatical since the head of the relative, the antecedent of the pronoun here, can function referentially. This account has some desirable consequences, but it creates the problem that (iii) is now predicted to be grammatical.

(iii) *the man it is illegal PRO to go

It seems that the constraints on what may function as an antecedent for an anaphor are stricter than those on the antecedents of pronominals. (Also compare *a man to fix the sink*.)

13 Structures like (i) and parasitic gap constructions like (ii) also support this view. The fact that these may be weak crossover violations is of course irrelevant to the argument in the text.

(i) ?Who$_x$ did his$_x$ father like t$_x$ best
(ii) Which book$_x$ did you criticize t$_x$ without reading t$_x$

14 Given structures like (i), we must allow for variables that are not arguments, presumably as a consequence of being in a chain with an argument/variable.

(i) Who$_x$ t$_x$ was seen t$_x$

15 Chomsky (LGB, 344) attributes (30a) to K. Safir.
16 Sportiche (1983) argues that the ungrammaticality of (27b) is due to a prohibition against Case-marking nonhead members of chains. I received this work, which contains both similar and diverging developments relating to topics discussed here, only after the final version of this article had been prepared. See Brody (forthcoming) for discussion.
17 That is, we modify conditions (b) and (c) of the definition of chains cited in note 2 as (i) and (ii), respectively:

(i) α_i locally BINDs α_{i+1}
(ii) For $i > 1$, either α_i is a nonpronominal non-Operator empty category
or α_i is A-BOUND.

Note that a minor problem with the earlier formulation disappears: NPs in $\bar{\text{A}}$-positions are no longer predicted to form one-member chains. (A stipulation still seems necessary, however, to prevent *wh*-phrases in resumptive pronoun structures from being chains.)

18 As for chains that are formed by cosuperscripting, there are two basic cases:

(i) e^i [$_{VP}$ arrivano molti studenti^i]
      arrive many students
    "Many students arrive."
(ii) e^i [$_{VP}$[$_{VP}$ telefonano] molti studenti^i]
      telephone many students
    "Many students telephone."

In the ergative structure exemplified in (i) the subject is a $\bar{\theta}$-position and the GF$_n$ a θ-position, as required. (Note that only one of the two reasons given in the text for the fact that at D-structure a GF$_i$ ($i \neq n$) cannot contain an argument is relevant here. Since there is no movement in (i), the Recoverability Condition need not be violated.)

In the case of (ii), where the preverbal D-structure position of the NP *molti studenti* appears not to be a GF$_n$, we may assume that the notion of GF$_n$ is ambiguous and that both the pre- and the postverbal NPs have it. (If the hypothesis that they c-command each other (in the sense of c-command relevant for chain formation) could be maintained, then this would essentially follow.)

19 Rizzi (1983) gives a very interesting argument for this claim.
20 In fact, we may assume in general that there are two main interpretations of coindexing between A-positions: "chain-internal," which holds between members of the same chain, and "antecedence," which holds between a head of a chain and some other chain. Note that we need not assume any specific stipulations about which type of empty category participates in which type of relation. Pronominals may have antecedents since they always head chains, whereas NP-traces are never heads. Thus, the interpretation of the relation between these and a coindexed category will be "chain-internal."
21 An antecedentless pronominal is necessarily an argument iff it is an anaphor. This is because a PRO without an antecedent is interpreted as a variable-like element, hence an argument. It follows that (35) is also excluded by the θ-Criterion if PRO is taken to be free in it, and that it can become grammatical when PRO is replaced by a pronominal nonanaphor.
22 Examples like (37) were noted independently by Neil Smith and Luigi Burzio.
Note also the contrast between (37) and (i), of which I was reminded by N. Chomsky (personal communication).

(i) ?*It^i was clear without e seeming that S^i

(34) cannot distinguish (37) from (i). Given the account in the text, however, this contrast reduces to the one between (ii) and (iii).

(ii) This is obvious
(iii) ?*This seems

Assume that this contrast arises because the subject of *is obvious*, but not that of *seem*, is a θ-position. The ungrammaticality of (i) is then a consequence of the fact that the PRO, which must be an argument (cf. the discussion of (35)), is in a $\bar{\theta}$-position.

23 Note that this argument gives independent support to the derivation of the Case Filter from the θ-Criterion proposed in LGB. Assuming that either cosubscripting or cosuperscripting is necessary for chain formation, it follows from (39a,d) that a nonargument that is not cosubscripted with an argument must be cosuperscripted with one. By (39a), a one-member chain containing only a pleonastic element would still have to be in a θ-position, resulting in a violation of (39d) at A-structure.

The impersonal passive construction in (i) has been claimed to contain a chain that contains no argument and to which no θ-role is assigned.

(i) Es wurde getanzt
it was danced
"There was dancing."

However, as Betts (1983) notes, these constructions are not really impersonal, in the sense that they are possible only if the external argument is animate. As he points out, this might suggest that the NP *es* is in a chain with a PRO-type argument.

24 (47b) is also excluded if *e* is an Operator for the same reason as (i); neither contains a category that could function as a variable.

(i) *Who e seems S'

(47c) is excluded redundantly by the θ-Criterion, since the Operator splits *he* and *e'* into two chains, only one of which has a θ-role.

25 (47b) is now also excluded by the principles that prevent a GF_i ($i \neq n$) from being a θ-position, as are (45a,b).

3 ON THE COMPLEMENTARY DISTRIBUTION OF EMPTY CATEGORIES

1 The Identification Principle allows pro to occur in positions associated with "strong" (Italian-type) agreement and possibly in positions associated with clitics.
2 As we have seen, (11) is excluded by the θ-Criterion if the EC in it is not taken to break the chain. In (2) the EC would be a nonpronominal by the definition of pronominals in Chomsky (1981) and would therefore be excluded by the ECP, whether or not it breaks the chain.
3 As noted, (12) is ruled out by the θ-Criterion if the chain is not maximal. In (6a) the EC would be a pronominal by the definition of pronominals and would thus be ruled out by the Identification Principle and the PRO Condition whether or not the chain is maximal.
4 The assumption in fact refers more generally to "contentive" elements, where these include arguments and Operators.
5 Note that PRO is like lexical anaphors and unlike lexical pronouns in that it may not function as a resumptive element in relative-type structures.

(i) ?The man$_x$ that the fact that it was illegal for him$_x$ to come did not disturb anybody arrived

(ii) *The man$_x$ that the fact that it was illegal for himself$_x$ to come did not disturb anybody arrived

(iii) *The man$_x$ that the fact that it was illegal PRO$_x$ to come did not disturb anybody arrived

Suppose that arguments in the position of head of a relative or perhaps in Ā-positions in general do not need a θ-role. (I shall not attempt to choose here among the various ways this could be made compatible with the θ-Criterion and the Projection Principle.) The contrast between (i) and (ii)–(iii) then could be due to the fact that anaphors that are heads of chains (PRO and lexical anaphors) must obey (19), whereas pronouns would have to obey only (iv). (See section 4 for other properties concerning choice of antecedent that PRO and lexical anaphors have in common.)

(iv) If a pronoun has an antecedent A, A must refer.

Note that *I found [a man [e to fix the sink]]* would now have to be analyzed as containing the chain [a man, e], with the EC governed, presumably by the N *man*.

(19) would account for the contrast between (v) and (vi) but not for the contrast between (vii) and (viii), since (as (viii) shows) it must allow an anaphor that heads some chain to use a "quasi-argument" antecedent.

(v) ??They would prefer for each other to go there
(vi) *It would be preferred for itself to be obvious that S
(vii) *It often rains without itself snowing
(viii) It often rains without e snowing

As one reviewer suggests, the ungrammaticality of (vii) may be due to some principle excluding lexical anaphors in general from the subject position of the *without*-clause. Alternatively, suppose that quasi-arguments do not refer at all, the fact that they can control PRO being due to the fact that they satisfy (19). To exclude (vii) we could extend (iv) from pronouns to all lexical categories. The rationale for this step would be that independently from the properties of PRO, we know that an EC E can be related to some other category C when E and C are not in any kind of referential relation with each other (where "referential relation" is taken to include coreference and binding) – for example, in NP-movement structures. Perhaps ECs lack some feature of overt categories that makes it necessary for an element of the latter kind to be in a referential relation with its antecedent. (The assumptions in this note differ from those of Brody (1984a), where (19) is extended not to head-of-chain anaphors but to pronouns. This difference does not affect the main line of the argumentation there concerning (19) and the θ-Criterion.)

6   Sportiche (1983) attributes to N. Chomsky the observation that in structures like (i) third person lexical anaphors do not need an antecedent either.

(i) Lies about each other trigger the fight

Because of the delicate judgments involved it is difficult to determine whether the implicit antecedent in examples like (29) is of the same type as the one in (i). Note also (ii), pointed out to me by R. Hudson.

(ii) John has been taking a lot of pictures lately. The ones of himself are pretty good.

See Sportiche (1983) for discussion of the fact that an antecedentless PRO may also pick a specific referent in a certain very restricted set of contexts.

7   It is sometimes claimed that PRO is like a pronominal in that it allows split antecedents. Again, however, we find that PRO shares this property with lexical anaphors in certain types of positions:

(i) John$_x$ told Mary$_y$ that PRO$_{x,y}$ to wash each other$_{x,y}$ would have been appropriate
(ii) John$_x$ told Mary$_y$ that each other's$_{x,y}$ pictures were on sale

Compare (i) and (ii) with (iii)–(v).

(iii) *John$_x$ promised Mary$_y$ PRO$_{x,y}$ to wash each other$_{x,y}$
(iv) *John$_x$ promised Mary$_y$ each other's$_{x,y}$ pictures
(v) *John$_x$ talked to Mary$_y$ about each other$_{x,y}$

The binding theory in section 4 will capture this parallel as well, if the indexing system is appropriately extended in the obvious way (see note 20).

8 Chomsky (1982, 78–79) states, "The most plausible general assumption is that the typology of ECs simply mirrors that of overt categories, that is, that no new principles are invoked to determine the types of EC."

One reviewer considers this remark as an argument for the existence of pro; another reviewer construes it as an argument for maintaining that ECs cross-classify as $+/-$ pronominal and $+/-$ anaphor categories. Chomsky's point seems to be, however, that the assumption that the typology of ECs mirrors that of lexical categories makes it possible not to introduce *new* principles to classify ECs. But this is an argument against introducing new typological principles for ECs, ones that are not independently motivated for lexical categories. It is not an argument against not applying principles of lexical category classification to ECs. So there is an argument here for making the lexical category typology carry over to ECs (and thus for the existence of pro) only if this assumption is necessary in order to avoid introducing new principles to establish the typology of ECs. I claim that this is not the case: the $+/-$ pronominal distinction (and, as I shall argue later, the $+/-$ anaphor distinction as well) can be dropped for ECs without introducing otherwise unmotivated principles.

9 From the assumption made in Brody (1984a) that at D-Structure only the GF$_n$ of a chain may contain contentive elements (arguments and Operators) it does not in fact follow that all chains involve movement (i.e. that only movement is chain-internal), even if we abstract away from chains that involve cosuperscripting in the theory of Chomsky (1981). This is because the assumption does not force the movement derivation in the case of chains that are headed by an expletive element, as in *It seems e to be obvious that S*. The correct conclusion appears to be that the (relatively) pretheoretical notion that the complementary distribution involves movement launching and other ECs is not precise enough.

10 Since we are assuming that the EC associated with Clitics and with Agr in "subject pronoun drop" languages is a nonpronominal anaphor and a nonhead member of a chain, Chomsky's (1981) proviso for (35) that PRO must have no superscript is unnecessary.

11 It is natural to take this as a consequence of a condition that Case-marked NPs must be phonetically realized. This condition is assumed to constrain pronominals in certain structural positions in Jaeggli (1980) and all pronominal NPs in Aoun (1982). It is unclear why the condition should be restricted in this way. Bouchard (1982) assumes as I do the truth of the more general statement that an NP is lexical iff it has Case at PF.

Certain types of contraction phenomena appear to be sensitive to Case properties. Analyses of contraction that refer to the distinction between Case-marked and Caseless ECs (e.g. Jaeggli (1980)) can be reformulated in the present framework using the distinction between ECs in Case and Caseless positions.

12 That is, we make what in a Case-assignment framework would be equivalent to the assumption that Case is assigned only under government.

13 This distinction between locality and Case-matching is the same as the distinction Vergnaud (1982) draws between Case-assignment and structural proximity, if the difference between Case-assignment and Case-checking is ignored. Note that the conjunction of Vergnaud's proximity condition, which may be rephrased as (i), and his condition (64), with essentially the import of (ii), is very close to the CLC.

(i) If x has Case, then x is governed.
(ii) If y with Case governs x, then x has Case.

14 Levin (1983), who develops an interesting account of the distribution of Operators in Comp that involves extending the Case-checking theory to Ā-positions, suggests that the fact that nonhead members of chains are ECs is a consequence of her Case Visibility Principle. According to this principle, Case is visible only on NPs in governed positions. Assuming that lexical NPs must have a *visible* Case, a lexical NP in an ungoverned position will be excluded. (Note that this notion of "visibility" is different from the one I shall make use of below. One concerns visibility of Case; the other pertains to visibility of a category or chain, which (I shall argue) depends on Case properties.)

15 Ignoring intervening Comp-to-Comp traces. I shall assume that non-Operators in Ā-position are not binders for the purposes of the binding theory either.

16 It is sometimes suggested that (in the terminology of the Case-assignment framework) it is in fact the *wh*-phrase and not the EC in A-position it locally binds that needs to be Case-marked (on local binding, see note 15). It may inherit Case from this EC or, when this EC is in a Caseless position, it may receive Case in its place (as for example in Hebrew free relatives; see Borer (1982)) or from an intermediate Comp-to-Comp trace (as for example in constructions like (i) and (iii), pointed out by Kayne (1980)).

(i) John who I assure you e e′ to be the best
(ii) *I assure you John to be the best
(iii) Jean, que Marie croit e e′ être intelligent, ...
    John who Mary believes to be intelligent
(iv) *Marie croit Jean être intelligent

Within Case-checking theory this would mean that a *wh*-phrase may be Case-linked not only to the governor of the locally bound EC in A-position but also to its own governor or to that of an intermediate trace. However, this proposal, whether or not it is stated in Case-checking terms, faces difficulties since it does not constrain strongly enough those structures that involve Case-assignment/Case-checking into Comp. The EC associated with a *wh*-phrase in these constructions can appear only in a restricted set of Caseless positions, contrary to what we would expect if Case-assignment/Case-checking into Comp could fulfill the Case requirements of these constructions in general. Thus, as discussed by Borer, in Hebrew free relatives the EC cannot appear (for example) in infinitival subject position. Constructions like (i) and (iii) are impossible when the EC in A-position is not adjacent to the Case-position.

(v) *John, who I assure you e it seems e e′ to be honest ...
(vi) *Jean, que Marie croit   e qu'il paraît e e′ être intelligent ...
    John who Mary believes that it seems   to be intelligent

Kayne assumes a formulation of the Nominative Island Condition that requires a coindexed binder to have Case (this translates straightforwardly into a system making use of the ECP), which is supplemented with Case-transmission conventions that ensure that the adjacent binder of the EC in subject position has Case in (i) and (iii) but not in (v) and (vi). Alternatively, the contrast between these examples may suggest a marked local rule that in the configuration "$x^0 e_x e'_x$," where x^0 governs e, transmits this relation to e'. The *wh*-phrase is now Case-linked in the position of e' in (i), (iii), (v), and (vi) but is Case-matched only in (i) and (iii). In (v) and (vi) it cannot be Case-matched, since its governor has no Case.

17 Constructions that involve an Operator that is never overt (e.g. Topicalization, "easy to please"-type adjectival complements) suggest that the latter hypothesis is preferable. The problem arises also with Clitic constructions. Given the assumption that Clitics (including Agr) are heads of chains, they must be Case-linked. If the situation is analogous to movement-to-Comp cases, then the Clitic will have to be Case-linked to the governor of

the EC associated with it. Since this EC is a nonhead member of a chain, it must be governed; hence, the Clitic must have Case. However, if the correlation between overt Agr and subject pronoun drop is only a tendency (and in general if there exist phonologically null Clitics), then again ECs in Ā-position must be allowed to bear Case.

18 SUBJECT is intuitively the "most prominent nominal." Agr is SUBJECT when present, otherwise the subject is. x is accessible to y iff x c-commands y and assigning the index of x to y would not violate (i), the i-within-i Condition (see Chomsky (1981)).

(i) *$[_v \ldots z \ldots]$, where v and z bear the same index

In the context of the assumption that the PRO Condition is derived from the binding theory, introducing the notion of accessible SUBJECT into the definition of governing category makes an extra principle necessary to ensure that a governed PRO always has a binding theory domain. Given the definition in (44), PRO in (i) and (ii) has no governing category.

(i) Pictures (of) PRO were on sale
(ii) PRO pictures were on sale

Chomsky (1981, 220) suggests that a principle like (iii) could be used to enable the binding theory to exclude (i) and (ii).

(iii) A root clause is a binding theory domain for a governed element.

Chomsky claims that (iii) is independently motivated by the behavior of lexical anaphors: (iii) makes it possible to exclude (iv) by the binding theory.

(iv) ?For each other$_x$ to win would be unfortunate (for them$_x$)

But the grammaticality of examples like (27) and (29) and (i) in note 6 strongly suggests that (iii) is incorrect (Sportiche (1983) notes this in connection with the example in note 6) and that the marginality of (iv) has some other source. It is not clear whether there is much difference between (iv) (when the required antecedent is present) and (v), or between (vi) and (vii), suggesting that the problem concerns the position of the anaphor and not that of its antecedent.

(v) ?They thought that for each other to win would be unfortunate
(vi) ?For himself to win would be unfortunate for Tom
(vii) ?Tom thought that for himself to win would be unfortunate

Therefore, if (contrary to our assumptions) the PRO Condition is derived from the binding theory, then it seems necessary to state (iii) as (viii).

(viii) A root S is a binding theory domain for a governed PRO.

19 The SUBJECT in the definition of governing category must be that of the minimal category in question; in (i) and (ii) the VP must not qualify as a potential governing category on the grounds that it contains a SUBJECT (that of the embedded clause).

(i) Mary [$_{VP}$ mentioned each other that Tom left]
(ii) Mary [$_{VP}$ promised John PRO to mention that Tom left]

If the NP *Tom* counted as a relevant SUBJECT, then the anaphor would not have a governing category in (i), (ii): the embedded SUBJECT does not c-command the anaphor and therefore is not accessible to it by definition.
20. Let us extend the theory of indexing in the natural and usual way in order to describe the phenomenon of split antecedents. Suppose that the referential index is a set of integers. Then

(i) x binds y iff x c-commands y and x, y have an identical referential index.

The PRO–lexical anaphor parallel, illustrated in note 7, again follows from the binding theory. Binding principle (A) allows the anaphors in (i), (ii) of note 7 to be free; they have no governing category. The anaphors in (iii), (iv), and (v) of note 7, however, do have a governing category in which they must be bound. But neither of the split antecedents binds the anaphor: their referential index set is not identical to that of the anaphor.

21. Huang (1983) proposes to modify the definition of governing category quoted in (44) by restricting the accessibility requirement to anaphors and dropping it for pronouns. He suggests that the head noun of an NP functions as a SUBJECT, nonaccessible for anaphors inside the NP. The NP is then the governing category for the pronouns but not for the anaphors inside it: the grammaticality of (54), (55), (56), and (57) follows. The hypothesis that the head noun of an NP is a nonaccessible SUBJECT for an anaphor inside the NP is not compatible with the theory we are adopting here. Given Manzini's assumption, well-motivated for anaphors, that if accessibility is not satisfied by the "nearest" SUBJECT, then the anaphor has no governing category, it would entail incorrectly that the anaphors in (54), (55) have no governing category and can refer freely.

Since PPs may contain subjects (see for example Stowell (1981)), examples where a pronoun in a PP has a binder in the S containing the PP are predicted to be well-formed. For example:

(i)   John$_x$ always keeps his wits about him$_x$
(ii) The melody$_x$ has a haunting character to it$_x$
(iii) John$_x$ pushed the book away from him$_x$
(iv) John$_x$ turned his friends against him$_x$
(v)   John$_x$ saw a snake near him$_x$

We must still appeal to independent considerations to exclude the anaphor in the place of the pronoun in (i) and (ii). This does not seem unnatural, given the set phrase character of these examples. In examples like *John talked to him, John was proud of him* we must assume that the PP may not contain a subject, presumably because of its close relationship with the verb.

22. Extensions of the binding theory to Ā-positions have been proposed by various authors, including Brody (1981), Aoun (1982), and Koster (1982). Koster defends the strong hypothesis adopted here that locally Ā-bound ECs are pure nonpronominal anaphors, using different arguments and arriving at somewhat different conclusions about the properties of these elements.

23. The implication (i) often assumed in the literature holds in the theory being developed here.

(i) An NP is an anaphor if it has no Case.

A different way of thinking about ECs would be to assume that they are neutral with respect to the $+/-$ anaphor, $+/-$ pronominal distinctions – that they do not have any of the four possible properties. If so, then being an anaphor would be a property of chains and not of categories; (i) would then hold for chains. ECs would cease to be constrained by principle (A) of the binding theory; the choice of an appropriately local antecedent would presumably have to be ensured by the bounding theory.

24 Sportiche (1983) notes that referential overlap is also prohibited in strong crossover configurations. Just as *this man* cannot be a member of the set denoted by *they* in (i), so there cannot be referential overlap between *they* and the EC in (ii). Thus, taking *Bill* to be a member of the set denoted by *they*, (ii) cannot mean "Bill wonders which man x is such that Bill and x think you saw x."

(i) They think you saw this man
(ii) Bill wonders which man they think you saw

Assuming that the referential index is a set of integers, the relevant structures of (i) and (ii) are (iii) and (iv), respectively.

(iii) *They$_{\{i,j\}}$ think you saw this man$_{\{j\}}$
(iv) *Bill$_{\{j\}}$ wonders which man$_{\{i\}}$ they$_{\{i,j\}}$ think you saw e$_{\{i\}}$

The definition of *bound* in (i) of note 20 and the further definitions in (v) take this extension into account. Note that *free* is not the same as *not bound any more*. In (v) I introduce the term *weakly bound*, which is equivalent to *not free*.

(v) a. x is bound by y iff y c-commands x and x and y have identical referential index sets.
b. x is weakly bound by y iff y c-commands x and the intersection of the referential index sets of x and y is a nonempty set.
c. x is free iff x is not weakly bound.
d. x is free in domain D iff x is not weakly bound in D.

Sportiche suggests that binding principle (C), which requires the overt NP *this man* in (iii) to be free, should be taken to generalize to the EC in (iv), thereby excluding both structures. (iv) could be ruled out also by extending principle (B) to Ā-positions. Sportiche argues against this. Although (iv) contains a pronominal that is not Ā-free, binding principle (B) could not make the proper distinction between (vi) and (vii); in neither case is the pronoun Ā-free.

(vi) *Which man$_{\{i\}}$ does Bill$_{\{j\}}$ think Comp they$_{\{i,j\}}$ saw e$_{\{i\}}$
(vii) Which man$_{\{i\}}$ e$_{\{i\}}$ told Bill$_{\{j\}}$ that they$_{\{i,j\}}$ should leave

Sportiche notes that using the EC in the intermediate Comp in (vi) to distinguish between the two structures would be a dubious move, since in French and Italian, where S is not a bounding node, no such EC need be present. But suppose that binding principle (B) is understood as prohibiting *local* weak binding inside the binding category. x locally weakly binds y with respect to an index i iff x is the nearest weak binder of y that has index i, where *nearest* is to be taken in its usual sense. We assume that the *wh*-phrase is in every binding category, a possibility mentioned above in connection with binding principle (A); also see appendix 1. The *wh*-phrase does not locally weakly bind the pronoun in (vii), whose local weak binders are the NP *Bill* (for index j) and the EC (for index i). However, since these are outside the binding category of the pronoun, they do not violate principle (B) either. In contrast, in (vi) the local weak binders of *they* are *which man* (for i) and *Bill* (for j). (It does not matter if there is an EC in Comp, since we assume that these are not binders for the binding theory.) The *wh*-phrase in (vi) is then a local weak binder, violating binding principle (B).

The violations in (iv) and (vi) are stronger than those of weak crossover, which (as I shall argue in appendix 1) are due to binding principle (B). We might attribute this to the fact that (iv) and (vi) also violate principle (A), if we assume that x locally (strongly) binds y iff x (strongly) binds y and it is the nearest weak or strong binder of y. The EC with index i in (iv) and (vi) is not locally strongly bound in its binding category. In both cases its local binder $they_{[i,j]}$ is a weak binder and its only strong binder is the *wh*-phrase. Although the *wh*-phrase is inside the binding category of the EC, it is not a local binder.

25 Chomsky (class lectures, MIT) has suggested an account of weak crossover based on binding principle (B), but without the assumption crucial to our account that S-adjoined positions are in every governing category.

26 Note that binding principle (A) must not hold after the predication rule since an EC locally bound by an Operator phrase x before predication (e.g. the EC in (68d)) would not be bound by x under the assumptions made here if the Operator status of x is revoked.

27 Sportiche (1983) attributes the grammatically of (72) to the stipulation in (i).

(i) An ungoverned subject (i.e. a PRO) is always bound by an empty Operator in the adjacent Comp.
(ii) An expletive PRO is governed.

PRO in (72) now has its own separate quantifier; thus, in (72) only one EC is locally bound by the *wh*-phrase, and the Bijection Principle is not violated. Sportiche argues that (i) is motivated by the following considerations as well. (a) In the context of Sportiche's assumption that locally $\bar{A}$-bound traces are pronominal elements (i) fills a gap in the paradigm of binding possibilities of ECs: anaphoric ECs can now also be $\bar{A}$-bound. This argument of course disappears in the present framework, where all ECs are anaphors. (b) Sportiche argues that (i) explains why the subject of a weather verb, a "quasi-argument" in an ungoverned position, must have a quasi-argument antecedent.

(iii) *It's impossible e to rain

According to Sportiche, it is in fact the Operator associated with this EC that has no available antecedent; therefore, "it is assigned an arbitrary range" and "must ... bind an element whose semantics allows [it] to range" (p. 311). (In contrast with Chomsky (1981) and note 5 above, Sportiche assumes that quasi-arguments refer to a designated element.) But it is not clear that this contributes to the explanation of the ungrammaticality of (iii), since it does not seem to matter whether the property of arbitrary interpretation is stipulated of the antecedentless empty head of the chain or of the putative Operator associated with it.

(i) entails (ii), Sportiche's Constraint on Expletive PRO (CEP), under assumption (iv).

(iv) Locally $\bar{A}$-bound categories are arguments.

Two further advantages claimed for the CEP and thus for (i) are (c) that the CEP entails that traces of NP-movement are governed (the Trace Condition) and (d) that it excludes structures with ungoverned expletives that are not NP-traces, such as (18). On the basis of the argument in section 1.1, we should reject the CEP (and (i)) on the grounds alone that it does not relate either to the principles that entail the Trace Condition for locally $\bar{A}$-bound traces or to those that entail the PRO Condition. Finally, consider the fact that the assumption that expletive ECs are governed excludes (18). Sportiche derives this assumption (the content of the CEP) from (iv) and (i), the latter a stipulation that we have had reason to reject. In contrast, in the framework proposed here (ii) (the content of the CEP) is derived partly from Case-checking theory (ungoverned ECs are heads of chains) and partly from (19), which entails that anaphors that head chains are arguments. The latter assumption in turn is also motivated independently from the behavior of PRO: it is also true of lexical anaphors (see the contrast between (v) and (vi) of note 5). Furthermore, it follows from the θ-Criterion for those cases where the anaphor has an antecedent (Brody (1984a)). It does have one stipulative component: that an antecedentless PRO (or perhaps CL-anaphor in general) must have the arbitrary reference "someone/oneself" interpretation, from which it follows that it must be an argument. But this stipulation is necessary even if the CEP is assumed or if (i) is also accepted, in order to specify the interpretation of the PRO or that of the empty Operator associated with the PRO in such cases.

28 Safir (1984) argues that relative clauses where two lexical pronouns (both in positions that are inaccessible to movement) are locally bound by the *wh*-phrase are also more acceptable than (restrictive) relative clauses like (68c). Given the marginality of the resumptive pronoun strategy in English and the fairly high acceptability of structures like (68c), this involves very delicate judgments. The binding-theory-based account proposed here excludes these examples, but makes the same predictions for the clearer cases as Safir's parallelism constraint.

29 Further elaborations are necessary to deal with the varying acceptability of (i), (ii), (iii), and (67), as well as for apparent weak crossover violations in structures like (iv), (v), and (vi). See Haïk (1983; 1984), Higginbotham (1983), Safir (1984).

  (i)   ?Whose$_x$ mother likes him$_x$
  (ii)   ?Everyone's$_x$ mother likes him$_x$
  (iii) Everybody in some city$_x$ likes its$_x$ climate
  (iv)   ??Every man who a donkey$_x$ kicked was afraid of it$_x$
  (v)   ??Which man who owns a donkey$_x$ did it$_x$ kick
  (vi)   ??(The man who she$_x$ loves)$_y$ kissed (his$_y$ wife)$_x$

30 More precisely, Sportiche proposes that an EC (and in general a category with φ-features only) without Case falls under principle (A) of the binding theory, and one with Case under principle (B). He restricts to arguments the condition that φ-categories with Case are interpreted as pronominals and those without are interpreted as anaphors.

Note that the import of (79) and (80) is somewhat different here than in the (obligatory) Case-assignment framework their originators propose.

31 The fact that (81) is a more complicated characterization of complementary distribution than the one proposed in the text is of course not an argument against it. As (81) is also assumed to follow from Case-checking theory, it would have no theoretical status in the grammar.

32 In this appendix I shall briefly discuss how some of the central claims of Brody (1984a) could be integrated with the theory developed above. I saw Chomsky (1985) only after the final version of the text and the first two appendices of this article had been prepared – hence the fact that references to this work appear only in this appendix. For a binding theory that integrates ideas in Chomsky (1985) and in this chapter, see Manzini (1985).

33 I assume that it is not necessary to use two kinds of indexing to distinguish trace binding from the expletive argument relations of (83), (84), as has been proposed (for example) in Safir (1982) and Chomsky (1985).

Earlier the definition in (9) was extended to allow Ā-binding relations to form chains. Part (a) of (9) may also have to be revised, if clauses can also head chains in structures where they are not bound by an expletive – for example, *I believe that S, That S was not believed e by anybody*. (See note 43.)

34 Not all θ-roles that are present in a lexical entry create syntactic positions; for example, there is no syntactic position for the lexically present *agent* in *The boat was sunk e* (see Chomsky (1985, section 4.2)). Suppose that a θ-role T that does create a syntactic position can be assigned to an argument A at D-Structure iff A is in the position T created. Then (i) and (ii) follow from the θ-Criterion in (85).

  (i)   Each argument is in a θ-position.
  (ii) Each θ-position contains some argument.

(i) and (ii) require a θ-role to be assigned to a unique argument, assuming that an argument may be at most in one position, but allow an argument to receive more than one θ-role. On the latter possibility, see Chomsky (1985), who considers (i) and (ii) as part of the hypothesis that D-Structure is a pure representation of GF-θ. Note that the derivation that a chain must contain a unique θ-position in this appendix and in Brody (1984a) allows a chain to have any number of θ-roles as long as they are all assigned in GF_n.

35 The argument that receives the θ-role T at D-Structure must be an argument of the chain C that receives T at S-Structure/LF, since the position in which T is assigned (the same at both levels) cannot contain any categories at D-Structure that are not part of C if all movement is chain-internal as assumed here (also see Sportiche (1983), Brody (1984a), Chomsky (1985)).

36 Chomsky in fact states (87a) in terms of a prohibition against a chain containing more than one θ-position rather than as a condition on the number of positions where θ-roles may be assigned. His formulation of (85) ((i) and (ii) in note 34) and (87a) leaves open the possibility that θ-roles are assigned directly only to positions, chains and arguments then inheriting θ-roles indirectly by virtue of containing or being contained in the relevant positions. Also, what Chomsky considers to be the θ-Criterion is in fact the conjunction of his formulation of (87a) with the visibility requirement.

37 It is configurationally possible for a chain to contain more than one x_n – that is, in a structure containing two or more members of some chain that do not c-command any element of the chain. If such chains exist, the theory predicts that they may contain more than one θ-position. (Under the revised GF_n hypothesis (see (88) below), they contain as many θ-positions as x_n's.) Parasitic gaps will not provide an example if they are Ā-bound by an empty Operator that does not bind the real gap, a suggestion attributed to Chomsky in Cinque (1984). Operators, we have assumed throughout, break the chain. As we shall see below, extending chains to Ā-chains forces this account of parasitic gaps in the context of the theory of appendix 3 (see note 44). The standard formulation of the local binding condition requires that each link of the chain be of the form $[x_i, x_{i+1}]$, where x_i, locally binds x_{i+1}. If this is understood in accordance with (i),

(i) For two positions x_i and x_j, if not $x_i = x_j$ then not $i = j$.

then the requirement is not met by forking chains.

38 In Brody (1984a) I have suggested that the fact that NP-traces are not arguments is due to a strengthened Recoverability Condition: arguments may not be deleted or inserted during the derivation. There may be other reasons why *John was seen e* cannot mean either "John and somebody were seen" or "John and himself were seen." For example, contrary to the assumptions of Brody (1984a), we may consider coindexing between arguments to entail a referential dependence not only when the arguments are members of different chains but also chain-internally. Then the first interpretation is impossible. As for the second, we would have to assume that this meaning is not well-formed for some independent reason, which is certainly conceivable. Given the extension of chains to expletive argument pairs, we must also rule out chains with two overt arguments in structures like (i) and (ii).

(i) *A man_x is $himself_x$ in the garden
(ii) *$This_x$ seems that S_x

Again it is not immediately obvious why (i) and (ii) cannot be interpreted as "There is a man in the garden" and "It seems that S," respectively. The GF_n hypothesis, together with the strengthened Recoverability Condition, will rule out (i) and (ii); but it is not difficult to imagine alternative solutions.

39 Or, to avoid having to insert lexical expletives during the derivation, we may allow $\bar{\theta}$-positions at D-Structure if linked to a θ-position. Note that we must allow $\bar{\theta}$-positions that contain null categories (as opposed to an EC; see Chomsky (1981) for the distinction) not

to be linked to enable NP-movement to apply. This would essentially follow Chomsky's (1985) analysis, which derives (86) from such a weakened statement of (89). (Chomsky requires *nonempty* categories to be linked to an argument, but this must be *nonnull* categories since otherwise expletive ECs (pro's in Chomsky's theory) would be able to form chains without a θ-role, violating (86).) But we have lost the real motivation for this weakening of (89), since the GF_n hypothesis entails (86). Furthermore, if Chomsky's suggestion that expletives are not present at LF is adopted, then it will be necessary to delete lexical expletives in the derivation in any case.

40 Chomsky (1985) derives (87c) partly from the assumption that subchains that are not expletive argument pairs are the "history" of movement. In "history-chains," then, x_n must be the D-Structure position of x_1. If x_1 is an argument, then by (85a) x_n is a θ-position, and it is unique by (87a). The assumption in (i)

(i) In expletive argument pairs the expletive c-commands the argument.

ensures that a chain always terminates in a "history-chain" headed by an argument and thus that (87b) holds in general. (i) in fact follows from other assumptions Chomsky makes. Consider structures where the argument c-commands the expletives. (ii) is ruled out since at D-Structure the argument is not in a θ-position (this is not a movement chain by hypothesis), and (iii) is impossible since $\bar{\theta}$-positions are all subject positions at D-Structure (where there are no Ā-positions); but, as Chomsky notes, there are no expletive argument pairs across a clause boundary.

(ii) argument   expletive
     $\bar{\theta}$-position   θ-position
(iii) argument   expletive
     θ-position $\bar{\theta}$-position

It seems a curious coincidence that all these various conditions result in (87c).

Other strange coincidences in the "history-chains" approach involve the local binding requirement on chains. Chomsky suggests that the requirement that each nonhead member of an A-chain must be bound is a consequence of the binding theory under the assumption that NP-traces are anaphors. Nonanaphor traces must also be bound but for independent reasons. The condition that for each chain link binding must be local is derived from various principles, each accounting for some part of the effects of this condition. The observation that this conspiracy is surprising is attributed by Chomsky to Luigi Rizzi. Chomsky argues that the local binding requirement does not hold in full generality on the basis of examples like (iv) where there is some reason to assume that the NP complement of the matrix verb c-commands the embedded subject position (as shown by (v)), apparently making the binding relation between the members of the chain [John,e] nonlocal.

(iv) John$_x$ seems to himself$_x$ e$_x$ to be clever
(v) *It seems to him$_x$ that John$_x$ is clever

But this account leaves open how to exclude (vi) and (vii), which (like (iv)) would not violate either the binding theory, the θ-Criterion, or Chomsky's (1985) Case theory but are more strongly unacceptable than typical Subjacency violations.

(vi) *John$_x$ is certain that it seems to him$_x$ e$_x$ to be clever
(vii) *It seems to John$_x$ e$_x$ to appear that he$_x$ is certain S'

(The derivation lowering *he* in (vii) is not excluded by the requirement that at D-Structure expletives must be coindexed with an argument of their own clause if (vii) is derived from a D-Structure where the subject of the most deeply embedded clause is the null category. See note 39.)

41 Suggesting that the basic level of representation is in fact not S-Structure (as suggested in Sportiche (1983)) but LF.

42 Also see Sportiche (1983).

43 Since there are clausal arguments, in order for them to be Case-linked it is necessary to assume that clauses also have Case. But clauses may appear in Caseless positions, so we conclude that the Case-matching requirement constrains only NPs. Note that since at LF all and only arguments are heads of chains it is not necessary to stipulate any more that a head of a chain is either NP or clause – only these categories may have the property of being Case-linked.

44 If parasitic gaps are bound by their own empty Operator, then they provide no argument against the assumption that ECs in A-position cannot have Case and thus cannot be Case-linked/visible when governed. If ECs may have Case only in Ā-position (see note 17), then parasitic gaps at D-Structure would have to move into Ā-position in order to be visible for θ-role assignment.

The inversion construction exemplified by the Italian (i) is another problematic case if chains are extended to Ā-chains (see Brody (1984a) for a suggestion).

(i) $e_x[_{vp}[_{vp}$ telefonano] molti studenti$_x$]
    telephoned many students
    "Many students telephoned"

45 Since NP-traces are also expletives, it is necessary to state more precisely which expletives need to be replaced at LF. Note that the first EC in (93), the trace of the expletive at S-Structure, is presumably licensed at LF, although it contains no argument. Apparently, then, at LF arguments and categories that are traces of arguments *at LF* are licensed. In other words, a category that may contain a D-Structure argument is licensed at LF if it is in a position that has contained an argument at some point in the derivation.

4 ON CHOMSKY'S *KNOWLEDGE OF LANGUAGE*

1 This review is based on research funded by the Economic and Social Research Council (UK), reference number C OO 23 2201.

2 This has in fact been proposed in May 1985.

3 A-positions are "those that are assigned grammatical functions such as subject and object (including the object of a preposition) ... The A-positions, then, are the positions in which semantic roles such as agent, patient and so forth can in principle be assigned, although whether they are in fact assigned depends on the choice of lexical items. Other positions we will call 'Ā-positions' in particular the clause-external position occupied by operators such as *who*."

4 Chomsky refers to chains in this extended sense as CHAINs.

5 The assumption in (7) is in fact implicit in Chomsky 1981, at least if all expletive elements must be Case-marked. This is because the derivation of the Case filter from the θ-Criterion in the form suggested there ensures the obligatoriness of Case-marking for expletives only if they are in a chain with some argument. In KL Chomsky argues that (7), supported by other principles of Case- and θ-theory (some of the latter we shall discuss below) makes it possible to derive a somewhat extended form of "Burzio's generalization":

(i) "A verb with a complement assigns Case if and only if it θ-marks its subject."

(i) restricts the lexicon in a strong and perhaps surprising way; one should certainly expect it to be a derived condition, a consequence of the interaction of the general principles of

Case- and θ-theory. Furthermore, the same general principles will provide a solution for another so far unresolved problem: the obligatoriness of subject-θ-marking (cf. the second paragraph of note 11).
6 I have changed "nonempty" to "nonnull" in (8) to correct what appears to be a minor oversight.
7 Suggested in Brody (1984).
8 Incidentally, one occurrence of "visible" is redundant here. If each θ-position (in a chain) is visible then a chain can only contain visible θ-positions.
9 Assuming that arguments can never be inserted or deleted during the derivation. In Brody 1984 this is attributed to a generalized recoverability condition. For a different approach see Sportiche (1983).
10 For example using the generalized recoverability condition referred to in the previous note.
11 The chain [John, e] in (11) might alternatively be excluded on the grounds that it contains two Case-marked positions. But (10a) would still be necessary to explain why there can be no construction like (11), involving movement between two θ-positions, differing from (11) only in that the object of the verb receives no Case. That is, why can there not be a verb *HIT* which has the thematic properties of *hit* but which assigns no Case to its object. The object would have to move away from its D-structure position to a position where it can receive Case exactly as in the examples in (4), resulting in the structure in (i), which would remain to be excluded.

(i)   *John HIT e

((i) would be excluded by Burzio's generalization quoted above in note 4, but that generalization is itself in need of an explanation. The explanation provided in KL is based partly on the principles of θ-theory discussed in the text.)

Note that we assume here that both the subject and the object position are θ-positions, that both of the θ-roles of *hit* are available and assigned. The problem discussed in the text should not be confused with a different one, – namely the question of what ensures that both θ-roles in the structure are available and assigned. For complements this follows from the projection principle: the position in the complement is created by the θ-role whose projection it is, but in the case of subjects some further assumptions are needed. (These are the ones referred to also in note 4 above.) This is because subjects are not obligatory in general ("the picture"), except probably in sentences ("*left"). However when they are present they must be assigned a θ-role if the relevant head of construction has a θ-role to assign: "*there's picture," "*There left."

12 We might exclude movement into a trace by appealing to the recoverability condition, or Sportiche's 1983 Isomorphy Principle. We assume throughout in the text that movement into θ-positions or into a trace is in fact excluded. If this is too strong (cf. KL para. 3.5.2.4), movement into the trace left by Wh-movement and NP-movement would still be excluded by other independently motivated principles.
13 For more discussion of these ideas see Brody 1984, 1985 and 1995.
14 Cf. e.g. Williams 1986 for a relevant proposal about S-structure indexing. Note, however, that he argues that there are no LF movement rules and that LF and S-structure can be collapsed.

5 A NOTE ON THE ORGANIZATION OF THE GRAMMAR

1 This note was written during the first half of 1991. Minor revisions were made in October 1991.

6 θ-THEORY AND ARGUMENTS

1. To say that an element is an argument iff it saturates a θ-role/fills a θ-position/etc. would of course make the θ-Criterion circular, causing it to lose its empirical content.
2. Chomsky 1992, which I saw only at the copyediting stage, makes a number of proposals that are similar or identical to claims put forward in sections 1 and 2 of this article. Two salient points of agreement are the rejection of the syntactic θ-Criterion (on essentially similar grounds) and the assumption that antecedent-trace type relations (chains or Move α) can be formed prior to any syntactic level of representation being fully assembled. See also note 13.
3. I assume that A-movement from the complement position must land in the next higher subject position. Empty categories cannot appear in place of the lexical NP *John* in (7) either since pro needs Case (and also a licensing environment; see Rizzi 1986 and also section 3 below) and PRO must be ungoverned. Pro then is just like the lexical NP in the relevant respect, and PRO is forced to move from the Caseless complement position since it is governed there.
4. Another respect in which (4b) might be too strong is that it requires each chain to have a θ-role. See note 16 and references cited there.
5. We thus proceed in the spirit of Sportiche's (1983) principle (i).

   (i) Partition the set of NPs into chains.

   For a potential problem posed by an analysis of the Italian impersonal clitic *si*, see Chomsky 1986b, Burzio 1986.
6. The logic of the argument here is the same as that of Chomsky's (1986b) argument against syntactic principles that rule out structures of vacuous quantification. Note also that in contrasting (5) and (5'), I do not wish to question the assumption that θ-position–argument relations are mediated by chains. My point is that the uniqueness requirements of (5) are not motivated by general considerations of interpretation.
7. Similarly, if Rizzi (1990), Cinque (1991), and others are correct and the distinction between movement constrained by Subjacency only and movement constrained also by the antecedent government clause of the Empty Category Principle (ECP) has to do with referentiality, then we need to assume that a θ-role that is not referential in a strong enough sense does not license a fully referential variable, thus incorrectly enabling long movement to occur.

   The converse of (14) would be false in a system like Rizzi's and Cinque's: an element with a referential θ-role is not necessarily referential enough to license long movement.

   Incidentally, (12d) and (13a) show that Rizzi's claim that categories with nonreferential θ-roles (i.e. ones constrained by Relativized Minimality) are quasi arguments leads to the conclusion that there are two kinds of quasi arguments: some may be questioned (like idiom chunks and measure phrases), and others (like the weather-*it* in (12) and (13)) may not.
8. For ease of exposition, I discuss structures in terms of movement rules. I do not assume, however, that movement rules operate between D- and S-Structure; see section 2.3.
9. Adapting an idea proposed by Browning (1987). See also Chomsky 1991.
10. The CUP is in effect a condition of relativized antecedence: it allows a (non-R-expression/Caseless) chain member in an X-position to have a (chain-internal) antecedent only in an X-position. This might suggest that perhaps the CUP could be collapsed with Relativized Minimality (Rizzi 1990). For this to happen, the two principles would have to refer to the same set of elements. Whether they can be taken to do so is unclear, and I shall not pursue the matter here. But see Manzini 1992 for a theory in which Case is crucial in determining whether an element falls under the strict locality requirement captured in Rizzi's theory by Relativized Minimality.

11 One might think of various stipulations that could exclude one or the other of these examples. One possibility would be to say that a moved element must be related to its D-Structure position through an empty trace. Since in (30) and (31) the trace in the D-Structure position of the moved subject is covered by the category illegally moving to a θ-position (in (31) the subject itself), this appears to exclude both cases. But it is not clear that the derivation in (31) can be straightforwardly excluded even in this rather *ad hoc* way. Since we have to allow an unmoved category not to have a trace in its D-Structure position, which it occupies throughout the derivation, the relevant condition can only require a category either to be in its D-Structure position or to have a trace there. But the first part of this disjunction is satisfied by the moved element in (31).

Furthermore, if the definition of an empty category is made dependent not on derivational history (as in the currently standard framework) but on its position in the chain (as I would propose), then another complication arises. If we take *trace* to refer to chain-internal elements rather than to empty categories left by movement, then the chain [John, e] in (31) can be derived by no movement at all, a derivation that also needs to be ruled out. (Of course this is the only possible derivation if movement rules operating between D- and S-Structure do not exist; see section 2.3.)

Note also that in the standard framework that assumes D-Structure-to-LF derivations, it seems unlikely that lowering rules can be excluded in principle, especially in view of the analysis of V-raising and affix hopping that has been advanced by Emonds, Pollock, and Chomsky (see, for example, Chomsky 1991). See Brody 1991 for a suggestion on how to treat the relevant French–English difference within an LF-based system like the one proposed here.

12 The fact that XP-chains can be headed by phrases rather than simple lexical items creates no new problems with lexical insertion. Once phrase structure rules are dispensed with, it is necessary to assume that phrasal nodes can be inserted into trees. Take, for example, an object NP. The grammar has no rules like VP → V NP, NP → N. The V projects a VP, the head N of the object projects an NP and thus it is this NP that is inserted into the VP created by V.

13 Chomsky (1992) eliminates D-Structure completely and thus loses the explanation of (the equivalent of) (9), as he notes. The explanation of (9) put forward here is perfectly compatible with his "minimalist" hypothesis, however. D-sets are included in LF representations; hence, the assumption that LF representations are projected through D-sets is a legitimate interface condition within this framework.

That chains can be defined before any syntactic level of representation is assembled and that LF is projected directly from the lexicon through D-sets, defined on chains (rather than being derived via Move α, from D-Structure representations) should clarify the claim that LF is the "basic" level of representation (cf. Brody 1985, 1987, 1991). If the minimalist hypothesis is correct and all constraints on representation hold at the interface levels LF and PF, then the claim that LF is the basic syntactic level of representation is of course considerably strengthened.

Chomsky dispenses with D-Structure essentially on the same grounds as I do: postulating D-Structure as a level of representation requires the dubious extension of the θ-Criterion from LF, where it holds by virtue of the interpretation, to this level. (His evidence for empirical difficulties with D-Structure representations from *easy to please* constructions appears weaker. He takes this construction in the standard GB framework to necessarily involve an argument inserted at some level later than D-Structure, in violation of the D-Structure θ-Criterion. But as we saw in section 1.4, under an improved analysis this problem does not arise. The construction does create serious problems for the uniqueness requirement of the syntactic θ-Criterion on chains and for the general prohibition against improper movement, but it is perfectly compatible with the D-Structure representations of standard GB Theory.) Chomsky also rejects the Projection Principle, which I keep here as an interface condition. See Brody 1992 for a more thorough discussion.

14 I take no stance here on the hypothesis that Infl should be broken up into two or more separately projecting heads. For presentational purposes, I adopt the Infl node that comprises at least [Tense] and [(S-)Agr]. All the claims in the article easily translate into a split Infl framework.

15 In Brody 1985 and in earlier versions of this article I derived the requirement that traces must be (head-) governed and the PRO Theorem (the condition that PRO must be ungoverned) from a condition similar to (37). I assumed (a) that arguments are always heads of (A-/Ā-) chains at LF and (b) that empty categories (other than pro) can never bear Case. This entailed that an empty category (other than pro) must be a chain head iff it is ungoverned, since by (37) Caseless categories are arguments iff they are ungoverned. Hence, PRO is ungoverned and trace is governed. But if governed empty categories are never arguments, then syntactic variable empty categories locally bound from A-positions are not arguments either. Taking variables to be nonarguments made sense on the assumption that argumenthood was defined for the D-Structure θ-Criterion: at this level the operator associated with the variable was in the θ-position of the variable. Therefore, it did not seem unreasonable to claim that in some sense relevant for the θ-Criterion the operator and not the variable was functioning as an argument.

But we have now argued that no D-Structure θ-Criterion is part of the grammar. The only notion of argument that appears to remain is the one relevant for the θ-Criterion taken as a principle of LF interpretation. Syntactic variables then must be arguments. So we are led to revise our assumptions about empty categories not being able to have Case: variables must be Case-marked, as is generally assumed, to enable (37) to take them to be arguments. Rather than stipulating that nonvariable empty categories cannot have Case, we shall allow empty categories to be Case-marked optionally. As a result, the requirement that traces must be governed and the PRO Theorem no longer follow from (37).

16 The LF empty category in the S-Structure position of the argument must be Caseless. If it had Case, it would be an argument by (37); thus, the argument *a man* could not form an A-chain with it, resulting in a violation of (5'). (Note that the empty category can occur in a position where Case can be assigned. Thus, if in expletive-associate structures the associate can receive Case from its governor (see, e.g. Belletti 1988, Chomsky 1991), the LF empty category in the S-Structure position of the argument can still remain Caseless.)

In fact, given the theory of expletive replacement, the condition in (i) follows from (37).

(i) Only heads of A-chains can be Case-marked.

Under expletive replacement, heads of A-chains are always arguments. Since A-chains cannot contain more than one argument, nonheads are nonarguments. Furthermore, they are necessarily governed categories; hence, by (37), they must be Caseless.

Alternatively, we could take the expletive to be able to simply delete between S-Structure and LF. Deletion may be necessary if the expletive does not always form a chain with the postverbal element (see, e.g. Borer 1986, Chomsky 1986b) – that is, if (ii) does not hold.

(ii) All chains contain some argument.

We could assume that both the replacement/adjunction and the deletion mechanisms are possible options. Thus, there would be two ways of satisfying the requirement of Full Interpretation, the former mechanism being applicable iff the expletive and the associate form a chain. If (ii) is false, then of course we lose the explanation it provides of the locality effects shown by expletive-argument associations.

But if (ii) is false and expletive deletion is necessary, then it may be preferable to dispense with the replacement mechanism altogether, since the deletion option makes it redundant and thus makes the problems that replacement appears to create avoidable.

17 I shall leave open the relationship between (37) and the Case Filter. Perhaps this condition is another visibility requirement, the PF correspondent of the LF condition in (37) (see Aoun 1979). See also Epstein 1987, where a different theory is developed, for relevant discussion.

The Case Filter ensures that neither lexical expletives nor lexical arguments can occur in ungoverned positions, and it excludes S-Structure representations like (iii), which can have the well-formed LF representation in (iv).

(i) *John to VP would be impossible.
(ii) *There to arrive a man would be impossible.
(iii) *There was seen John.
(iv) John was seen t

I take the visibility condition in (37) to constrain NPs and ignore here the problem of how and whether it should be extended to sentential categories.

18 Suppose that the improper movement chain is headed by an expletive, as in (i).

(i) *There seems t that Mary saw t'.

Again, if t' is Caseless, the CUP is violated. If t' has Case, it is Case-linked and thus an argument by (37). However, this does not exclude (i): A-chains containing an expletive and an argument are legitimate. We can attribute the ungrammaticality of (i) to the necessity of expletive replacement: if at LF t' replaces the expletive, then it ends up without a binder. Where an appropriate binder is provided, as in (ii),

(ii) *Who t seems t' that Mary saw t''?

we again have a situation like (40): no chain can be formed that includes both variables (both are arguments by (37)); but then the matrix subject variable violates (5'), not being related to any θ-role.

19 Rizzi argues that arb-assignment can only apply to affected θ-roles: we shall instead restrict the affectedness condition on arb-assignment to internal θ-roles.

20 For evidence that the PRO Theorem should not be taken to be a consequence of the binding theory, see, for example, Brody 1985. One of the arguments given there is that this view makes the complementary distribution of PRO and trace result from an accidental interplay of the ECP and the binding theory. If we think of the proper head government condition for traces as their formal licensing requirement, then the complementary distribution of trace and PRO will not be accidental under the present theory. Traces must be governed and PRO ungoverned so that they can satisfy the formal licensing conditions.

21 Rizzi argues that pro must be formally licensed by a Case assigner. This is quite compatible with my proposal: the Case will be assigned to the empty category only if it is identified. I assume that there is no Case transmission in expletive-associate structures (see Chomsky 1991, Belletti 1988), so the postverbal argument in such constructions receives Case from its governor.

22 We explain the distinction between (i) and (ii) in the usual way.

(i) *It's difficult e to rain.
(ii) It often rains without e snowing.

The default interpretation in (i) is incompatible with the quasi θ-role assigned by weather verbs. (ii) however, is a control structure, where the interpretation of PRO is determined by its antecedent.

7 PROJECTION AND PHRASE STRUCTURE

1 In Brody 1995a I argued against theories where central concepts are duplicated by being captured both representationally and derivationally. The choice between a purely representational and a purely derivational theory is of course a more difficult matter. Note that we cannot in principle exclude mixed theories either, when these succeed in avoiding the unwanted redundancies and duplications. A rather strong consideration that argues against the existence of syntactic derivations is the lack of genuine feeding–bleeding relations in syntax. We would expect these to be commonplace if derivations involving successive steps existed (see Brody 1995a,b for related discussion). The versions of the theory I present in this article – a single-step degenerate derivational alternative and a representational alternative – both exclude feeding–bleeding relations in principle.

2 It may be possible to consider a phrase to be "pure" if the properties determined by its head are marked on and thus attributed to the head only. Thus, a category that subcategorizes for a DP, for example, would in effect subcategorize for a "pure" phrase headed by D. I will not explore this possibility here mainly because it appears to be incompatible with Chomsky's (1995) principle of inclusiveness.

3 The projection or copy relation involved in the PCP is a two-place relation, and I assume that an element can be copied only once. In other words, there cannot be two distinct projections of some category C such that both dominate C but neither dominates the other; that is, there can be no "upward-branching" projections. (Note here that we cannot attribute the exclusion of upward branching in general to Kayne's (1994) Linear Correspondence Axiom (LCA). For example, a terminal element immediately dominated by two distinct categories will not violate the LCA.)

4 A phrase that immediately dominates no nonphrasal element and at least two phrases that contain terminal elements violates the LCA. A headless phrase that either contains nothing, or contains a single phrase of a different type, or contains two or more phrases that in turn dominate nothing does not seem to violate the LCA.

5 In Brody 1994 I raised an apparent problem for this approach to the question of the intermediate X' level: with heads that assign no θ-role to their subjects, specifier and complements could be distinguished only at the price of postulating a fully empty head. For example, *seem* would have to decompose into a higher head that does not select its subject and that does not appear to contribute in any other way and a lower one that is exactly like *seem*. However, the problem arises only if the expletive subject is generated VP-internally. If a verb like *seem* simply has no VP-internal subject, then the question of how such a subject can be distinguished from the complements will never arise, and such considerations will never make decomposition necessary.

6 In (11) I take the specifier to be the element that undergoes checking for the case of the minimal domain of functional heads, and the "external argument" for the case of (decomposed parts of) lexical heads.

7 It is interesting to note that ordering Project so that it always precedes Chain would capture the "target projects" generalization. If Project cannot apply to copies created by Chain, then a "moved" category cannot provide a "label" for a higher node. We could order Chain and Project by assuming that the former but not the latter is a strictly lexical operation. Project would then create lexicon-internally the form in which lexical entries are presented to syntax (i.e. PLs), whereas Chain would be an operation between the lexicon and the input list (in effect, an aspect of the selection operation). An open question would remain in this approach, however: how to ensure, nonstipulatively, that copies of a PL are always inserted higher in the tree than the original PL, which would have to correspond to the most deeply embedded "trace." In section 4 I develop a different approach.

8 The condition probably does not require full identity. In principle, it allows elements like adjuncts to be missing from one chain member that are present in another (see Brody

NOTES

1995a and section 3.3). Notice that an element may only be missing from "traces" and not from the head of the chain. Presumably this is due to a recoverability requirement.

9 In Brody 1994 I took *Near John he saw a snake* to be grammatical on the coreferential reading. If this reading is in fact not better than (15b), then it needs no additional comment. If, however, it *is* significantly better, then we can attribute this improvement to the option of not chain-relating the adjunct PP to the IP-internal position – an option not available in the case of the selected PP.

10 The remarks in this section were prompted by several discussions of the derivational-representational issue with Michal Starke and by the comments of an *LI* reviewer.

11 Ignoring this aspect of the principle created complications in earlier versions of this article with respect to categorial projection. In an XP chain the XP is also projected in the nonroot position, apparently counterexemplifying a simple formulation of the GPP. But this XP is projected by a chain-member-internal element, the head of XP; hence, it is no more relevant to the GPP than the fact that the head of XP can also select its complement in the nonroot positions of this XP chain.

12 Of course, either or both chains involved may be trivial, one-member chains.

13 Or checking. The account is neutral between checking and assignment technology. This is not to say that projectional features behave similarly to features usually called checking features. The point is only that the differences between the two types of features do not force the distinction to be made in terms of checking versus assignment.

14 Or checked; see note 13.

15 The similarity between selectional features and categorial projection casts some doubt on the idea that categorial features can serve as formal checking features. As we have seen, there is some reason to think that the features participating in categorial projection behave like other nonformal semantic selectional properties and unlike formal checking features.

16 In fact, only the property of being a $+/-$ maximal projection is defined relationally in (27) – being a lexical item is an inherent property.

17 In the richer system that assumes multiple adjunctions to a given X^0, and thus multiple X^0 projections, parallel to the multiple XP projections created by multiple adjunctions/specifiers, probably X^0 chains should be restricted to maximal X^0s, just as phrasal chains are restricted to maximal phrases. The problem would not arise in the present, more impoverished framework with a single X^0 and XP level for a given X^{min} head. (An additional issue in both frameworks is whether X^{min} chains exist.)

18 Note incidentally that in the standard minimalist framework even the status of "ordinary" morphology is rather unclear. Morphology must presumably be somewhere on the Spell-Out branch. Since conditions exist only at the interface in the minimalist grammar, Morphology would have to be located at the PF level, which does not have the structure necessary for this component to operate. In contrast, in the framework proposed in Brody 1993a, 1995a, where Spell-Out applies to the LF level. Morphology can be identical to WI and its principles will hold at this level.

19 The fact that uniformity gives a partial account of one aspect of the GPP does not seem to be an argument in its favor. If anything, it is an argument against uniformity since it is seen to be redundant here; see section 6.

20 That chains consist of copies is an independently necessary assumption in minimalist frameworks, where representational conditions, like the binding theory, can hold only at or beyond the interface level of LF. For example, as discussed in section 3.3, in order to rule out the Principle C violation indicated by the indices in (i), the trace must be (at least a partial) copy at LF (and perhaps beyond).

(i) whose$_x$ mother did he$_x$ like (whose$_x$ mother)

21 Given the independently necessary full identity requirement on the top PLs of chain copies, ensured either by the Chain operation or by an interface condition; see section 3.5.

22 Alternatively, the impossibility of the configuration could be attributed to the GPP, parallel to the case of (31).
23 There are various ways of treating clitics in the literature that take account of the fact that they are X^{min} or X^0 elements linked to an XP position without assuming that the clitics themselves have dual projectional status. I know of no advantage that the dual-status assumption might have over such treatments.

9 THE MINIMALIST PROGRAM AND A PERFECT SYNTAX

1 Noam Chomsky, *The Minimalist Program*. Cambridge, MA: MIT Press, 1995, pp. 420. This note was written during the summer of 1996. I am very grateful to Neil Smith and Michael Starke for helpful comments.
2 Cf. Brody 1995a, pp. 35–40 for discussion.
3 Cf. Brody 1993.
4 Originally written in 1989–90. Cf. also Brody 1995a, pp. 25–9 for discussion.
5 Apart from some revisions, written in 1991/2.
6 Cf. chapter 2 of Brody, 1995a, among a number of other recent publications in a similar vein.
7 As in Brody, 1998 and 1995b.

10 ON THE STATUS OF REPRESENTATIONS AND DERIVATIONS

1 Brody (1997a,b, 1998a,b). Although in these works I referred to the framework of elegant syntax as perfect syntax, the operative sense of perfection was invariably that of theoretical elegance. Hence the change of terminology.
2 Brody (1995, 1997a,b, 1998b). As has been noted before, in Brody (1995a), the argument against mixed theories (which include both the pure derivational and the pure representational alternatives) and the argument for the representation option (as opposed to the derivational one) are clearly distinguished. A certain amount of confusion has been generated in subsequent literature by not always keeping these two points distinct.
3 See esp. Brody (1995, 2000a). For more recent discussions of the "architectural" duplication see Epstein *et al.* (1998) and Starke (2000). See also Hornstein (1999, 2000) and Brody (2000b,c), among other related matters, for a discussion of a somewhat curious position that retains the architectural redundancy but wishes to eliminate the chain–move duplication. Hornstein (1998) also argues for eliminating chains rather than move, but on the basis of flawed arguments (Brody 2000b). He attempts unsuccessfully to defend one of these in Hornstein 1999. See Brody (2000c).
4 A possible argument against the approach I'm taking here might be that it focuses narrowly on LF. When we take the full theory of expressions generated by the grammar this seems to include a derivational component: a mapping from narrow syntax to PF. Therefore, one could argue, the overall theory of grammar would be simpler if the theory of the lexicon–LF relation was also derivational. But we seem to know too little about Spell Out for this argument to carry much force. First, it is not clear that the Spell Out component is indeed derivational (i.e. sequential) and not just a one-step mapping. Second, even if they are derivational, we do not know if the principles of Spell Out are different or similar to those of narrow syntax. The general idea of syntax being a generative and Spell Out an interpretive component would not make it unexpected that Spell Out principles have a different cluster of properties from the principles of narrow syntax. If this is the case that would make at least the intuitive simple version of the simplicity argument inapplicable. More complex versions – like, for example, that the same principles apply differently in the two domains (the differences being due to the different properties of the elements to which they apply) – may still hold. But again we seem to know too little about Spell Out to make any such point with more confidence than its opposite.

5 It is sometimes suggested that a representational approach simply translates a derivational approach and with the cost of involving richer set theoretical assumptions. It is not clear how the richness of the set theory involved is relevant to what is an empirical issue: which system is instantiated in the mind of the speaker. This is an empirical matter to which both empirical considerations and conceptual considerations of sharpening the concepts involved may be relevant, but the mathematical properties of the object postulated to exist will have to be whatever empirical research (with concepts adequate for the task) determines them to be. Once the set theoretical point is eliminated from the picture, as I think it should be, it is clear that a priori we do not know if the derivational theory is a (perhaps misleading) translation of the representational approach or conversely.

Recursivity of LF structures is also sometimes cited as entailing derivationality, at least in spirit. Note, however, that we can define LF without employing rules that reapply to their output. LF could be structurally characterized, for example, by some relation R (e.g. immediate domination) that all nodes have to enter (with special clauses for roots and terminals). For more discussion see e.g. Brody (2000a). It is expected that in the framework of ES no narrow syntactic principles will refer to the notion of constituent. That is, it would not be necessary to define constituents for narrow syntax, but only for the interpretive modules. But in any case the notion of constituent would not necessarily have to be defined recursively in terms of immediate domination. If the primitive notion is domination, then a node together with every node it dominates is a constituent – and immediate domination can also be defined nonrecursively in terms of domination without intervention.

Remnant movement is also sometimes taken to provide evidence for derivations. In a derivational theory the context for a simple statement of the c-command relation between the element moved out from a constituent to be moved itself (the remnant) is destroyed by the later step of moving the remnant. The problem, however, does not seem to arise in a representational theory with copies, given the assumption that c-command of traces inside chain members, like anaphoric connections in general, have to hold only with respect of a single chain member. This corresponds to the fact that in a derivational approach c-command has to hold only at one step of the derivation. That is, with X forming a chain with a copy (indicated here by "t") inside the bracketed chain-forming remnant ("X extracted from the remnant"), X needs to c-command only one of the relevant copies ("t's") inside the members of the chain formed from the two bracketed remnants in (i):

(i) [… t …] … … X [… t …]

Another question raised by David Pesetsky (personal communication) about representationality and remnant movement concerns principles of Spell Out, in particular, what ensures that in (i) the copy in the position indicated by the first "t" is silent. Concentrating on two-member "overt" chains without resumption, this appears to follow from the cyclic derivational theory. Move involves copy and delete. If X remerges and deletes before the remnant does (as it must, given the cycle), the original position of X in the copied remnant will be empty.

Note first that cyclicity of syntax does not in fact follow; the same result is translatable to a grammar with a representational syntax, if Spell Out is cyclic. Spell Out might have the two rules of identity check of chain members (corresponding to the identity requirement of copy) and +silent marking of the lower member (corresponding to part of delete). If these apply cyclically then identity check for the remnant will cover also the +silent mark on the lower copy of X in the lower remnant in (i), hence the higher remnant will have silent X. But even cyclicity of Spell Out can also apparently quite straightforwardly be avoided if we assume that the identity requirement on chain members covers also the +silent marking quite generally, but only up to recoverability. Thus in a remnant chain, if one member properly contains a +silent element, so must the other. But in an ordinary nonremnant chain, where the lower member is silent marked, the requirement will not entail that the higher member is also silent, since this would violate recoverability.

6 Heycock (1995) was one early case where it was explicitly argued that both derivational and LF conditions are necessary. For critical discussion see Brody (1997b) and Fox (1999). To take a somewhat random choice from relatively recent work that assumes and attempts to argue for a mixed theory, take first Nunes (2000), who argues that Move should be decomposed into copy (C), merge (M), form chain (FC) and chain reduction (CR). In fact M is not different from the usual merge operation that puts together phrase structures, CR is a Spell Out issue and C need not be separate from selecting from the lexicon the same thing twice. (The difference between the relation linking the two pronouns in "He said he left" and "He was seen (he)" does not have to do with different lexical access, as is sometimes suggested.) It is plausible to attribute that to FC having applied (or being able to apply legitimately) to the two pronouns in the second but not in the first structure. So only FC remains. In other words, it is not clear that this approach really needs to be different from a representational account. It looks different, of course, for Nunes C applies as part of a derivation. That a derivation exists and that C is part of it are thus additional assumptions.

In support of the assumption of keeping copy and (re)selection from the lexicon distinct Nunes refers to Chomsky's (1995) argument from expletive construction where greater cost is assigned to move than to merge to rule out (i).

(i)   *There seems a man to have left

The strength of this argument is questionable since (i) may be excluded by independent reasons: for example, that no lexical element, expletive or not, is ever permitted in the infinitival subject position that follows *seem*-type predicates. On accounts that exploit this fact, assigning different cost to different derivations would become irrelevant.

In support of the assumption that derivation exists, Nunes cites also the following contrast:

(ii)   *Which book did you review this paper without reading?
(iii) Which book did you review without reading?

This is supposed to motivate derivations on the grounds that *which book* moved sideward from an island in (iii) before it became an island and then to the front while a similar non-island-violating derivation is not possible in (ii). But there are no reasons why a largely similar alternative account could not be given in a representational vocabulary. In (ii) *which book* is separated from its trace (theta position) by an island. In (iii) it is not, since there is a trace in object position of the matrix clause. The trace in the island causes no violation if the wh-phrase needs only a single thematic trace to be subjacent to it (see e.g. Richards' (1997) principle of minimal compliance, a major and very interesting generalization of a proposal in Brody (1995), or this latter work for a somewhat different approach). All this seems straightforward, and makes no direct reference to parasitic chains. It is not clear why the derivational approach would be better. In fact for there to be an argument for derivations here, it would be necessary to argue that something along these representational lines cannot be right, otherwise Nunes' account (and the derivational equipment it is supposed to motivate) is redundant and therefore undesirable.

Lechner (2000) proposes an interesting analysis of NP-comparatives, where an empty operator raises to an intermediate spec-C position and the AP moves into the matrix:

(iv)   Mary met [young-er men]$_i$ [$_{CP}$ Op$_j$ than Peter met [$_{DegP}$ [$_{AP}$ young men] Deg t$_j$]]

He suggests an argument for a mixed theory based on the following observation: "empty operators in spec-CP of the than-XP [do] not interfere with AP-movement" (p. 16). He observes that the two APs should not form a chain for thematic/semantic reasons, hence he suggests that these APs are linked by a move operation that applied countercyclically to avoid the island effect induced by the empty operator. Note that countercyclic operations seem to be (a) quite problematic (see section 2.2 below) and (b) they also seem to be beside the point if the relevant locality constraints (like on Lechner's assumptions of the thematic requirements) apply only to chains. Furthermore, no crossing problem will arise if the matrix AP and the empty operator are coindexed and the operator in turn is related to the whole degree phrase in the lower clause – as in other similar constructions analyzed in terms of empty operator movement since the late 1970s. Lechner provides arguments from principle C, etc. that the structure does not involve pure deletion only but movement/chain, but his evidence does not seem to distinguish between linking the AP to its matrix clause correspondent or linking it only to the operator at the edge of the embedded clause.

Pesetsky and Torrego (2000) provide an interesting and intricate new analysis of the *that*-t effect and various related matters. They argue for what they call "relativized extreme functionalism," which appears to be an approach essentially identical to Brody's (1997a) bare checking theory. (I think the colourful name they give is misleading: the issue involved in eliminating features that are in principle uninterpretable is one of restrictiveness and has little to do with functionalism.)

In bare checking theory all features must be interpreted in principle, but in a given sentence some occurrences of features may be in positions where their usual interpretation cannot be assigned to them, where interpreting them would not make sense. In such cases occurrences of features of type t (say *wh* for example) in position(s) where they cannot be interpreted will have to merge (presumably via the chain and the spec–head relation) with another feature of type t that is in a position where interpreting it would make semantic sense. Pesetsky and Torrego's approach is not completely identical to bare checking theory because they wish to retain the otherwise apparently dispensable operation of feature deletion (as it follows feature checking) in order to integrate into their system the anti-*that*-t effects in sentences with topicalization like:

(v) Mary said *(that) John she liked

However it is not clear if such sentences should or can be integrated with other data they analyze. Anti-*that* trace effects constitute a much less clear class of facts than *that*-t effects. Maybe a pause in cases like (v), where the matrix verb does not select for *that*, suffices, suggesting perhaps an approach in terms of parsing. Pesetsky and Torrego attempt to extend their theory to cover such facts, but at the cost of a set of otherwise unnecessary and *ad hoc* assumptions that in turn question the claim that these facts have genuinely been "integrated." It is necessary to reengineer their notion of locality into a less appealing form specifically to cover this case; it is necessary to retain the otherwise unnecessary operation of feature deletion; and it is even necessary to adopt a gamma-marking type mechanism, essentially identical to that of Chomsky (1999), that distinguishes deletion of a feature from the feature being marked for deletion – the latter carried part way through the derivation.

It seems fair to say that even if we assume that the anti-*that*-t effects must be treated syntax internally, Pesetsky and Torrego have not successfully integrated these into their theory. Assuming that anti-*that*-t effects need to be treated differently, all dubious theoretical adjustments and innovations just mentioned can be dispensed with. The argument for derivations that they consider to have provided then disappears, together with the curious gamma-marking type distinction between marking for deletion at one derivational stage and deleting at a later one. (Gamma marking for deletion as in Chomsky (1999) and Pesetsky and Torrego (2000) is clearly undesirable, and it is also dispensable in general since the deletion operation itself is in fact unnecessary – see e.g. Brody (1997a) on this latter point.)

7 To make the point of restrictiveness more concrete, recall for example that (as noted in Brody 1997a), Chomsky (1995) proposes a representational definition in addition to the

derivational system of interface assembly (in effect an additional definition) of what counts as a well-formed syntactic object (cf. also Brody 1998a for some discussion). Or take the additional distinction he makes between deletion (interface invisibility only) and erasure (essentially invisibility also for Move), where erasure occurs only if this would not violate the representational duplicate definition of well-formed syntactic object. Such duplications that exploit the derivational–representational duplication and distinctions that in turn might build on these additional duplications should probably have no place in a restrictive system of syntax and are indeed excluded in principle by avoiding the less restrictive mixed theory that makes them possible in the first place.

8 Remotely – and at least here irrelevantly – resembling syntactic chains.
9 See Brody (1995, 1997a,b, 1998b, 1999a, 2000b) and Epstein *et al.* (1998) for more discussion of the redundancy issue and related matters.
10 Actual PDTs and PRTs may have other restrictions, relating, for example, to the number of branches of nodes, etc.
11 If chain members are linked interpretively and at a single interface level, and furthermore the status of z can switch from opaque during the derivation to transparent at LF, then the theory may not be multirepresentational, but would still be mixed. The same conclusion seems to hold also for the various older and more novel multiply dominated single-element theories of chains, since the multiple positions of the relevant category need (also) to be interpretively linked. (Incidentally, this fact might render syntactic multiple domination unnecessary.)
12 In fact I argued that neither categorial projection (Brody 1997b, 2000a), nor the chain relation (Brody 1998b, 1999a) should exist narrow syntax internally, but I put these matters aside here.
13 Note that the examples in the text are not simply cases analyzed representationally that are translatable derivationally without any gain or loss in understanding – something that often seems to be the case with putative arguments for derivations. The examples here illustrate the point that there are several derivations for a single representation, some of which need to be stipulatively exluded by some principle that is not entailed by the derivational nature of the grammar. So it does not matter, for example, if in (1b) *when* in the lower spec-C is in the (intermediate) trace position of *what* or that there are two positions available here, one for each wh-phrase. The pure derivational theory that contains no traces / copies (if it did, it would encode earlier stages of the derivation into later representations) will not exclude (1b) without some auxiliary assumptions that prohibit the countercyclic derivation.

Similarly in (2) it is not relevant that the subject island constraint apparently holds of subjects only. This is not a stipulation that is additional to what would be necessary to exclude the structure in a derivational framework. Derivationally, the assumption translates as the constraint holding only for extraction from subjects. This much is necessary so that the structure be excluded on the cyclic derivation, but does not suffice to rule out by itself the countercyclic derivation. On the representational approach, the representational statement of the subject island does not need to be similarly supplemented by (some equivalent of) the cycle.

Consider a different line of attack. On the representational approach we need to ensure that the trace/copy inside the subject is part of the chain that includes *who* in spec-C and the trace/copy inside the object. But again this is not an extra statement that would correspond to the stipulation of the cycle on the derivational view. If one A-position copy of *who* would be a trace and the other would not be, then the two copies of the subject-to-object chain of *pictures of who* would not satisfy the identity requirement on chain members that corresponds to the identity requirement of move, which is "copy (involving identity) and delete" on the derivational view. But properties of move in the derivational theory do not ensure the ungrammaticality of the countercyclic derivation, while given a representational approach, the corresponding properties of chain do.

NOTES

14 Sections 3.1 and 3.2 correspond, with minor changes, to sections of Brody (1997b). For the purposes at hand "term" in (3) can be taken as a synonym of "constituent." Citations of and references to Epstein's work in these sections relate to Epstein (1995).
15 Or, if binary branching was not assumed then:

(5′)   x c-commands all and only the terms of its sisters

Note that sisterhood is taken not to be reflexive in (5)/(5′).
16 In Brody (1998a), I argued that the best hypothesis to explain the invisibility of intermediate projections (for chain theory) is that they do not exist. See also note 12 for references to a later and stronger hypothesis ("telescope") that subsumes this one.
17 The problem of intermediate projections does not arise in the framework of mirror theory referred to in note 12, where no categorial projection exists.
18 Note that presupposing the cycle in the explanation of c-command and c-command in the explanation of the cycle (see section 2.2 above), as in Epstein et al. (1998), makes the explanation of these notions circular in addition to the other problems discussed in the text.
19 More precisely, no two unconnected subtrees have been formed that respectively properly include x and y.
20 More precisely, K_1 and K_2 have not yet undergone merge or the merge part of move.
21 Notice that "syntactic relation" here must mean: not yet part of the tree, and not as before, c-command.
22 Again, read "merge part of move" for "move" in (6′).
23 It is often suggested that c-command follows from the way semantics works but proponents of this view typically do not raise the question of why the semantics they assume has to work in the way that the strange asymmetry of the notion of c-command/scope comes into existence, why this relation must be what it is. So in effect such accounts often restate c-command in semantics but do not attempt to explain its surprising property. In fact as far as I am aware, all attempted explanations in syntax or semantics so far simply define c-command differently and stipulate the asymmetry differently rather than explain it.
24 In Brody (1999a), some empirical advantages of this view are sketched. Additionally, the substitution of domination for c-command may solve the antisymmetry problem of the well-motivated instances of c-command from the right (see Brody 1997b, 2000a, Brody and Szabolcsi 2000). The latter work discusses also the extension of this view, that semantic scope is similarly a matter of domination.
25 See Brody (1999a).

11   MIRROR THEORY

1 Mirror theory is the theory of narrow syntax in Perfect Syntax, a general framework I have discussed elsewhere. See Brody 1997b, and also 1997c, 1998a,b.
2 I argue in Brody 1995, 1997c that the cycle is an unnecessary construct. Accordingly, I make the terminological adjustment and refer to excorporating "successive-cyclic" XP and X^0 movement/chains as *successive chains*.
3 For some discussion, see Phillips 1996 (esp. p. 191, n. 17, and the text to which that note relates). See also Bošković 1997.
4 In Chomsky 1995: chap. 3, where checking theory is introduced, the verb would have remained in place only in overt syntax. In Brody 1995 and later in Chomsky 1995: chap. 4, there is no covert displacement of phonological material and the verb remains in situ throughout. See also Brody 1998b.
5 Checking of the "V + elements of I" unit involves a set of chains in a "roll-up" structure when the analysis is detailed enough to take account of more than one I position. As in Brody, to appear, I consider a series of chains to be in a roll-up structure if each chain

(except the last) takes the top of the previous chain together with the host of this top member to be the root of the next chain. In the theory to be developed below, head roll-ups are treated in terms of MWs, but "phrasal" roll-ups remain (i.e., roll-ups into syntactic specifier positions of constituents that correspond to heads together with whatever these heads dominate).

6 Given checking theory, the No Excorporation Condition can be translated as the requirement that in each nonroot position of a head chain some suffix must be checked. Thus, a version of checking theory might allow a successive-step (non-roll-up) head chain of for example the V + v + I unit, linking the V, the word-internal [Spec, v], and the word-internal [Spec, I] positions. The chain of V + v +I still cannot have a member in an additional (word-internal specifier) position between V and v or between v and I given the requirement that in each (nonroot) position some suffix must be checked. Further auxiliary assumptions would be necessary to make this account compatible with bare checking theory in Brody 1997b,c.

Note also that the comments about checking theory in the text refer to the standard version. One can imagine an improved version that avoids some of the problems raised. For example, given checking theory, the matching requirement on word structure and complementation structure (the first problem in the text) can be eliminated. If complements are generated in a random order, the correct complement order will be forced by the requirement, which as we have seen restates the mirror generalization, that checking order must respect the order of suffixes. Such an approach, which also needs to assume additionally the HMC and the No Excorporation Condition (or the above-mentioned equivalent), still would not help with most of the other problems raised. I shall therefore propose a more radical solution below.

7 As mentioned in note 6, under a (nonstandard) version of checking theory the No Excorporation Condition may be dispensable, but the suggestion there does not explain why X^0 and XP chains differ in this regard any more than other solutions in the literature. For example, Baker (1988) suggests prohibiting word-internal traces. But if separate heads can come together to form a word in syntax, why can they not separate again? Note also that under checking theory excorporation would not result in a word-internal trace anyway.

8 See Brody 1997b for further empirical differences between head chains and XP chains having to do with reconstruction and ellipsis phenomena.

9 As we shall see, head-complement order follows under mirror theory from specifier-head order. The latter, however, must be stipulated. Kayne (1994) has attempted to relate this to the direction of time (for a critical discussion, see Brody 1997b).

10 For more recent attempts to simplify the theory of phrase structure in terms of dependencies, see Brody (1994) and Manzini (1995). The latter work, like Hudson's and others' in the Dependency Grammar tradition, also dispenses with phrasal nodes, but it adopts the assumption made in Brody (1994) that all dependencies in the syntactic representation exhibit left-to-right order, which I crucially reject here in favor of a principled alternative.

11 Hudson (1990) defines a constituent as a category together with its dependents and assumes that the theory makes no use of this notion, as he treats movement/chains in alternative ways. His is thus a conceptually different notion of constituent from the one outlined in the text.

12 A phonological distinction between free and bound forms appears to be necessary whether or not Mirror is a biconditional, just as in standard terms it appears to be necessary in addition to head chains and the X^0/XP distinction. If Mirror is not biconditional, then this free versus bound distinction would have to play a role also in determining which syntactic specifiers form words with an element that is not their complement.

To strengthen Mirror to a biconditional, we might take apparently nonmirroring compounds like English *blackbird* and French *ouvre-boîte* "can opener" to be created only in phonology/Spell-Out. Another logical possibility is that (some of) these are created in the lexicon and then function in morphosyntax as a single unit, corresponding to a single head position.

NOTES

Similar problems arise with VP-external clitics, which probably reach their higher position via phrasal chains (Sportiche 1992, Cardinaletti and Starke 1994, Roberts 1997, Brody, to appear) and may also form only a phonological unit with their host. As an alternative to the phonological account, I assume in Brody, to appear, that the top member of the phrasal chain of the clitic can be expressed by an I domain head of which it is the specifier. This could capture Kayne's (1994) generalization that VP-external clitics occur only in null subject languages. Both null subjects and VP-external clitics (as opposed to weak and strong pronouns in Cardinaletti and Starke's sense) must be specifiers of a licensing head. If furthermore the head H that expresses the clitic is lower in the extended word than the morphological host H' of the clitic (i.e. H is (in) the complement of H'), then H and H' will form an MW.

Further problems for strengthening (15) to a biconditional arise from VP-shift type structures like those proposed by Barbiers (1995), Cinque (1999), Kayne (1994, 1998a,b), and others; see note 18.

13 But see section 5 for a different approach to "XP" chains.
14 To avoid confusion, perhaps it would be better to change the terminology and use XF (X-family) instead of XP to refer to X and all categories that depend on X (equivalently: and all categories that X reflexively dominates). I will not adopt this usage here, however.
15 I made a version of this assumption in an early version of this work (Brody 1997a).

In the present theory "extended projections" become "extended words" since not even nonextended phrasal projection is taken to exist.

16 This explanation is also lost if both inflectional morphology and open-class incorporation are assimilated to XP chains, as is sometimes suggested (e.g. Koopman and Szabolcsi 1998).
17 Note the possible analysis of "VP-internal" SOV: same structure (i.e. (18)) but with weak Agr.
18 Kayne (1998b) argues that English constructions with an *only* phrase in focus as in (i) involve preposing the *only* phrase to [Spec, F] and subsequently preposing the (remnant) VP to [Spec, F'] (Kayne notates F' as W) as in (ii), an analysis he extends to related phenomena such as negative and *even* phrases.

(i) Mary read [only one book]
(ii) Mary [read t] F' [only one book] F t_{VP}

Mirror theory, with its extended words that are allowed to span syntactic specifier-head links, provides a natural account of how the VP in the preposed position is licensed: V is allowed to continue its extended word there. If furthermore F and F' are in some relevant sense the same type of node, then c-command of the trace can be ensured by allowing the *only* phrase in [Spec, F] to count as a (derivative) [Spec, F'] (see the discussion of c-command in section 5). Interesting problems remain: in particular, (a) how the V + I unit is composed here and (b) what parameter distinguishes Hungarian (which does not allow this VP-shift) and English. The question in (a) is relevant to determining whether the statement of Mirror in (15) can be strengthened to a biconditional. Various approaches suggest themselves that I will not explore here.

19 For arguments that the binding theory should be stated in terms of θ-roles, see Williams 1994. Under the present suggestion implicit arguments could correspond to θ-roles represented configurationally as features/properties of heads that have no specifier.
20 For a different instantiation of the same idea see Brody 1999, where r(estricted)-chains are taken to involve only features of heads and all specifier constituents, including the lowest one, associated with these heads are external to the r-chain.
21 See Brody 1997b for a critical discussion of the derivational solution proposed by Epstein (1995; also Epstein *et al.* 1998). Neeleman and van de Koot (1998) conceptualize c-command as involving a function that expresses the dependency of a c-commanded dependent element. This function can percolate to any dominating node and is then satisfied by an argument in specifier-head relation with it. Their solution thus also merges two apparently distinct relations: the postulated percolation of a function and function

satisfaction. My proposal in the text is that the two relations involved in c-command are distinct and therefore they are best kept separate.
22 This is because heads in mirror theory dominate and do not c-command (categories in) their complement; hence, only specifiers ever need to c-command.
23 Kayne (1994) argues that c-command by the specifier S of a specifier S' of a node N into the complement of N is possible. This is incompatible with the proposal in the text. In Brody 1997b I provide evidence that such cases are better analyzed as involving a chain that links S to a higher specifier position S", where S" is the specifier of a node that dominates N.

12 "ROLL-UP" STRUCTURES AND MORPHOLOGICAL WORDS

1 This paper is a slightly revised version of chapter 4 of Brody 1997b, with references and some other more or less technical matters updated. Chapter 3 of that ms. corresponds to Brody 2000. For more discussion of the proposals made in section 1. See now Brody and Szabolcsi to appear.
2 As the argument crucially uses the presence of the complement C, the derivation of the lack of word-dominated phrases needs the assumption, as Kayne notes, that the source for the phrase P must be internal to the complement C. i.e., if there is no complement then there is no source for the phrase. This might still be problematic if empty categories, hence empty complements do not need to be ordered by the LCA.
3 On these see Kayne 1994 section 3.7.
4 The strength of this argument is weakened by the apparent existence of another reason for the difference. As Phillips 1996 points out there seems to be a preference for fronted VPs to be potentially complete. He gives examples like the following (the goal argument is optional with *give* but obligatory with *hand*):

(i) ?... and [give candy] he did to the children on weekends
(ii) *... and [hand candy] he did to the children on weekends

5 Another issue (raised e.g. by Manzini 1995 against the family of solutions I am considering here) that we can also put aside here is that of extraction.

(i) Who did you say that we sent there in order to please John's mother
(ii) ?*"Who did you say that we sent him there in order to please t"

Extraction on this analysis must be possible from a left branch as in the case of (1) but not from the main branch (ii). But at least the former is a general problem in the antisymmetry framework, not directly linked to the analysis of (1). Indeed the problem arises in the minimalist framework even without antisymmetry given object shift to AgrO. In these approaches extraction from left branches will often be necessary creating problems for connectedness (Kayne 1983, Manzini 1992) type approaches to locality.
6 Cinque in fact assumes also another, VP internal, source for "circumstantial" adverbials.
7 Most Hungarian examples that follow are from Szabolcsi 1996 and from references cited there.
8 It is not clear if the tensed deficient verb will have the requirement (34) for VMs when there is a focussed element in the clause.

(i) MOST fogom szét [fogom] próbálni szedni a rádiót

Szabolcsi 1996 and others take structures of this type to be impossible, but (i) seems acceptable to me. If there are grammatical structures like (i) then we may assume that (34) needs to be satisfied by some member of the chain of V. In (i) *szét* satisfied (34) for the trace of *fogok*. The verb is then spellt out in the position of F, the (empty) focus morpheme.

If structures like (i) are invariably bad then (34) must be restricted to verbs that are not associated with focus. If in such a structure the tensed verb has a focus feature (Brody 1990, 1995b), then we may take this feature to transform a deficient V into a nondeficient one, or essentially equivalently, serve as a VM for (34).

9 In a series of infinitives only the last one can be taken as a VM. For example (35a) cannot be analyzed as *akarni* (want-INF) being a VM that is linked to a position under *kezdeni* (begin-INF), the relevant interpretation of (35a) (i.e. "will begin to want to...") is not available. The restriction does not appear to be simply that only infinitives without complements can serve as VMs: infinitives with noninfinitive complements can be spelt out higher, without any special (emphatic/contrastive) interpretation:

(i) MOST fogok (/fogom) olvasni akarni [olvasni] egy (/a) könyvet
NOW will-I read-INF want-INF a (/the) book
I will want to read a/the book NOW

(ii) MOST fogom közölni akarni [közölni] hogy Mari elment.
NOW will state-INF want-inf that Mary left
I will want to state that Mary left NOW

10 Recall that last resort does not need to be a derivational condition. Translated to representational terms, it requires all non-root positions of chains to be licensed by some (checking) requirement. Under the representational version, the relationship of last resort and full interpretation is immediately brought out, and it is natural to generalize the condition to require that all positions (in chains/ in syntactic structures) are licensed by some (checking or thematic) relation.

11 Notice that in this MW the focus marked *akar* is not directly the spec of F, but rather the spec of the spec of the spec of F. Putting aside the technical question (percolation or satisfaction of the checking relation at a distance) note that the problem here is a special case of a much more general issue. Thus in (i) the syntactic spec of F position is occupied by a nonfocus category whose spec is the actual focus.

(i) JÁNOS barátja hivott fel
John's friend called up

The same problem arises also in the definition of wh-phrases etc.

12 In fact the generalization that roll-up structures are not able to form long distance chains does not hold in all types of structures. As noted earlier, nontrivial cascades like the ones in (29) do not qualify as VMs and therefore cannot appear before the finite verb in the VM position. The focussing structures in (ibcd) however contain a nonlocal chain of the roll-up structures *szétszedni, szétszedni kezdeni* and *szétszedni kezdeni akarni* respectively.

(i) a. SZÉT fogom akarni kezdeni szedni a rádiót
"I will want to begin to take APART the radio"
b. SZÉTSZEDNI fogom akarni kezdeni a rádiót
c. SZÉTSZEDNI KEZDENI fogom akarni a rádiót
d. SZÉTSZEDNI KEZDENI AKARNI fogom a rádiót

Consider the nonlocal relations between the focus position and the position where the roll-up structure is assembled. The prediction of the mirror theory is of course that these relations must be chains and not MWs.

Thus a roll-up structure can form a chain when such chain formation is triggered by some checking requirement, e.g. focus in (i). The chain structure in (44c) is not legitimate however, since the higher chain member satisfies no requirement (of its own or of its host) there.

INDEX

Ā-/A-bound categories 18, 19, 21, 22, 24, 26, 30, 38, 44–5, 50, 56, 57–61; Case-marked 108; see also anaphors; empty categories; pronominals
Ā-/A-/A'-chains 44–5, 50, 52, 55, 93, 101, 106, 107, 108, 169, 215, 238; Case-checking theory and 56–7; covert, MLC and 161–7; intermediate links 173; PRO can head 106; reconstructed positions 234
Abels, K. 188
abstract noun argument 97
a-c (anaphoric-compositional) dependency 8–9, 10, 11, 12, 13; superfluous 16
accessibility condition 60
adjectival complement constructions 94, 98–9
adjectivals 123
adjunct argument asymmetry 167
Adjunct Condition 162, 163–4
adjunction 120, 122–6, 130, 132, 139, 140, 143, 194; c-command out of 214, 215; complements and 234, 235, 238; dubious status of 156; general problem in 142; multiple 228
adverbials 123, 145, 156, 208, 211, 219, 225, 259, 262; on the right 232–42
affixes 208
Agr features 167, 168, 223, 224, 226, 234
anaphoric expansion 14–15, 16
anaphoric expression 7, 8, 9, 10
anaphors 11, 12, 19, 25, 161, 173; Ā-bound 23, 62; ECs as 25, 57–63; lexical 27, 47, 57–9, 60; nonpronominal 17, 22, 27, 36, 49, 58; nonvariable empty categories as 18; pure 59; see also anaphoric expansion; anaphoric expression; PRO

Andrews, A. 235
annotation 14, 15
antecedents 7, 8, 11, 12, 13, 16, 18, 31; asymmetric 9; c-commanding 14, 15; coreferentiality with 32, 41, 46; definite nonarbitrary referent 111; must have θ-role 50, 51; non-c-commanding 58, 59; nonreferential 23–4; potential 215; PRO 46, 47, 57; quasi-argument 33; referential 24, 36, 94; syntactic (coindexed) 47
antisymmetry hypothesis 194, 224, 227–8, 232, 233, 234, 235
Aoun, J. 41, 147
Arad, M. 220
arguments 30, 32, 33, 46, 82, 84, 165; and "Arb"-interpretation 106–12; expletive 81, 85; interpreted "quantificationally" as "for someone" 45; LF θ-criterion for 97–8; θ-theory and 93–113; unique 43, 83
A-structure 33, 34, 36

Baker, Mark 205, 209, 222
Barbiers, S. 225, 237
bare output conditions 150, 152, 188
Barss, A. 101
base-generation 28, 29
Beghelli, F. 238
Belletti, A. 256
biconditionals 44, 50, 52, 56, 219, 223
binary branching 122, 124, 125, 194, 220, 228
binding theory 17, 19, 21, 22, 23, 25, 29, 33, 35, 36, 37, 101, 173; ECP and 41, 42, 44, 46; locally A-bound categories and 57–61; locally Ā-bound ECs 61–3; PRO Condition and 48; see also LGB

biuniqueness 95, 96, 102
bleeding relations 178, 191, 192
Bobaljik, J. 223, 256
Borer, H. 220
Bouchard, D. 41
Brody, Michael 21, 41, 42, 44, 45, 61, 62, 81, 104, 106, 117, 118, 124, 126, 127, 129, 130, 131, 134, 146–53 *passim*, 156, 159–72 *passim*, 174, 178, 182, 188, 189, 192, 197, 198, 199, 205, 214, 215, 216, 219, 220, 222, 225, 227, 228, 232, 233, 238, 240, 241, 251, 262, 263
Browning, M. A. 96, 109
Burzio's Generalization 95

Cardinaletti, A. 255, 258, 262
Case 45–6, 81, 95, 101, 103, 106–7, 108, 111, 112, 144, 145, 170, 171; uninterpretable 238
Case-checking theory 52–7, 61, 220
Caseless complements 95, 101, 103, 107
Caseless object position 144
categorial projection 118, 136, 140, 146, 153, 172, 233, 253; principle of 119–22, 123
causal efficacy 78
c-command 14, 15, 37, 42, 59, 96, 118, 120, 135, 136, 151, 155, 165, 173, 183, 233, 235; "almost" 164; and asymmetry/antisymmetry 121, 125, 126, 193, 226–8, 232; by Merge 158–9; cyclicity and 159–61, 172; definitions 193–9, 214, 215
c-domain 57–8, 59
chain composition mechanism 93
Chain/Move relation 118, 150, 151, 152, 153, 154, 164, 172, 187
chains 81, 82, 83, 84, 98, 134, 135, 222, 226; adjunct movement 100; anaphoric 13, 14, 15, 16; Chomsky's maximality requirement on 44; complementary distribution and 42–52, 56; definition of 42–5, 46, 50, 85; distributed 189; expletive-associate 132, 146, 180; head 209, 213–15, 219, 220, 221, 227, 240, 243, 246, 247, 254, 263, 264; levels and 102–6; LF θ-criterion for 94–6; long distance 242; nonuniform 133, 137, 138, 140; NP-movement 100; overt 227; perfect 150–75; phrasal 242, 262, 264; projects, inserts and 126–9, 133; referential 12–14; role of 17–39;

S-structure concept of 86; transitive 12; *see also* CUP
chain-theoretic requirement 101, 135
characterizations 139, 140, 146, 210; *see also* RC
checking features 131, 135, 136; interpretable 152; strong 152, 155–8; weak 155
checking relations 129, 140, 143, 156, 163, 166, 172, 181; licensing of "categoriality" 154
checking theory 154, 155, 206, 211–13; bare 167–70, 238; minimalist 170–2
Chierchia, G. 164
Chomsky, Noam 18, 33, 34, 41, 43, 45, 49, 50, 52, 56, 57, 58, 61, 63, 87, 95, 96, 97, 98, 99, 102, 103, 106, 107, 119, 120–1, 124, 125, 129, 130, 131, 132, 134, 138–9, 140, 141, 142, 143, 144, 145, 146, 147, 151, 152, 155, 156, 157, 158, 159, 161, 162, 163, 164, 167, 168, 170, 171, 211, 214, 227, 255, 256; *see also* Identification Principle; *Knowledge of Language*; LGB; *Minimalist Program*
Cinque, G. 123, 156, 166, 208, 209, 219, 221, 223, 225, 235, 237, 238, 257
Circularity Principle 10–11, 12
CL (Case-linked) anaphors 60–1
clauses 255, 256; adverbial 225, 236, 237, 238; complement 130, 233; embedded 19, 38, 132, 163, 166, 262; matrix 179
CLC (Case-linking Condition) 53, 54, 55, 56, 57
clefting 99
clitics 50, 54, 55, 61, 62, 111, 138, 139; climbing 255, 257, 258–9, 262; Romance 210; verbal modifiers and 260–2
CMC (Case-matching Condition) 53, 54, 55, 57
Collins, C. 124
competence theory: grammar 188; syntax 186
complementary distribution 19–21, 42–52, 56, 59
complementation structure 210, 211, 213
complements 123, 124, 126, 130, 134, 208, 219, 220, 236, 259–60; adjectival 94, 98–9; adjunction and 234, 235, 238; Caseless 95, 101, 103, 107; infinitival 161; nonempty 125; specifiers and 220–6

INDEX

Complex NP Constraint 162
Comp-to-Comp violations/traces 35, 36, 37, 38, 56, 57, 62, 63
constituents 232, 235; remnant 238
"construct chains" 85
contentive elements 30, 80, 81, 227
contextual definitions 17–19, 20, 21, 37, 38, 41–2, 44
continuations 151
contradictions 9, 139, 233; "near" 105
copy relation 153, 154, 182
coreference relations 24, 32, 40, 41, 46, 50, 101, 109, 234
"covert movement" structures 129, 131–2, 152, 153
crossover structures 22, 35–8, 62; weak 165
CRs (circular readings) 7–8, 10, 11, 12, 13; unacceptability of 16; ungrammaticality of 16
C-structures 33, 34, 36
CUP (Chain Uniformity Principle) 101, 108
cyclicity 154, 155, 158, 159–61, 173

definitions *see* contextual definitions; relational definitions; representational definition; syntactic definition
deictic expression 12
deletion 34, 57, 84, 118, 235, 236, 238; trace-copy 133
dependency 165, 216, 224, 226, 227; anaphoric 8, 10, 12, 13, 16; circular 12; compositional 8, 12, 13, 16; illegitimate 164; interpretive 9; referential 7, 12; *see also* a-c dependency
derivations 21, 28, 29, 33, 34, 87, 88, 94, 104, 118, 140, 152, 158, 160, 167, 183; converging 151, 171; crashing 161, 171; D-structure-LF 90, 91; improper movement 99, 100; "movement history" of 103; nonmovement 30; overt 162; representations and 177–80, 185–201; RNR 233; syntactic 89, 90, 159, 178, 179, 180
disambiguation 11, 12, 16
disjointness 233, 234, 236
dominance/domination relations 126, 127, 188, 198–9, 216, 219, 224, 226, 227
D-structure 28, 29, 30, 32, 33, 34, 43, 45, 80, 87, 99, 100, 105, 133; constraints imposed on 89–90; defined in terms of chains 105; LF and 91, 177, 178;

reasons for rejecting 146; residue of 133; S-structure and 79, 85, 88, 90, 179, 180; θ-criterion 81, 82, 83, 84, 85, 86, 93, 94, 98, 102, 103, 104, 106
Dummett, M. 78
duplication 102, 118, 151, 156, 211, 212, 213; derivational 150; restrictiveness and 185–6

Earliness 153
easy to please-type constructions 94, 98–100, 101
ECM structures 237
economy conditions 151, 161, 183, 184
ECP (Empty Category Principle) 17, 18, 21, 23, 26, 28, 29, 31, 32, 33, 43; binding theory and 41, 42, 44, 46; theta theory and 88
Edmonds, J.-Y. 211
E-language (Externalized language) 77, 78
ellipsis chains 160
embedded heads 125
embedded position 135; object 93; subject 173
embedded structure 151
empty categories 22, 24, 27, 36, 37, 38, 81, 106, 179; A-bound 35; as anaphors 25, 49, 57–63; complementary distribution of 19–21, 40–73; expletive-bound 31; governed 41, 44, 46, 53, 110, 111; intermediate nonoperator 101; nonpronominal 32, 36, 41, 43, 49, 50, 51, 61; nonvariable 18, 25; optimal theory of classification 94; ungoverned 23, 41, 46, 49, 50, 52, 54, 55, 110; *see also* ECP
empty shell approach 124
Epstein, S. D. 109, 159, 192, 193, 194, 195, 196
equidistance solution 255, 256
expletive-associate structure 107, 132, 146, 153, 180
expletives 31, 32, 33, 36, 47, 81, 85, 93, 161, 165; governed and Case-marked 107
extended structure preservation 120–1, 122, 169, 219, 232

feature-chains 169
feature-movement 153, 180
feeding–bleeding relations 178
Ferris Wheel theory 87–8, 89, 90
FFs (Formal Features) 129, 132

303

INDEX

FI (Full Interpretation) principle 107, 142, 152, 167, 169, 170, 172, 177, 179
F-Movement 129–31
"forking" chains 96
Freidin, R. 192
French 211, 219, 258

GB (Government-Binding) theory 41, 42, 50, 61, 78, 80, 93, 94; outstanding problem for 99; *see also* LGB
generalization 96, 98, 103, 105, 127, 138, 167, 169, 172; mirror 208–15, 218; *see also* Burzio's Generalization; GPP
generative grammar 77
GF (grammatical functions) 28, 29–30, 36, 38, 45
governing category 57, 58, 59, 60, 61, 62, 63
governors 52–4, 55, 56, 57, 58, 59, 60, 61, 110; as anchors 107
GPP (Generalized Projection Principle) 160, 220, 241; effects in Chomsky (1994, 1995) 144–6; nonsyntactic explanation of 133–7; "target projects" condition and 124, 136, 138, 140–4, 214
grammar 13, 17, 30, 80, 82, 95, 98, 123; accidental interaction of two unrelated modules 41; core 158; discourse 14, 16; independently necessary subsystems 19; organization of 78, 87–92, 178; phonological material in 180; phrase structure 213; principles of 84; rules of 7; structure 131; theory of 89, 177, 188; weakening 186; *see also* generative grammar; transformational grammar; UG
grammaticality 9, 161, 173, 246, 261; degraded 162
Greed principle 140, 141, 142, 143, 144, 145
Grimshaw, J. 221
Groat, E. 197–8

Haider, H. 233
Hale, K. 145
heads of chains 49, 50, 51, 52, 55, 56
Hindi 225
HM (Higginbotham/May) 7–8, 10, 12, 13, 14, 15
HMC (Head Movement Constraint) 132, 138, 140, 208, 209, 210, 211, 213, 215, 219, 242, 264
Hornstein, N. 161, 163, 164, 166, 233, 235

Hudson, R. 216
Hungarian 156, 172, 208, 262–4; verbal clusters 259–60; VMs 261; V-raising in 242–9

identification 110–12
Identification Principle (Chomsky) 44, 45
identity condition 9, 133
I-language (Internalized language) 77, 78; principles of 186–7
imperfections 180, 181, 182, 183
improper movement structure 51, 94, 99, 100–1, 108
inclusiveness 119
infinitivals 161, 244, 245, 257, 259, 260, 261, 262, 263, 264
inflection 172, 211, 217, 222, 225
Insert 126–7, 129, 136–7, 140
instantiations 79, 103, 123, 147; lexical and empty 27
intermediate projections 122–6, 194
interpretability condition 169
interpretation 11, 12, 15, 16, 17, 22, 24, 25, 239, 263, 264; arb(itrary) 94, 106–12; coreferential 40, 41, 50; meaningful 97, 98, 99; pair-list 164; phonological 54; post-LF 133; semantic 14, 117, 150, 154; unambiguous 235; word 138–9; *see also* FI; radical interpretability
interpretative condition 102
interpretive components 151–5, 165, 188
interrogatives 169, 237
"inverse heavy shift" constructions 234
invisibility: interface 118, 151, 154; PF 168
Italian 43, 94, 109, 111, 172, 256, 258

Jacobson, P. 14, 15
Jaeggli, O. 162
Japanese-type languages 162
Johnson, K. 173
Jones's attained state 78

Kayne, R. 119, 121, 122, 123, 158, 159, 162, 163, 192, 208, 214, 215, 216, 223, 224, 225, 227, 233, 234, 236, 251, 256, 257, 258, 259
Keyser, S. J. 145
Kiss, É. 261
Knowledge of Language (Chomsky) 77–86, 177
Koizumi, M. 124, 173, 223, 256

Koopman, H. 125, 210, 242, 243, 259, 260
Kripke, S. 78
Kuno, S. 227

language(s) 87, 109, 153, 172, 181, 209; head-final 225; multiple subject 165; natural 8, 22; *see also* E-language; French; Hindi; Hungarian; I-language; Italian; Japanese-type; Romance; Slavic; Spanish
Larson, R. 124, 220
Lasnik, H. 57, 164, 173, 176
Last resort condition 144, 151, 172
law of pre-existence 195, 196
LCA (Linear Correspondence Axiom) 119, 121, 122, 125, 159, 192, 208, 216, 227, 228, 232, 233
least effort assumption 156
Lebeaux, D. 130, 147, 227
left-adjunction 125
lexicon 87, 89, 90, 95, 105, 110, 111, 117, 119, 216–17; LF and 184, 185; *see also* LIC
LF (Logical Form) 79, 86–90 *passim*, 111, 130, 131, 132, 138, 142, 146, 155, 160, 167, 183, 184, 185, 191; D-structure and 91, 177, 178; Move creates copies 182; PF and 158, 159, 168, 177; possible representations 190; S-structure 104, 105, 106, 177, 178, 179, 180; thematic visibility requirement 107; θ-criterion 80, 93–101, 102, 103; *see also* LLF
LGB (Chomsky's Government-binding theory) 17, 19, 20, 21, 25, 28, 33, 34, 36, 37; definition of chains 30; R-expressions 38; θ-roles assigned to chains 31
LIC (lexical item copy) 126, 128, 129
licensing 94, 97, 100, 101, 102, 110, 111, 154, 169, 172, 173, 218; structural 133
LLF (Lexico-Logical Form) theory 90, 117–18, 126, 128–9, 133, 136, 150, 152, 156
locality 120, 122, 129, 163, 164, 166, 183, 211, 212, 214, 215, 219, 255, 263, 264; strict 222, 242
Longobardi, G. 162, 163, 166

Manzini, M. R. 41, 48, 57, 58, 59, 60, 146, 233, 234, 238
mapping 15, 79, 88, 90, 91, 94, 150, 152; D- to S-structure 179; lexicon–LF 185

markedness 238
Martin, R. 172
matrix subject 29, 36, 38, 60, 93, 99, 100, 104, 105, 259; anaphoric element bound by 132; nonthematic position 98; PRO coindexed with 45
May, Robert 102; *see also* HM
meaning 7, 11, 77
mediating features 168, 169
Merge operation 155, 158–9, 167, 180, 189–90, 191, 192, 193, 194, 196, 197, 216
minimal category 57, 60, 61; *see also* Relativized Minimality; standard minimalist framework
Minimal Chain Link 151; *see also* MLC
Minimalist Program, The (Chomsky) 176–84
mirror theory 199, 205–31, 232, 233, 237, 240, 242, 251–4, 258, 264; and word order 254
mixed theory 185–7
MLC (Minimal Link Condition) 118, 144, 145, 155, 160, 172; and covert A′-chains 161–7
morphemes 210, 225, 251, 252, 254, 255, 259
morphological features 119, 120, 126, 137, 140
morphology 128, 129, 139, 153, 154, 169, 205, 213, 219, 242, 252, 253, 264; affixes 208; inflectional 217, 222
movement 85, 95, 103, 135, 164, 167; covert 129, 131–2, 152, 153, 169, 180; improper 51, 94, 99, 100–1, 108; "last resort" 144, 151; NP 81, 99, 100, 101; overt 129, 131, 152, 153, 155, 156, 162, 171, 174; successive-cyclic 143; *see also* HMC
Move rule 150, 152, 154, 155, 156, 158, 159, 161, 180, 181–2, 183, 189, 190, 191, 192, 193, 194, 196, 197, 216
multirepresentational theory 189, 190, 191

"near circularity" 105
negation 211
neg-phrases 162, 163
No Excorporation Condition 209, 211, 213, 215, 219
nonanaphors: nonpronominal 22, 23, 25, 36, 37, 38, 61, 62; pronominal 18, 19, 21, 22, 23, 25, 49

nondistinctness requirement/condition 127, 128, 129, 130, 132, 227
nongrammaticalized selection 140
nonheads of chains 49, 50, 51–2, 55, 56, 57
nonidentity condition 60
noninterface structures 127
noninterpretable features 170, 172
nonreferential categories 23–4, 80
nontrivial chains 105, 172, 209
nouns 128, 170, 260–1; *see also* NPs
NPs (Noun-Phrases) 8, 9, 13–23 *passim*, 34, 35, 44, 50, 84, 127, 128, 168; base-generated in surface position 28; Case and 52–3, 54, 55, 56, 108; c-commanding coindexed 37, 42; complex constructions 166; control of PRO 109; expletive 31; lexical 45, 54, 55, 57; movement structures 81, 99, 100; nonpronominal 41; partitioned 17; phonetically unrealized 40; postverbal 19, 32; referential 80, 99
NP-traces (nonpronominal anaphor) 17, 20, 21, 30, 31, 95; Caseless 165; incorrect 107; PRO and 48–9; pronoun and 59–61
null elements 79, 109, 172, 258–9

objects 143, 145, 173; Caseless 144; embedded 93; syntactic 151
Occam's razor 89
OFS (One Fell Swoop) EC Condition 48–9, 50, 51; and Case theory 52–3, 55, 56
Opacity Conditions 61, 173
open classes 217, 222
Operators 30, 34, 37, 38, 44, 45, 56, 57, 61, 98, 101, 102; empty 99, 100, 166
Orwell's problem 77
overt chains 153

Pairing 194
parallel structures 15
parasitic gap structures 93, 96, 163, 164, 234, 236, 237
parsing 188
PDT (purely derivational theory) 188
percolation 135, 136, 165–6, 173
perfect syntax 117–19, 150–5, 159, 160, 180–4; syntactic representation in 205–31
Pesetsky, D. 41, 153, 164, 235
PF (Phonetic Form) 79, 87, 88, 89, 90, 91, 129, 130, 131, 133, 155, 156, 184;

convergence forces 181; exhaustive ordering of terminals 192; interpretive pressures 152; LF and 158, 159, 168, 177; recoverability condition and 182; S-structure and 179
phi (Φ)-features 23, 26, 27, 31, 167, 168, 170
phonetic matrix 27, 54
phonology 88, 154, 159, 178–9, 180, 211
phrase structure 213; minimal theory of 119–26, 177; projection and 117–49
pied-piping theory 129–31, 152, 156
Plato's problem 77
PLs (projection lines) 205, 207, 215, 219, 228
Pollock, J. 211, 212
poverty of stimulus argument 77
pragmatic solution 7–8; inadequacy of 10–12
precedence 227, 228
Predicate Opacity Condition 173
predicates 165, 238; adverbial 239; matrix ECM 237
predication relation 100
predictions 168, 226; incorrect 245; phrase structure 128–9
prefix incorporation 242
prepositions 128; hypothetical 144
presyntactic chains 104–6
Principle B 109
Principle C 100, 101, 127, 130, 147, 173, 226, 227, 233, 234, 236
Principles and Parameters theory 150, 160, 176, 177, 178, 180
PRO (pronominal anaphor) 17, 18, 19, 20, 21, 25, 26, 35, 41, 52, 93; antecedentless 32, 47, 109, 110; "arb"-assignment and 94, 108–10; argument that can control 97; as nonpronominal 46–8; can head A-chain 106; cannot be expletive 32, 33, 47; c-domain of 58, 59; choice of antecedents for 57; complementary distribution of 56; identification and 110–12; invariably an argument 107; lexical anaphor and 57–9; nonreferential 23, 24; not coindexed 45; NP-trace and 48–9; null case of 172
PRO Condition 44, 46; OFS 48–9, 50, 51; violations 43
Procrastinate condition 151, 172, 173
projection 105–6, 205, 213, 233; extended 254, 255, 256; internal 253;

phrase structure and 117–49; *see also* categorial projection; GPP; PLs
Projection Principle 28, 29, 33, 34, 81, 82–3, 94, 102, 105; D-structure constrained by 106; *see also* GPP
pronominals 17, 18, 20, 47, 48, 49, 173; Ā-bound 23, 31, 32, 33, 37; A-free 57; definition of 26–34, 37, 38, 44; empty 25; object-oriented 234
pronouns 8, 10–14 *passim*, 18, 24, 26, 35, 63, 234; binding 235, 238; lexical 20, 47; NP-trace and 59–61; represented *in situ* by antecedents 15; resumptive 104
PRO Theorem 94
PRT (purely representational theory) 188
"pseudo-gapping" structures 236

Quantifier Raising 9, 102
quantifiers 9, 13, 24, 37, 80, 93, 166; existential 235, 237
quantum theory 187
quasi-argument 32, 33, 97, 98
Quine, W. V. O. 78

radical interpretability 154, 168, 172
random marking 133; *see also* RC
RC (Random Characterization) system 42, 43, 45, 46, 48, 49, 62
reconstructed positions 234, 238
reconstruction effects 101
recoverability approach 103
Recoverability Condition 28, 29, 30, 32, 34, 36, 38, 84, 182
redundancy 19, 21, 22, 23, 38, 84, 95, 125, 132, 150, 152, 156, 167, 187, 232, 253; eliminated 217
referential apparatus 80
referential categories 97, 98, 99
referents 11, 12, 16, 24
reflexive relation 14
regularity 41
Reinhart, T. 173, 193, 197
relational definitions 137, 138, 139
relativization 99
Relativized Minimality 144, 145, 167, 215, 242, 262
representational conditions 150
representational definition 151
representational/derivational difference 132
representations 45, 87, 88, 89, 253; abstract 102, 106, 108; derivations and 177–80, 185–201; D-structure 100; ill-formed 129; interface 117, 150;

(L)LF 117, 118, 133, 135; morphological 218–19; pure 28, 29, 30, 82, 84; semantic 12, 13, 15; syntactic 34, 81, 94, 105, 128, 135, 154, 179, 205, 216, 217, 218
restrictiveness 185–6, 187, 190–3
restructuring 262; and (covert) roll-up 254–6; as "I in C" 256–8
Reuland, E. 173
rewriting rule 15
R-expression 100, 101, 226, 227
right-adjunction 125
Rizzi, L. 50, 55, 61, 94, 107, 109–10, 111, 162, 166, 167, 169, 209, 215, 256
Roberts, I. 255, 256, 260
roll-up structures 225, 226, 262–4; and morphological words 232–50
Romance languages 162, 210, 238, 251, 255, 259, 261

Safir, K. 227
Saito, M. 164
scope reconstruction 166–7
scope relations 235
Searle, J. 78
selectional requirements 123, 124, 128, 129, 130, 134, 144, 241
"self-attachment" 140
semantic content 168
semantic effects 130
semantic role 79
sensory/motor systems 88, 89, 90
sentence grammar binding processes 14, 15
sentences 58, 93, 105, 158, 188, 207, 225, 235; uninterpretable 97
Sentential Subject Condition 162, 163
Slavic languages 210
SOV order 254
Spanish 225
specifiers 123, 124, 134, 143, 154, 156, 177, 207, 208, 215, 216, 217, 219, 227, 228, 252, 254; complements and 220–6; overt 169
Spell-Out component 130, 131, 147, 150, 152, 153, 154, 155, 156, 159, 169, 178–9, 179–80, 181, 182, 184, 210, 219, 221–2, 225, 260, 261
Sportiche, D. 37, 41, 45, 48, 63, 123, 228, 255, 256
S-structure 28, 29, 30, 33–4, 36, 80, 84, 87, 103; D-structure and 79, 85, 88, 90, 179, 180; eliminating 178; LF 104, 105, 106, 177, 178, 180; PF and 88, 91

standard minimalist framework 151, 154, 157, 187, 188, 219, 240
Starke, M. 209, 255, 258
Stowell, T. 172, 238
subjacency effects 162, 234
SUBJECT 57, 58, 59, 60, 61
subject non-subject difference 172
subject–predicate relation 165
"subject pronoun drop" 50
subjects 160; embedded 29, 173; expletive 161; nominative 172; nonovert 40; null 258–9; thematic 95
subject verb agreement 167
substitution 14, 15, 142
suffixes 211, 212, 213, 225, 251
superiority effects 161, 164, 165
superraising case 161, 165, 171
SVO order 122
syntactic conditions 98, 150
syntactic definition 11
syntactic effects 49
syntactic structures 83, 105, 118, 119, 212, 218; assembly of 126–33
syntactic theory 78
syntactic tree 106
syntax 88, 110, 111, 177, 222, 264; elegant 185, 186, 187, 198; interpretive systems and 152, 161; narrow 186, 188, 191; restricting 150; single interface 89; *see also* perfect syntax
Szabolcsi, A. 210, 242, 246, 259, 260, 262

Target Condition 14, 15
"target projects" condition 124, 136, 138, 140–4, 214
technicalities 78
Telescope 205, 207, 215–17, 228
Tense 172
thematic positions 144, 145
theory of knowledge 78
theta (θ)-criterion 22, 29, 32, 33, 34, 38, 42–3, 51, 79; arguments for 111; D-structure 81, 82, 83, 84, 85, 86, 93, 94, 98, 102, 103, 104, 106; LF 80, 93–101, 102, 103; satisfied 110; unresolved problems 93; violations 18, 24, 28, 36, 44, 45, 46, 48, 49, 56, 111
theta (θ)-roles 18, 22, 28, 33–4, 43, 45, 46, 56; antecedent must have 50, 51; assignment of 79, 145; categories that require 80, 104; chain must have 32; independent 26, 27, 31, 38, 47;
inherited from NP-trace 165; internal and external 110; quasi 98; receipt of 146
theta (θ)-theory 45, 89; and arguments 93–113
Thráinsson, H. 124
Trace Condition 41, 43, 44, 45, 46; OFS 49, 51; violations 50
traces 160, 165, 212, 213; deeply embedded 101
trace theory 90
transformational grammar 177
transivity 9
Transparency principle 153, 172

UG (Universal Grammar) 33, 34, 41, 77, 78, 90; principles of 87
unacceptability 8, 10, 12, 13, 16
unconnected tree law 195, 196
ungrammaticality 7, 9, 23, 24, 26, 32, 38, 46, 47, 48, 51, 60, 95, 97, 144, 145, 161, 171, 172, 173, 234, 244; contradiction and 139; CRs 16; improper movement structures 94; Principle C structure 100; uniformity condition 142
uniformity 101, 118, 121, 133, 137–40, 142, 151, 172
uniqueness 129, 219, 232, 233
uniqueness condition/requirement 30, 56, 84, 93, 94, 99, 103, 121–2
Ura, H. 165

vacuous quantification 45, 51, 104
variables 14, 15, 17, 18, 38, 93; as arguments 99; Caseless 101; definition of 21–4, 61; free 8, 22; syntactic 101, 107, 111
VEC (V-Element Condition) 22–3, 25, 26, 29, 33, 44, 61
verbal modifiers and clitics 260–2
verb-raising: in Hungarian 242–9; in Italian 256
verbs 95, 125, 144, 145, 167, 220, 221, 252; direct object θ-role of 110; hypothetical 144; matrix 37; multiple-argument 124; nonexistent 103, 145; nonpassivized transitive 99; *see also* VMs; VPs
Vergnaud, J.-R. 41
visibility principle 108
visibility requirement 56, 83, 84; LF thematic 107

VMs (verbal modifiers) 242–3, 244–5, 247, 248, 260, 261, 262
VPs (Verb Phrases) 9, 12, 127, 145, 165, 194, 211, 213, 219, 235–42, 258; layered 256; multi-layered 169, 220; shift operations 254

Watanabe, A. 162, 163, 179
well-formedness condition 120, 188, 189–90
wh-islands 166
"wiggly" extended words 224–6
Williams, E. 16, 153, 161, 164, 165, 166, 173, 233
Window theory 88, 89, 90

word-internal phrases 169
word order 211, 212, 213, 214, 225; mirror theory and 254; universal 126
words 119, 120, 121, 122, 123, 136, 153; complex 217; extended 221–3, 224–6, 253, 254, 258; morphological 207, 208, 218–25 *passim*, 227, 232–50, 254, 255, 258, 259–60, 261, 263, 264; phrases and 137–40, 215, 216, 217

XPs *see* phrase structure

Zubizarreta, M. L. 41

For Product Safety Concerns and Information please contact our EU
representative GPSR@taylorandfrancis.com
Taylor & Francis Verlag GmbH, Kaufingerstraße 24, 80331 München, Germany

www.ingramcontent.com/pod-product-compliance
Lightning Source LLC
Chambersburg PA
CBHW060553230426
43670CB00011B/1811